C++
In Plain English

Third Edition

C++
In Plain English

●━━━━━━━━━━━━━━━━━━━━●

Third Edition

Brian Overland

M&T Books

An imprint of IDG Books Worldwide, Inc.

Foster City, CA • Chicago, IL • Indianapolis, IN • New York, NY

C++ In Plain English, Third Edition

Published by
M&T Books
An imprint of IDG Books Worldwide, Inc.
919 E. Hillsdale Blvd., Suite 400
Foster City, CA 94404
www.idgbooks.com (IDG Books Worldwide Web site)

ISBN: 0-7645-3545-5

Printed in the United States of America

10 9 8 7 6 5 4 3 2 1

1O/RU/RS/QQ/FC

Distributed in the United States by IDG Books Worldwide, Inc.

Distributed by CDG Books Canada Inc. for Canada; by Transworld Publishers Limited in the United Kingdom; by IDG Norge Books for Norway; by IDG Sweden Books for Sweden; by IDG Books Australia Publishing Corporation Pty. Ltd. for Australia and New Zealand; by TransQuest Publishers Pte Ltd. for Singapore, Malaysia, Thailand, Indonesia, and Hong Kong; by Gotop Information Inc. for Taiwan; by ICG Muse, Inc. for Japan; by Intersoft for South Africa; by Eyrolles for France; by International Thomson Publishing for Germany, Austria, and Switzerland; by Distribuidora Cuspide for Argentina; by LR International for Brazil; by Galileo Libros for Chile; by Ediciones ZETA S.C.R. Ltda. for Peru; by WS Computer Publishing Corporation, Inc., for the Philippines; by Contemporanea de Ediciones for Venezuela; by Express Computer Distributors for the Caribbean and West Indies; by Micronesia Media Distributor, Inc. for Micronesia; by Chips Computadoras S.A. de C.V. for Mexico; by Editorial Norma de Panama S.A. for Panama; by American Bookshops for Finland.

For general information on IDG Books Worldwide's books in the U.S., please call our Consumer Customer Service department at 800-762-2974. For reseller information, including discounts and premium sales, please call our Reseller Customer Service department at 800-434-3422.

For information on where to purchase IDG Books Worldwide's books outside the U.S., please contact our International Sales department at 317-572-3993 or fax 317-572-4002.

For consumer information on foreign language translations, please contact our Customer Service department at 800-434-3422, fax 317-572-4002, or e-mail rights@idgbooks.com.

For information on licensing foreign or domestic rights, please phone +1-650-653-7098.

For sales inquiries and special prices for bulk quantities, please contact our Order Services department at 800-434-3422 or write to the address above.

For information on using IDG Books Worldwide's books in the classroom or for ordering examination copies, please contact our Educational Sales department at 800-434-2086 or fax 317-572-4005.

For press review copies, author interviews, or other publicity information, please contact our Public Relations department at 650-653-7000 or fax 650-653-7500.

For authorization to photocopy items for corporate, personal, or educational use, please contact Copyright Clearance Center, 222 Rosewood Drive, Danvers, MA 01923, or fax 978-750-4470.

Library of Congress Cataloging-in-Publication Data

Overland, Brian R.
    C++ in plain English / Brian Overland.-- 3rd ed.
        p. cm.
    ISBN 0-7645-3545-5 (alk. paper)
    1. C++ (Computer program language). I. Title.
QA76.73.C153 O835   2000

00-050076

 is a registered trademark or trademark under exclusive license to IDG Books Worldwide, Inc. from International Data Group, Inc.in the United States and/or other countries.

 is a trademark of IDG Books Worldwide, Inc.

ABOUT IDG BOOKS WORLDWIDE

Welcome to the world of IDG Books Worldwide.

IDG Books Worldwide, Inc., is a subsidiary of International Data Group, the world's largest publisher of computer-related information and the leading global provider of information services on information technology. IDG was founded more than 30 years ago by Patrick J. McGovern and now employs more than 9,000 people worldwide. IDG publishes more than 290 computer publications in over 75 countries. More than 90 million people read one or more IDG publications each month.

Launched in 1990, IDG Books Worldwide is today the #1 publisher of best-selling computer books in the United States. We are proud to have received eight awards from the Computer Press Association in recognition of editorial excellence and three from Computer Currents' First Annual Readers' Choice Awards. Our best-selling ...For Dummies® series has more than 50 million copies in print with translations in 31 languages. IDG Books Worldwide, through a joint venture with IDG's Hi-Tech Beijing, became the first U.S. publisher to publish a computer book in the People's Republic of China. In record time, IDG Books Worldwide has become the first choice for millions of readers around the world who want to learn how to better manage their businesses.

Our mission is simple: Every one of our books is designed to bring extra value and skill-building instructions to the reader. Our books are written by experts who understand and care about our readers. The knowledge base of our editorial staff comes from years of experience in publishing, education, and journalism — experience we use to produce books to carry us into the new millennium. In short, we care about books, so we attract the best people. We devote special attention to details such as audience, interior design, use of icons, and illustrations. And because we use an efficient process of authoring, editing, and desktop publishing our books electronically, we can spend more time ensuring superior content and less time on the technicalities of making books.

You can count on our commitment to deliver high-quality books at competitive prices on topics you want to read about. At IDG Books Worldwide, we continue in the IDG tradition of delivering quality for more than 30 years. You'll find no better book on a subject than one from IDG Books Worldwide.

John J. Kilcullen
John Kilcullen
Chairman and CEO
IDG Books Worldwide, Inc.

WINNER

*Eighth Annual
Computer Press
Awards 1992*

WINNER

*Ninth Annual
Computer Press
Awards 1993*

WINNER

*Tenth Annual
Computer Press
Awards 1994*

WINNER

*Eleventh Annual
Computer Press
Awards 1995*

IDG is the world's leading IT media, research and exposition company. Founded in 1964, IDG had 1997 revenues of $2.05 billion and has more than 9,000 employees worldwide. IDG offers the widest range of media options that reach IT buyers in 75 countries representing 95% of worldwide IT spending. IDG's diverse product and services portfolio spans six key areas including print publishing, online publishing, expositions and conferences, market research, education and training, and global marketing services. More than 90 million people read one or more of IDG's 290 magazines and newspapers, including IDG's leading global brands — Computerworld, PC World, Network World, Macworld and the Channel World family of publications. IDG Books Worldwide is one of the fastest-growing computer book publishers in the world, with more than 700 titles in 36 languages. The "...For Dummies®" series alone has more than 50 million copies in print. IDG offers online users the largest network of technology-specific Web sites around the world through IDG.net (http://www.idg.net), which comprises more than 225 targeted Web sites in 55 countries worldwide. International Data Corporation (IDC) is the world's largest provider of information technology data, analysis and consulting, with research centers in over 41 countries and more than 400 research analysts worldwide. IDG World Expo is a leading producer of more than 168 globally branded conferences and expositions in 35 countries including E3 (Electronic Entertainment Expo), Macworld Expo, ComNet, Windows World Expo, ICE (Internet Commerce Expo), Agenda, DEMO, and Spotlight. IDG's training subsidiary, ExecuTrain, is the world's largest computer training company, with more than 230 locations worldwide and 785 training courses. IDG Marketing Services helps industry-leading IT companies build international brand recognition by developing global integrated marketing programs via IDG's print, online and exposition products worldwide. Further information about the company can be found at www.idg.com.   1/26/00

Credits

Acquisitions Editor
Debra Williams Cauley

Project Editor
Sharon Nash

Technical Editor
Allen Wyatt

Development Editor
Kezia Endsley

Copy Editor
Richard H. Adin

Proof Editor
Cordelia Heaney

Project Coordinators
Danette Nurse
Louigene A. Santos

Graphics and Production Specialists
Robert Bihlmayer
Jude Levinson
Michael Lewis
Victor Pérez-Varela
Ramses Ramirez

Quality Control Technician
Dina F Quan

Book Designers
London Road Design
Kurt Krames

Illustrator
Karl Brandt

Proofreading and Indexing
York Production Services

Cover Image
© Noma/Images.com

About the Author

Brian Overland worked for Microsoft for 10 years, where he was a software tester, senior technical writer, and manager. Before that, he was an applications programmer using both C and Basic. While at Microsoft, he was on the development teams of both Visual C++ 1.0 and Visual Basic 1.0, the latter as project lead of documentation. He also worked on Assembler and Interactive Television. His books have been translated into several languages, including French, German, Polish, and Croatian. He is currently at work on his second novel.

*To my Uncle Reid, riding a soft, sunny wave
to a far horizon*

Preface

If you've used previous versions of this book, you should find this edition to be the most useful and comprehensive yet. If you need quick but thorough answers to C++ questions, this may be the most useful book you can acquire. Now it has specific improvements to make it even better than earlier editions. These improvements are in two areas: improvements that the publisher has made to the format, and coverage of new language features.

A New and Better Format

In the new millennium, books must compete not only with each other, but also with the Internet. In reference books, the name of the game is ease of access. How quickly can you get to what you want?

One virtue of the *In Plain English* books is that they provide many ways to look something up. We have strengthened this virtue in several ways.

- You can look up tasks in the "C++ In Plain English" section. Now, instead of getting just a reference to the appropriate language element, you also get a page reference, pointing you directly to the information you need.

- You can look up items by their place in the reference. Reference sections are now equipped with dictionary-style running heads, so that every page tells you immediately where you are in the alphabetical order.

- Cross-references now specify exact pages, so that you can find what you need more quickly.

If you've used earlier versions of this book, you'll notice another big change: the tutorial section is now Part II. This change supports the book's central goal: to make it easy to get information. The task-oriented section, "C++ in Plain English," is now at the front of the book, making it easier than ever to pick up the book and find what you need. Yet, all the old tutorial information is still there, with some updating.

Of course, information is useless if badly done. It's not just a matter of how quickly you get somewhere, but when you get there, does it help you? To uphold quality, I've included at least one example for every topic, as well as explained, where appropriate, the *why* of the feature.

Readers who've used earlier editions should find higher quality here than ever. I've provided examples for the few topics that lacked them. Additionally, each topic is organized by subheading, such as Purpose or Example. As I worked with this format, I found it made topics sharper, tighter, and more readable.

Expanded Coverage of the New C++

C++ has the virtue of having a worldwide standard: the ANSI specification. Every so often, the ANSI committee meets and discusses changes, and, fortunately, the specification has been increasingly stable over the past few years.

There have been some changes, however, mandated by the increasing importance of international applications and by the fact that we live in a world of astronomical improvements in capacity and memory.

Amendment 1

This addition to the ANSI specification, first proposed in the mid-1990s and now widely accepted, mandates support for the wide-character (wchar_t) format. This type is necessary to support human languages with more than 255 text characters. The type itself is not hard to document, but Amendment 1 also mandates a large set of functions, such as wprintf and wscanf, to support operations on wide-character strings. This book now describes all these functions.

C99

This is a more recent change, although its effects are smaller than those of Amendment 1. ISO C, the state-of-the-art specification of the C language, now mandates support for two new primitive types that take advantage of bigger, faster processors and increased memory: long long int and long double. Most vendors of C++ compilers support these additions to the C language as a part of C++. This is logical, because C++ is designed to be a superset of C, with few limitations. This book describes the two new types.

I/O Stream Classes

The I/O stream classes have always been an important part of the standard library of C++. In recognition of their increasing importance, this book now describes these classes — along with functions and objects — more completely and systematically.

Using This Book

This book is aimed primarily at intermediate and advanced C++ programmers, although it does provide background for the novice. The book is useful as a supplement to a course or to another, carefully guided tutorial. I believe that you could learn C++ from this book alone, but of necessity, the tutorial is concise. If you're just beginning, you'd do well to have another book to help you, such as *C++ For Dummies, 4th Edition* (ISBN: 0-7645-0746-X).

Part I: C++ Reference

Part I is designed for people who have a basic understanding of C++ and want to get quick answers. If you know the language element (keyword, function, class, or operator) you need to look up, you can find it

directly in Sections 3 to 7. There are only a few of these sections — for
example, keywords are all in one section, functions in another — so it's
usually obvious where to look. If in doubt, you can find exact page
locations in Section 2, "C++ Elements A to Z." Dictionary-style running heads make it easy to navigate within each section.

If you know what you want to do but aren't sure what the name
of the appropriate function or keyword is, start by looking up the
task in the "in Plain English" section. This is now the first section
in the book. It specifies both the item you need and exactly where to
find it. With C++, such a reference is particularly helpful, because
C++ inherits C's approach of using compact but sometimes obscure
function names, such as strftime.

Although you might not know that you needed to use strftime,
you might know that you want to print the day of the week. By using
the "in Plain English" section, you could find strftime by looking up
"day of the week," "month," "time data," or "print time display."

This book helps you with obscure function names in other ways
as well. Each topic has both a plain-English description, which is
placed on the same line as the name of the element itself, and a
concise statement of purpose.

Part II: C++ Tutorial

If you want to start by getting an overview of C++ and object-oriented
programming, turn to Part II, "C++ Tutorial," starting on page 296.

Part II also serves another purpose, which helps to explain why it
has been moved to the back of the book. After you look up a language
element in Part I, you may want to get more background on the subject. For example, after reading about the class keyword in Section 4,
you might want to read more about the theory and use of classes; this
material starts in Chapter 5. Part I includes cross-references to Part II
wherever these are helpful. In Part II, you'll find extended description
and examples — some spanning multiple chapters.

For those of you who'd rather start with the tutorial, I hope
that the placing of the tutorial in the back won't be too disruptive.
Remember that all the tutorial material from previous editions is still
there, along with some updating and revision. You simply have to start
on a different page.

Glossary

The glossary, which begins on page 522, fills in conceptual gaps by
describing language features not tied to specific keywords. For example, you can look up topics such as "functions," "pointer arithmetic,"

"arrays," and "inheritance." These topics contain cross-references to Parts I and II where helpful.

The glossary also performs another important role: translating object-oriented jargon into plain English. After you're familiar with the real meanings behind incantations such as *polymorphism* and *abstraction*, you no longer have to be so intimidated by the object-oriented gurus and C++ veterans around you. You can feel like a C++ insider.

Conventions

C++ sometimes employs complicated syntax, reflecting the power and flexibility of the language. To summarize the possibilities, this book makes use of some typographical conventions. Although overuse of such conventions can make life complicated, I've employed them wherever I thought I could use them to simplify things.

The main convention is that anything in **bold** is meant to be typed in exactly as shown. Anything in both *italics* and monospace is a placeholder, which means that you replace it with an item of your own choosing. For example, in the following syntax, *type* is the name of any C++ type you choose. You could therefore apply this syntax by using sizeof(int), sizeof(long), or sizeof(float).

```
sizeof(type)
```

Occasionally, brackets are used to indicate an optional item. In the following syntax, the brackets mean that "C" can be either included or omitted. You don't type the brackets themselves.

```
extern ["C"] declaration;
```

If brackets are meant literally, they are in bold font. This happens only where arrays are concerned and with the new and delete operators. For example, to apply the following syntax, you could enter new int[100] or new long[56]:

```
new type[size]
```

Section 6 includes a declaration of each function. The declaration lists each argument and its type. When using the function, never enter the type, just the argument. For example, the following declaration means that abs gets and returns an integer (int).

```
int abs(int num);
```

Here's an example of a call to this function.

```
int i = abs(-75);
```

Other Icons

This book employs several types of icons to draw attention to different kinds of notes.

●─ANSI

This icon points out a language feature in the ANSI specification not present in early versions of C++.

●─NOTE

This icon signifies a technical note that digresses from the main discussion. There are many ands, ifs, and buts in C++. To be technically correct without being too distracting, the text relegates additional information to Notes.

●─C/C++

This icon points to information about a common language feature that is supported by both C and C++ but that is handled differently by each. C has some restrictions that C++ does not have, and vice versa. Pay special attention to these notes if you're porting C code to C++, or if you're a C programmer moving to C++.

●─TIP

A Tip recommends an alternative way to do something that might be faster or more convenient. These tips are always in the form of a suggestion.

Why C++?

Along with Visual Basic and Java, C++ is the language to know for the programming work of the future. Of these three languages, C++ still provides the most complete realization of object orientation and is best suited for writing serious, commercial applications as well as for doing systems programming. In short, mastery of C++ helps put you into the league of alpha programmers.

One of the hurdles in learning C++ is that function names are compact and often not at all user-friendly. This book comes to the rescue with the plain-English approach, providing task-oriented access, as well as one-line summaries of each function and keyword.

Another hurdle is C++'s reliance on operator symbols where Basic might use an English word (for example, the AND operation.) This book comes to the rescue again by providing several different summaries of operators and their use in Section 3.

Final Thoughts

C++ is a largely elegant and powerful language. It has some idiosyncrasies, however, stemming from the fact that C++ grew out of C, an older and less powerful language; C++ must retain old features for the sake of backward compatibility. It also suffers a bit from its lack of concession to beginning programmers, who resist concepts such as pointers and references. Perhaps unfairly, C and C++ have the reputation of being "geek" languages, although a couple million people have learned them or at least tried to.

I hope that your use of C++ is as free of confusion as possible. I've tried to give you the benefit of insight gleaned from both successes and mistakes — mistakes I wouldn't have made if someone had been there to steer me around the redundancies and pitfalls I know about now. May your coding be pleasant, elegant, and bug-free.

One last note. You can send feedback to Briano2u@aol.com and find code for the examples online at:

http://www.idgbooks.com/extras/cipe/

Acknowledgments

From the first edition

The book that you're holding contains many tables, diagrams, and contrasting fonts, all in the name of simplifying some rather abstract concepts. Many people contributed their production and editing talents to make this happen, including Shari Chappell, Betsy Hardinger, Gay Nicols, and Stephanie Doyle. Special thanks go to the series editor, Debra Williams Cauley, who managed the whole process, showing the patience of a saint while dealing with frequently changing deadlines and page counts. Michael Sprague also played an important role in helping to get the project started.

On the technical side, Will Iverson made some excellent suggestions that have since been incorporated into the book, particularly Chapter 8. In the process of writing, it was extremely encouraging (if occasionally frustrating) to know what was working and what wasn't.

Much of the content of the book was influenced by conversations I had with Rich Knoph, a talented full-time programmer I work with here in the Northwest. Not only have we had many discussions about programming languages over the years, but he pointed me toward some helpful resources on the history, evolution, and fine points of C++.

And thanks to my cat Purrly, who has been understanding during my long writing sessions when I've ignored him.

From the second edition

The Second Edition involved a heavy rewrite of the last half of the book. This wouldn't have happened without Laura Lewin, who encouraged me to take on the job, or without Matthew Lusher and Michael Gaebler, the developmental and technical editors, respectively, for this edition. Matthew made many helpful suggestions, and Michael did a superb job of testing and improving all the code. The book is much better than it might have been because of their contributions.

For the third edition

This edition came about because of the urging and encouragement of Debra Williams Cauley, the acquisitions editor. It was made considerably better by the efforts of Allen Wyatt, who checked every word and every figure with exquisite care, finding things that others should have seen years earlier. The result is that this edition is much stronger than any other edition. Finally, I would like to extend my thanks to the other editors — Sharon Nash, Kezia Endsley, and Richard Adin — for their flexibility and long-suffering patience with an author who basically just wants everything to be perfect. Now, that's not asking much, is it?

Contents at a Glance

C++
In Plain English

Third Edition

C++ Reference

english in plain english in p
ain english in plain english in
plain english in plain english
english in plain english in p
plain english in plain english
english in plain english in p
ain english in plain english in
plain english in plain english
english in plain english in p
ain english in plain english in
plain english in plain english
english in plain english in p

Part I provides detailed reference to C++ elements such as operators, keywords, and the function and I/O class libraries. Use Section 1, "C++ in Plain English," to look up a topic by task. This section is organized alphabetically by key phrase. Use Section 2, "C++ Elements A To Z," to find the location of any element instantly. In this edition of the book, these two indexes give direct page references so that you can use them to get to the right topic quickly. For a general background on any of the fundamentals of C++, see Part II, "C++ Tutorial."

IN THIS PART

- C++ in Plain English
- C++ Elements A to Z
- Operators
- Keywords
- Preprocessor Elements
- Library Functions
- I/O Stream Classes

in plain english in p
sh in plain english in
glish in plain english
in plain english in p
sh in plain english in
glish in plain english
in plain english in p
glish in plain english
in plain english in p
sh in plain english in
glish in plain english
in plain english in p
sh in plain english in
glish in plain english
in plain english in p
lish in plain english
in plain english in p
sh in plain english in
glish in plain english
in plain english in p
sh in plain english in
lish in plain english
in plain english in p

C++ in Plain English

This section is for people who understand the basics of C++ and need to look up a specific keyword, directive, class, or function. For an introduction to object orientation or C++ in general, see Part II, "C++ Tutorial."

C++ builds on the foundation of the C language, which was originally created for system programmers. Consequently, names in C++ sometimes look like a foreign language. It's not obvious that `fscanf` reads values from a file or that `strstr` finds a substring. When you want to accomplish a specific task, you might wonder: Where do I start?

To look up an item by task, start with this section. The tasks are organized in the left column by key phrase; these key phrases are also italicized. The second and third columns give the applicable element and the page or pages containing more information.

If you want to...	Use these elements:	Located on these pages:
label *case* statement	case	73
cast between polymorphic types	dynamic_cast	82
cast between primitive types	static_cast	109
cast between related classes	static_cast	109
cast away const attribute	const_cast	78
cast pointer to different type	reinterpret_cast	103
change name of file	rename	214
prevent *changes* to a variable	const	76
enable *changes* to field of a const object	mutable	96
access *changing data object*	volatile	134
use *character data*	char	74
get next *character* from file	fgetc, getc	179, 179
print *character* to a file	fputc, putc	178, 179
print *character* to a file	putchar	170, 207
push back *character*	ungetc	179
test single *character*	is<cond>	195
get *character* from keyboard	getchar	170
link to *C-language modules*	extern	86

If you want to...	Use these elements:	Located on these pages:
write a *class template*	`template`	113
declare *class*	`class, struct, union`	75, 111, 129
clear errors	`clearerr`	180
clear file buffer	`fflush`	178
close and reopen file	`freopen`	178
close file	`fclose`	178
combine bits	bitwise OR (`|`)	60
combine strings (concatenate)	`strcat`	288
combine wide-character strings	`wcscat`	245
use system *command*	`system`	234
get *command-line input*	`main`	95
compare strings	`strcmp`	288
compare wide-character strings	`wcscmp`	245
compare two memory blocks	`memcmp`	202
report time of *compilation*	`__TIME__`, `__DATE__`	154, 153
compile on condition	`#if`	147
report *compile-time error*	`#error`	146
concatenate strings	`strcat`	288
concatenate wide-character strings	`wcscat`	245
conditionally compile	`#if`	147

Continued

If you want to...	Use these elements:	Located on these pages:
print data to the *console*	putchar, puts, printf	170
read data values from the *console*	scanf	171
read character from the *console*	getchar	170
read string from the *console*	gets	170
read string from *console* to stream object	getline	268
read wide-char string from the *console*	getws	170
use a *constant variable*	const	76
define symbolic *constant*	#define, enum	143, 83
enable changes to *constant*	mutable	96
continue to next cycle of a loop	continue	79
prevent *conversion*	explicit	85
convert data type (cast)	const_cast, dynamic_cast, reinterpret_cast, static_cast	78, 82, 103, 109
convert number to digit string	sprintf	222
convert string to floating point	atof, strtod	166, 230
convert string to integer	atoi, atol, strtol, stroul	166, 167, 231, 232
convert to lowercase	tolower	239
convert to uppercase	toupper	240

If you want to...	Use these elements:	Located on these pages:
copy array	`memcpy`	202
copy memory block	`memcpy`	202
copy string	`strcpy`	288
copy wide-character string	`wcscpy`	245
get *cosine*	`cos`	175
use loop with a *counter variable*	`for`	87
place variable in *CPU register*	`register`	103
get pointer to *current object*	`this`	120
get *current source-file line*	`__LINE__`	154
get *date*	`time`	236
get compile-time *date*	`__DATE__`	153
print *day of the week*	`strftime`	228
get *day of the week*	`mktime, time`	236, 236
declare pointer	`*`	53
declare reference variable	`&`	53
decrease size of memory block	`realloc`	212
decrement value	`--`	51
define alias for a type	`typedef`	125
define symbol	`#define`	143
delete file from disk	`remove`	213
delete object	`delete`	80
dereference pointer	`*`	53

Continued

If you want to...	Use these elements:	Located on these pages:
get current source file	`__FILE__`	154
get formatted input from a *file*	`fscanf`	179
get next character from *file*	`fgetc, getc`	179, 179
open *file*	`fopen`	187
print character to a *file*	`fputc, putc`	178, 179
print formatted string to a *file*	`fprintf`	178
print string to a *file*	`fputs`	178
read binary data from a *file*	`fread`	179
read string from a *file*	`fgets`	179
create *file-stream* object	`fstream, ifstream, ofstream`	265, 269, 274
find substring location	`strstr`	288
set format *flags*	`setf, unsetf`	287, 292
floating-point type	`double, float`	81, 86
flush a file buffer	`fflush`	178
flush stream-object buffer	`flush`	263
set *format flags*	`setf, unsetf`	287, 292
get *formatted* input from a file	`fscanf`	179
print *formatted* string	`printf`	170. 205
print *formatted* wide-char string	`wprintf`	174, 253
4-byte integer data type	`long`	93
get *fractional* portion of number	`modf`	203

If you want to...	Use these elements:	Located on these pages:
free allocated memory	free, delete	189, 80
exit function	return	104
write generalized class or function	template	113
generate random number	rand	211
get data from a string	sscanf	224
get data from a wide-char string	swscanf	233
get data from input stream	ifstream	269
get data from the console	scanf	171, 214
get data pointed to	*	53
get file position	ftell, fgetpos	179
get file position in stream object	tellg, tellp	291, 291
get string length	strlen	288
go to file position	fseek, fsetpos	180, 180
go to file position in stream object	seekg, seekp	285, 286
go to statement	goto	90
greater than	>	59
greater than or equal to	>=	59
convert to Greenwich Mean Time	gmtime	236
handle exception	catch	74
handle signal	signal	219
include header file	#include	150
use hexadecimal format with stream object	hex	491

Continued

If you want to...	Use these elements:	Located on these pages:
get *hyperbolic sine*	sinh	222
get *hyperbolic tangent*	tanh	235
identify type	typeid	126
import symbols from namespace	using	132
include header file	#include	150
increase size of memory block	realloc	212
increment value	++	51
index character in a memory block	memchr	202
test for *inequality*	!=	60
compile function as *inline*	inline	92
input binary data from a file	fread	179
input from file as a stream	ifstream	269
input line from the keyboard	gets	170
input object from stream	istream	271
get data from *input stream*	cin	259
input string from a file	fgets	179
input wide-character string from a file	fgetws	184
input values from a string	sscanf	224
input values from a wide-character string	swscanf	233
input values from the keyboard	scanf	171
use an *input-file stream*	ifstream	269

If you want to...	Use these elements:	Located on these pages:
install signal handler	signal	219
integer data type	int	92
long *integer* data type	long	93
get *integer portion* of number	modf	203
get *inverse of cosine*	acos	162
get *inverse of sine*	asin	163
get *inverse of tangent*	atan, atan2	164, 164
join strings (concatenate)	strcat	288
jump based on test value	switch	111
jump between functions	longjmp	200
jump to statement	goto	90
read data values from *keyboard*	scanf	171
read character from *keyboard*	getchar	170
read string from *keyboard*	gets	170
label target of switch	case	73
declare *late-bound function*	virtual	133
left-shift bits	<<	58
get *length of a string*	strlen	288
get *length of wide-character string*	wcslen	245
less than	<	59
less than or equal to	<=	59
read *line of input*	gets	170
get current source *line*	__LINE__	154
define *list of constants*	enum	83
set *location for longjmp*	setjmp	217

Continued

If you want to...	Use these elements:	Located on these pages:
release *object* from memory	delete	80
get pointer to current *object*	this	120
allocate one or more *objects*	new	98
use *octal format with stream object*	oct	491
get *one's complement*	~	50
open existing file-stream object	open	275
open file	fopen	178
open file-stream object for input	fstream, ifstream	265, 269
open file-stream object for output	fstream, ofstream	265, 274
write *operator function*	operator	99
perform bitwise *OR*	|	60
perform logical *OR*	||	62
output binary data to a file	fwrite	179
print to *output stream*	cout	260
output to file stream object	ofstream	274
force *output to physical device*	fflush	178
output variables to screen	printf	170, 205
enable *outside access of members*	public	102
declare *overlapping types*	union	129
overload operator	operator	99
use *parameterized type*	template	113

If you want to...	Use these elements:	Located on these pages:
pass data by reference	&	53
pass variables along to printf	vprintf	243
permit outside access of members	public	102
get value of *pi*	atan	164
place character back on file stream	ungetc	179
place character back on stream object	putback	281
get data *pointed to*	*	53
change type of *pointer*	reinterpret_cast	103
get *pointer to current object*	this	120
access member through a *pointer*	->	55
dereference or declare *pointer*	*	53
use *pointer-to-member* operators	.* ->*	55
apply *polymorphic cast*	dynamic_cast	82
declare *polymorphic function*	virtual	133
get file *position*	fgetpos, ftell	179
set file *position*	fsetpos, fseek	180
raise number to a *power*	pow	204
preserve value between function calls	static	108
prevent changes to a variable	const	76
prevent conversion	explicit	85
print character to a file	fputc, putc	178, 179

Continued

If you want to...	Use these elements:	Located on these pages:
print character to the console	putchar	170
print data to file output stream	ofstream	274
print formatted data to a string	sprintf	222
print formatted data to wide-character string	swprintf	232
print formatted string to a file	fprintf	178
print formatted string to the console	printf	170, 205
print string to a file	fputs, fputws	178, 184
print string to the console	puts	171, 208
print time display	strftime	228
print to output stream object	ostream	277
print to standard-output stream object	cout	260
print values of variables	printf	170, 205
specify *private access*	private	100
enable access to *private members*	friend	89
write the *program entry point*	main	95
get *program running time*	clock	235
specify *protected access*	protected	101
specify *public access*	public	102
put character back on file stream	ungetc	179

If you want to...	Use these elements:	Located on these pages:
put character back on stream object	putback	281
use quick-sort algorithm	qsort	209
raise any number to a power	pow	204
raise e to a power	exp	177
raise exception	throw	121
raise signal	raise	211
get random number	rand	211
read binary data from a file	fread	179
read data from a string	sscanf	224
read data from the keyboard	scanf	171
read from file input stream	ifstream	269
read data from a wide-character string	swscanf	233
read in header file	#include	150
read next character from a file	fgetc, getc	179, 179
read next character from the keyboard	getchar	170
read string from a file	fgets	179
read string from a stream object	getline	268
read string from the keyboard	gets	170
read wide-character string from a file	fgetws	184
reallocate memory block	realloc	212
recast data	static_cast	109
recast pointer type	reinterpret_cast	103

Continued

If you want to...	Use these elements:	Located on these pages:
install *signal handler*	`signal`	219
raise *signal*	`raise`	211
get *size of data type*	`sizeof`	106
skip characters from stream object	`ignore`	271
sort an array	`qsort`	209
get current *source file line*	`__LINE__`	154
get current *source file name*	`__FILE__`	154
specify class or namespace scope	`::`	49
get *square root*	`sqrt`	223
start the program	`main`	95
allocate *static data*	`static`	108
extend *stream operators* (<<, >>)	`istream, ostream`	271, 277
use *stream operators* (<<, >>)	`<<, >>`	58, 58
copy *string*	`strcpy`	288
print *string* to a file	`fputs`	281
print *string* to the console	`puts`	171, 208
print formatted data to a *string*	`sprintf`	222
read *string* from a file	`fgets`	179
read *string* from stream object	`getline`	268
read *string* from the keyboard	`gets`	170
read data from a *string*	`sscanf`	224
use *string as input stream*	`istrstream`	273

If you want to...	Use these elements:	Located on these pages:
use *string as output stream*	ostrstream	278
get *string length*	strlen	288
perform *string operations*	str<op>	224
test *strings for equality*	strcmp	288
search for *substring*	strstr	288
subtract and assign	-=	63
subtract numbers	-	57
subtract one from a value	--	51
use *switch/case logic*	switch	111
define *symbolic constant*	#define, enum	143, 83
access *symbols* from a namespace	using	132
get *system time*	time	236
execute *system-level command*	system	234
get *tangent*	tan	234
write class or function *template*	template	113
get *temporary file*	tmpfile	239
terminate abruptly	abort	162
register *termination* routine	atexit	165
test for equality	==	60
test for greater than	>	59
test for greater than or equal to	>=	59
test for inequality	!=	60
test for less than	<	59

Continued

If you want to...	Use these elements:	Located on these pages:
test for less than or equal to	<=	59
test single character	is<cond>	195
test strings for equality	strcmp	288
jump based on *test value*	switch	111
throw exception	throw	121
get *time and date*	time	236
print formatted *time data*	strftime	228
get *time of compilation*	__TIME__	154
tokenize a string	strtok	288
use *true/false* value	bool	72
turn off bits	bitwise AND (&)	60
turn off file buffering	setbuf, setvbuf	180
two-byte integer type	short	105
use a *type as argument*	template	113
create *type definition*	typedef	125
get *type information*	dynamic_cast, typeid	82, 126
declare new *type*	class, struct, union	75, 111, 129
undo symbol definition	#undef	152
unset format flags	unsetf	292
convert to *uppercase*	toupper	240
test if character is *uppercase*	isupper	195
declare *user-defined type*	class, struct, union	75, 111, 129

If you want to...	Use these elements:	Located on these pages:
use *variable-length argument list*	va_arg, va_end, va_start	242
declare *variant record type*	union	129
declare *virtual function or base class*	virtual	133
execute *while condition is true*	while	136
use *wide-character data type*	wchar_t	132
copy *wide-character string*	wcscpy	245
print *wide-character string*	wprintf	174, 253
print *wide-character string* to a file	fputws	184
read *wide-character string* from a file	fgetws	184
get *wide-character string length*	wcslen	245
get *width of data type*	sizeof	106
get *width of string*	strlen	288
write binary data to a file	fwrite	179
write class or function template	template	113
write data to a string	sprintf	222
write data to the console	printf	170, 205
write string to the console	puts	171, 208
write to file output stream	ofstream	274
write wide-character string to console	wprintf	174, 253
XOR (exclusive OR) operation	^	60

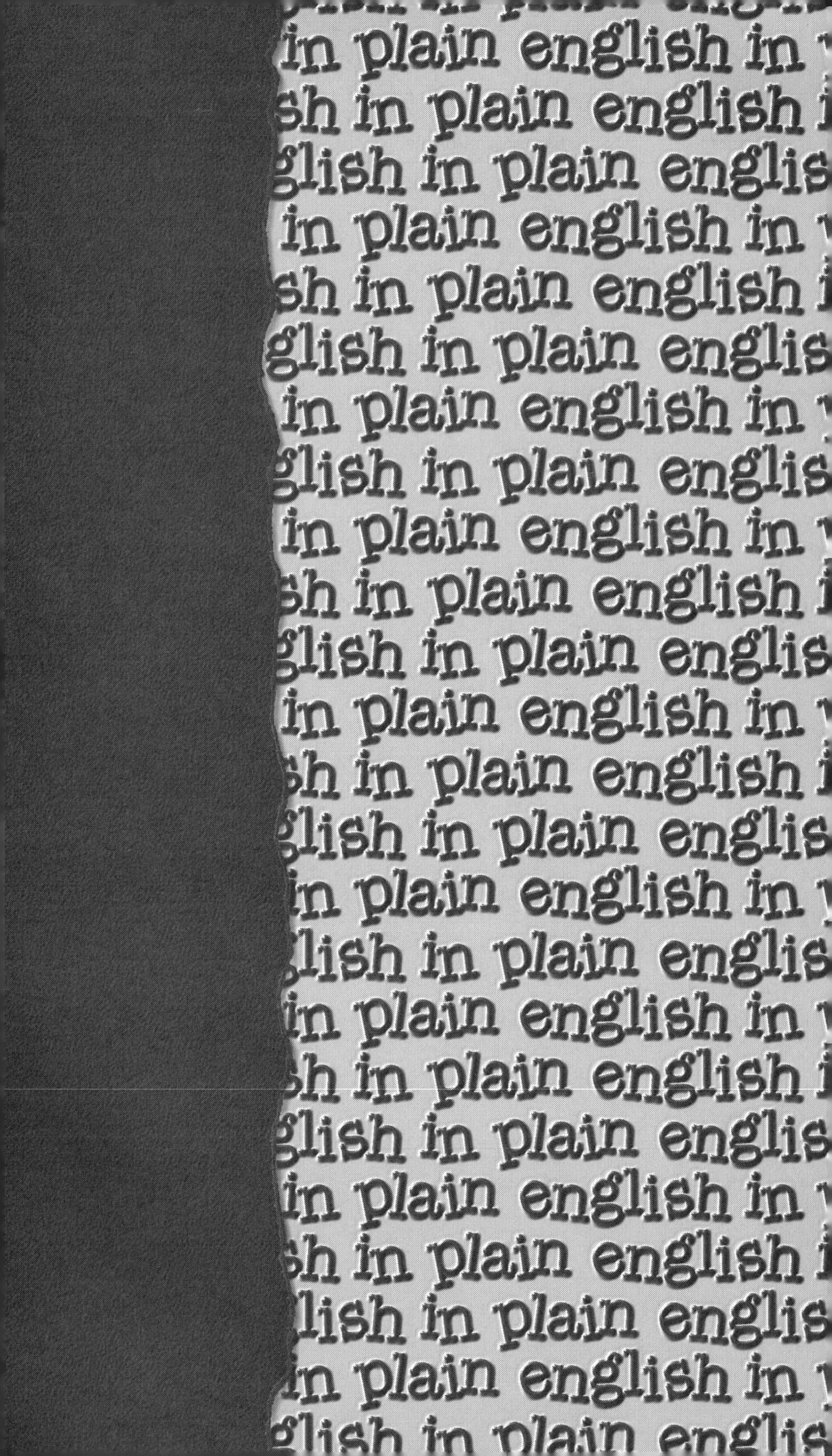

C++ Elements
A to Z

This section provides a chapter cross-reference for the language and library elements described in Part I. These elements include keywords, directives, functions, classes, and operators. Look up the element that you want to find in the left-hand column, and then turn to the page given in the right-hand column to get more information.

In some cases, an element is listed with a *stream* prefix (for example, *stream*.clear). In these cases, the element is a member function of one of the stream classes described in Section 7 as well as in Chapters 4 and 10.

C++ Elements A to Z

C++ Elements A to Z

Continued

Element	Covered on this page of Part I:
inequality, test for (!=)	60
inline	92
int	92
is<condition>	195
isw<condition>	196
istream	271
istrstream	273
labs	197
ldexp	198
ldiv	198
less than (<)	59
LINE	154
#line	151
localeconv	199
localtime	236
log	199
log10	200
logical operators	44
long	93
longjmp	200
main	95
malloc	201
member access (.)	44
member access through pointer (->)	48
memchr	202
memcmp	202
memcpy	202
memmove	202
memset	202
mktime	236
modf	203
modulus operator (%)	58
multiplication (*)	57
mutable	96

C++ Elements A to Z

Continued

C++ Elements A to Z

C++ Elements A to Z

Continued

C++ Elements A to Z

Element	Covered on this page of Part I:
wcslen	245
wcsncat	246
wcsncmp	246
wcsncpy	246
wcspbrk	246
wcsrchr	246
wcsspn	246
wcsstr	245
wcstod	246
wcstok	246
wcstol	247
wcstoul	247
wcsxfrm	246
while	136
stream.width	293
wmemchr	251
wmemcmp	251
wmemcpy	252
wmemmove	252
wmemset	252
wprintf	253
stream.write	293
wscanf	174
XOR operator (^)	60

C++ Elements A to Z

Operators

C++ supports operators for combining smaller expressions into larger expressions. (Each variable and constant is, itself, a simple expression.) The expressions that operators are applied to are called its *operands*.

Operators can be unary, binary, or trinary. Operators that apply to one operand at a time are *unary operators*. Operators that apply to two operands at a time are *binary operators*. The conditional operator (?:) is the only trinary operator; it has three operands.

Table 1 lists C++ operators in order of precedence, placing operators with the same precedence in the same row; items with greatest precedence are listed highest in the table. (Operators with higher precedence are applied first.) Except where otherwise noted, all operators are binary and associate from left to right.

Table 1 *Short Summary of C++ Operators*

Associativity (and type)	Operator
	`()` `[]` `->` `::` `.`
Right to Left (unary)	`!` `~` `++` `--` `-` `*` `&` `sizeof` `new` `delete` `typeid` *casts*
	`.*` `->*`
	`*` `/` `%`
	`+` `-`
	`<<` `>>`
	`<` `<=` `>` `>=`
	`==` `!=`
	`&`
	`^`
	`|`
	`&&`
	`||`
Right to Left (trinary)	`?:`
Right to Left	`=` `+=` `-=` `*=` `/=` `%=` `>>=` `<<=` `&=` `^=` `|=`
	`,`

Table 2 lists operators along with brief descriptions and syntax. Precedence runs from highest (level 1) to lowest (level 16). Association is left to right, except at levels that have an "R" next to the number. (For example, "2R" means that operators at the second level associate right to left.)

Table 2 *Descriptions of C++ Operators*

Level	Operator	Description	Syntax
1	`()`	Function call	`func(args)`
1	`[]`	Array access	`array[int]`
1	`->`	Member access	`ptr->member`
1	`.`	Member access	`obj.member`
1	`::`	Scope resolution	`class::symbol` `::symbol`

Level	Operator	Description	Syntax
2R	!	Logical negation	*!int*
2R	~	Bitwise negation	*~int*
2R	++	Increment	*++lval* *lval++*
2R	--	Decrement	*--lval* *lval--*
2R	-	Arithmetic negation	*-num*
2R	*	Pointer dereference	**ptr*
2R	&	Address of	*&lval*
2R	sizeof	Get size of data	**sizeof**(*expr*) **sizeof**(*type*)
2R	new	Allocate data	**new** *type* **new** *type*(*args*) **new** *type*[*size*]
2R	delete	Remove data	**delete** *ptr* **delete** [] *ptr*
2R	typeid	Get type info	**typeid**(*expr*)
2R	*casts*	Type cast	(*type*) *expr*
3	.*	Pointer to member	*obj.*ptr_mem*
3	->*	Pointer to member	*ptr->*ptr_mem*
4	*	Multiplication	*num * num*
4	/	Division	*num / num*
4	%	Modulus (remainder)	*int % int*
5	+	Addition	*expr + expr*
5	-	Subtraction	*expr - expr*
6	<<	Bitwise left shift	*expr << int*
6	>>	Bitwise right shift	*expr >> int*
7	<	Less than	*expr < expr*
7	<=	Less than or equal to	*expr <= expr*
7	>	Greater than	*expr > expr*
7	>=	Greater than or equal to	*expr >= expr*
8	==	Is equal to	*expr == expr*
8	!=	Is not equal to	*expr != expr*

Continued

Operators

Table 2 *Continued*

Level	Operator	Description	Syntax
9	&	Bitwise AND	*int* **&** *int*
10	^	Bitwise XOR (exclusive OR)	*int* **^** *int*
11	|	Bitwise OR	*int* **|** *int*
12	&&	Logical AND	*expr* **&&** *expr*
13	||	Logical OR	*expr* **||** *expr*
14R	?:	Conditional operator	*expr* **?** *expr* **:** *expr*
15R	=	Assignment	*lval* **=** *expr*
15R	+=	Addition assignment	*lval* **+=** *expr*
15R	-=	Subtraction assignment	*lval* **-=** *expr*
15R	*=	Multiplication assignment	*lval* ***=** *expr*
15R	/=	Division assignment	*lval* **/=** *expr*
15R	%=	Modular-division assignment	*lval* **%=** *expr*
15R	>>=	Right-shift assignment	*lval* **>>=** *int*
15R	<<=	Left-shift assignment	*lval* **<<=** *int*
15R	&=	Bitwise AND assignment	*lval* **&=** *int*
15R	^=	Bitwise XOR assignment	*lval* **^=** *int*
15R	|=	Bitwise OR assignment	*lval* **|=** *int*
16	,	Comma operator (return *expr2*)	*expr1*, *expr2*

In Table 2, *expr* is an expression of any type; *int* is an integer expression (you can use whole numbers or an integer variable);

num is any numeric expression — this includes any expression of primitive type, including char, int, float and double. *ptr* is an address expression, such as p, where p is declared as a pointer, an array name, or &n. *lval* is an lvalue, which is an expression that can appear on the left of an assignment. (See "lvalue" on p. 549 of the glossary.) The other placeholders are more self-explanatory.

The topics in this chapter discuss operators in order of precedence as shown in Tables 1 and 2. Table 3 gives the page reference for each topic.

Table 3 *Operator Topics (Organized by Precedence)*

Operator(s)	Page	Operator(s)	Page
[ ]	47	(*type*)	54
->	48	.*, ->*	55
::	49	*, /, +, –	57
!	50	%	58
~	50	<<, >>	58
++	51	<, <=, >, >=	59
--	51	==, !=	60
–	52	&, ^, !	60
*	53	&&, ||	62
&	53	?:	62
new	98 (Section 4)	=	63
delete	80 (Section 4)	+=, -=, etc.	63
sizeof	106 (Section 4)	,	64
typeid	126 (Section 4)		

[ ]   **Get array element**

Purpose
Gets access to an array element according to an index number (actually an offset).

Syntax
    array[integer]

```
CAuto::go_faster(double inc) {
    speed += inc;
    ::speed = speed;  // Assign to global var.
    return speed;
}
```

! Logically negate (NOT)

Purpose

Reverses a true/false value, returning true if the value is false and vice versa.

Syntax

```
!integer
```

Although the test value should be Boolean, any integer is accepted. The operator returns 0 (false) for any nonzero operand and 1 (true) for a zero operand.

Example

The following example prints a message only if character c is not an uppercase letter.

```
#include <iostream.h>
#include <ctype.h>
//...
if (!isupper(c))
    cout << "Character is not uppercase.";
```

~ Negate bits (bitwise NOT)

Purpose

Negates all bits in a value so that each 1 produces a 0 in the result and vice-versa.

Syntax

```
~integer
```

Examples

The following example applies bitwise negation to the hexadecimal number 0000FFFF, thereby producing FFFF0000:

```
long val = 0x0000FFFF;
cout << hex << ~val << endl;
```

As with all integer operators, ~ converts its result to the prevailing int type, which is 32 bits on most systems. To stick with 16 bits, use data casts:

```
short val = 0x00FF;
cout << hex << (short) ~val << endl;
```

++   Increment

Purpose

Increases the value stored in a variable by 1.

Syntax

The operator comes in two forms:

```
++lvalue     // Pre-increment; return old value + 1

lvalue++     // Post-increment; return old value
```

Both versions add 1 to *lvalue*; the first version, however, increments the operand before it returns a value. An *lvalue* is anything that can appear on the left of an assignment (for example, a variable). For more information on *lvalues*, see page 549 in the glossary.

Examples

These two statements do the same thing: increase the value of n by 1:

```
n++;
++n;
```

Here is another version of the factorial function. This version features the increment operator. Note how post-increment is used here so that n is incremented only *after* being used to multiply the value of amt.

```
long fact(int i) {
     long amt = 1;
     int n = 2;
     while (n <= i)
          amt = amt * n++;   // <= post-increment
     return amt;
}
```

--   Decrement

Purpose

Decreases the value stored in a variable by 1.

Operators

Syntax

The operator comes in two forms:

```
--lvalue      // Pre-decrement; return old value - 1

lvalue--      // Post-decrement; return old value
```

Both versions subtract 1 from *lvalue*; but the first decrements the operand before it returns a value. An *lvalue* is anything that can appear on the left of an assignment (for example, a variable). For more information on *lvalues*, see page 549 in the glossary.

Example

These two statements do the same thing: decrease the value of n by 1:

```
n--;
--n;
```

The difference between pre-decrement and post-decrement is important in this next example. The loop stops executing as soon as n is decremented to 0:

```
long fact(int i) {
    long amt = i;
    int n = i;
    while (--n)              // <= pre-decrement
        amt = amt * n;
    return amt;
}
```

As you can easily verify, if post-decrement were used (n--), fact would always return 0. At some point n would evaluate to 1 and *would then be set* to 0, causing amt to be multiplied by 0 in the statement amt = amt * n.

Arithmetic negation (take "minus of")

Purpose

Returns a positive number for a negative input and vice versa. This is the same as multiplying by –1.

Syntax

```
-number
```

Example

The following example implements an absolute-value function for integers. (The standard library provides this capability as the abs function.)

```
int absval(int n) {
    if (n < 0)
```

```
            return -n;
        return n;
}
```

Purpose

Gets the contents at an address. This is sometimes called the "at" operator.

Syntax

```
*pointer
```

pointer can be any valid address expression, so that *(ptr + 2), for example, is legal.

This symbol is also the binary multiplication operator (see p. 57). C++ uses context to differentiate the two uses.

Examples

Here is an elementary use of the operator.

```
int i = 5;
int *p = &i;
cout << "The variable pointed to contains " << *p;
```

The operator is often used in declarations. The following declaration means that p, when dereferenced, results in an integer. In other words, p is a pointer to an integer:

```
int *p;
```

Multiple levels of reference are possible because a pointer can point to another pointer. A typical case is an array of strings. The following code prints the first character in the first string in the array argv:

```
cout << **argv;
```

This statement is equivalent to the following:

```
cout << *(argv[0]);
```

Purpose

Returns the address of the operand; this creates an address expression which is a constant.

Syntax

```
&lvalue
```

An *lvalue* is anything that can appear on the left of an assignment (for example, a variable). For more information on *lvalues*, see page 549 in the glossary.

Examples

This example sets a pointer p so that it contains the address of integer i:

```
int i, *p;
p = &i;
```

The symbol & is used in declarations to create *references* (see p. 562 in the glossary) and also, depending on context, as the binary AND operator (see p. 60). In initializations, & retains its simple meaning as an address operator.

```
int *p = &i;
```

For an introduction to the subject of pointers and addresses, see Part II, Chapter 3.

(type)	**C-style type cast**

Purpose

Converts the data type of an expression.

Syntax

This operator comes in two versions:

```
(type) expression
type (expression)
```

The resulting expression has the same value as the *expression* operand, but with data type converted to specified *type*. You can use this operator to perform any of the tasks fulfilled by the ANSI C++ keywords const_cast (p. 78), reinterpret_cast (p. 103), and static_cast (p. 109).

Remarks

Although, in theory, a cast does not change value, it may actually modify data significantly. For example, this code converts integer 10 to floating point 10.0:

```
int i = 10;
float f = (float) i;
```

Although the face value 10 is preserved, the cast changes the underlying bits. Similarly, you can cast between objects of different classes if the conversion is supported, but the result usually alters the data. Suppose class B has a constructor B(A). In that case, you can apply the (B) cast:

```
A a_obj;
B b_obj = (B) a_obj;
```

The result is that the value of a_obj is "converted" to B, but what actually happens is that constructor B(A) gets called.

The C-style cast operator is supported mainly for backward compatibility. The C++ cast operators are now preferred, because each has a narrow, well-defined purpose; this makes for better programming discipline as well as being more self-documenting. These operators are const_cast (p. 78), dynamic_cast (p. 82), reinterpret_cast (p. 103), and static_cast (p. 104).

Examples

The most common practical uses for the cast operator are:

- Suppressing a compiler warning when you assign a larger type to a smaller type. In some cases, this involves involve rounding:

```
double d = 4.25;
int n = (int) d;   // Assign 4 to n.
```

- Casting a void* pointer, such as the value returned by malloc, to a more specific pointer type:

```
short *p = (short*) malloc(100 * sizeof(short));
```

- Casting a base-class address to a derived-class pointer (note that you can go in the reverse direction without a cast):

```
B b_obj;
D *pd = (D*) &b_obj;
```

- Adding or removing the const attribute, especially from an address.

```
const int n = 12;
funk((int*) &n);   // Remove const from &n.
```

.*, ->*   **Apply pointer-to-member offset**

Purpose

Gets a member of an object in which the member is determined by a variable offset. (This offset can point to different members at different times.) These are rarely used, so feel free to skip this topic!

Syntax

These operators are used with a special type of variable (called a *pointer-to-member* variable) declared with a class prefix:

```
type class::*ptr_to_mem;
```

Such a variable is not a real pointer at all, but an offset within a class. A pointer-to-member variable can represent different members at different times. Here is a summary of the syntax for operations on these variables:

Operator (with syntax)	Description
object.*ptr_to_mem	Applies offset stored in ptr_to_mem to access a member of object.
ptr->*ptr_to_mem	Dereferences ptr to get an object, and then applies offset in ptr_to_mem to access a member of that object.

Examples

Assume you have declared a class CHorse, along with an object called horse:

```
class CHorse {
  public:
      int   breed;
      int   age;
      int   race(void);
} horse;
```

You can declare a pointer-to-member variable as in the following statement. This declaration states that pData can point to any int data member of CHorse:

```
int CHorse::*pData;   // Declare pData as ptr-to-mem
                      //  for an int data member.
```

The next statement sets up the relationship between pData and the age data member. This statement gets the offset of age.

```
pData = &CHorse::age;  // Store offset of age within
                       //  the CHorse class.
```

At this point, pData stores the offset from the beginning of the CHorse class to the age data member. This offset, in turn, can be used to access the age member, given a CHorse object (horse, in this example). Note the use of the operator .* here.

```
int i = horse.*pData; // Get data at offset
                      //  pData (=age).
```

At this point, you may object that accessing a member this way is no different from doing this:

```
int i = horse.age;
```

If you made this objection, you are correct. The only versatility provided by a pointer-to-member variable such as pData is that it can act as a stand-in for different members at different times. For example, you can use it to represent age, and then you can use it later to represent breed (another int field).

```
pData = &CHorse::age;
int i = horse.*pData;   // Get horse.age.


pData = &CHorse::breed;
int j = horse.*pData;   // Get horse.breed.
```

Alternatively, you can access the object through a pointer, using ->*:

```
CHorse * ptr = &horse;
int i = ptr->*pData;
```

You can also use a pointer-to-member object to store an offset to a function. Some extra parentheses are necessary during declaration of the pointer-to-member object, but otherwise, the basic procedure is roughly the same as for data members.

```
int (CHorse::*pFunc)();   // Declare pFunc as ptr to
                          //   an int member function.
pFunc = &CHorse::race;
int k = (horse.*pFunc)();   // Call horse.race().
```

Pointer-to-member operations are most likely to be useful in situations in which a class has a large number of members of the same type, and you want to refer to different members at different times. You can pass a pointer-to-member variable to a function instead of having to use some other scheme (such as an enumerated constant) to indicate on which member the function should operate.

*, /, +, -	Perform arithmetic

Purpose

Adds, subtracts, multiplies, or divides, and returns results. Each of these operators takes two operands.

Syntax

```
x * y      // Multiply; higher precedence
x / y      // Divide;   higher precedence
x + y      // Add;      lower precedence
x - y      // Subtract; lower precedence
```

In this syntax, x and y can be any two numbers. Also, with addition, exactly one of the operands can be an address; the result is another address. With subtraction, the first operand (x) can be an address; if both operands are addresses, the result is a scaled number. (See "Pointer arithmetic" in the glossary, p. 557.)

Operators

Examples

These four operators follow standard mathematical conventions: multiplication and division have higher precedence. For example, this statement:

```
x = y * 2 + z / 3;
```

is equivalent to this one:

```
x = (y * 2) + (z / 3);
```

%	Get remainder (modulus)

Purpose

Divides one integer by another and returns the remainder (modulus function).

Syntax

```
integer % integer
```

This operator has the same precedence as multiplication and division (*, /).

Examples

The operator divides the first integer by the second and returns the remainder. For example:

```
cout << 21 % 2;    // Prints "1"
cout << 20 % 2;    // Prints "0"
cout << 18 % 5;    // Prints "3"
```

A common application for this operator is to determine whether one number divides another evenly; if it does, the operator returns 0. The following function returns true for even numbers, false for odd.

```
boolean is_even(int n) {
    return (n % 2 == 0);
}
```

<<, >>	Shift bits

Purpose

Shifts position of 1s and 0s within the binary representation of a number and returns results.

Syntax

```
value << number_of_bits    // Shift left
value >> number_of_bits    // Shift right
```

In this syntax, both value and number_of_bits must be integers.

Examples

The following loop prints the leftmost bit of test_val, shifts bits to the left
by one, and then repeats. The effect is to print out test_val in binary radix.

```
unsigned short test_val = 255, i, c;

for(i = 0; i < 16, i++)
    c = (test_val & 0x8000) ? '1' : '0';
    cout << c;
    test_val = test_val << 1;    // <= Shift bits.
}
```

Note that as bits are shifted to the left, 0 is placed in the rightmost digits.
(Similarly for right shifts.) The following figure illustrates how bit patterns
change with each shift.

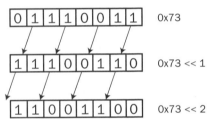

Effect of bit shifts.

<, <=, >, >=   **Compare values**

Purpose

Tests two numbers by comparing their values. The result in each case is
a Boolean: either true (1) or false (0).

Syntax

```
x < y       // Is x less than y?
x <= y      // Is x less or equal to y?
x > y       // Is x greater than y?
x >= y      // Is x greater than or equal to y?
```

In each case, x and y can be any two numbers or any two address expressions
(pointers). It is not valid to compare a pointer to a nonpointer. Address comparisons are meaningful within arrays. For example, &array[10] is always
greater than &array[5].

| &&, || | **Combine Boolean expressions (AND, OR)** |

Purpose

Performs logical AND or OR, using short-circuit logic where appropriate, and returns true (0) or false (1).

Syntax

```
integer && integer     // Logical AND
integer || integer     // Logical OR
```

Each operand can be any integer expression, but generally, each should be a Boolean. All nonzero inputs are considered "true."

C and C++ use short-circuit logic for these operators: With AND (&&), if the first operand evaluates to false (0), the second is not evaluated. With OR (||), if the first operand evaluates to true (nonzero), the second is not evaluated. Unlike & and |, these operators do not compare individual bits.

Example

These operators are best used to combine Boolean expressions. This example says, "If x is greater than or equal to min and x is less than or equal to max, print a message." This example works without additional parentheses because of precedence rules.

```
if (x >= min && x <= max)
    cout << "x is in range."
```

| ?: | **Conditional operator** |

Purpose

Evaluates a conditional expression and selects a different value depending on whether the expression is true (nonzero) or false (0).

Syntax

```
condition ? true_value : false_value
```

C++ first evaluates condition. If it is nonzero, true_value is evaluated and returned as the value of the overall expression; otherwise, false_value is evaluated and returned.

Example

The purpose of the conditional operator is to let you write if-else structures more compactly. It also makes it possible to squeeze if-else logic into macros.

Consider this if-else structure:

```
if (0x8000 & test_val)
    c = '1';
```

```
else
    c = '0';
```

With the help of the conditional operator, this four-line example can be
rewritten as a compact expression:

```
c = (0x8000 & test_val ? '1' : '0');
```

| **=** | Simple assignment |

Purpose

Places a value inside a variable (or other *lvalue*).

Syntax

```
lvalue = source_value
```

lvalue is an expression that can be assigned a value. The most typical case
is a variable, but other cases include array elements and data members. For
more information on *lvalues*, see page 549 in the glossary.

The assignment expression, *lvalue = source_value*, returns the value
assigned; assignment can therefore appear within a larger expression. Be
careful not to confuse it with test-for-equality (==), described on page 60.

Example

The simplest use of assignment is to put a value in a variable:

```
n = 5 + i;      // Assign 5 + i to n
```

You can also assign values to elements, data members, and dereferenced
pointers. For example:

```
int p = &n;      // Initialize p
*p = 5 + i;      // Assign 5 + i to *p
```

The first statement in this example *initializes* pointer p (because it is part of a
declaration); the second *assigns* the data (5 + i) to dereferenced pointer *p.
Although initialization and assignment are not precisely the same, C++
makes little distinction, permitting (unlike C) any valid expression on the
right side in both cases.

| **+=, -=, *=, etc.** | Operate and assign |

Purpose

Performs an operation and places the result in the left operand.

Syntax

```
lvalue @= operand2
```

In this syntax, replace @ with one of these binary operators: +, -, *, /, %, >>, <<, &, ^, |. The result is the same as:

```
lvalue = lvalue @ operand2
```

lvalue is an expression that can be assigned a value, such as a variable. See page 549 in the glossary for more information on *lvalues*.

The expression returns the value that was assigned.

Example

These statements add 5 to n and then double it:

```
n += 5;
n *= 2;
```

The effect is the same as these two statements:

```
n = n + 5;
n = n * 2;
```

So, for example, if n contained 10, it will contain 30 after the two statements are executed.

, Evaluate sequence of expressions

Purpose

Evaluates two expressions and returns the value of the last one.

Syntax

```
expression1, expression2
```

The value of *expression2* is returned.

Example

This operator is useful when you want to squeeze a series of operations into a place that takes only a single expression. For example:

```
while (a = func1(), b = a * 2, b > 0) {
// Do some stuff...
}
```

Here, the comma operator is used to combine several expressions into one. At runtime, all of these are evaluated, in the sequence given.

```
a = func1(), b = a * 2, b > 0
```

The beauty of this code is that it lets you carry out a couple of different operations before evaluating the actual loop condition (b > 0).

Keywords

The keywords of a language are the predefined names that have universal meaning within the language. You cannot use them for your own variable and functions names. The major groups of keywords covered in this section are:

- Data types: bool, char, short, int, long, float, double, long double, as well as unsigned versions of the integer types.
- Cast operators: const_cast, dynamic_cast, reinterpret_cast, static_cast.
- Other operators: new, delete, sizeof, and typeid.
- Control statements: if-else, while, do, for, try-catch, switch, case, default, goto, break, and continue.
- Miscellaneous keywords.

Table 1 summarizes C++ standard data types.

Table 3 *C++ Primitive Data Types*

Casting operator	Major use
if (*cond*) *stmt* [**else** *stmt*]	If condition is true, execute first statement; otherwise execute statement after else (if present).
while(*cond*) *stmt*	While condition is true, execute statement.
do *stmt* **while**(*cond*);	Execute statement; then while condition is true, repeat.
for (*init*; *cond*; *inc*) *stmt*	Execute *init* once; then while condition is true, execute statement and increment (*inc*).
switch(*test_val*) { *stmts* }	Evaluate *test_val*, then jump to the matching case value, if any, within the statements.
case *val*: *stmt*	Identify a case value within a switch statement block.
default: *stmt*	Identify the default case within a switch statement block.
break;	Exit out of nearest enclosing loop or switch statement block.
continue;	Advance to next iteration of loop.
goto *label*;	Jump directly to target labeled statement.

The syntax for each of these keywords forms a complete, executable statement. This makes it easy to nest structures inside of other structures to any level. For example, the syntax of if is:

```
if statement1 [else statement2]
```

This syntax includes one or two statements, but at the same time forms a complete statement itself, so that the whole thing can be placed inside another if statement, as well as within a do, while, or for statement.

Remember also that wherever syntax calls for a statement, you can use a compound statement; this consists of any number of statements placed between braces ({}). See page 532 in the glossary.

Keywords

Purpose

Translates one or more symbolic machine instructions. Assembly is useful for people adapting to the low-level requirements of hardware. Otherwise, it is nearly a dead art.

Syntax

Here is the universal ANSI C++ syntax:

```
asm ("assembly_instruction");
```

Some compilers, such as Borland C++, support three other versions. In the second version, (newline) denotes the end of a physical line.

```
asm assembly_instruction;

asm assembly_instruction    (newline)

asm {
    assembly_instructions
}
```

Microsoft Visual C++ supports similar syntax, but uses the __asm keyword. In the first version, __asm is a statement separator, so multiple instructions can appear on the same line.

```
__asm assembly_instruction

__asm {
    assembly_instructions
}
```

Example

This example uses the Microsoft Visual C++ keyword __asm to load a variable into a register, add 1 to it, and store the result. The AX register is pushed onto the stack, which in general is a good practice, because you can't assume that the register isn't being used for some other purpose.

```
#include <iostream.h>

main (void) {
    short var = 0;
    __asm {
      push ax
      mov ax,var
      add ax,1
```

```
            mov var,ax
            pop ax
        }
        cout << var << endl;
        return 0;
    }
```

auto   Allocate automatic variable

Purpose

Specifies automatic storage class, which means that each call to the function gets its own copy of the variable. Local variables have this storage class by default.

Syntax

```
auto data_declaration
```

bool   True/false data type

Purpose

Declares a value that can be either true (1) or false (0).

Syntax

The following syntax creates a data declaration.

```
bool var [, var]... ;
```

Examples

The following example uses a bool variable to build a condition.

```
bool b1, b2, b3;
b1 = (32 * y) / 2 < x;
b2 = x < 500;
b3 = b1 && b2;           // b3 = b1 AND b2
if (b3)
    func1();
```

The next example uses a Boolean flag variable, initialized to true:

```
bool do_more = true;
while (do_more) {
    // Do some stuff...
    if (x > 100)
        do_more = false;
    // Do some more stuff...
}
```

Any nonzero value assigned to a bool variable is converted to true (1). Although you can use int in most situations in which you can use bool, use of the bool type enforces better programming discipline.

break — Exit current loop or switch

Purpose

Exits out of the nearest enclosing switch statement or loop.

Syntax

```
break;
```

This statement is valid only within a switch statement or a loop (do, for, or while). Execution jumps to the first statement after the switch or loop.

Example

break is needed at the end of each case inside a switch, unless you want control to fall through.

```
case 1:
     strcpy(strNum, "One");
     break;
case 2:
     strcpy(strNum, "Two");
     break;
     //...
```

See page 111 for more information on the switch statement.

case — Define target for switch

Purpose

Labels a target statement within a switch statement block.

Syntax

```
case constant_value:
     statement
```

Within a switch block, control is transferred to *statement* if *constant_value* matches the switch test value.

Example

In this example, control transfers to the statement if the test value matches any of the ASCII values a, e, i, o, or u. Any number of labels can precede a single statement.

```
case 'a':
```

Keywords

```
case 'e':
case 'i':
case 'o':
case 'u':
    cout << "Letter is a vowel."
    break;
```

See the switch topic on page 111 for more information.

---

catch   **Define exception handler**

Purpose

Defines an exception handler within a try-catch block. An exception is an
unusual program occurrence that demands immediate attention.

Syntax

```
catch (exception_type [object]) {
    statements
}
```

The object, if included, refers to the exception object that was passed by the
code raising the exception. The brackets indicate that object is optional; if it
is present, the statements can refer to this object, which may contain useful
information about the event.

You can also use case to write a default exception handler, which catches
any exception thrown but not yet caught. Here the ellipses (. . .) are
intended literally:

```
catch (...) {
    statements
}
```

See page 122 for more information on try statements.

---

char   **One-byte character**

Purpose

Declares a single-byte integer that's large enough to store a single ASCII
character.

Syntax

The following syntax creates a data declaration.

```
char var [, var]... ;
```

Range

Usually the same as signed char (–128 to 127), depending on implementation.

Examples

Technically, the char type is an integer. When you assign a character to it, you actually transfer an ASCII value.

```
char ch = 'A'    // Set ch to numeric value 65, which
                 //  is the ASCII code for A.
```

The char data type is mainly used to build strings, which are arrays of characters. You can initialize a char array with a string literal. In this example, a storage space of 20 bytes is allocated, and the first three characters are initialized.

```
char message[20] = "Hi!";
```

In the next example, the compiler allocates exactly as many bytes as are needed to hold the string, including one for the terminating null.

```
char message2[] = "This is a warning.";
```

The char type is equivalent to either signed char or unsigned char, depending on the compiler implementation.

●—NOTE

Some character sets, particularly the Unicode character set, require a larger storage space for each character. The wchar_t type is provided for use with these sets.

When coding a char value, you can enclose a standard printable character in single or double quotation marks. You can also use one of the escape sequences shown in Table 2 of Section 3 on page 44.

class	Declare user-defined type

Purpose

Declares a user-defined data type, or *class*, which can contain both variables and functions.

Syntax

```
class name [: base_class_declarations] {
    declarations
} [object_definitions];
```

The brackets indicate that the base class declarations and object definitions are optional. See page 383 in Chapter 5 for more information on base class declarations. The effect is the same as the struct keyword, except that member access is private by default.

The *declarations* can include variables, function declarations, or both.

Example

The following code declares a class CIoStr derived from base class CStr. This declaration also declares several objects (str1, str2, and str3). status is private, because members are private by default.

```
class CIoStr : public CStr {
     int status;
public:
     void input(void);
     void output(void);
} str1, str2, str3;
```

In this case, the declarations of member functions input and output must be provided later. Functions can also be defined within the class declaration, in which case they are inlined. See Chapter 5 for more information.

---

const   Prevent changes to variable

Purpose

Prevents changes to a variable, argument, or (in the case of pointers) a value pointed to.

Syntax

The simple version prevents changes to *item*:

```
const type item
```

const can also modify a pointer declaration. This prevents changes to the item pointed to.

```
const type *pointer
```

The const keyword can also be used *inside* a pointer declaration. Using const this way prevents changes to the pointer itself.

```
type * const pointer
```

It's even possible to declare a const pointer to a const type — which means that neither the pointer nor the thing it points to can be changed.

```
const type * const pointer
```

Usage 1: const Variables

You can apply const to a simple variable. After the variable is defined, the compiler rejects all statements in which the variable is the target of an assignment. However, initialization is permitted.

```
const int id = 12345;   // This is valid; id may be
                        //   initialized.
...
id = 10000;   // ERROR! attempt to assign new value.
```

You can also declare compound types, such as arrays and classes, as const. In that case, all members and elements of the object are protected from change.

Usage 2: const Pointers

The following declaration says that "p points to a const integer." In other words, p points to an integer that cannot be changed.

```
const int *p;
```

Although p itself can change in this case, *p cannot. C++ has these rules regarding the interaction of pointers and const data:

- A const pointer can point to both const and non-const data.
- An ordinary pointer cannot point to const data.

The second rule is necessary to prevent sneaky tricks like this one:

```
const int id = 12345;
int *p = &id;           // ERROR! This is not allowed.
(*p)++;
```

You can try to get around the rules with a const pointer, but that won't work because if p is a pointer to const data, *p cannot be changed.

```
const int id = 12345;
const int *p = &id;   // This is okay.
(*p)++;               // ERROR! *p is const!
```

Usage 3: const Argument Types

Here's a question that comes up sometimes: how do you pass an address, yet prevent changes to the data at that address? The technique for doing this is to declare a const pointer argument. The function gets a pointer to data, but it agrees not to use that pointer to change the data. For example:

```
void fnct(const char str[], const double *px,
     const double *py);
```

Within the function, the values of *str, *px, and *py can all be read. Nevertheless, the following statements — which attempt to assign values to the data pointed to — cause errors:

```
*str = 'a';           // ERROR!
str[2] = 'z';         // ERROR!
*px = 0.0;            // ERROR!
*py = 98.6;           // ERROR!
```

It is an error to use a const pointer to change data pointed to even if an offset is involved (as in the expression str[2] above).

Usage 4: const Member Functions and Objects

If you declare an object with const, you can only call const member functions of this object. Such functions agree not to change any data members.

You can declare a member function as const by placing the keyword at the end of the declaration, but before the definition, if any. For example:

```
class:CStr {
        int getlength(void) const {return nLength;}
        char *get(void) const {return pData;}
        //...
```

You can overload a member function so that it has both a const version and a version that is not const (with no difference in the signature than the use of the const keyword).

const_cast   Remove const attribute

Purpose

Removes or adds the const attribute from an address expression.

Syntax

const_cast<type>(expr)

This expression has the same value as expr, converted to the specified type. The type can differ from expr's original type only by the addition or removal of const or volatile.

Examples

Assume that x has type const double:

```
const double x = 2.1714;
```

Here is a correct use of const_cast, converting &x from type const double* to double*:

```
const_cast<double*>(&x)
```

The need for const_cast arises because there are some functions that should be declared with const pointers but are not. For example, it is safe to pass const data to this function, because it does not use the pointer to change data:

```
void display_num(double *p) {
   printf("The value is %2.3f\n", *p);
}
```

Yet you cannot pass the address of x to this function unless you first use const_cast. Remember that it's an error to pass a const address to a non-const argument.

```
display_num(&x);        // ERROR!! &x is const double*!
```

But const_cast removes the const attribute from &x, yielding a standard double* argument:

```
display_num(const_cast<double*>(&x));
```

Remember that const_cast is a workaround for special situations like these. If you use it in other situations, the result can cause errors. const_cast is a loaded gun. Be careful not to shoot yourself.

●—ANSI

The const_cast operator is an extended ANSI feature, not supported in earlier versions of C++.

continue | Go to next iteration of loop

Purpose

Advances to the next cycle of the nearest enclosing for, do, or while loop.

Syntax

```
continue;
```

Example

The following loop prints out all the prime numbers between 1 and n. If a number is not a prime, the loop immediately advances to the next value of i. Otherwise, it prints out the number and increments num_of_primes before continuing. It's assumed that is_a_prime is a function defined somewhere in the program.

```
for(i = 1; i <= n; i++) {
    if (! is_a_prime(i))
        continue;
    printf("%d\n", i);
    num_of_primes++;
}
```

Note that continue causes the loop counter i to be incremented, but not num_of_primes.

delete   Release objects

Purpose

Deletes a data item previously allocated with new. If the item's type has a destructor function, that destructor is called before the memory is freed.

Syntax

The delete operator has two versions:

```
delete pointer;
delete [] pointer;
```

pointer must contain the address of memory previously allocated with new (see p. 98). If new was used to create multiple items, use the second version of the delete syntax when you want to remove the items. Note that brackets ([ ]) are intended literally.

Examples

```
int *p1, *p2;
p1 = new int;
p2 = new int[100];   // Allocate array.
//...
delete p1;
delete [] p2;        // Note use of [] to delete array.
```

default   Define "else" target for switch

Purpose

Labels a statement inside a switch-case block; the switch statement transfers control to this statement if none of the case values match the test value.

Syntax

```
default: statement
```

See page 111 for more information on the switch statement.

do   Execute loop at least once

Purpose

Executes a statement as long as a specified condition is true (similar to while, except that do ensures that the statement is executed at least once).

Syntax

```
do
     statement
while (expression);
```

The loop executes the *statement* and then evaluates *expression*. If it is true (nonzero), the process is repeated; otherwise, the loop terminates. The *statement* is frequently a compound statement, although it is not required to be.

Example

The following code prints characters from a file until the end of the file is reached.

```
#include <stdio.h>
//...
do {
    c = getc(fp);
    putchar(c);
} while (c != EOF);
```

See also while on page 136.

double | Double-precision floating point

Purpose

Declares an eight-byte floating-point number.

Syntax

The following syntax creates a data declaration.

```
double var [, var]... ;
```

Range

Between plus and negative 1.797693×10^{308}. The type has 10 digits of precision. I shudder at the thought that anyone needs this large a range, but there it is.

Other than zero itself — which can be represented precisely — the tiniest numbers supported are positive and negative $2.225074 \times 10^{-308}$ (10^{-308} is the same as $1/10^{308}$).

Examples

You can form floating-point constants by using either standard decimal notation or by using exponential form, in which *numEexp* equals *num* times 10 to the power of *exp*. (You can use either uppercase or lowercase "E.") For example:

```
double amt = 0.0;      // amt assigned zero precisely.
double x = 25.72;      // Standard decimal form.
double y = 3.5e2;      // y = 350.0
double tiny = 3.1e-3;  // tiny = 0.0031
double biggie = 2e5;   // biggie = 200,000
```

All of these statements store constants as double values, because double is the default floating-point type. This is true even with constants that fall into the smaller float range, as these constants do.

| **dynamic_cast** | Verify runtime type (polymorphic cast) |

Purpose

Casts a pointer to a more specific type, after first verifying that the object pointed to has that type.

Syntax

```
dynamic_cast<class*>(ptr)
```

At runtime, the program checks the type of the object pointed to by *ptr*. If this type is *class* or a type derived from *class*, the expression returns a *class** pointer to the object. Otherwise, it returns a null pointer.

There are two restrictions: (a) the classes involved must have at least one virtual function, and (b) some compilers require a runtime-type information (RTTI) option to be set, such as /GR for Microsoft Visual C++.

Example

What makes dynamic_cast useful is that a base-class pointer can point to many different subtypes (derived classes). There may be times you want to cast the base-class pointer back to the derived class. This example declares a class B and a class D derived from B.

```
class B {
public:
    virtual void func1(int);
};

class D : public B {
public:
    void func2(void);
};

D od;
B *pb;
pb = &od;    // Point to object of subclass D.
```

Although pb's declared type is B*, the actual type pointed to is D.

The following function uses dynamic_cast to check whether the argument, which has type B*, actually points to an object of class D. If it does, the function can take advantage of this fact by calling func2, which is defined only in D and classes derived from D.

```
void process_B(B* arg) {
   D *pd;
   pd = dynamic_cast<D*>(arg);   // <- cast
   if (pd)
      pd->func2();
   //...
}
```

If arg points to an object of class D or a class derived from D, the cast succeeds, and it is therefore safe to call func2 through the pointer. Otherwise,
the cast fails and pd is assigned NULL.

●─ANSI

The dynamic_cast operator is an extended ANSI feature that is not
supported in earlier versions of C++. Note that some compilers only provide this feature when it is explicitly turned on through the use of a compiler flag (e.g., /GR for Microsoft Visual C++ 6.0).

else   Execute alternative

Purpose
Specifies an alternative statement in an if block.

Syntax
```
if (condition)
   statement1
else
   statement2
```

See if on page 90 for examples and more information.

enum   Define list of sequential constants

Purpose
Declares a list of symbolic constants, each of which is assigned a different
value. (The word *enumeration* is a fancy word for list.)

Syntax
```
enum [enum_type_name] {
     item_1, item_2, ... item_n
} [variable_declarations];
```

The effect is to define each *item* as a symbolic constant. Each item can
optionally be assigned a specific integer value:

```
item = integer_value
```

Keywords

extern
Share externally defined variable

Purpose
Gives a variable external storage class, which means that it may be defined in another module. A variable is shared among all modules that include an extern declaration for it.

Syntax
```
extern ["C"] declaration
```

The brackets indicate that "C" is optional. If included, "C" tells the compiler that the variable is declared in a C-language source file.

Example
This example defines the variable amount in module1.cpp and makes the variable available to all modules. Note that the variable must be defined in exactly one place.

```
// MODULE1.CPP
extern int amount;
int amount = 0; // <- Variable defined here.

// MODULE2.CPP
extern int  amount;

// MODULE3.CPP
extern int  amount;
```

false
Boolean constant

Purpose
Specifies the Boolean value false (0).

Syntax
```
false
```

Example
The following declaration creates a Boolean value and initializes it.

```
bool flag1 = false;
```

float
Single-precision floating point

Purpose
Declares a four-byte floating-point number.

Syntax

The following syntax creates a data declaration.

```
float var [, var]... ;
```

Range

Between plus and negative 3.4×10^{38}. The type has six digits of precision. Other than zero itself — which can be represented precisely — the tiniest numbers supported are positive and negative 1.175×10^{-38} (10^{-38} is the same as $1/10^{38}$).

Examples

You can form floating-point constants by using either standard decimal notation or by using exponential form, in which *numEexp* equals *num* times 10 to the power of *exp*. (You can use either uppercase or lowercase "E.") However, an F suffix is needed to tell the compiler to store the constants as float values. For example:

```
float amt = 0.0F;      // amt assigned zero precisely.
float x = 25.72F;      // Standard decimal form.
float y = 3.5e2F;      // y = 350.0
float tiny = 3.1e-3F;  // tiny = 0.0031
float biggie = 2e5F;   // biggie = 200,000.0
```

Without the use of the F suffix — or, alternatively, a (float) type cast — the constants are stored as double. The compiler may issue an annoying warning message about possible loss of data. The best policy is to use the F suffix when initializing a float variable.

●—NOTE

The float type is not the best choice for most floating-point operations. When C++ evaluates a floating-point expression, it promotes it to double for better precision. The principal use of the float type is for declaring large arrays where space is at a premium. See double on page 81.

Keywords

for — Execute loop a fixed number of times

Purpose

Executes a loop a fixed number of times, using a counter ranging from 1 to N (0 to N-1 in the case of array indexes). for is actually much more versatile than this, but this is how it's typically used.

Syntax

```
for (initializer; condition; increment)
    loop_statement
```

This syntax is equivalent to the following while statement. (I've added comments relating the syntax to the upcoming example.) *initializer* is executed just once, and *increment* is executed after each trip through the loop.

```
initializer;           // Set i = 1.
while (condition) {     // While i <= 100, do more.
    loop_statement
    increment;          // i = i + 1
}
```

These two code blocks are identical in effect, except that with the for statement, continue causes *increment* to be executed before continuing.

Examples

The typical way to use for is with a loop variable, such as i in the following example. This code prints all the numbers from 1 to 100.

```
#include <iostream.h>
//...

for (i = 1; i <= 100; i++) {
    cout << i;
    cout << ", ";
}
```

The *initializer* expression (i = 1) is executed exactly once.

Then *condition* (i <= 100) is tested. If true, the statements in the block are executed, then *increment* (i++) is executed, and then the process is repeated. If the condition is false (zero), the loop terminates immediately.

Note that although this is a typical use, the three expressions *increment*, *condition*, *increment* can be any valid C++ expressions.

Array indexes run from 0 to N-1. A common use of for is to initialize all the elements of an array. Here the code sets every element of the_values to 0:

```
int i, the_values[50];
for (i = 0; i < 50; i++)
    the_values[i] = 0;
```

The comma operator (,) can be useful within a for statement because it enables you to squeeze multiple operations into an expression. For example, this loop initializes and increments two loop variables, i and j:

```
for (i = 0, j = 0; i < MAX_SIZE; i++, j++)
    //...
```

friend   Enable access to class

Purpose

Gives a global function access to all members of a class. This is mainly useful for writing operator functions, which need access to class internals. The keyword can also be applied to an entire class, although this is rare.

Syntax

To declare a function as a friend of a class, include a prototype of the function inside the class declaration, preceded by the friend keyword. The access level, in this case, does not matter.

```
class name {
     //...
     friend function_prototype;
```

To declare another class as a friend, use the following syntax. (Substitute struct or union for class, as appropriate, if the friend class is declared with struct or union.)

```
class name {
     //...
     friend class class_name;
```

Example

In C++, friendship should usually be avoided, because it weakens encapsulation. Friend functions have one main purpose: to help write binary operator functions.

In this example, the operator+ function is written as a global, but it needs access to a private member of class CFix, which it gets as a friend. See Chapter 7 for background on operator functions.

```
class CFix {
private:
     long amount;
     friend CFix operator+(long lng, CFix cf);
     //...
};
// Operator function for long + CFix.
// Because this function is a friend, it can access
//   amount, a private member.
//
CFix operator+(long lng, CFix cf) {
     CFix result;
     result.amount = (lng * 1000) + cf.amount;
     return result;
}
```

Friendship has two rules of nontransitivity, which matter only in rare situations:

- If class C1 is a friend of C2, and C2 is a friend of C3, C1 is not automatically a friend of C3. The friend of my friend is not necessarily my friend.
- If class C1 is a friend of C2, then a derived class D of C1 is not automatically a friend of C2. The child of my friend is not necessarily my friend.

goto   Jump to labeled statement (create spaghetti code)

Purpose

Transfers control to a particular statement. The danger of using goto with wild abandon is that you can create programs that look like spaghetti.

Syntax

```
goto label;
```

goto unconditionally transfers control to the target labeled statement, which must be in the same function.

Example

```
goto the_end;
//...
the_end:
    return n;
```

A goto statement can be useful as a way of breaking out from several levels of enclosed loops. In most cases, the availability of the break and continue statements makes goto unnecessary. If you're using a structured language, why use goto?

if   Execute conditionally

Purpose

Executes a statement if a particular condition is true; also supports optional else clause.

Syntax

```
if (expression)
    statement1
[ else
    statement2 ]
```

Here the brackets indicate that the else clause is optional. Note that
statement1 and statement2 are frequently compound statements, using
opening and closing braces ({}), although this is not required.

If *expression* is nonzero (true), *statement1* is executed If *expression* is zero
(false) and else *statement2* is included, *statement2* is executed. The expression can be any valid C expression of integer type, although it's wise to stick
with Boolean expressions.

Examples

Here is a simple use of if.

```
if (x == y) puts("x equals y!");
```

By nesting an if statement inside an else clause, you can create a virtual
"elseif" keyword:

```
if (a < b)
    return -1;
else if (a == b)
    return 0;
else
    return 1;
```

This statement is equivalent to:

```
if (a < b)
    return -1;
else {
    if (a == b)
        return 0;
    else
        return 1;
}
```

Occasionally braces are required to associate else with a certain if statement. By default, an else clause associates with the nearest matching if
statement.

Keywords

●─NOTE

Within a condition, remember not to confuse test for equality (==) with
assignment (=). Chapter 2 discusses this problem in more depth.

inline   Place function code inline

Purpose

Indicates that a function should be expanded into the body of the calling
function rather than implemented through a CALL instruction. (See p. 546
in the glossary.)

Syntax

```
inline function_definition
```

Example

```
inline double cube_it(double x) {
     return x * x * x;
}
```

The inline keyword is a suggestion to the compiler. Some compilers optimize a program by automatically inlining some functions. A member function is automatically inlined whenever its definition is inside the class
declaration.

int   Signed integer

Purpose

Declares a standard-sized integer, which can store both positive and negative
values.

Syntax

The following syntax creates a data declaration.

```
int var [, var]... ;
```

Range

−32,768 to 32,767 (16-bit systems), or approximately negative to positive
2 billion (32-bits systems), depending on implementation.

Example

```
int i, j, kount, hexno, octno;
i = 25;
j = -1;
kount = 10500;
hexno = 0xFF;   // hex FF = 255;
octno = 010;    // octal 10 = 8;
```

The int type was developed as the "natural" integer size — the same size
as the processor's own registers. By its nature, the type doesn't make for

portable code. However, it's used in the standard library, so to some extent you're stuck with it. By now, 32-bit processor width is so universal that int is almost equivalent to long. Be careful about porting to 16-bit systems, however; in that case, int should be handled as you would handle a short.

In C and C++, you can use hexadecimal or octal radix to write integer constants. Both use a leading zero:

```
0Xdigits    // Hex ('x' may be upper or lowercase)
0digits     // Octal
```

Also, you can use the L suffix to force storage of a constant as a long:

```
int x = 0L;   // Constant 0 is stored in 32 bits.
```

long   Signed four-byte integer

Purpose
Declares a four-byte integer, which can store both positive and negative values.

Syntax
The following syntax creates a data declaration.

```
long var [, var]... ;
```

Range
–2,147,483,648 to 2,147,483,647 (approximately plus or minus 2.1 billion).

Examples
```
long i = 350100, j = -5, k = -123000555;
```

You can use the L suffix to specify that a constant be stored as a long. Without this suffix, the compiler stores numbers as short, as long as they fit in that range.

```
long i = 5L;    // 5L is stored as a long.
```

In this case, the use of the L suffix makes no difference, because on assignment to i, the number is promoted to long anyway. However, there are some rare situations in which the suffix makes a difference: for example, function arguments in which you need to guarantee that data pointed to has a particular size.

For more information on the notation of integer constants, see unsigned short (p. 132) and int (previous topic).

Keywords

long double
Extra-long floating point

Purpose

Declares a floating-point number at least eight bytes wide; potentially larger on some systems.

Syntax

The following syntax creates a data declaration.

```
long double var [, var]... ;
```

Range

Depends on implementation; at least as large as double. See page 81.

Remarks

The C++ ANSI specification provides the long double floating-point type in addition to the float and double types. The only thing guaranteed about long double is that its range and precision is *at least* as big as double. Check your compiler documentation for more information.

long long
64-bit integer

Purpose

Declares an eight-byte (64-bit) integer.

Syntax

The following syntax creates a data declaration.

```
long long var [, var]... ;
```

Range

Plus or minus 2 to the 63rd power.

Examples

```
long long          n;
long long int      n2;
unsigned long long amount;
```

Remarks

This data type is a new addition to the language, contributed by the C99 specification. Note that long long and long long int are equivalent. You can also use the unsigned long long type, which ranges from 0 to 2 to the 64th power.

| main | Program entry point |

Purpose

Serves as entry point for standard console applications.

Syntax

The function definition for main can take either of the forms shown in the following figure.

Here, the expression {int | void} indicates that main must be qualified by the int or void return type, but not both. In the case of *argv[ ], the brackets are intended literally.

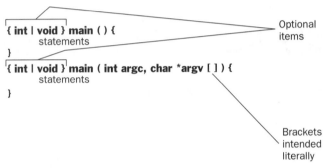

```
{ int | void } main ( ) {
     statements
}
{ int | void } main ( int argc, char *argv [ ] ) {
     statements
}
```

Optional items

Brackets intended literally

Syntax of the main function.

Example

This code defines main with no return type.

```
void main () {
    init_vars();
    prompt_for_input();
    print_results();
}
```

You can use the special arguments argc and argv to get command-line arguments. For example, suppose you wrote an application called sort.exe, which accepts an input file and an output file. A sample command line might be:

```
sort datafile.txt results.txt
```

The argc argument contains the total number of items on the command line, including program name itself. (In this case, argc is three). The argv argument is an array of strings. In this case, argv[0], argv[1], and argv[2] point to the strings "sort," "datafile.txt," and "results.txt," respectively.

Keywords

This code prints an error message and exits if exactly two arguments are not entered:

```
int main(int argc, char *argv[]) {
    if (argc != 3) {
        printf("Bad number of arguments.\n");
        printf("Syntax: sort infile outfile.\n");
        return -1;
    }
    //...
```

The following code prints out the first two arguments:

```
puts(argv[1]);
puts(argv(2]);
```

mutable   Enable changes to const

Purpose

Permits changes to a data member, even when part of an object is declared const.

Syntax

mutable *data_member_declaration*

Example

In this example, a is a mutable member. Even when an object of the class is declared const, changes to a are still allowed.

```
class CSilly {
public:
    mutable int a;
    int b, c;
    CSilly() {};
};
//...
const CSilly thingie;
thingie.a = 1;
```

Normally, if an object is declared const, none of its members can be changed. The mutable keyword permits an exception. This violates the purpose of const and should not be used often. It might make sense, however, if the member served a special purpose such as temporary storage for calculations.

●─ANSI────────────────────────────

The mutable keyword is a relatively new feature in ANSI C++ and is not supported by all versions of C++.

namespace	Create separate namespace

Purpose

Creates a separate group of names; the same name can be used both inside and outside the namespace without conflict.

Syntax

```
namespace name {
    declarations
}
```

In this syntax, declarations refers to any valid C++ function, class, and variable declarations — in other words, to any valid code.

Outside of the namespace, you need to take special action to refer to anything inside. You can refer directly to a symbol by using the scope-resolution operator (::).

```
namespace_name::symbol
```

A using statement causes the compiler to recognize all further use of the symbol without qualification:

```
using namespace_name::symbol;
```

A using namespace statement causes the compiler to recognize all the symbols in the namespace:

```
using namespace namespace_name;
```

Example

Suppose that global variables Hugh and Cary are declared in a namespace.

```
namespace grants {
    int Cary = 0;
    int Hugh = 1;
}
```

Outside of the namespace, the variables can be referred to as grants::Cary and grants::Hugh, but you can remove the need for the prefix if you choose. For example:

```
using grants::Cary;
```

Keywords

Now the name Cary can be used in subsequent statements without qualification. For example:

```
Cary = 0;  // Set grants::Cary to 0.
```

Alternatively, you can make both the names available with the using namespace syntax.

```
using namespace grants;
Cary = 0;  // Set grants::Cary to 0.
Hugh = 0;  // Set grants::Hugh to 0.
```

●─ANSI

The namespace keyword is a required part of the ANSI specification, but is not supported in some early versions of C++.

new	Create objects

Purpose

Creates one or more data items, which can be primitive data or objects of a class; calls a constructor after allocating memory for an object.

Syntax

The new operator has several versions. In each case, new returns a pointer to the data allocated, and the type of the pointer is *type**. The last version allocates multiple items; *number* can be any nonnegative integer expression.

```
new type
new type(args)
new type[number]      // Allocate multiple items
```

Examples

In both of these uses of new, the pointer returned has type int*:

```
int *p1, *p2;
p1 = new int;        // Allocate one int.
p2 = new int[50];    // Allocate 50 ints.
```

When you create objects of a user-defined type (class), you can specify arguments as long as the appropriate constructor exists.

```
CAuto *pcar1, *pcar2, *pcar3;
pcar1 = new CAuto;
pcar2 = new CAuto("Jag", 97);
pcar3 = new CAuto[10];        // Allocate 10 objects.
```

The second use of new here calls the constructor CAuto(char*, int). The first and second uses of new call the default constructor (10 times, in the last case, because 10 objects are created).

After you're done using the data items, you should remove them with delete (p. 80).

●—**NOTE**

It is valid to use the syntax new type[size] to create just one object, as in new CAuto[1]. When you do this, you should use delete [] type to remove the object later.

operator | **Overload operator behavior**

Purpose

Defines a function for an operator (such as + or *) when applied to particular types. This tells the program how to "add" (or multiply or divide) objects of those types.

Syntax

```
return_type operator@ (args) {
    statements
}
```

In this syntax, @ stands for any valid C++ operator. You can't make up your own operators, such as ##%@$!!

Example

The following code defines how addition is carried out on two objects of class CPnt:

```
CPnt operator+ (CPnt pnt1, CPnt2 pnt2) {
    CPnt new_pnt;
    new_pnt.x = pnt1.x + pnt2.y;
    new_pnt.y = pnt1.y + pnt2.y;
    return new_pnt;
}
```

This example assumes that the CPnt class has two members x and y. An operator function can be defined as either a member function or a global function. If it is a member function, the first operand is implicit. The previous example could have been written as a member function of the CPnt class:

```
CPnt CPnt::operator+ (CPnt2 pnt2) {
    CPnt new_pnt;
    new_pnt.x = x + pnt2.y;
```

```
          new_pnt.y = y + pnt2.y;
          return new_pnt;
      }
```

The advantage of writing an operator function as a global function is that *any* type — including a primitive type — can be used for each operand. For more information on operator functions, see Chapter 7, starting on page 422.

private   Limit member access

Purpose

Restricts access for one or more members. An object's private members are truly private; no one else can get at them — not even another object of the same class.

Syntax

To declare members with private access, place the private keyword in front of the declarations. All the declarations that follow, up to the next access keyword (private, protected, or public) are private.

private:
> *declarations*

The private keyword can also be used as part of a base-class specifier. This has the effect of making all the inherited members private.

private *base_class*

Examples

In this code, the members a, b, and c all have private access. a and b are private by default.

```
class AClass {
      int a, b;
public:
      AClass();
      double x, y;
private:
      int c;
};
```

Because a, b, and c are private members, the only functions that can refer to them are member functions of AClass. No object can refer to another object's private data, regardless of class.

```
AClass this_object;
this_object.a = 1;      // ERROR! Access not permitted.
```

However, a member function (in this case, the constructor) can refer to its own data:

```
AClass::AClass() {
     a = 1;
     b = 2;
}
```

As a base-class access specifier, the private keyword modifies inherited members so that all of them become private in the derived class.

```
class CDerived : private CBase {
     // Some declarations
};
```

private is the default base-class specifier, so use public (p. 102) if you don't want this effect.

protected   Limit access to class hierarchy

Purpose
Restricts access for one or more members of a class; similar to private, except that protected members can be referred to in derived classes.

Syntax
To declare members with protected access, place the protected keyword in front of the declarations. All the declarations that follow, up to the next access keyword (private, protected, or public) are protected.

```
protected:
     declarations
```

The protected keyword can also be used as part of a base-class specifier. This has the effect of making all the inherited members protected or private. Public members inherited from the base class become protected in the derived class.

```
protected base_class
```

Examples
In the following code, members x, y, and c are protected. The members a and b are private by default.

```
class AClass {
     int a, b;
protected:
     double x, y;
```

```
        int c;
public:
        void set_vars(int i, int j, int k);
};
```

Consequently, function code in a derived class could refer to all members except a and b.

As a base-class access specifier, the protected keyword modifies inherited members so that a member that is public in the base class (CBase) becomes protected within the derived class (CDerived). Note that private is the default base-class access.

```
class CDerived : protected CBase {
        // Some declarations
};
```

Although private and protected access have roughly the same purpose, protected is helpful to people deriving classes from your class. If most of the members are private, programmers deriving new classes must treat your class like a "black box" to which they can add new functions but can't see inside. Protected access grants greater freedom.

public   Enable member access

Purpose

Extends access for one or more members of a class, so they can be manipulated from outside an object as well as from within.

Syntax

To declare members with public access, place the public keyword in front of the declarations. All the declarations that follow, up to the next access keyword (private, protected, or public) are public.

```
public:
        declarations
```

The public keyword can also be used as part of a base-class specifier. This enables the derived class to inherit all members without modification.

```
public base_class
```

Examples

In the following code, members x and y are public, as is the constructor. The members a and b are private by default.

```
class AClass {
        int a, b;
public:
```

```
    AClass();
    double x, y;
private:
    int c;
};
```

Because x, and y are public members, the program can create AClass objects and then access x and y directly.

```
AClass this_object;
this_object.x = 1;    // Valid, because x is public.
```

As a base-class access specifier, the public keyword enables the derived class to inherit all base-class members without modification. Note that private is the default base-class access.

```
class CDerived : public CBase {
    // Some declarations
};
```

register   Place variable in CPU register

Purpose

Requests that a variable be allocated in one of the processor's internal registers.

Syntax

```
register data_declaration
```

Example

This statement declares the integer i as a register variable:

```
register int i;
```

The use of the register keyword is not binding on the compiler. It is only a suggestion. With their state-of-the-art optimizing, modern compilers tend to make their own decisions about register allocation.

reinterpret_cast   Convert pointer

Purpose

Casts between pointers of different types with almost no restrictions; can also cast between pointers and integers.

Syntax

```
reinterpret_cast<type>(expr)
```

Keywords

This expression returns data with the same value as *expr*, but converted to the specified *type*. The types involved are usually pointers. Unlike static_ cast (p. 109), reinterpret_cast cannot alter the actual bits contributed by *expr*; the data is simply reinterpreted. const and volatile attributes cannot be added or removed; that requires const_cast (p. 78).

Examples

The most common use for this operator is to cast a void* return value or argument to a specific pointer type. In C++, it is illegal to assign a void* pointer to another pointer type without first casting it. For example:

```
char *p = reinterpret_cast<char*>(malloc(100));
```

Although the malloc return value does not have to be immediately cast to another pointer type, it must be cast before being dereferenced. One advantage of the new operator over malloc is that new does not require a cast.

reinterpret_cast is dangerous, so don't use it unless you have a good reason for doing so. For example, it is possible to cast an int* pointer to float* pointer type, causing the program to interpret integer data *as if it were floating-point data,* thereby printing garbage.

```
int i = 100;
int *p_i = &i;
float *p_f = reinterpret_cast<float*>(p_i);
cout << *p_f;  // THIS OUTPUTS GARBAGE
```

The effects of casting pointers are quite different from casting objects. Applying static_cast<float> takes a value and duly converts it to the correct floating-point representation of that value:

```
int i = 100;
float f = static_cast<float>(i);
cout << f;     // This prints 100.0
```

● ANSI

The reinterpret_cast operator is an extended ANSI feature that is not supported in earlier versions of C++.

---

return	Exit function (with return value)

Purpose

Causes a function to immediately exit, optionally returning a value.

Syntax

The syntax of return has two versions:

```
return expression;
return;
```

Use the first version in functions that return a value. Use the second version in functions with void return type. In the latter case, the use of the statement is optional and is used only to exit early.

Example

If a function is declared with any return type other than void, the use of return is required. In the following example, the keyword is used to return a long integer.

```
long factorial(int n) {
    long result = 1;
    while (n)
        result = result * n--;
    return result;
}
```

short   Signed two-byte integer

Purpose

Declares a two-byte integer that can hold positive or negative values.

Syntax

The following syntax creates a data declaration.

short *var* [, *var*]... ;

Range

–32,768 to 32,767.

The ANSI spec only requires support for values as low as –32,767, but platforms that use two's complement arithmetic (which includes virtually all personal computers in use today) support this slightly larger range.

Examples

You can use the short type to declare signed integers within this range.

short i = 2500, j = -5, k = -1000;

By default, the compiler stores integer constants in the short range as long as they fit. See the int topic on page 92 for information on notation of integer constants.

signed char   Signed one-byte integer

Purpose

Declares a one-byte integer that can hold positive or negative values.

Keywords

Syntax

The following syntax creates a data declaration.

```
signed char var [, var]... ;
```

Range

-128 to 127.

The ANSI spec only requires support for values as low as -127, but platforms that use two's complement arithmetic (which includes virtually all personal computers in use today) support this slightly larger range.

Examples

Like the other char types, signed char can be used to define buffers of raw data.

```
signed char buffer[1000];
```

When using signed char, be aware of the potential effects of sign extension. For example:

```
signed char sbuf[100];
unsigned char ubuf[100];
sbuf[0] = 255; // All bits set to 1; represents -1.
ubuf[0] = 255; // All bits set to 1; represents 255.
short i = sbuf[0];   // Extend to 11111111 11111111.
short j = ubuf[0];   // Extend to 00000000 11111111.
```

Typically, arrays of unsigned char are easier to work with, because you can assign values from 0 to 255 (hex 0x00 to 0xFF) without getting a warning. See page 564 in the glossary for more information on sign extension.

sizeof | Get width of data structure

Purpose

Returns the width, in bytes, of an expression or a type.

Syntax

sizeof has two versions; both return a value of type size_t.

```
sizeof(expression)
sizeof(type)
```

Remarks

There are several rules that apply to handling of complex types:

- If the operand is a statically allocated array, sizeof returns the total size of the array in bytes.

- If the operand is a pointer rather than an array, sizeof returns the width of the pointer — in other words, the address width.
- If the operand is an array whose size cannot be determined at compile time, the operation is illegal.
- If the operand is a class, structure, or union, or an instance of one, sizeof returns the total size of an instance, including padding, if any.

Examples

```
#include <iostream.h>
//...
cout << sizeof(short) << endl;      // Prints 2
cout << sizeof(short*) << endl;     // Prints 2 or 4
cout << sizeof(short[10]) << endl;  // Prints 20

long arr[100];
long *p = arr;
cout << sizeof(arr[1]) << endl;     // Prints 4
cout << sizeof(p) << endl;          // Prints 2 or 4
cout << sizeof(arr) << endl;        // Prints 400
```

●—NOTE

The sizeof operator does not return string length; it returns either address width (if the operand is a pointer) or total allocated space (if the operand is an array). To get current length, use the strlen library function (p. 288).

size_t	Size-of-type field

Keywords

Purpose
Declares an integer large enough to hold any value returned by the sizeof operator; also used by functions and macros that return the size of a data type.

Syntax
The following syntax creates a data declaration.

```
size_t var [, var]... ;
```

Range
Depends on implementation; typically the same as unsigned long.

Example
```
size_t n;
n = sizeof(my_array);
```

This expression takes the value stored in *expr*, converts it to the specified *type*, and returns the results.

static_cast can be used in any situation in which the *reverse* cast is automatic. For example, a short is automatically cast to a long before it's assigned to a long, but assigning from long to short requires an explicit cast to suppress a warning message.

Examples

Here the cast is used to suppress a compiler warning. This cast says, in effect, "Yes, I really want to do this." It is your responsibility to ensure that the data is not too large to be stored in the new type — in this case, short.

```
long j = 17;
short i = static_cast<short>(j);
```

You can also cast between pointers to any classes in which one is derived, directly or indirectly, from the other. It is your responsibility to ensure that the underlying data supports the cast. In this example, assume that B is a base class of D. Going from general to specific (base-class address to derived class pointer) requires a cast.

```
B *pb;  // B is base class of D.
D *pd;
pd = static_cast<D*>(pb);  // Cast B* -> D*.
```

Such a cast might cause problems unless the object pointed to by pb actually has type D or a class derived from D. Note that an explicit cast is not necessary when you go in the reverse direction (derived-class address to base-class pointer).

There are some other situations in which static_cast is useful, but they are infrequent. For example, you can use it to create a chain of data conversions. Assume that there is a conversion function for going from type A to B, and another for B to int.

```
A oa;
int i = static_cast<int>(static_cast<B>(oa));
```

Certain situations require one of the other casts: const_cast, dynamic_cast, or reinterpret_cast. Unlike dynamic_cast, static_cast does not perform any runtime checks and does not require virtual functions.

●—ANSI

The static_cast operator is an extended ANSI feature that is not supported in earlier versions of C++.

struct   Declare structure class

Purpose

Declares a class in which member access is public by default. In every other respect, struct is identical to class. struct is provided mainly for backward compatibility with C.

Syntax

```
struct name [: base_class_declarations] {
    declarations
} [object_definitions];
```

The brackets indicate that base class declarations and object definitions are optional. See page 383 in Chapter 5 for more information on base class declarations. The declarations can include variables, function declarations, or both.

Example

The following declaration creates a class, movie_ratings, with four data members. Because the class is declared using the struct keyword, the members are public.

```
struct movie_ratings {
    char movie_name[20];
    char director_name[30];
    int  Roger;  // 1 = thumbs up, 0 = thumbs down
    int  Jean;
};
```

switch   Select between alternatives

Purpose

Evaluates a test value, and then uses that value to jump to one of several blocks of code.

Syntax

```
switch (test_value) {

[case constant_value:
    statements ] ...

[ default:
    statements ]
}
```

The brackets here indicate optional elements, and the ellipses (. . .) indicate that any number of case blocks may appear. The typical case block has this form:

```
case constant_value:
    statements
    break;
```

Although the use of break is optional, execution falls through to the next case if break is omitted.

Examples

Suppose you have a program that prints a number not as 1, 2, or 3, but as one, two, or three. One way to do this is with a series of if else statements:

```
if (n == 1)
    printf("one");
else if (n == 2)
    printf("two");
else if (n == 3)
    printf("three");
```

You can get the same functionality from a switch statement, which is leaner and a little easier to follow. Note the use of the break statement at the end of each case.

```
switch (n) {
  case 1:
    printf("one"); break;
  case 2:
    printf("two"); break;
  case 3:
    printf("three"); break;
}
```

Without the use of break, execution falls through to the next case. This is because case is a statement label, not a control structure. Sometimes you can use this execution fall through to your advantage. In the following example, the y case falls through to the a, e, i, o, u case.

```
switch(c) {
  case 'y':
    printf("sometimes ");
  case 'a':
  case 'e':
  case 'i':
  case 'o':
  case 'u':
```

```
    printf("is a vowel");
    break;
  default:
    printf("is a consonant");
    break;
}
```

If the test expression is 'y', this switch statement prints this result:

```
sometimes is a vowel
```

The following figure summarizes the flow of control in this statement.

Flow of control in a switch statement.

The switch statement does not support string or object test values, because these are not integers. If you need to supply a series of alternative actions depending on a string value, the only way to do so is to use a series of if else statements and to use the strcmp function to test for equality.

template   Use generalized type

Purpose

Creates a generalized class or function using a *parameterized type* that is to be filled in later. For example, you can create a general collection class (such as a stack) and then apply it to int, long, float, or another type.

Syntax

The following syntax declares a template:

```
template<class T> declaration
```

The *declaration* is a class declaration or function definition. The argument *T* can have any valid name; it stands for a type to be filled in later.

Once a template is defined, you can use it to generate a declaration based on a specific type. You apply a template by filling in the argument *T*:

```
template_name<type>
```

Templates can be more complex, taking several arguments, one or more of which is a **class** *T* argument:

```
template<args> declaration
```

You would apply such a template by filling in all the arguments:

```
template_name<arg_values>
```

Example 1: A Simple Class Template

Here is the syntax for a class template taking a single type as argument:

```
template <class T>
class template_name {
    declarations
};
```

The parameterized type, *T*, is expanded into the declarations. Wherever *T* appears in *declarations*, an actual type (such as int or double, or a class name) replaces *T* when the template is used. The following figure shows how template expansion works.

template <class arg**>**
class name {   name <type> vars;
        declarations

};

Simple template expansion.

Here's a simple template example. For any given type T, the template called pair defines a new type consisting of two members of type T.

```
template <class T>
class pair {
    T a, b;
};
```

To use this template, specify a type as pair<T>, in which T is an actual type:

```
pair<int>    jeans;   // jeans contains two ints
pair<double> gloves;  // gloves contains two doubles
pair<CStr>   glasses; // glasses contains two strings
```

The following figure shows how the int type is expanded in the case of pair<int>.

```
template <class T>              pair<int> jeans;
class pair {
      T   a,b;
};
```

Template expansion for pair < int >.

The type specification pair<int> is therefore expanded into a class containing two members:

```
class pair<int> {
      int a, b;
};
```

Similarly, pair<double> and pair<CStr> are expanded as follows. You don't actually see this expansion, but this is how C++ interprets the meaning of the pair<double> and pair<CStr> type specifications.

```
class pair<double> {
      double  a, b;
};
```

```
class pair<CStr> {
      CStr   a, b;
};
```

Example 2: A Simple Function Template

Another use of templates is with functions. The syntax is similar to that for template classes. A simple function template has this form:

```
template <class T>
type name (args) {
      statements
}
```

A function template is just the template <class T> syntax followed by a function definition. The parameter T, which is a stand-in for a type to be specified later, can appear as many times as you like in the function definition code. Here is an example of a simple function template, switch_values.

```
template <class T>
void switch_values(T &a, T &b) {
      T temp;
```

```
    temp = a;
    a = b;
    b = temp;
};
```

Here the stand-in type T is used in the argument list; this function template therefore operates on any two variables of type T. The code also uses this type to create another variable, temp. Here is an example of this template in use:

```
#include <iostream.h>
//...
int x = 2.0, y = 10.0;
cout << "x = " << x << endl;
cout << "y = " << y << endl;
switch_values<int>(x, y);    // Switch x and y!
cout << "x = " << x << endl;
cout << "y = " << y << endl;
```

The key line of this example is:

```
switch_values<int>(x, y);    // Switch x and y!
```

The use of switch_values<int> causes a hidden function definition to be generated. This function behaves as if you had entered the following statements. (I produced this function definition by replacing each occurrence of T with int, which, in effect, is what the compiler does.)

```
void switch_values<int>(int &a, int &b) {
    int temp;
    temp = a;
    a = b;
    b = temp;
};
```

● NOTE

This example uses the name switch_values because switch is a C++ keyword and is therefore already taken. Also note that this example uses the address operator (&) to declare two reference arguments. For more information, see the topic "reference" in the glossary (p. 562). Finally, note that this template only works correctly with types for which assignment (=) is defined.

Example 3: A Generalized Stack Class

Although it's a minimal implementation, the following example shows a generalized collection class that might be useful. Notice how the parameterized type T appears four times inside the class declaration.

```
template <class T>
class stack {
    T *stackp;
    int size;
    int index;
public:
    T pop(void) {return stackp[--index];}
    void push(T item) {stackp[index++] = item;}
    stack(int sz) {stackp = new T[size = sz];
                   index = 0;}
    ~stack() {delete [] stackp;}
};
```

This template is weak in the area of error checking, a fault that is addressed
in the next section. Because only one constructor is defined, you must use
this constructor in creating stack variables. For example:

```
stack<int>  things(30);
stack<CStr> strings(20);
```

This creates things as a stack of up to 30 integers and strings as a stack of
up to 20 CStr objects. As soon as these stacks are defined, you can push and
pop items on and off the stacks. For example:

```
strings.push("A string");
strings.push("B string");
cout << strings.pop(); // Prints "B string"
cout << strings.pop(); // Prints "A string"
```

The type specification stack<CStr> generates the following class. I produced
this code by replacing each occurrence of T with CStr, which is essentially
what the compiler does when interpreting what stack<CStr> means.

```
class stack<CStr> {
    CStr *stackp;
    int size;
    int index;
public:
    CStr pop(void) {return stackp[--index];}
    void push(CStr item) {stackp[index++] = item;}
    stack(int sz) {stackp = new CStr[size = sz];
                   index = 0;}
    ~stack() {delete [] stackp;}
};
```

This generated type works because assignment (=) and copy operations are
defined for CStr (see Chapter 7). It would not work correctly on arrays, for
example.

Example 4: Stack Class with Function Templates

The previous section included function definitions in the class declaration, but you can define a function outside the class by giving it its own template.

```
template <class T>
T stack<T>::pop(void) {
    //...
}
```

This approach helps make it possible to write better push and pop implementations. The following version improves error checking.

```
template <class T>
class stack {
    T *stackp;
    int size;
    int index;
public:
    T pop(void);
    int push(T item);
    stack(int sz) {stackp = new T[size = sz];
                    index = 0;}
    ~stack() {delete [] stackp;}
};


// Template to define stack template's pop function.
// Check index: if stack empty, return dummy object.
// Type T must have a default constructor!
//
template <class T>
T stack<T>::pop(void) {
    if (index > 0)
        return stackp[--index];
    else
        {T dummy; return dummy;}
}


// Template to define stack template's push function.
// Check index: if stack full, return 0 (failure).
// Otherwise, return 1.
//
template <class T>
int stack<T>::push(T item) {
    if (index < size)
        stackp[index++] = item;
```

```
    else
        return 0;
    return 1;
}
```

The following variable definition creates a stack called `strings` that is a maximum size of 50:

```
stack<CStr> strings(50);
```

This statement instantiates the `stack<CStr>` type, which causes the compiler to generate the type. As the type is generated, the compiler declares two member functions — pop and push — that have `stack<CStr>` scope. Here are the resulting prototypes:

```
CStr stack<CStr>::pop(void);
int stack<CStr>::push(CStr item);
```

These declarations, in turn, apply the function-definition templates for `stack<CStr>::pop` and `stack<CStr>::push`, causing the compiler to generate the appropriate code.

In the final example, the code demonstrates how a template can take multiple arguments. This approach eliminates the constructor, using instead a template argument to determine size.

```
template <class T, int sz>
class stack {
    T arr[sz];
    int index;
public:
    T pop(void);
    int push(T item);
    stack () {index = 0;}
};

// Template to define stack template's pop function.
// Check index: if stack empty, return dummy object.
// Type T must have a default constructor!
//
template <class T, int sz>
T stack<T, sz>::pop(void) {
    if (index > 0)
        return arr[--index];
    else
        {T dummy; return dummy;}
}
```

```
// Template to define stack template's push function.
// Check index: if stack full, return 0 (failure).
// Otherwise, return 1.
//
template <class T, int sz>
int stack<T, sz>::push(T item) {
    if (index < sz)
        arr[index++] = item;
    else
        return 0;
    return 1;
}
```

To use these templates, specify both type and size in the declaration. Here are some examples:

```
stack<int, 10>    ten_little_integers;
stack<float, 20>  float_my_boat;
stack<CStr, 50>   tons_o_strings;
```

The first declaration here creates a stack, ten_little_integers, which has a maximum size of 10. When the compiler generates this type, two functions are declared:

```
stack<int, 10>::push
stack<int, 10>::pop
```

These declarations, in turn, cause the compiler to generate the appropriate function definitions.

●—ANSI

The ANSI C++ specification requires support for templates, but earlier versions of C++ often lacked this support.

this	Pointer to current object

Purpose

Points to the current object being operated on within a member function.

Syntax

this

Examples

Use of this is usually implicit, because references to class members are automatically resolved as members of the current object — that is, the object through which the function was called.

One use for this is to clarify that a variable is referring to a class member rather than something else. For example, the following code uses the this keyword to assign values to data members x and y. This usage is necessary here because names are matched to local variables and arguments before they are matched to class members.

```
CPoint::set(double x, double y) {
    this->x = x;    // Init the object's copy of x.
    this->y = y;    // Init the object's copy of y.
}
```

Another use for this is to return the current object, which is necessary in certain operator functions (see Chapter 7, starting on p. 422). Because this is a pointer to the object, *this refers to the object itself.

```
CStr& CStr::operator=(const CStr &source) {
    cpy(source.get());
    return *this;       // Return myself!
}
```

| **throw** | Raise exception, or pass the buck |

Purpose

Raises an exception or passes it along. An exception, as described in the section about try, is a runtime event that demands immediate attention.

Syntax

The syntax of throw has two versions:

```
throw;
throw exception_object;
```

The first version can be used inside an exception handler. The effect is to say, "I can't handle the exception," and to pass it along to the next catch block that can.

The second version raises an exception. The effect is to transfer control to the nearest appropriate exception handler. The *exception_object* can be an object of any type. Control goes to the first catch block that accepts an argument of this type.

Example

The following code raises an exception if a file was not successfully opened. It's assumed that file_err is a class defined somewhere in the program.

```
if (fp == NULL)
    throw file_err(fname, "r");
```

| **true** | **Boolean constant** |

Purpose

Specifies the Boolean value true (1).

Syntax

```
true
```

Example

The following declaration creates a Boolean value and initializes it.

```
bool flag1 = true;
```

| **°try** | **Define exception-handling block** |

Purpose

Declares an exception-handling block. This is a structured approach to handling errors and other events.

Syntax

```
try {
     statements
}
catch (arg1_declaration) {
     statements
}
catch (arg2_declaration) {
     statements
}
...
catch (argN_declaration) {
     statements
}
```

The code executes the statements following try unconditionally; these are part of the normal flow of execution. If an exception occurs during execution of these statements (even inside a function call), control transfers to the nearest try catch structure.

The system looks for the first arg_declaration whose type matches that of the exception thrown. The type matches if the exception has the same type as the argument's class or any type derived from that class. For example, if arg1_declaration has type ioerror, it catches any exception having type ioerror or any type derived from ioerror.

Each *arg_declaration* includes an exception type and, optionally, an argument name. The *object*, if specified, refers to the exception object that was passed when the exception was raised. (See throw.)

    exception_type [object]

arg_declaration syntax also accepts ellipses (. . .), which indicate that the block catches any exception. This syntax can be used to write a default exception handler.

• • •

After an exception is successfully handled, execution resumes after the end of the try catch structure. If an exception is raised without being caught, the program terminates.

Exception Handling: General Concepts

An exception is an unusual program occurrence that demands immediate attention. Most, but not necessarily all, exceptions are runtime errors.

The traditional approach to error handling is to test each function as it is called, returning an error code if something goes wrong. This approach is fine for simple cases, but when an error is encountered deep within a program, the error must be propagated back through a series of returns, as shown in the following figure.

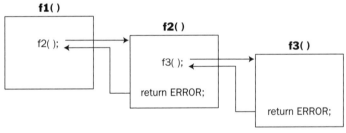

Error propagation in C.

C++ exception handling, as illustrated in the following figure, lets you centralize all your error handling in one location. When an exception is raised, control transfers directly to the appropriate handler. This is true even if the exception occurs deep in the function hierarchy.

Given this definition, you can use LSTRING to create several strings, just as if it were a primitive type.

```
LSTRING a, b, c;
```

The effect of this declaration is the same as the following:

```
char a[256], b[256], c[256];
```

Once declared, a typedef type can be used just like other types. For example, in the following declarations, sarray is declared as an array of 100 char* pointers and get_name is a function returning a single char* pointer.

```
typdef char *STYPE;    // STYPE = a char* pointer

STYPE sarray[100];     // sarray is array of 100 ptrs.
STYPE get_name(void);  // get_name returns char*.
```

●—NOTE

The typedef keyword has one other effect. Each use of typedef creates a distinct type as far as the typeid operator is concerned. For example, the following statement creates SILLYTYPE as a distinct type, even though it works exactly like an integer:

```
typedef int SILLYTYPE;
```

A typedef statement is typically placed in a header file, so that every module gets the same type definitions. Note that typedef performs a stronger action than #define. The following two statements have different consequences, even though they look similar.

```
typedef int *PTI;   // Declare PTI as alias for int*.
#define PTI int*    // Replace "PTI" with "int*".
```

The difference is clear when you attempt to define several variables, as in the following statement. If PTI was created with #define, then only the first variable, p1, is made into a pointer. If typedef was used, then all three variables are made into pointers.

```
PTI p1, p2, p3;
```

typeid   Get type information

Purpose

Uniquely identifies the type of an expression to the compiler by returning a type_info data structure.

Syntax

To use typeid, you must include the file typeinfo.h. This syntax indicates that the operand can either be an expression or a type (such as int or C, where C is a class).

```
#include <typeinfo.h>

typeid(expression | type)
```

Remarks

The most important use of typeid is to identify the type of an object at run-time. A base-class pointer can point to many different derived types; there-fore, the precise type pointed to may be undetermined at compile time.

To use typeid to identify type dynamically at runtime, there are two require-ments: (a) the base class must have at least one virtual function, and (b) your compiler may require you to set an option to enable runtime-type informa-tion (RTTI) support.

● NOTE

To enable RTTI, Microsoft Visual C++ requires the use of the /GR option. For other compilers, consult your compiler documentation.

The typeid operator returns an object of class type_info, which is defined in typeinfo.h. This type supports two operators, == and !=, as well as two mem-ber functions, before and name. The before function is not used except inter-nally, but the others are useful:

Usage	Action
typeid(a) == typeid(b)	Return true if a and b have the same type.
typeid(a) != typeid(b)	Return true if a and b differ in type.
typeid(a).name()	Return a string containing the type name.

Examples

This sample program illustrates the use of typeid to determine the class of an object pointed to by pb, a base-class pointer:

```
#include <iostream.h>
#include <typeinfo.h>

class B {
public:
    virtual int func1(void) { return 0; }
};
```

```
class D : public B {
public:
    int func1(void) { return 1;}
    int func2(void) { return 2;}
};

void main() {
    B *pb;
    D objd;
    pb = &objd;
    cout << typeid(objd).name() << endl;
    cout << typeid(pb).name() << endl;
    cout << typeid(*pb).name() << endl;
}
```

Here is the output of the program. The last statement prints "class D," correctly identifying that pb points to an object of class D, even though pb itself has type B*.

```
class D
class B *
class D
```

This follow-up example tests a pointer (pb) to determine whether it points to an object of class D. If it does, then it is safe to call func2, a function declared in D. Another way to get this same functionality is to use dynamic_cast (see p. 82).

```
void test_func(B *pb) {
    if (typeid(*pb) == typeid(D)) {
        D *pd = reinterpret_cast<D*>(pb);
        pd->func2();
    //...
```

Testing for equality (= =) is the most common thing to do with a value returned by typeid. Calling the name function — as done earlier — enables you to print the type name, which can be useful for debugging.

●—ANSI

The typeid operator is an extended ANSI feature that is not supported in all the earlier versions of C++.

union
Use location to store different kinds of stuff

Purpose

Enables multiple data formats to be used at a single location. For example, a union can store integer, floating-point, or string data — but only one of them at a time.

Syntax

```
union [name] [base_class_declarations] {
    declarations
} [object_definitions];
```

Here brackets indicate optional items. The syntax of the union keyword is similar to class and struct. As with struct, declarations can include variables, function declarations, or both, and access is public by default. The *name* declares the name of the union as a type; *object_definitions* creates one or more instance of the union in memory.

You can choose to omit both the name and object definitions, to create an anonymous union. See page 525 in the glossary for more information.

Example

In this example, a union named data is declared inside a structure class named variant. The union has four members — c, i, s, and f — all of which share the same address.

```
struct variant {
    short type;
    union {
        short c;
        long  i;
        char  *s;
        double f;
    } data;
};
```

The following figure shows what the resulting type looks like in memory.

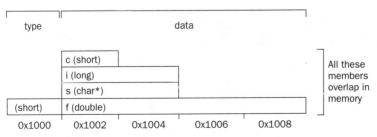

Memory layout of the variant type.

This structure creates a variant type that can store string, integer, or floating-point data — but only one of them at a time. The following code creates two objects. It then assigns a floating-point value to the first and a string to the second.

```
enum { CHAR, INT, STR, FLOAT};

struct variant v1, v2;

v1.type = FLOAT;        // Use v1 to store a float.
v1.data.f = 27.5;

v2.type = STR;          // Use v2 to store a string.
strcpy(v2.data.s, "Hello");
```

unsigned char   Unsigned one-byte integer

Purpose
Declares a one-byte data object that holds only nonnegative values.

Syntax
The following syntax creates a data declaration.

```
unsigned char var [, var]... ;
```

Range
0 to 255

Example
The unsigned char type can be useful for defining buffers to hold raw binary data. Here is an example of unsigned char used to define a buffer for binary data:

```
unsigned char buffer[1000];
```

Unlike the char type, the range of unsigned char is guaranteed to be 0 to 255. This is often more convenient, particularly if you are assigning hexadecimal values in the range 0x0 to 0xFF.

unsigned int   Unsigned integer

Purpose
Declares an integer that can hold only nonnegative values; this provides twice as large a positive range as int.

Syntax

The following syntax creates a data declaration.

```
unsigned int var [, var]... ;
```

Range

0 to 65,535 on 16-bit systems; approximately 0 to 4 billion on 32-bit systems.

Examples

```
unsigned int i = 55;
unsigned int j = 60100;
unsigned int mask = 0xFFFA;
```

A notable feature of unsigned int is that it is the recommended type on which to base bit fields. This prevents confusion due to sign extension. For example:

```
struct card {
    unsigned int rank:4;
    unsigned int suit:2;
    unsigned int marked:1;
} hand[5];
```

For information on bit-field declarations, see page 339 in Chapter 2.

You can use the U suffix to force storage of a constant as an unsigned value. For more information on notation of integer constants, see int on page 92.

unsigned long   Unsigned four-byte integer

Purpose

Declares a four-byte integer that can hold only nonnegative values; this provides twice as large a positive range as long.

Syntax

The following syntax creates a data declaration.

```
unsigned long var [, var]... ;
```

Range

0 to 4,294,967,296 (approximately 4.3 billion).

Examples

```
unsigned long i = 500;
unsigned long j = 4123000123;
```

You can force a constant to be stored as an unsigned long by using the U (unsigned) and L (long) suffixes. By default, the compiler stores a constant as a short if it is small enough, or a long.

For more information on notation of integer constants, see int on page 92.

Keywords

unsigned short | Unsigned two-byte integer

Purpose

Declares a two-byte integer that can hold only nonnegative values.

Syntax

The following syntax creates a data declaration.

```
unsigned short var [, var]... ;
```

Range

0 to 65,535

Examples

```
unsigned short i = 251;
unsigned short j = 25000;
```

This type can represent twice as many positive numbers as a short. Usually when you need use of this upper range, it makes sense to use a long. Occasionally, however, unsigned short may be preferable because of its compactness.

By default, the compiler stores a constant in the short range and, if this range isn't large enough, the compiler stores the constant as a long. You can, however, use the U suffix to specify that a constant be stored as an unsigned short. For example:

```
unsigned short j = 65000U;
```

For more information on the notation of integer constants, see int on page 92.

using | Enable direct use of namespace item

Purpose

Enables direct access to a name defined in another namespace; it can also be used to enable access to all the names in a namespace.

Syntax

The using syntax has two versions:

```
using namespace_name::symbol;
using namespace namespace_name;
```

The first version enables direct access to a particular symbol. The second version enables access to all the symbols in the namespace.

Examples

The first two examples enable access to the variables CB and BillTheCat declared in the namespace cats, so they can be referred to directly rather than as cats::CB and cats::BillTheCat. The last example enables direct access to everything in the namespace.

```
using cats::CB;
using cats::BillTheCat;
using namespace cats;
```

For more information, see namespace on page 97.

virtual	Defer resolution until runtime

Purpose

Defers resolution of a member function until runtime. No matter how an object is accessed, the correct code is executed, even if the caller does not know the object's precise type. See Chapter 9, starting on page 468, for more information.

The virtual keyword can also declare virtual base classes.

Usage 1: Virtual Functions

To declare a member function virtual, place the virtual keyword in front of the function prototype.

```
class name {
//...
    virtual function_prototype;
//...
};
```

A virtual function must be a member function of a class (the class can be declared with class, struct, or union). You cannot place the function definition inside the class declaration, because a virtual function cannot be inlined. Once a function is declared virtual, it's automatically virtual in all derived classes.

Usage 2: Virtual Base Classes

virtual can also be applied to base classes. A virtual base class contributes only one copy of its members to each descendent class, even if the base class is inherited several times. This only arises in complex hierarchies involving multiple inheritance. For example, CKid inherits only one copy of CAncestor members even though CKid inherits through both CMom and CDad base classes.

```
class CMom : virtual public CAncestor {
//...
};
```

Keywords

```
class CDad : virtual public CAncestor {
//...
};
class CKid : public CMom, public CDad {
//...
};
```

void — Declare empty type (being and nothingness)

Purpose

Declares an empty type or a generic pointer (pointer to nothing).

Remarks

The keyword is best understood as a way of supporting three specific uses:

- Declaring a function with no return value:

  ```
  void print_num(int n);
  ```

- Declaring a function with exactly zero arguments. This provides more information than an empty argument list, which can be ambiguous.

  ```
  int get_num(void);
  ```

- Declaring a generic pointer:

  ```
  void* p = malloc(n);
  ```

Several rules apply to void pointers: They cannot be dereferenced without first being recast. Other pointers, however, may be assigned to a void pointer without a cast. In addition, void pointer arithmetic has a scaling factor of 1, just like pointers of type char*.

● C/C++

The C language is more lax than C++ and permits void pointers to be assigned to other pointers without a cast. C++ disallows this.

volatile — Unstable, handle with care

Purpose

Tells the compiler that a particular data item may change without warning.

Syntax

```
volatile data_declaration
```

The word *volatile* suggests something unstable. In C++, a volatile object is one that may be changed by an outside agent (such as the system clock or an

I/O port). Every time the program refers to the data, it must do a fresh memory access. With most variables, the program can place the value in a register and assume that the value won't change.

Examples

The following example declares two volatile items — x and y — and one volatile pointer, *p_sys. The pointer itself doesn't require special handling, but each reference to what it points to does. Consequently, the compiler will generate code that does a direct memory refresh for each reference to x, y, or *p_sys.

```
volatile int x, y, *p_sys;
```

The syntax rules for volatile mirror those for const: specifically, only a volatile pointer can point to volatile data. Paradoxically, an item may be both const and volatile:

```
extern const volatile int *p_to_sys_clock;
```

This declaration states that an outside agency may alter *p_to_sys_clock without warning, but the program code must not change it.

●—NOTE

The need for volatile arises mainly in systems programming.

wchar_t   Wide character

Declares a wide character, large enough to represent international character sets.

Syntax

The following syntax creates a data declaration.

```
wchar_t var [, var]... ;
```

Range

Depends on implementation; typically the same as unsigned short.

Examples

Increasingly, applications are required to support international uses in which the character set may be a natural language that requires two bytes to represent each character.

To initialize a wide-character string, use the L prefix.

```
wchar_t wstr = L"This is a wide char string."
```

The standard library now provides a set of functions to handle wide-character strings. For a list of functions that manipulate wide-character strings, see

page 173 in Section 6. Each of these corresponds to a traditional string-handling function. In addition, for nearly every file I/O function that uses a tradi-
tional-string (char*) argument, there is now a corresponding function that
uses a wchart_t* argument. The wchart_t* versions require the wchar.h file.

For example, this code prints the wide string declared earlier.

```
#include <wchar.h>
//...
wchar_t wstr = L"This is a wide char string."
wprintf("%s\n", wstr);
```

●—ANSI

The wchar_t data type, along with its support functions such as
wprintf, is an extended ANSI feature that is not supported in earlier versions of C++.

while   Execute loop repeatedly

Purpose
Executes a statement as long as a condition is true.

Syntax
```
while (condition)
    statement
```

The loop evaluates the specified *condition*. If it is true (nonzero), then
statement is executed and the process is repeated. Otherwise, the loop terminates. The *statement* is frequently a compound statement, although this is
not required.

Example
This code prints all the numbers between 1 and 100.

```
#include <stdio.h>
//...
int i = 1;
while (i <= 100) {
    printf("%d, ", i);
    i++;
}
```

See also for (p. 87), which can efficiently create a loop with a counter, and
do (p. 80), which provides a variation on while.

wint_t   Wide character return type

Purpose

Declares a return value for functions such as getwc, which returns a wide
character or an error condition.

Syntax

The following syntax creates a data declaration.

    wint_t var [, var]... ;

Range

Depends on implementation; typically the same as long.

Example

The wint_t type is large enough to store any wchar_t value, as well as the
special WEOF value sometimes returned by the functions getwc and getwchar,
as well as by others. (WEOF indicates end-of-file or error conditions.) The use
of wint_t is analogous to the use of int with the getc and getchar functions.

```
#include <wchar.h>
//...
wint_t c;
c = getwchar();  // Put next character in c.
```

Keywords

Preprocessor Elements

Before the compiler translates a program, it runs a preprocessor that performs special actions: it reads in header files, decides what lines of code to compile, and performs text replacement.

Having a separate preprocessing phase used to irk some people because it meant a longer compile time, but modern CPU speeds make preprocessing incredibly fast. In return, the use of a preprocessing phase gives great flexibility to C and C++ programmers.

One of the main uses of the preprocessing phase is conditional compilation. If you need to support multiple versions of a program (for example, if you run different compiles for different platforms), conditional compilation is extremely helpful. It lets you set a single option to determine which lines are compiled. The conditional compilation directives are explained in the following table.

Directive	Description
#if	Starts a conditional compilation block; compiles on condition.
#ifdef	Similar to #if, but compiles if specified name is defined.
#ifndef	Similar to #if, but compiles if specified name is *not* defined.
#elif	Specifies an alternative condition to compile on.
#else	Specifies default conditional compilation block.
#end	Ends a conditional compilation block.

The other six directives support capabilities such as header files and macro definition.

Directive	Description
#define	Defines symbolic constant or macro.
#error	Stops compile immediately and prints error.
#include	Similar to #if, but compiles if specified name is *not* defined.
#line	Sets line number and (optionally) source filename.
#pragma	Specifies a compiler-specific command.
#undef	Removes a symbolic constant or macro definition.

In addition to directives, the preprocessor supports predefined macros and preprocessor operators. Although these are not used that often, they can be useful for reporting the version of the program and for debugging. The predefined macros are listed in the following table.

Predefined macro	Description
__cplusplus	Defined if the source file is being compiled as a C++ file.
__DATE__	Quoted string that contains the date of compilation.
__FILE__	Quoted string that contains the source file name.
__LINE__	Current line number.
__TIME__	Quoted string that contains the time of day of compilation.

Finally, the preprocessor has its own operators. These are recognized only during the preprocessing phase, and have no meaning otherwise.

Operator syntax	Description
defined(*symbol*)	Returns 1 if *symbol* is defined, 0 otherwise.
#*str*	Turns a string *str* into a quoted string.
text1##*text2*	Concatenates *text1* and *text2*.

Because the features in this chapter involve funny characters (_ and #), alphabetical order is somewhat arbitrary. The order used here is:

- preprocessor operators
- directives
- predefined macros

Quoted-string operator

Purpose

Puts quotation marks around a string. This is a compile-time operator used mainly with #define replacement text, where it is the only way to put quotes around an argument.

Syntax

    #string

The preprocessor expands this as "string".

Example

Suppose you want to write a macro using the #define directive (p. 143) that puts a string in quotation marks and calls the puts function. Here's our first attempt:

    #define pr(s) puts("s")

Unfortunately, this produces the wrong results. Each and every call to the macro, such as pr(Here is some text), results in this:

    puts("s")

which is not what was wanted. The problem is that the preprocessor takes quoted strings literally. The solution is to write the macro this way:

    #define pr(s) puts(#s)

Now the preprocessor correctly expands the call pr(Here is some text) as:

    puts("Here is some text")

Concatenation operator (come together)

Purpose

Joins together two strings. This is a compile-time operator whose most common use is with #define replacement text (p. 143).

Syntax

```
text1##text2
```

The preprocessor expands this as *text1text2*.

Examples

The need for this operator is obvious if you consider what happens with the following macro:

```
#define call(verb, adj, obj)   verb_adj(obj)
```

The problem is that the preprocessor considers verb_adj to be a new identifier, which it interprets literally. Therefore, a macro call such as

```
call(cut, yellow, trees)
```

is incorrectly expanded as:

```
verb_adj(trees)
```

because verb_adj was interpreted literally, rather than as concatenation of the arguments verb and adj. The correct way to write the macro is:

```
#define call(verb, adj, obj)   verb##_##adj(obj)
```

Now call(cut, yellow, trees) is correctly expanded as:

```
cut_yellow(trees)
```

When is this operator useful? One case is this: A macro might involve calls to different functions depending on compile-time conditions. For example, you may or may not want to call wc (wide character) functions. The following macro builds a function name from previous symbols:

```
#define STRINGF PREFIX##str##OP
```

Given these definitions:

```
#define PREFIX wc
#define OP cpy
```

the STRINGF macro would be translated into this function name:

```
wcstrcpy
```

defined   Is symbol defined?

Purpose

Returns 1 if the specified symbolic name is defined; 0 otherwise.

Syntax

```
defined(symbolname)
```

This is a compile-time operator whose use is mainly limited to working with the #if and #elif directives.

Example

The following code tests whether the symbol HEADER_INCLUDED is defined. If it is not defined, it compiles #include "myproj.h" and defines the symbol so that myproj.h is not included again. This way, no matter how many times these four lines appear, myproj.h is included only once.

```
#if !defined(HEADER_INCLUDED)
#include "myproj.h"
#define HEADER_INCLUDED
#endif
```

See also #ifdef (p. 149) and #ifndef (p. 150).

#define   Define symbol or macro

Purpose

Defines a symbolic constant or creates a macro function. You can also define a symbol just to set an #ifdef condition.

Syntax

The directive has several versions:

```
#define identifier replacement
#define identifier(arg [, arg]...) replacement
#define identifier
```

Here the brackets and ellipses (. . .) indicate that you can have any number of arguments separated by commas. The first whitespace character not enclosed in parentheses or quotation marks terminates the *replacement* text.

The *identifier* must conform to standard rules for identifier names. See "identifier" on page 544 in the glossary. The *replacement* text, however, can consist of any text.

The line-continuation character (\) can be used to build long *replacement* strings.

Usage 1: Symbolic Constants

Some programs deal with numbers that are important but difficult to remember. These are good candidates for symbolic constants. By convention, symbolic constants are always uppercase to distinguish them from variable names. For example:

```
#define PI 3.14159265
```

Given this #define directive, wherever PI appears in your program, the preprocessor replaces PI with the numeral 3.14159265.

Preprocessor Elements

●—NOTE

The symbol is not replaced if it appears in a comment, a quoted string, or as part of a larger word; for example, PI inside PIG is not replaced.

Alternatively, you can achieve similar results by defining PI as a const variable. For example:

```
const double PI = 3.14159265
```

However, there are some differences. If PI is a symbolic constant, its status is the same as a literal constant; the effect of using PI in your program is the same as if you had typed the number directly. As a literal constant, PI can be *folded in* to constant expressions before the program is ever run, thus optimizing speed. For example, in the following code, PI / 2 is completely evaluated at compile time rather than at runtime:

```
x = sin(y * (PI / 2));
```

Another feature of symbolic constants is that they can be used to set dimension sizes during array definition. This is another consequence of symbolic constants being translated into literal constants rather than stored as variables.

```
#define ROWSIZE 30
#define COLSIZE 20
//...
int matrix1[ROWSIZE][COLSIZE]
int matrix2[ROWSIZE][COLSIZE]
```

On the other hand, const variables help with compilation errors and debugging, because the compiler and debugger can refer to the variables by name. The names of symbolic constants are replaced by literals, which the debugger does not recognize.

Usage 2: Macro Functions

Macro functions look like function calls, but they are carried out through text replacement. For example, given the definition:

```
#define max(A, B)  ((A)>(B)?(A):(B))
```

the preprocessor replaces the expression max(i,j) with the following, just before compiling:

```
((i)>(j)?(i):(j))
```

Macro functions are fine for simple situations such as this. However, there are a number of weaknesses in macro functions compared to true function calls; for example, you cannot restrict argument types. Another weakness is that you cannot use statements because everything in the macro must be squeezed into a single expression. The use of inline functions (p. 546 in the glossary) corrects these weaknesses. Similar to macro functions, inline functions are expanded into the body of the code.

The use of parentheses around each argument in the replacement pattern (as shown in the previous example) is a good idea because it forces evaluation of each argument before the surrounding operators are resolved. Otherwise, if the arguments themselves contain operators, you can get unexpected (and wrong) results.

Usage 3: Controlling Compilation

A symbol can be defined as a way of turning on a condition recognized by an #ifdef directive. The #ifdef and #ifndef directives don't care *how* a symbol is defined, merely that it *is* defined. You can define a symbol without giving it a replacement value; in that case, the symbol is replaced with an empty string. However it is still a valid symbol as far as #ifdef and its friends are concerned.

In the following example, the symbol USE_8086 is defined; this causes the preprocessor to compile the code between #ifdef and #endif.

```
#define USE_8086
//...

#ifdef USE_8086
// Optimize for 8086 processors...
#endif
```

#elif	Compile on alternative condition

Purpose

Specifies an alternative condition within a conditional compilation (#if) block.

Syntax

    #elif constant_expression

If previous conditions were not met and *constant_expression* evaluates to true (any nonzero value), the lines following #elif are compiled.

As with the #if directive, the *constant_expression* can involve constants as well as most C++ operators, but it cannot include the sizeof operator, type casts, or enum constants. The expression can include the special define(*symbol*) operator, which evaluates to 1 if *symbol* is previously defined and to 0 otherwise.

For more information, see the #if directive on page 147.

#else Compile if condition false

Purpose

Specifies the default statement block within a conditional compilation (#if) block.

Syntax

```
//...
#else
statement_block_n
#endif
```

The statement block is compiled only if all preceding #if and #elif conditions are false. Syntactically, this directive appears similar to the else statement, but it is used in conditional compilation, not to control flow at runtime.

For more information, see the #if directive on page 147.

#endif End conditional block

Purpose

Ends a conditional compilation (#if) block.

Syntax

The #endif directive appears on a line by itself:

```
#endif
```

This terminates the syntax that begins with an #if directive. See the #if directive on page 147.

#error Terminate and cry uncle

Purpose

Stops compiling and prints source file, line, and a specified message. This is reported to the person *compiling* the program, not the person running it.

Syntax

```
#error message
```

Example

This code causes the compiler to stop if both BIT16 and BIT32 are defined.

```
#if defined(BIT16) && defined(BIT32)
#error Too many bits. Bombed out big time.
#endif
```

When the compiler processes this #error directive, it stops and prints the current source file and line number, along with the message, to the standard error stream (generally, the console of the person running the compile). In this case, the message reads:

```
Too many bits. Bombed out big time.
```

The #error directive provides a way to stop when some basic program assumption has been violated. Typically, you would use it where further compilation would serve no purpose.

Note that this directive prints out the *message* text as is, treating it like a quoted string. The preprocessor does not translate any macros inside this text.

#if   Compile if condition is true

Purpose
Starts a conditional compilation block; can also be used to "comment out" lines.

Syntax
An #if directive marks the beginning of a conditional compilation block. If the expression specified by the #if directive is true (any nonzero value), the C++ processor compiles the statements that follow it, up to the next matching #elif, #else, or #endif directive.

```
#if constant_expression
statement_block_1
[ #elif constant_expression
statement_block_2 ]
[ #elif constant_expression
statement_block_3 ]
    .
    .
    .
[#else
statement_block_n ]
#endif
```

The brackets here indicate optional items; only #if and #endif are required. You can use any number of #elif directives. You can use at most one #else directive.

The C++ preprocessor examines each *constant_expression* until one of them evaluates to true (nonzero). The corresponding *statement_block* gets compiled. Each *statement_block* can contain any kind of C++ code.

Each `constant_expression` is made up of constants and/or C++ operators. Such constants often involve symbols previously defined by #define directives or by command-line options. The expression cannot include the sizeof operator, type casts, or enum constants.

Usage 1: Conditional Compilation

Conditional compilation is an efficient way to maintain multiple versions of a program. You might be writing a program for multiple platforms and find that certain sections of code have to be rewritten for each platform. You also might want to build a debug version, which prints periodic diagnostic messages, as well as a release version.

This creates a dilemma. If you altered the program each time you compiled for a different platform, you'd have to do a lot of extra work. If you kept multiple versions, you'd eat up extra disk space and have major headaches due to source-code control.

The answer is *conditional compilation* — a technique for isolating portions of code specific to one version or another. For example, suppose I have a program that uses different coordinate systems for different platforms. First, I define a series of constants:

```
#define SHORT    0
#define LONG     1
#define REAL     2
```

Now, to recompile for a different coordinate system, I need only change one line — the line that defines the value of the symbol COORDSYS. For example:

```
#define COORDSYS REAL
```

Many compilers support a command-line or development-environment option that lets you define a symbol as part of the compile command, so you don't have to rewrite a single line of code. See your compiler documentation for more information.

The program checks the value of COORDSYS whenever needed to decide what to compile:

```
#if COORDSYS == SHORT
short x, y;
#elif COORDSYS == LONG
long x, y;
#elif COORDSYS == REAL
double x, y;
#endif
```

Usage 2: Commenting Out Lines

Occasionally, you may need to *comment out* lines of code; that is, remove the lines temporarily from the program in such a way that they are easy to put back. An obvious way to do this is to place the C-style multiline comment symbols around a block of code. However, this approach causes errors if you try to nest comments inside of other comments.

One solution is to use #if 0 and #endif to temporarily stop a group of statements from being compiled. The compiler then skips the lines, just as if they were placed in a comment block. For example:

```
#if 0
int i, j;      /* Declare i and j as int. */
double x, y;   /* Declare x and y as double. */
#endif
```

Unlike multiline comment symbols, #if and #endif directives can be nested to any level.

● NOTE

Don't confuse the #if directive and the if keyword, despite their apparent similarity; they are used for completely different situations. The if keyword controls decision-making at runtime, whereas the #if directive controls decision-making at compile time. This second kind of decision-making enables you to maintain multiple versions of the program.

#ifdef   Compile if symbol defined

Purpose

Starts a conditional compilation block, just as #if does; compiles a block if a symbolic name is defined.

Syntax

In place of the #if directive, you can use #ifdef:

#ifdef *symbol*

This means exactly the same as:

#if defined(*symbol*)

If *symbol* (a symbolic name) is defined, the lines of code following #ifdef are compiled up to the next matching #elif, #else, or #endif. The value of the *symbol* is not significant. It can even be defined as an empty string, as in the following definition of BIT32:

```
#define BIT32
```

Many compilers support a compiler option for defining symbols. Using such an option lets you control compiling from a command line, batch file, make file, or development environment. See your compiler documentation.

For the rest of the conditional compilation syntax, see #if, the previous topic.

Preprocessor Elements

#ifndef

Purpose

Starts a conditional compilation block, just as #if does; compiles a block if a symbolic name is *not* defined.

Syntax

In place of the #if directive, you can use #ifndef:

```
#ifndef symbol
```

This means exactly the same as:

```
#if ! defined(symbol)
```

If symbol (a symbolic name) is not defined, the lines of code following #ifndef are compiled, up to the next matching #elif, #else, or #endif.

Example

One practical use of #ifndef is to ensure that certain code is compiled only once. This is useful when you have a large project involving many different header files. For example, these four lines could appear multiple times, but myproj.h would get included only once.

```
#ifndef HEADER_INCLUDED
#include "myproj.h"
#define HEADER_INCLUDED
#endif
```

For more information on conditional compilation, see the #if directive on page 147.

#include

Purpose

Suspends compilation of the current file and compiles another file. This other file is usually a header file, with common declarations for a project or library.

Syntax

The directive has two versions:

```
#include "filename"    // Project header file
#include <filename>    // Standard lib header file
```

On encountering #include, the compiler suspends reading of the current file and instead compiles the file specified by filename. All the files read in this way are compiled as if they were part of one continuous source file. (This process can be nested to any level, so an included file can include other files.)

The difference between the two versions is that in the first version (*"filename"*), the preprocessor searches the current directory before looking elsewhere. Both versions search the standard include-file directory. (On DOS and Windows systems this directory is specified by the INCLUDE environment variable.)

You should use #include *"filename"* for your own project files. The second version is preferred for standard header files such as stdio.h and stdlib.h.

Example

```
#include <stdio.h>
```

●—ANSI

In ANSI C++, you can use #include to get standard library declarations directly from a *virtual header file*, as in #include <cstdio>. Such directives may or may not map to a physical header file. This is the preferred way to support standard libraries in the future, because it enables possible efficiencies for the compiler. Each topic in Section 6 shows both approaches.

#line   Set line number and source file

Purpose

Sets a new line number and a new source file name, as reflected by the __LINE__ and __FILE__ macros. The directive has no effect on the physical source file.

Syntax

```
#line num ["filename"]
```

The brackets here indicate that *"filename"* is optional.

After this line is processed, the value of __LINE__ for the next line is set to *num*; line numbers then resume incrementing normally. The *filename*, if specified, becomes the new value of __FILE__. The setting of __FILE__ retains quotation marks.

Example

```
#line 100 "source1"
#include <stdio.h>
```

__FILE__   Current source file

The __FILE__ macro is translated into a quoted string that contains the name of the current source file. (Note: This name can be set by using the #line directive). For example, consider this code:

```
#include <stdio.h>
//...
printf("Error in file %s.\n", __FILE__);
```

If the source file is c:\samples\test.cpp, the __FILE__ macro is translated into these characters during preprocessing:

```
"c:\\samples\\test.cpp"
```

The example would print this string:

```
Error in file c:\samples\test.cpp.
```

__LINE__   Current line of source code

The __LINE__ macro is translated into the current line number of the source file being compiled. (Note: this number can be reset by using the #line directive). For example, consider this code:

```
#include <stdio.h>
//...
printf("Error occurred at line %d.\n", __LINE__);
```

If the current line is 17, the __LINE__ macro is translated into these characters during preprocessing:

```
17
```

The example would print this string:

```
Error occurred at line 17.
```

__TIME__   Current time of day

The __TIME__ macro is translated into a quoted string that contains the time of compilation in the form *hours : minutes : seconds*. For example, consider this code:

```
#include <stdio.h>
//...
printf("TIME of compilation is %s.\n", __TIME__);
```

A sample value for __TIME__ might be:

"10:05:30"

Given this time, the example would print this string:

Time of compilation is 10:05:30.

in plain english

Library Functions

The C++ standard library includes a rich set of functions. You can use the functions to read and write to files, read and write to the console, get the time of day, and perform advanced math. Amendment 1 to the ANSI specification includes full support for wide-character strings, making it easier to write applications for international use.

Although the library is not the same as the language itself, compiler vendors always supply at least the standard library. Some vendors supply additional functions for specific platforms such as Microsoft Windows or UNIX. Because of space limitations, this book focuses on just those functions supported by all ANSI-conforming libraries.

Note that nearly all the I/O operations can also be performed by the C++ I/O classes, described in Section 7.

Function Summary

Math functions

This group includes trigonometric, exponential, rounding, and random-number functions. Although most of these are declared in math.h, some are declared in stdlib.h, so remember to check the include file.

abs	Cosh	labs	rand
acos	Div	ldexp	sin
asin	exp	ldiv	sinh
atan	fabs	log	sqrt
atan2	floor	log10	srand
ceil	fmod	modf	tan
cos	frexp	pow	tanh

Memory-allocation functions

This group enables you to allocate memory dynamically, requesting any size block. The new and delete operators are usually better, but these functions are supported for backward compatibility with C.

calloc	free	malloc	realloc

Memory-block functions

These functions take advantage of special processor instructions, if available, to efficiently manipulate large blocks of memory.

memchr	memcpy	memset
memcmp	memmove	

Conversion functions

These functions read strings containing digits and return numeric values.

atof	atol	strtol
atoi	strtod	strtoul

General I/O

These functions read from and write to the console (monitor and keyboard) or to strings.

getchar	printf	scanf
gets	putchar	sprintf
perror	puts	sscanf

Files

These functions read from and write to disk files, as well as support some miscellaneous operations. Except for remove and rename, these are all covered in this section; several, including fopen, have their own topic as well.

clearerr	fgets	fscanf	remove
fclose	fopen	fseek	rename
feof	fprintf	fsetpos	rewind
ferror	fputc	ftell	setbuf
fflush	fputs	fwrite	setvbuf
fgetc	fread	getc	tmpfile
fgetpos	freopen	putc	ungetc

Single-character functions

Most of these functions test an individual character for a particular condition. In addition, tolower and toupper convert the case of an individual character.

isalnum	isgraph	isspace	toupper
isalpha	islower	isupper	
iscntrl	isprint	isxdigit	
isdigit	ispunct	tolower	

String functions

These functions let you manipulate and analyze standard null-terminated strings, which are simple arrays of char. All of these are covered in the topic "str < op > (p. 224).

strcat	strcspn	strncpy	strtok
strchr	strerror	strpbrk	strxfrm
strcmp	strlen	strrchr	
strcoll	strncat	strspn	
strcpy	strncmp	strstr	

Time functions

These functions provide support for getting and storing sytem time, as well as for displaying it in a variety of formats. All of these functions are covered in the "Time" topic (p. 235). strftime also has its own topic as well as being discussed under the section "Time."

asctime	difftime	mktime
clock	gmtime	strftime
ctime	localtime	time

Variable-length argument support

This group includes a combination of macros and regular functions. The va_ macros enable you to process a variable-length argument list. The other items in this group make it possible to write wrappers around printf or a related function.

va_arg	vprintf	vwprintf
va_end	vfprintf	vfwprintf
va_start	vsprintf	vswprintf

Wide-character support

Amendment 1 to the ANSI specification mandates support for wide-character strings, including the following functions. These strings, consisting of arrays of wchar_t, make it possible to represent a wider character set than the ASCII set. Nearly all of these functions correspond to a traditional string, character, or text I/O function.

fgetwc	iswlower	wcscmp	wcsxfrm
fgetws	iswprint	wcscoll	wcstod
fputwc	iswpunct	wcscpy	wcstol
fputws	iswspace	wcscspn	wcstoul
fwide	iswupper	wcsftime	wmemchr
fwprintf	putwc	wcslen	wmemcmp
fwscanf	putwchar	wcsncat	wmemcpy
getwc	swprintf	wcsncmp	wmemmove
getwchar	swscanf	wcsncpy	wmemset
iswalnum	towlower	wcspbrk	wprintf
iswalpha	towupper	wcsrchr	wscanf
iswcntrl	ungetwc	wcsspn	
iswdigit	wcscat	wcsstr	
iswgraph	wcschr	wcstok	

●—ANSI

ANSI Amendment 1 was put forth in 1995. Not all earlier versions of C++ support the wide-character functions.

Miscellaneous functions

This last group includes program termination, array searching and sorting, and use of signals to handle special situations. In C++, the try keyword (p. 122) provides a better way to handle exceptions, but everything in the C library is still supported for the sake of backward compatibility.

abort	exit	qsort	signal
assert	getenv	raise	system
atexit	localeconv	setjmp	
bsearch	longjmp	setlocale	

More about binary I/O

The fread and fwrite functions use a char* argument to read and write data. This use of the char* type does not mean that you are limited to using character data. However, you must use a (char*) pointer cast to read and write individual values.

For example, if you want to write an integer to a file in binary mode, get a pointer to the integer, cast this pointer to type char*, and then call the fwrite function. The following code writes the value of the integer total to the next four bytes of the file. This operation writes the actual binary representation of the value, rather than text characters.

```
long total = 5;
fwrite((char*)&total, sizeof(long), 1, fb);
```

Notably, a pointer cast never changes the underlying bit patterns; it only changes the way data is interpreted. You can also write an array of values, f any type:

```
short array[] = {2, 55, 27};
fwrite((char*)array, sizeof(short), 3, fb);
```

You can use a similar technique to read a value from a binary file. The following code reads four bytes from the current file location into the long integer total.

```
fread((char*)&total, sizeof(long), 1, fb);
```

In ANSI C++, the preferred technique for pointer casts is now to use the reinterpret_cast operator (p. 103). Here is the previous example, rewritten with reinterpret_cast.

```
fread(reinterpret_cast<char*>(&total), sizeof(long),
    1, fb);
```

| **atof** | **Convert string to floating-point** |

Purpose

Takes a string containing a floating-point expression and returns a number.

Syntax

```
#include <stdlib.h>    // OR #include <cstdlib>


double atof(const char *str);
```

The function skips past leading whitespace characters and reads characters as long as they form a valid floating-point expression. Subsequent characters are then ignored. For example, " –24.56xy7" is interpreted as –24.56. The function reads "E" and "e" as exponent signs, so that "5E2" is interpreted as 50.0. If no valid number can be read, most implementations return 0.

Example

This example gets a string from the keyboard and stores the number in the variable x. Maximum line length of 80 characters is assumed.

```
#include <stdlib.h>
#include <stdio.h>
//...
char input_str[81];
double x = atof(gets(input_str));
```

Related functions are atoi and atol, which return integers. See also strtod (p. 230) and wcstod (p. 246).

| **atoi** | **Convert string to int** |

Purpose

Takes a string of digit characters and returns an int.

Syntax

```
#include <stdlib.h>    // OR #include <cstdlib>


int atoi(const char *str);
```

The function skips past leading whitespace characters and stops reading at the first nondigit character. For example, the string " –23.9x" is read in as –23. If no valid number can be read, most implementations return 0.

Example

This example gets a string from the keyboard and stores the number in the variable n. A maximum line length of 80 characters is assumed.

```
#include <stdlib.h>
#include <stdio.h>
//...
char input_str[81];
int n = atoi(gets(input_str));
```

Related functions are atol, which returns a long integer, and atof, which returns a floating-point value. Also, strol (p. 231) and stroul (p. 232) read integers in any radix; wcstol (p. 245) and wcstoul (p. 245) perform the same operations on wide-character strings.

atol	Convert string to long int

Purpose

Takes a string of digit characters and returns a long integer.

Syntax

```
#include <stdlib.h>   // OR #include <cstdlib>

long atol(const char *str);
```

The function skips past leading whitespace characters and stops reading at the first nondigit character. For example, the string " –23.9x" is read in as –23. If no valid number can be read, most implementations return 0.

Example

This example gets a string from the keyboard and stores the number in the variable n. A maximum line length of 80 characters is assumed.

```
#include <stdlib.h>
#include <stdio.h>
//...
char input_str[81];
long n = atol(gets(input_str));
```

Related functions are atoi, which returns an int, and atof, which returns a floating-point value. Also, strol (p. 231) and stroul (p. 232) read integers in any radix; wcstol (p. 245) and wcstoul (p. 245) perform the same operations on wide-character strings.

bsearch   Perform binary search

Purpose

Searches an array, which can be any length and type, but must be presorted (which you can do by calling qsort).

Syntax

```
#include <stdlib.h>   // OR #include <cstdlib>

void *bsearch(const void *key,
    const void *buf, size_t num, size_t size,
    int (compare)(const void *, const void *) );
```

key points to a copy of the target value to find.

The three arguments *buf*, *num*, and *size* describe the array to be searched. *buf* points to the beginning of the array, *num* is the number of items, and *size* is the size of each element.

The *compare* argument is the address of a function you supply, which returns a negative number, zero, or a positive number, depending on whether the first value pointed to is less than, equal to, or greater than the second. The function gets pointers to elements; these pointers are declared as void* and must be recast to their actual type. (See "Example.")

bsearch returns a pointer to the first element equal to *key*, if found, or NULL otherwise.

Example

This example sorts an array of integers. The cmp function gets pointers of type int* *that are passed as type* void*. The function casts them to int* and then dereferences them.

```
#include <stdlib.h>
#include <iostream.h>

int cmp(const void *p1, const void *p2) {
    int i = *(int *)p1;  // Get ints pointed to.
    int j = *(int *)p2;
    return i < j ? -1 : (i == j ? 0: 1);
}

void main() {
    int dat[] = {1, 4, 9, 34, 39, 40, 45, 50, 51, 99};
    int i = 45;
    void *p = bsearch(&i, dat, 10, sizeof(int), &cmp);
    if (p == NULL)
```

```
        cout << "i was not found.";
    else
        cout << "i was found.";
}
```

See qsort (p. 209) for a note concerning arrays of strings.

calloc   Allocate collection of stuff

Purpose
Allocates memory just as malloc does, but also aligns each of *num* items properly for its size, as well as initializing each to zero.

Syntax
```
#include <stdlib.h>   // OR #include <cstdlib>

void *calloc(size_t num, size_t size);
```

Like malloc, this function allocates a memory block of the appropriate size (*num * size*) and returns a pointer to the first element, or NULL if there is insufficient memory.

The memory is properly aligned for objects of the indicated *size*.

Example
```
#include <stdlib.h>
int n;
int *p;
//...
p = reinterpret_cast<int*>(calloc(n, sizeof(int)));
if (p == NULL)
    // Print error message and end.
```

This example allocates n integers, each of which is initialized to 0. For more information, see free (p. 189), malloc (p. 201), and realloc (p. 212).

ceil   Round upward to integer

Purpose
Takes a floating-point value and rounds it upward to the nearest integer.

Syntax
```
#include <math.h>   // OR #include <cmath>

double ceil(double x);
```

In the following table, *fmt* is a format string in wide-character format and *ch* is a character of type wchar_t.

Function	Action
getwchar()	Returns the next character from the keyboard as a wide character, or WEOF if there is an error. Return type is wint_t. Similar to getchar.
putwchar(ch**)**	Writes character *ch* to standard output. If successful, it returns the character written; otherwise, it returns EOF. Similar to putchar.
wprintf(fmt, ...**)**	Writes wide-character-format string to standard output and returns the number of characters written. See printf (p. 205) for format specifiers.
wscanf(fmt, ...**)**	Uses wide-character-format string *fmt* to read data from the keyboard and to return the number of variables assigned values. See scanf (p. 214) for format specifiers.

The library provides no wide-character versions of gets and puts ("get string" and "put string"). However, you can get and print strings to the console by calling the file-stream functions fgetws and fputws, using stdin or stdout, respectively, for the file-pointer argument. (stdin and stdout are defined in the file stdio.h, which you would need to include.) You can also print a string by calling wprintf.

Examples

This function prints a wide-character string to the console.

```
#include <wchar.h>

void putws(const wchar_t wstr) {
    wchar_t *pwc = wstr;
    while(*pwc)
        putwchar(*pwc++);
}
```

This next example declares a wide-character string and prints it. Note that the string is initialized with the "L" prefix, because it uses wide characters.

```
#include <wchar.h>
//...
wchar_t *wcs = L"Here is a message.\n";
wprintf(wcs);
```

cos
Cosine

Purpose

Returns the cosine of its argument.

Syntax

```
#include <math.h>   // OR #include <cmath>

double cos(double x);
```

The function takes an angle in radians and returns a value between 1 and –1.

Example

This code prints the cosine of pi/2. The result should be extremely close to zero.

```
#include <math.h>
#include <iostream.h>
//...
double pi = atan(1) * 4;
cout << "cos(pi/2) = " << cos(pi / 2) << '\n';
```

See also acos, asin, atan, atan2, sin, and tan.

cosh
Hyperbolic cosine

Purpose

Returns the hyperbolic cosine of its argument.

Syntax

```
#include <math.h>   // OR #include <cmath>

double cosh(double x);
```

The function returns an angle in radians. If the result is out of range, the function returns HUGEVAL and sets the global variable errno to ERANGE. See also sinh and tanh.

div
Divide integers

Purpose

Performs division on two integer inputs, returning both quotient and remainder (as integers).

Syntax

```
#include <stdlib.h>   // OR #include <cstdlib>

div_t div(int numerator, int denominator);
```

The results are returned in a div_t structure, which has the following format. The quotient (quot) represents the largest integer that *denominator* can be multiplied by without exceeding *numerator*.

```
struct div_t {
    int quot;
    int rem;
};
```

Example

```
#include <stdlib.h>
#include <iostream.h>
//...
div_t dv = div(255, 2);
cout << "255/2 = " << dv.quot << ", with remainder ";
cout << dv.rem << endl;
```

A related function is ldiv (p. 198), which performs the same action but works with integers of type long. The modulus operator, % (p. 58), provides another way of getting a remainder. See also fmod (p. 187), which gets a remainder for floating-point division.

exit   Terminate graciously

Purpose

Exits the program normally, flushing all output buffers and executing all termination procedures. (See atexit, p. 165.)

Syntax

```
#include <stdlib.h>   // OR #include <cstdlib>

void exit(int exit_code);
```

The stdio.h file defines at least two values for *exit_code*: EXIT_SUCCESS (0) and EXIT_FAILURE (nonzero). Your implementation may define other values.

Example

This function call terminates the program and indicates success:

```
exit(0);
```

exp   Raise e to a power

Purpose

Raises the mathematical value e to a specified power x and returns the result.
(For a function that raises any number to a specified power, see the pow function, p. 204.)

Syntax

```
#include <math.h>    // OR #include <cmath>

double exp(double x);
```

Example

One of the more obvious uses of exp is to get the value of e directly:

```
#include <math.h>
//...
double e = exp(1);
```

fabs   Absolute value (floating point)

Purpose

Gets the absolute value of a floating-point number.

Syntax

```
#include <math.h>    // OR #include <cmath>

double fabs(double x);
```

Example

The absolute value converts a negative number to positive, but returns a non-negative number as is. This code prints the number 5.07:

```
#include <stdio.h>
#include <iostream.h>
//...
cout << abs(-5.07);
```

Related functions are abs (p. 162), which takes the int type, and labs
(p. 197), which takes a long integer.

Files	File I/O functions

Purpose

This family of functions provides support for opening, reading, and writing to files, as well as moving file and accessing file position.

Syntax

```
#include <stdio.h>  // OR #include <cstdio>
```

This first table summarizes functions that open and close files. The argument f, which has type FILE*, is a pointer to a file stream, and *fname* is a string containing a filename.

Function	Action
fclose(f)	Closes file stream f.
fopen(*fname*, m)	Opens file *fname* using mode string m. Returns a file-stream pointer if successful; otherwise returns NULL. See page 187 for more information.
freopen(*fname*, m, f)	Same action as fopen, but it first closes file stream f.
tmpfile()	Opens a temporary file in binary read/write mode and returns file-stream pointer. See tmpfile topic for more information.

Once you get a file-stream pointer, you can use it as the f argument in a file I/O function. The following functions perform output. All have int return type.

Function	Action
fflush(f)	Flushes output stream f, immediately sending output to the physical device. Returns EOF on error; otherwise, returns 0.
fprintf(f, *fmt*,...)	Writes formatted string to f. Returns number of characters written. See page 205 for information on formats.
fputc(*ch*, f)	Writes character *ch* to f. Returns EOF on error; otherwise, returns character written.
fputs(s, f)	Writes string s to f, not including null terminator. Returns EOF on error; otherwise returns nonnegative value.

Function	Action
fwrite(p, size, n, f)	Writes n items to f from char* buffer pointed to by p. Returns number of items written. Each item has specified size.
putc(ch, f)	Same as fputc.

The next group of functions read data from an input file. Each of these has an int or char* return type, as appropriate.

Function	Action
fgetc(f)	Returns next character from f; if the character cannot be read, returns EOF. Character is returned as an int.
fgets(s, n, f)	Reads up to n-1 bytes from f into string s, stopping at newline or end-of-file, and appending a null. Includes newline, if read. Returns null pointer on error; otherwise, returns the string. (End-of-file is not an error in this context.)
fread(p, size, n, f)	Reads n items from f into char* buffer pointed to by p. Returns number of items read. Each item has specified size.
fscanf(f, fmt, ...)	Uses format string fmt to read input from f. Returns number of items read, or EOF on error. See page 214 for formats.
getc(f)	Same as fgetc.
ungetc(ch, f)	Pushes character ch back onto file stream f. Returns EOF on error; otherwise, returns ch. The capability to push one character back is guaranteed, but not necessarily more. Return type is int.

Several functions deal with getting and setting file position. These are especially useful for random-access operations. The pos argument has type fpos_t, which is defined in stdio.h; fpos_t is an integer or structure large enough to record every file position.

Function	Action
feof(f)	Returns nonzero (true) if end-of-file has been reached.
fgetpos(f, *pos)	Returns current position in file f and copy to value pointed to by *pos. This value can be used with fsetpos. The return type is fpos_t.

Continued

Function	Action
fseek(f, off, org)	Moves current position in file f to offset off. org is an integer specifying one of several modes. (See below.)
fsetpos(f, pos)	Moves current position in file f to pos. Use with fgetpos.
ftell(f)	Returns current position in file f as a long.

With the fseek function, the org argument can take one of these values: SEEK_SET, which seeks from the start of the file; SEEK_CUR, which seeks from the current position; or SEEK_END, which seeks past the end of the file.

The rest of the file I/O functions deal with errors and user-defined buffers. The argument p has type char*. By default, C/C++ file streams provide their own buffer, of size BUFSIZ, to minimize disk access.

Function	Action
clearerr(f)	Clears error flags for f.
ferror(f)	Returns an integer containing current error number for f; this number is 0 if the file has no errors.
rewind(f)	Clears error flags for f and resets file position to the start of the file.
setbuf(f, p)	Sets buffer of file stream f to bytes pointed by p. Buffer must be BUFSIZ long. If p is a null pointer, buffering is turned off.
setvbuf(f, p, m, size)	Same action as setbuf, except that m specifies mode (see below) and size specifies size of the buffer. Returns zero on success and nonzero on failure.

With the setvbuf function, mode is an integer argument set to one of the following: _IOFBF, which enables full buffering; _IONBF, which turns buffering off; or _IOLBF, which flushes the buffer each time a newline is written to an output stream.

Reading and writing text files

The starting point of file operations is to open a file stream by calling fopen. The function, if successful, returns a pointer of type FILE*, which you can use as input to other functions.

```
#include <stdio.h>
//...
FILE* fp;
fp = fopen("C:\\test.txt", "w");
```

Function	Action
fwscanf(*f*, *fmt*,...)	Uses format string *fmt* to read input from *f*. Returns number of items read, or EOF on error. See page 214 for formats. Similar to fscanf.
getwc(*f*)	Same as fgetwc.
putwc(*ch*, *f*)	Same as putwc.
ungetwc(*ch*, *f*)	Pushes wide character *ch* back onto file stream *f*. Returns WEOF on error; otherwise, returns *ch*. Return type is wint_t.

The fputws, fwprintf, and fwscanf functions all have int return type, and fgetws returns a wchar_t* pointer. The other functions have wint_t return type, as indicated.

An interesting quirk of these functions is that although all the I/O is performed with wide-character (wchar_t) text, the file must first be opened with a file name stored in an ordinary char* string. This is why there is no alternative version of fopen. (See "Examples.")

Examples

Here is the first complete program example from the "Files" topic (p. 178), converted to work with wide-character strings. The file is still opened with single-byte characters, as before.

```
#include <stdio.h>
#include <wchar.h>
//...
void test_files(void) {
    FILE* fp;
    int i = 12;
    fp = fopen("C:\\test.txt", "w");
    if (fp)
        fwprintf(fp, L"Here is a number: %d\n", i);
    else
        fputws(L"Error opening the file.\n", stderr);
}
```

Here is the second program example from the "Files" topic, converted to work with wide characters.

```
#include <stdio.h>
#define LINESZ 256
```

```
void main(void) {
   FILE *inf, *outf;
   char s[LINESZ];

   inf = fopen("c:\\test.txt", "r");
   outf = fopen("c:\\test1.txt", "w");
   if (inf == NULL || outf == NULL){
      putws("Could not open files.\n", stderr);
      return 1;
   }
   fgetws(s, LINESZ, inf);
   while (!feof(inf)) {
      fputws(L"> ", outf);
      fputws(s, outf);
      fgetws(s, LINESZ, inf);
   }
}
```

For this example to work properly, the file c:\test.txt must have been previously created as a text file and then written using wide-character functions only.

floor   Round downward to integer

Purpose

Takes a floating-point value and rounds it downward to the nearest integer.

Syntax

```
#include <math.h>   // OR #include <cmath>

double floor(double x);
```

Although the amount returned is an integer amount, it still has type double, so you may need to cast the result. This function always rounds downward, so that –2.05, for example, is rounded down to –3.0.

Example

For example, the following function returns an integer ranging from 0 to n – 1.

```
#include <math.h>
#include <stdlib.h>

int random_0toN_1(int n) {
     return (int) floor(n * (rand()/RAND_MAX));
}
```

See also the ceil (p. 169) and modf (p. 203) functions.

fmod   Get remainder from division

Purpose

Divides one floating-point number by another and returns the remainder.

Syntax

```
#include <math.h>   // OR #include <cmath>

double fmod(double x, double y);
```

The function determines the largest integer *i* such that *y* * *i* does not exceed
x. Then it returns x – yi. The action is similar to that of the modulus operator
(%), except that the function takes floating-point arguments and returns a
floating-point result.

Examples

```
#include <math.h>
#include <iostream.h>
//..
cout << fmod(31, 2) << '\n';      // Prints 1
cout << fmod(31.05, 2) << '\n';   // Prints 1.05
cout << fmod(7.6, 2.5) << '\n';   // Prints 0.1
```

fopen   Open file for reading or writing

Purpose

Opens a file and returns a file-stream pointer, which can be used in other file
I/O functions. (See "Files" on p. 178.)

Syntax

```
#include <stdio.h>   // OR #include <cstdio>

FILE *fopen(const char *fname, const char *mode)
```

The *fname* argument contains a filename, which can include a path specification. If you use a literal string, remember that C/C++ strings use double
backslashes (\\) to represent a single backslash (\). For example, suppose you
want to open the following file:

```
c:\programs\drawing.dat
```

To open this file for binary reading, you would use the following statement:

```
FILE *fp;
fp = fopen("c:\\programs\\drawing.dat", "rb");
```

Mode specifiers

The mode argument is a string that contains one of the values listed in Table 1.

Table 1 *Modes Used with fopen*

Mode string	Action
"r"	Opens text file for reading
"w"	Creates new text file for writing
"a"	Opens text file for appending
"rb"	Opens binary file for reading
"wb"	Creates new binary file for writing
"ab"	Opens text binary for appending
"r+"	Opens text file for reading and writing
"w+"	Creates new text file for reading and writing
"a+"	Opens text file for reading and writing
"rb+"	Opens binary file for reading and writing
"wb+"	Creates new binary file for reading and writing
"ab+"	Opens binary file for reading and writing

Technically, the only difference between text and binary modes is the handling of newlines. In text mode, file output functions translate each newline (hex 0A) by writing out a carriage return/linefeed pair (hex 0D 0A); and file input functions translate each carriage return/linefeed by reading in a newline.

Consequently, program strings represent the end of a line of text with a single, convenient character — denoted in C/C++ strings as "\n" — even though an end-of-line is represented in files as a two-character sequence (0D 0A).

In practice, of course, there are other differences between text and binary files. In text files, all data is usually represented in ASCII, human-readable format, so that a numeric field is represented as a digit string rather than stored directly as a binary value. (It's therefore common to use fprintf to write to a text file but not to a binary file.)

Example

The following example gets a file name from the console and uses it to open a file for reading in text mode. A NULL return value indicates that the file cannot be opened.

```
#include <stdio.h>
#include <stdlib.h>
```

```
//...
FILE *fp;
char fspec[81];
printf("Enter a file specification:\n");
gets(fspec);

fp = fopen(fspec, "r");

if (fp == NULL) {
   printf("Could not open file %s\n", fspec);
   exit(1);
}
// Perform file operations with fp...
```

Other rules

Several rules apply to the use of fopen in its various modes.

- If the function cannot successfully open the file, it returns NULL.
- When you open a file for reading or appending, the file must previously exist or fopen is not successful.
- When you open a file for writing, the major requirement is that *fname* contain a valid file name. If there is an existing file with this name, the file is erased and then opened as a new file.
- When you open a file for both reading and writing (read/write mode), the named file is opened if it exists. Otherwise, a new file is created.
- If a file has been opened in read/write mode, you cannot switch from doing input to output, or vice versa, without first calling one of these functions: fflush, fseek, fsetpos, or rewind. (See "File I/O Functions" for information on these functions.)

free   Liberate memory

Purpose

Releases a previously allocated memory block. This function and its relatives are supported mainly for backward compatibility with C.

Syntax

```
#include <stdlib.h>   // OR #include <cstdlib>

void free(void *pointer);
```

The pointer must point to a block previously allocated with malloc, calloc, or realloc, or the result is a runtime error.

Example

This code allocates a block of n characters and later frees it.

```
#include <stdlib.h>
int n;
char *p;
//...
p = reinterpret_cast<char*>(malloc(n));
//...
free(p);
```

Note that new and delete (Section 4, pp. 98 and 80) can be used wherever malloc and free are, and provide a number of advantages. new and delete are simply better.

frexp   Free exponent

Purpose

Takes a floating-point argument and returns its mantissa and exponent portions. Few programs ever have a need for this function. Not to be confused with the "free Willy" and "free Mandela" functions, which the ANSI committee has no plans to add.

Syntax

```
#include <math.h>    // OR #include <cmath>

double frexp(double x, int *expptr);
```

The function returns the mantissa of floating-point value x; it also copies the exponent of x to the location *expptr. Because the base is binary, the mantissa is always less than 1.0, and the exponent represents a power of 2.

Example

For example, the following code breaks down the number 48 into a mantissa and an exponent of 0.75 and 6, respectively (48 = 0.75 * 2 to the 6th power):

```
#include <math.h>
#include <iostream.h>
//...
int exp;
double man = frexp(48, &exp);
cout << "man = " << man << endl;
cout << "exp = " << exp << endl;
```

fwide
Orient stream to char or wchar_t

Purpose

Determines whether a file stream is oriented to char or wchar_t text operations; also returns the current orientation, after being set.

Syntax

```
#include <wchar.h>   // OR #include <cwchar>

double fwide(FILE *stream, int mode);
```

The function changes the orientation of the stream as follows:

- If mode is greater than zero, the stream is set to wide-character orientation.
- If mode is less than zero, the stream is set to char orientation.
- If mode is zero, the orientation does not change; the function simply returns the current orientation state.

The return value is similar to the mode value. Greater and less than zero represent wide-character and char orientation, respectively. Return value of zero indicates that orientation has not been set.

Remarks

A file stream can handle text I/O with wchar_t or char strings, but not both. (These restrictions are relaxed for console I/O.) The first text I/O function called determines orientation. For example, printf uses char orientation. The fwide function enables you to test the orientation of a file stream as well as set it explicitly.

Example

```
#include <wchar.h>
//...
FILE *fp;
fp = fopen("c:\\test.txt", "r");
fwide(fp, 1);    // Set to wide-char orientation.
```

getc
Get character from file

Purpose

Returns the next character from the specified input stream, or EOF if no more characters are available.

Syntax

```
#include <stdio.h>    // OR #include <cstdio>

int getc(FILE *stream);
```

getc works exactly as the fgetc function does. The reason for this redundancy is that getc is often implemented as a macro with better performance; therefore, getc is preferred to fgetc. (Exception: getc, as a macro, may evaluate the stream argument more than once and is therefore unreliable if stream is returned by a function call.)

Example

This code prints out all the characters in a file previously opened as fp.

```
#include <stdio.h>
//...
int c;
while ((c = getc(fp)) != EOF)
    putchar(c);
```

The while condition stores the character in variable c and then compares it to EOF. This complex expression — frequently used by C/C++ programmers — actually performs two complete operations: assignment to c and comparison.

```
(c = getc(fp)) != EOF
```

For more information on file-stream operations, see the topic "Files" on page 178.

getchar   Get character from keyboard

Purpose

Returns next character from standard input (usually the keyboard).

Syntax

```
#include <stdio.h>    // OR #include <cstdio>

int getchar(void);
```

Example

```
#include <stdio.h>
//...
int c;
c = getchar();
```

Note that most platforms buffer console input one line at a time. Consequently, getchar may not return until the user presses Enter. Also note that pressing

Enter itself generates characters: the newline character sequence, interpreted in text mode as "\n".

getenv — Get environment variable

Purpose
Returns a string containing a setting for a specified environment variable.

Syntax
```
#include <stdlib.h>   // OR #include <cstdlib>

char *getenv(const char *str);
```

Syntax
This example prints the setting of the PATH environment variable.

```
#include <stdlib.h>
#include <iostream.h>
//...
cout << "PATH = " << getenv("PATH") << '\n';
```

Note that the name and meaning of environment variables are implementation-defined.

gets — Get string from keyboard

Purpose
Gets keyboard input, up to the next newline or EOF, and stores in the specified string.

Syntax
```
#include <stdio.h>   // OR #include <cstdio>

char *gets(char *str);
```

The function places input in the string argument *str* and returns the string. To avoid errors, the string should be large enough to hold any line of input that can be physically entered. (To specify a string-size maximum, use fgets and specify stdin as stream.) gets does not copy the terminating newline to the string.

Example
```
#include <stdio.h>
//...
char input_line[256];

gets(input_line);
```

The call to gets waits for the user to enter input and press Enter. The input is then stored in the string input_line. Note that in this case, errors occur if more than 255 characters are entered; fgets (p. 179) is safer in this respect.

For more information on this and other console I/O functions, see the topic "Console" on page 170.

getwc — Get wide character from file

Purpose
Returns next character from the specified input stream as a wide character, or WEOF if no characters are available; similar to getc.

Syntax
```
#include <wchar.h>    // OR #include <cwchar>

wint_t getwc(FILE *stream);
```

Example
This code prints out all the characters in a file previously opened as fp.

```
#include <wchar.h>
//...
wint_t c;
while ((c = getwc(fp)) != WEOF)
    putwchar(c);
```

For more information on wide-character file operations, see the topic "Files, wide-character" on page 184.

getwchar — Get wide character from console

Purpose
Returns next character from standard input as a wide character; similar to getchar.

Syntax
```
#include <wchar.h>    // OR #include <cwchar>

wint_t getwchar(void);
```

Value returned is a character of type wchar_t, or WEOF if there is an error.

Example
```
#include <wchar.h>
//...
```

```
wint_t c;
c = getwchar();
```

is<cond> — Character-testing functions

Purpose

This family includes functions for testing individual characters.

Syntax

```
#include <ctype.h>  // OR #include <cctype>
```

The functions are summarized below. Each takes an argument of the type int containing a character. In addition, each function returns an int value: either true (nonzero) or false (0).

Function	Action
isalnum(ch)	Is character a letter or digit?
isalpha(ch)	Is character a letter?
iscntrl(ch)	Is character a control character such as backspace, line feed, Del, or tab? These are nonprintable characters that perform some action. Most are in the range 0x to 0x1F.
isdigit(ch)	Is character a digit?
isgraph(ch)	Is character visible — that is, a printable character other than a space?
islower(ch)	Is character a lowercase letter?
isprint(ch)	Is character a printable character? (This includes spaces.)
ispunct(ch)	Is character a punctuation character — that is, printable but not a letter, or a digit, or a space?
isspace(ch)	Is character a space character? (This includes tab, newline, and form feed, as well as a standard space.)
isupper(ch)	Is character an uppercase letter?
isxdigit(ch)	Is character a hexadecimal digit? (This includes digits plus the letters A through E, both upper- and lowercase.)

Remarks

Although each of these functions takes an int argument, only the low byte of the argument is used. An individual char value is promoted to int within expressions; this is why these functions take an int argument rather than char.

The following example prints a message if a certain character, taken from a string, is a space character:

```
#include <ctype.h>
#include <iostream.h>
//...
char *s = "Here is a sample string.";
if (iswspace(s[4]))
    cout << "Character is a space.";
```

Remember that although the is functions have int return value, they should be treated as Boolean (true/false) expressions, as in this example.

isw<cond>   Wide-character-testing functions

Purpose

This family of functions contains a wide-character version of each of the functions in the previous topic; each of these functions tests a single character.

Summary

```
#include <wctype.h>  // OR #include <cwctype>
```

The functions are summarized below. Each takes an argument of type wint_t containing a wide character and each returns an int value: either true (nonzero) or false (0).

Function	Action
iswalnum(ch)	Is character a letter or digit?
iswalpha(ch)	Is character a letter?
iswcntrl(ch)	Is character a control character such as backspace, line-feed, Del, or tab? These are nonprintable characters that perform some action. Most are in the range 0x to 0x1F.
iswdigit(ch)	Is character a digit?
iswgraph(ch)	Is character visible — that is, a printable character other than a space?
iswlower(ch)	Is character a lowercase letter?
iswprint(ch)	Is character a printable character? (This includes spaces.)
iswpunct(ch)	Is character a punctuation character — that is, printable but not a letter, or a digit, or a space?
iswspace(ch)	Is character a space character? (This includes tab, newline, and form feed, as well as a standard space.)

Function	Action
iswupper(*ch*)	Is character an uppercase letter?
iswxdigit(*ch*)	Is character a hexadecimal digit? (This includes digits plus the letters A through E, both upper- and lowercase.)

Remarks

Although each of these functions takes a wint_t argument, you should pass a character of type wchar_t.

Wide characters were developed to support any natural language, for international applications. With some languages, some categories may not apply — such as uppercase and lowercase. In those cases, zero (false) is returned.

Examples

The following example prints a message if a certain character, taken from a string, is a space character:

```
#include <wchar.h>
#include <iostream.h>
//...
wchar_t *wcs = L"Here is a sample string.";
if (iswspace(wcs[4]))
    cout << "Character is a space.";
```

Remember that although the is functions all have int return value, they should be treated as Boolean (true/false) expressions, as in this example.

labs   Absolute value (long)

Purpose

Returns the absolute value of a long integer.

Syntax

```
#include <stdio.h>   // OR #include <cstdio>

long labs(long num);
```

Example

The absolute value function converts a negative number to positive, but returns a nonnegative number as is. This code prints the number 5.

```
cout << labs(-5);
```

See also abs (p. 162), which takes an integer of type int, and fabs (p. 177), which takes a double.

ldexp Load exponent and mantissa

Purpose

Combines a mantissa and exponent of a floating-point number and returns the result. Like its cousin, `frexp`, it rarely sees use in most programs.

Syntax

```
#include <math.h>    // OR #include <cmath>

double ldexp(double mantissa, int exp);
```

The function returns the value *mantissa* * (2 to the power of *exp*).

If your program doesn't do a lot of work pulling apart floating-point numbers and putting them back together, you can ignore this function. Note that the pow function (p. 204) can be used to achieve similar results, although not necessarily as efficiently.

ldiv Divide integers (long)

Purpose

Performs integer division, returning both quotient and remainder.

Syntax

```
#include <stdlib.h>    // OR #include <cstdlib>

ldiv_t ldiv(long numerator, long denominator);
```

The results are returned in an `ldiv_t` structure, which has the following format. The quotient (quot) represents the largest integer that *denominator* can be multiplied by without exceeding *numerator*.

```
struct ldiv_t {
    long quot;
    long rem;
};
```

Example

```
#include <stdlib.h>
#include <iostream.h>
//...
ldiv_t dv = ldiv(255, 2);
cout << "255/2 = " << dv.quot << ", with remainder ";
cout << dv.rem << endl;
```

A related function is div (p. 175), which performs the same action but works with integers of type int. The modulus operator % (p. 58) provides another way of getting a remainder. See also fmod (p. 187), which gets a remainder for floating-point division.

localeconv   Get locale settings

Purpose
Gets the current locale setting, which provides country-specific information about numeric displays.

Syntax
```
#include <locale.h>   // OR #include <clocale>


struct lconv *localeconv(void);
```

Example
```
#include <stdio.h>
#include <locale.h>
//...
lconv *lc = localeconv();
```

The structure returned by localeconv should not be changed. Be aware that subsequent calls to localeconv and setlocale overwrite the structure. For the layout of this structure, see Appendix E.

log   "Natural" logarithm

Purpose
Returns natural logarithm, which is the logarithm using base e. (This is a concept of "natural" only a mathematician could love.)

Syntax
```
#include <math.h>   // OR #include <cmath>


double log(double x);
```

The number returned is the exponent necessary to raise e to the value specified for x. The function returns NaN (which stands for "Not a Number") if x is negative, and INF (which, more intuitively, stands for "Infinity") if x is zero.

Example
```
#include <math.h>
//...
cout << "log(5), base e = " << log(5) << endl;
```

log10

Base-10 logarithm

Purpose

Returns logarithm using base 10.

Syntax

```
#include <math.h>   // OR #include <cmath>


double log10(double x);
```

The number returned is the exponent necessary to raise 10 to the value specified for x. The function returns NaN (which stands for "Not a Number") if x is
negative, and INF (which, more intuitively, stands for "Infinity") if x is zero.

Example

This code outputs the numbers 2, 3, and 3.47712.

```
#include <math.h>
#include <iostream.h>
//...
cout << "log of 100 is   " << log10(100) << endl;
cout << "log of 1000 is  " << log10(1000) << endl;
cout << "log of 3000 is  " << log10(3000) << endl;
```

longjmp

Jump to saved address

Purpose

Jumps to a program location previously saved by setjmp, enabling you to
jump between functions. This is not recommended but is included for backward compatibility with C. If C programmers ran the Olympics, they'd probably have a "long jmp."

Syntax

```
#include <setjmp.h>   // OR #include <csetjmp>


void longjmp(jmp_buf envbuf, int status);
```

The envbuf argument is an environment buffer previously set by a call to
setjmp. This records the state of the system stack, including the instruction
pointer.

The status argument specifies a new return value for setjmp. The effect of
longjmp is to jump back to the statement containing the setjmp call, causing
setjmp to be executed again. This time, however, setjmp will return the number you specify for the status argument to longjmp. This number should not
be zero; if the number is zero, the longjmp function may change it to a
nonzero value.

Example

```
#include <setjmp.h>

jmp_buf envbuf;
//...
longjmp(envbuf, 5);
// This call to longjump causes setjmp to be
//   executed again and return 5.
```

For a more complete example, see setjmp (p. 217).

malloc   Allocate raw memory

Purpose

Allocates a memory block of requested size. Unlike new (p. 98), this function does not call constructors. It is supported mainly for backward compatibility with C.

Syntax

```
#include <stdlib.h>   // OR #include <cstdlib>

void *malloc(size_t size);
```

The function returns a pointer to a memory block if the requested size is available; otherwise, the function returns NULL. The block is suitably aligned for any type of object. The type size_t is an integer large enough to hold the size of any type (usually equivalent to unsigned long).

Example

This example allocates enough space for n integers:

```
#include <stdlib.h>
int n;
int *p;
//...
p = reinterpret_cast<int*>(malloc(sizeof(int) * n));
if (p == NULL)
     // Print error message and end.
```

The malloc return value must be cast to another pointer type before the pointer is used. Also note that the memory block should eventually be released by calling free (p. 189). See also calloc (p. 169) and realloc (p. 212).

●—TIP

The C++ keywords new and delete offer significant advantages over malloc and free and are easier to use. See pages 98 and 80.

mem<op>   Memory-block functions

This family includes several functions for operating efficiently on blocks of memory. Although the same operations can be performed other ways, most C and C++ compilers optimize these functions to make best use of memory-block instructions on the processor (if available).

Summary

```
#include <string.h>  // OR #include <cstring>
```

The following table summarizes the memory-block functions. The arguments p, p1, and p2 are each a memory block represented by a pointer of type void*. The argument n is an integer that generally specifies the number of bytes to operate on. The argument ch is of type int and represents a single character; only the low byte is significant.

Function	Action
memchr(p, ch, n)	Returns pointer to first byte in memory block that matches low byte of argument ch.
memcmp(p1, p2, n)	Compares two blocks and returns negative, 0, or positive, depending on whether first block is less than, equal to, or greater than the second block; the value returned has type int.
memcpy(p1, p2, n)	Copies up to n bytes from block p2 to p1.
memmove(p1, p2, n)	Copies up to n bytes from block p2 to p1; these may overlap.
memset(p, ch, n)	Sets each byte of memory block to low byte of argument ch.

All the pointer arguments accept both const and non-const pointers, except the first argument in memcpy and memmove; these cannot be const because the data they point to gets changed.

Remarks

All of these functions, except memcmp, return void* pointers. The memcpy, memmove, and memset functions each return their first argument, a void* pointer to a buffer. The memchr function returns a void* pointer to the first byte matching ch. Because a void* pointer is returned, it usually must be cast to a particular type before being used. For example:

```
#include <string.h>
//...
char *p, *buf = "This is a character X array."
```

```
p = (char *) memchr(buf, 'X', strlen(buf));
int index = p - buf;   // Use ptr arithmetic to get
                       //  index.
```

The memcpy and memmove functions are similar to each other. memcpy can be used to assign all the values in one array (arr1) to another array (arr2) and is generally faster than *memmove*.

```
short arr1[100], arr2[100];
//...
memcpy(arr2, arr1, 100 * sizeof(short));
```

But memmove, which is more versatile, can be used to shift values within an array. Here it is used to shift 100 values down by one array position, so that array positions 1 to 100 are copied to array positions 0 to 99.

```
short arr1[500];
//...
memmove (arr1, arr1 + 1, 100 * sizeof(short));
```

modf   Return integer and fraction portions

Purpose
Returns integer and fractional portions of a floating-point value. In effect, the integer portion is always rounded in the direction of zero.

Syntax
```
#include <math.h>   // OR #include <cmath>

double modf(double x, double *intptr);
```

The function returns the fractional portion, if any, of the argument x and copies the integer portion to the location *intptr. Both of these quantities have the same sign as x.

Example
This example places -3.0 in the variable f and -0. 14159265 in the variable d:

```
#include <math.h>
//...
double d;
double f = modf(-3.14159265, &d);
```

See also ceil (p. 169) and floor (p. 186).

perror   Print error just committed

Purpose

Prints an error message determined by the current value of global variable errno; this variable contains a number corresponding to the most recent run-time error.

Syntax

```
#include <stdio.h>   // OR #include <cstdio>

void perror(const char *string);
```

The function prints an error message of the form *"string: error-message"* in which *string* is specified in the function call and *error-message* is a string determined by the current error conditions. This latter string is determined by the current value of the global variable errno; the compiler defines a string for each errno setting.

The message ends with a newline and is sent to standard error (usually, the monitor).

Syntax

```
#include <stdio.h>
//...
errno = 1;
perror("ERROR MESSAGE");
```

With Microsoft Visual C++ version 6.0, the code prints this message:

```
ERROR MESSAGE: Operation not permitted
```

pow   Raise number to a power

Purpose

Raises a specified base (*x*) to a specified power (*y*); for example, pow(5, 2) returns 5 to the second power, or 5 squared.

Syntax

```
#include <math.h>   // OR #include <cmath>

double pow(double x, double y);
```

Examples

```
#include <math.h>
#include <iostream.h>
double x = 4.0;
```

```
//...
cout << "x to 2nd power is " << pow(x, 2) << endl;
cout << "x to 3rd power is " << pow(x, 3) << endl;
cout << "x to 0.5 power is " << pow(x, 0.5) << endl;
```

printf   Print formatted string

Purpose

Translates zero or more numeric values, along with other characters if desired, and then prints the resulting string.

Syntax

```
#include <stdio.h>   // OR #include <cstdio>

int printf(const char *format,...);
```

The format string contains zero or more placeholders called *format specifiers*; the ellipses (. . .) indicate that the *format* string can be followed by any number of arguments. For each format specifier, there must be a data-field argument. The first specifier corresponds to the first data field, the second specifier corresponds to the second data field, and so on. For example, the following function call contains one format string with two specifiers (%d and %f), along with two data-field arguments, i and x:

```
printf("i = %d and x = %f\n", i, x);
```

printf returns the number of characters printed.

Format specifiers

Table 2 summarizes the specifiers that can appear in the printf format string.

Table 2   *Format Specifiers for printf*

Specifier	Description
%c	Prints value as a single ASCII character. (Use low-order byte.)
%d, %i	Prints value as a decimal integer.
%u	Prints value as an unsigned decimal integer.
%o	Prints integer in octal format.
%x, %X	Prints integer in hexadecimal format.
%e	Prints floating-point in exponential format; for example: 1.273110e+01.
%E	Same as %e, but uses E as exponent sign

Continued

Table 2 *Continued*

Specifier	Description
%f	Prints floating-point number in standard format.
%g	Uses either %e or %f format, whichever is shorter.
%G	Same as %g, but uses E as exponent sign if exponential format is used.
%s	Prints null-terminated string pointed to by data.
%p	Prints pointer value in hexadecimal format.
%%	Prints a literal percent sign (%).

Format modifiers

When you call printf, you may want to control how many characters are printed. The printf syntax lets you modify the meaning of each format by using up to two numbers, represented here as *min* and *precision*. c represents a format specifier from Table 2.

```
%[-]minc
%[-]min.precisionc
```

Here the brackets are not intended literally, but indicate that the negative sign (–) is optional. If included, it indicates that data is to be left justified within the print field, rather than right justified (the default).

The *min* modifier is a decimal number that indicates the size of the print field. For example, the following format specifies a decimal integer printed into a field at least five characters wide:

```
%5d
```

The *precision* modifier is also a decimal integer, but its meaning varies with the format:

- If the field is a string format (%s), *precision* specifies the maximum number of characters to print.
- If the field is a floating-point format (such as %f or %e), *precision* specifies the number of digits to appear after the decimal point.
- If the field is an integer field (such as %i or %d), *precision* specifies the minimum number of digits to print. The data is padded with leading zeroes, as needed, to print this many characters.

Example

The following code prints a format string along with two values: a string and a number.

```
#include <stdio.h>
```

```
//...
char *state = "Alaskan";
double temp=25.7;

printf("The %s temperature is %5.4f.\n", state, temp);
```

When the program is run, the output is:

```
The Alaskan temperature is 25.7000.
```

putc
Print character to file

Purpose
Sends a single character to the specified file output stream.

Syntax
```
#include <stdio.h>    // OR #include <cstdio>

int putc(int ch, FILE *stream);
```

The function sends a character to the specified file-output stream; the character is taken from the low byte of *ch*. If there is an error, putc returns EOF; otherwise, it returns the character that was written.

putc works exactly as the fputc function does. The reason for this redundancy is that putc is often implemented as a macro with better performance; therefore, putc is preferred to fputc. (Exception: putc, as a macro, may evaluate the stream argument more than once and is therefore unreliable if *stream* is returned by a function call.)

Example
This example writes the letter A to the file c:\stuff.txt.

```
#include <stdio.h>
\\...
FILE *fp;
fp = fopen("c:\\stuff.txt", "w");

putc('A', fp);
```

putchar
Print character

Purpose
Prints a character to standard output (usually the monitor).

Syntax

```
#include <stdio.h>   // OR #include <cstdio>

int putchar(int ch);
```

The function sends a character to standard output; the character is taken from the low byte of *ch*. If there is an error, putc returns EOF; otherwise, it returns the character that was written.

Example

```
#include <stdio.h>
//...
putchar('A');
```

puts   Print string

Purpose

Prints a string to standard output (usually the monitor); appends a newline.

Syntax

```
#include <stdio.h>   // OR #include <cstdio>

int puts(char *str);
```

The function prints string *str* to standard output, appending a newline at the end of the string. If there is an error, putchar returns EOF; otherwise, it returns a nonnegative value. To print a string without appending a newline, you can call fputs and specify stdout for the file-argument; you can also make a simple call to printf.

Example

```
#include <stdio.h>
//...
puts("Hello!");
```

putwc   Print wide character to file

Purpose

Sends a wide character to the specified file output stream; similar to putc.

Syntax

```
#include <wchar.h>   // OR #include <cwchar>

wint_t putwc(wchar_t ch, FILE *stream);
```

If there is an error, putwc returns WEOF; otherwise, it returns the character written.

Example

This example writes wide-character A to the file c:\stuff.txt.

```
#include <wchar.h>
\\...
FILE *fp;
fp = fopen("c:\\stuff.txt", "w");

putwc(L'A', fp);
```

Library Functions

putwchar   Print wide character

Purpose

Prints a wide character to standard output (usually the monitor).

Syntax

```
#include <stdio.h>    // OR #include <cstdio>

wint_t putwchar(wint_t ch);
```

If there is an error, putwchar returns WEOF; otherwise, it returns the character written.

Example

This example prints the letter A.

```
#include <wchar.h>
//...
putwchar(L'A');
```

qsort   Perform quick sort

Purpose

Sorts an array of any size, containing any type of data.

Syntax

```
#include <stdlib.h>    // OR #include <cstdlib>

void qsort(void *buf, size_t num, size_t size,
    int (compare)(const void *, const void *) )
```

The three arguments buf, num, and size describe the array to be sorted. buf points to the beginning of the array; num is the number of items; and size is the size of each element.

The *compare* argument is the address of a function you supply, which returns a negative number, zero, or a positive number, depending on whether the first value pointed to is less than, equal to, or greater than the second. The function gets pointers to elements; these pointers are declared as void* and must be recast to their actual type. (See "Example.")

Example

This example sorts an array of integers. The cmp function gets pointers of type int* *that are passed as type* void*. The function casts them to type int* and then dereferences them.

```
#include <stdlib.h>
#include <iostream.h>

int cmp(const void *p1, const void *p2) {
    int i = *(int *)p1;   // Get ints pointed to.
    int j = *(int *)p2;
    return i < j ? -1 : (i == j ? 0: 1);
}

void main() {
    int dat[] = {1, 99, 17, 40, 39, 16, 45, 7, 51, 3};

    qsort(dat, 10, sizeof(int), &cmp);
    for (int i = 0; i < 10; i++)
        cout << dat[i] << "\n";
}
```

NOTE

If you're sorting an array of strings, each element is itself a pointer of type char*. The cmp function therefore receives data of type char**, which must be cast to the correct type and dereferenced to get data of type char*.

```
#include <stdio.h>

int cmp(const void *p1, const void *p2) {
    char *a = *(char **)p1; // Get char* pointed to.
    char *b = *(char **)p2;
// strcmp returns values as required for qsort
    return strcmp(a, b);
}
```

This may seem confusing at first, but remember that p1 and p2 point to array elements, not to individual characters. Each element in the array to be sorted has type char*; therefore, the true type of p1 and p2 is actually char**.

raise   Propagate signal

Purpose
Sends a signal to the program that indicates that one of several runtime error conditions has occurred; supported mainly for backward compatibility with C.

Syntax
```
#include <signal.h>   // OR #include <csignal>

int raise(int signal);
```

The function returns zero if successful, nonzero if unsuccessful. The C/C++ standard library defines several values for *signal*, although some implementations may define additional settings.

Signal	Description
SIGABRT	Program aborted
SIGFPE	Floating-point error
SIGILL	Bad machine instruction
SIGINT	Interruption: user pressed Ctrl+C
SIGSEGV	Illegal access of memory
SIGTERM	Program terminating normally

Example
```
#include <signal.h>
//...
raise(SIGFPE);  // Raise floating-pt error.
```

The effect of raise is to transfer execution to the appropriate signal handler, if any. Signal handlers are installed by use of the signal function (p. 219).

●—NOTE ─────────────────────────────────

The try keyword (p. 122) provides a better mechanism for handling runtime errors. As mentioned, raise and signal are supported mainly for backward compatibility.

rand   Get random number

Purpose
Generates a random floating-point number between 0 and RAND_MAX (a predefined constant).

Syntax

```
#include <stdlib.h>   // OR #include <cstdlib>

int rand(void);
```

The function returns the next number in the random-number sequence. (This is actually a pseudo random sequence in which each number is produced by a complex transformation of the previous number.) To simulate true randomness, first set a seed for the sequence by calling srand and time.

Examples

The following code prints 10 random numbers:

```
#include <stdlib.h>
#include <time.h>
#include <iostream.h>
//...
srand(time(NULL));  // Call time() function for seed.
rand();             // Ignore first rand() call.
for (int i = 0; i < 10; i++)
   cout << rand();
```

You can divide the results by RAND_MAX to produce a floating-point number between 0 and 1.0. (RAND_MAX is a constant declared in stdlib.h.) You can then convert this number to an integer by multiplying it and rounding up or down. For example, the following version of the code returns the integers 0, 1, 2, 3, and 4 with equal frequency. The floor function rounds downward.

```
#include <stdlib.h>
//...
cout << floor(5 * (rand()/RAND_MAX)) << endl;
```

You could rewrite this function to return numbers from 1 to 5 (instead of 0 to 4) by rounding upward instead; see ceil function, page 169.

realloc   Reallocate raw memory

Purpose

Reallocates and resizes a block of memory previously allocated with malloc, calloc, or realloc; moves the block, if necessary. This function preserves all values in the block, unless the new block is smaller; in which case, it preserves as many values as fit.

Syntax

```
#include <stdlib.h>   // OR #include <cstdlib>

void *realloc(void *memblock, size_t size);
```

The function returns the new location of the memory block, which differs from the old address (*memblock*) only if realloc has to move the block. If the memory requested is not available, realloc returns NULL and the original memory block does not change. *size* specifies a new size for the block.

Most of the rules that apply to malloc also apply to realloc.

Example

This example allocates a memory block and then later allocates a block twice as big.

```
#include <stdlib.h>
int n;
char *p;
//...
p = reinterpret_cast<char*>(malloc(n));
if (p == NULL)
    // Not enough memory. Print error message and end.
//...
p = reinterpret_cast<char*>(realloc(p, n * 2));
if (p == NULL)
    // Not enough memory. Print error message and end.
```

For more information, see malloc (p. 201), calloc (p. 169), and free (p. 189).

remove   Blow away target file

Purpose

Deletes the specified file from the system.

Syntax

```
#include <stdio.h>   // OR #include <cstdio>

int remove(char const *fname);
```

The function returns zero if successful and nonzero if not successful. *fname* may include a relative or absolute directory path. Note that you must use double backslashes (\\) to represent a single backslash (\) in a C/C++ string.

Example

```
#include <stdio.h>
//...
remove("c:\\junk.txt");
```

rename	Rename file or directory

Purpose

Renames or moves the specified file or directory.

Syntax

```
#include <stdio.h>   // OR #include <cstdio>

int rename(char const *oldfname, char const *newfname);
```

The name *oldfname* refers to an existing file or directory. If *oldfname* refers to a file, you can specify a new directory for *newfname*; this causes the rename function to move the file. The function returns zero if successful and nonzero if not successful.

Example

This example renames junk.txt as useful.txt, and then moves memo.txt from c:\ to the c:\mydocs directory.

```
#include <stdio.h>
//...
rename("c:\\junk.txt", "c:\\useful.txt");
rename("c:\\memo.txt", "c:\\mydocs\\memo.txt");
```

scanf	Read data from keyboard

Purpose

Reads text from the keyboard, interprets it, and places the results in one or more data fields.

Syntax

```
#include <stdio.h>   // OR #include <cstdio>

int scanf(const char *format,...);
```

The format string contains zero or more placeholders called *format specifiers*. For each format specifier, there must be a data-address argument. The first specifier corresponds to the first data address, the second specifier corresponds to the second address, and so on. For example, the following call to scanf has one format specifier (%d) and one data-address argument (&i, the address of an integer):

```
scanf("%d", &i);   // Place decimal integer in i.
```

The function returns the number of data fields successfully read.

scanf formats

Table 3 describes the specifiers accepted in a scanf format string. In this table, the term *scan* means that a character is read but discarded.

Table 3 *Format Specifiers for scanf*

Specifier	Description
%c	Reads the next individual character, even if whitespace.
%d	Reads an integer in decimal format only.
%I	Reads an integer. This format interprets a leading 0 to mean octal and leading 0x to mean hexadecimal.
%u	Same as %i, but destination address is an unsigned integer.
%o	Reads an integer in octal format.
%x, %X	Reads an integer in hexadecimal format.
%e, %f, %g	Reads a floating-point number, accepting either standard or exponential format.
%s	Reads characters up to the next whitespace, copying to a string address.
%p	Reads a pointer value in hexadecimal format.
%[chars]	Scans a character in the range chars.
%%	Scans a literal percent sign (%).

All arguments to scanf after the format string must be data addresses. This usually means that you combine a variable with the address operator (&). However, the name of a string is already an address, so you do not apply the address operator in the case of a string. For example:

```
#include <stdio.h>
//...
int d;
char name[256];
printf("Enter name and id number: ");
scanf("%s %i", name, &id);
```

When scanf reads a string, it reads skips to the first non-whitespace and then reads characters up until the first whitespace character (space, tab, or newline). To read all the way up to the next newline — which is usually more useful — you need to use gets or fgets.

Format modifiers

Between the percent sign (%) and the format specifier, a letter l can appear, which indicates that the format is long. This is necessary in the case of arguments with a destination of type double, which gets incorrect data unless l is used to indicate the type. For example:

```
double x, y, z;
float  f;

scanf("%lf %lf %lf %f", &x, &y, &z, &f);
```

You can also use h (short) and l (long) to modify integer formats. It's a good idea to use these modifiers if a variable is specifically declared short or long rather than int (which uses the default size).

Another modifier is the asterisk or "star" (*). When you place a star between the percent sign (%) and a format character, it causes scanf to read the indicated field but not assign it to an address. For example, the following format specifier causes scanf to read and ignore the next character:

```
%*c
```

Other characters in the format string

A scanf format string typically has characters other than just the format specifiers. scanf responds to these characters by matching and discarding the characters.

When a whitespace appears between the format specifiers, scanf reads and discards any number of whitespace characters found in the input stream. Both of the examples featured earlier in this topic separate each field with a whitespace.

When nonwhitespace characters appear, scanf attempts to match them precisely. If it cannot match them, scanf terminates and does not read any further data.

●—**NOTE**————————————————————————

printf and scanf support a limited range of types, and scanf requires you to specify the precise type; you cannot rely on promotion or rounding. The newest compilers support primitve types (such as long long) not recognized by scanf. The solution is to use cin and cout. These objects — and their classes, istream and ostream — are extensible to all types. You can expect cin and cout to support all the primitive types recognized by the compiler.

setjmp   Save address for longjmp

Purpose

Registers a program location so that you can jump back to it with longjmp
(p. 200). These functions are provided mainly for backward compatibility
with C.

Syntax

```
#include <setjmp.h>   // OR #include <csetjmp>

int setjmp(jmp_buf envbuf);
```

The effect of setjmp is to save contents of the system stack in *envbuf*. This
saves a program location you can jump back to by calling longjmp.

The first time setjmp is called, it returns 0. However, a jump back using
longjmp causes setjmp to be called again. In that case, setjmp returns the
nonzero value specified as the *status* argument to longjmp. See "Example"
for clarification.

Example

```
#include <setjmp.h>
#include <iostream.h>

jmp_buf envbuf;
int status;

void test_func(void) {
   cout << "I'm in test_func. " << endl;
   longjmp(envbuf, 5);  // Jump back to top of main.
}

void main()
{
   status = setjmp(envbuf);

// If setjmp has executed AFTER jumping back from
//  longjmp, status is set to 5.

   cout << "This is just after setjmp. " << endl;
   if (status == 0)
      test_func();
   cout << "status = " << status << endl;
}
```

The program first calls setjmp to register a location. During this call, it returns 0. Then the program calls test_func, which uses longjmp to jump back to the setjmp location. This causes setjmp to execute again, but this time it returns a nonzero value for status (5). This value is then compared to 0, preventing test_func from executing a second time. The program prints the following output:

```
This is just after setjmp.
I'm in test_func.
This is just after setjmp.
status = 5
```

For longjmp to successfully execute, the function that called setjmp must not have terminated; that is, it must still be running. In addition, if a function calls setjmp and then changes the value of its local variables, the values of those variables become undefined when longjmp is executed. (Exception: Locals declared volatile do not suffer from this problem.)

C++ programmers should avoid the use of longjmp and setjmp as much as possible, because they are inconsistent with the goals of structured and object-oriented programming. They are mainly supported for backward compatibility with C, which requires them for use with some signal handlers. C++ provides exception handling with try (p. 122), which is superior in a number of ways to use of signal handlers.

setlocale — Set new locale formats

Purpose

Specifies a locale setting; this determines the country for the character set or a display format. setlocale can also query settings.

Syntax

```
#include <locale.h>   // OR #include <clocale>

char *setlocale(int type, const char *locale);
```

The type argument specifies which category the locale string applies to.

Value of type	Description
LC_ALL	All categories.
LC_COLLATE	Character set used by the strcoll function.
LC_CTYPE	Character functions such as isalnum.
LC_MONETARY	Format of monetary amounts.
LC_NUMERIC	Format of numbers displayed by functions such as printf.
LC_TIME	Format used by functions such as asctime.

The *locale* argument is a string containing a new locale setting. ANSI recognizes the strings "C" and "". "C" specifies use of standard minimum C settings. "" specifies the use of implementation-defined defaults. Other settings may be defined by individual implementations. (See "Example.") The *locale* argument may also be set to NULL, in which case the function only performs a query.

In any case, the setlocale function returns a string containing the current locale setting. If the locale argument is any value other than NULL, setlocale returns the new setting.

Example

```
#include <stdio.h>
#include <locale.h>

void main()
{
    puts( setlocale(LC_NUMERIC, "French") );
    printf("%f\n", 8.007);
}
```

When run in the Microsoft Visual C++ 6.0 environment, this example prints the following results. Note that with French locale settings, the comma (,) is used as the decimal point; six decimal places are shown because that is the default for printf.

```
French_France.1252
8,007000
```

signal   Register signal handler

Purpose

Registers a signal handler for responding to the raise function (p. 211); supported mainly for backward compatibility with C.

Syntax

```
#include <signal.h>   // OR #include <csignal>

void (*signal(int signal, void (*func)(int))) (int)
```

Although this declaration appears complex, it really takes only two arguments. Here is a simplified version of the syntax:

```
signal(signal, func)
```

The *signal* argument takes one of the signal numbers listed for the raise function, such as SIGINT, SIGILL, or SIGFPE.

The *func* argument can be one of these special values: SIG_DFL (default handling) or SIG_IGN (ignore the signal). It can also be the address of a function that takes a single int argument (the signal number) and has no return value. (See "Examples.")

Examples

This code causes the program to ignore the signals SIGINT, SIGILL, and SIGTERM:

```
signal(SIGINT, SIG_IGN);
signal(SIGILL, SIG_IGN);
signal(SIGFPE, SIG_IGN);
```

You can also supply the address of your own signal handler, which must be a function that takes an integer as an argument and has void return type (it returns no value). For example, the following code registers a handler for two different signals, and then it raises each signal as a test. The *sig* argument enables the function to determine which signal was raised.

```
#include <signal.h>
#include <iostream.h>

void handler(int sig) {
    cout << "Signal received: " << sig << '\n';
}
//...
signal(SIGINT, &handler);
signal(SIGILL, &handler);
raise(SIGINT);
raise(SIGILL);
```

After the signal handler returns, execution automatically returns to the statement after the one that raised the signal, except in the case of SIGFPE, where behavior on return is undefined.

Signal handler rules

A number of rules apply to the signal handler. Consult your compiler documentation for platform specifics. The general ANSI rules are summarized here:

- In the case of SIGFPE, you need to use the setjmp and longjmp functions to reset execution to the place that raised the signal.
- Do not call setjmp and longjmp for signals other than SIGFPE.
- Avoid calling these functions: stdio.h functions (such as printf), memory-allocation functions (such as malloc), and functions that get the system time.
- Windows NT and Windows 95 (and later) systems do not generate SIGINT in response to Ctrl+C. However, you can generate any signal by calling raise.

Library Functions

Return value

The `signal` function returns the address of the previous handler for the given signal. For example, if `signal` is used to register a handler for `SIGINT`, the function returns the value of the previous `SIGINT` handler. You can save this address, if you choose, in order to restore it later.

```
void (*saved_handler)(int);
saved_handler = signal(SIGINT, &handler);
//...
signal(SIGINT, saved_handler);
```

The fact that `signal` returns a pointer to a function helps account for its unusual (and to many, confusing) declaration.

●—NOTE

The `try` keyword (p. 122) provides a better mechanism for handling run-time errors. As mentioned, `raise` and `signal` are supported mainly for backward compatibility.

sin	**Sine**

Purpose

Returns the sine of its argument.

Syntax

```
#include <math.h>   // OR #include <cmath>

double sin(double x);
```

The function takes an angle in radians and returns a value between 1 and –1.

Example

This example prints the sine of pi/2, which is equal to 1:

```
#include <math.h>
#include <iostream.h>
//...
double pi = atan(1) * 4;
cout << "sin(pi/2) = " << sin(pi / 2) << '\n';
```

See also acos, asin, atan, atan2, cos, and tan.

sinh   Hyperbolic sine

Purpose

Returns the hyperbolic sine of its argument.

Syntax

```
#include <math.h>   // OR #include <cmath>

double sinh(double x);
```

The function returns an angle in radians. If the result is out of range, the function returns HUGEVAL and sets the global variable errno to ERANGE. See also sinh and tanh.

sprintf   Write data to string ("sprint F")

Purpose

Translates any number of numeric values into text-string representation; this function is similar to printf but uses a buffer string as destination rather than the monitor.

Syntax

```
#include <stdio.h>   // OR #include <cstdio>

int sprintf(char *buffer, const char *format, ...);
```

As with the printf declaration, the ellipses (. . .) indicate that the *format* string can be followed by any number of arguments. For each format specifier (such as %s, %d, or %f) in the format string, there must be a corresponding data argument.

The output is written to the string pointed to by *buffer*.

Example

For example, the following code places an ASCII representation of the floating-point number x into the string buf, along with the characters "x = ":

```
#include <stdio.h>
//...
char buf[256];
double x = 2.50e3;
sprintf(buf, "x = %f", x);  // Place output in buf.
puts(buf);                   // Print buf.
```

The output of this program is:

```
x = 2500.000000
```

For a list of format specifiers and their meanings, see printf (p. 205).

sqrt   Square root

Purpose
Returns the square root of its argument.

Syntax
```
#include <math.h>    // OR #include <cmath>

double sqrt(double x);
```

Example
These statements return the square root of 2:

```
#include <math.h>
#include <iostream.h>
//...
cout << "square root of 2 is " << sqrt(2) << '\n';
```

srand   Set seed for random numbers

Purpose
Starts a pseudo random number sequence, in which numbers are read by subsequent calls to the rand function (p. 211).

Syntax
```
#include <stdlib.h>    // OR #include <cstdlib>

void srand(unsigned int seed);
```

The random number sequence is strictly determined by the value of seed; each subsequent number is based on a mathematical transformation. If you want to set the seed to best simulate true randomness, the most convenient approach is to use system time. (See "Example.")

Example
```
#include <stdlib.h>
#include <time.h>
//...
srand(time(NULL));
rand();
```

The first random number should be thrown away, because it is based on system time; subsequent calls to rand produce a good simulation of random behavior.

sscanf · Read data from string

Purpose

Reads text from a string, interprets it, and places the results in one or more data fields; similar to scanf, but inputs from a string rather than from the keyboard.

Syntax

```
#include <stdio.h>   // OR #include <cstdio>

int sscanf(char *buffer, const char *format, ...);
```

The function reads characters from the string pointed to by *buffer*.

The format string contains zero or more placeholders called *format specifiers* such as %i or %lf. For each format specifier, there must be a data-address argument following *format*. The first specifier corresponds to the first data address, the second specifier corresponds to the second address, and so on. The function returns the number of data fields successfully read.

Example

This example reads "1.2345" from a string and then stores the value 1.2345 in a floating-point variable, x:

```
#include <stdio.h>
//...
char data[] = "1.2345";
double x;
sscanf(data, "%lf", &x);   // Read from data into x.
```

For a list of format specifiers and their meanings, see scanf (p. 214).

str<op> · String functions

Purpose

This family of functions provides ways to manipulate and search null-terminated strings of char.

Syntax

```
#include <string.h>  // OR #include <cstring>
```

Here are the most commonly used string functions. The arguments s, s1, and s2 are strings represented by pointers of type char*. n is an integer of type size_t. Except where otherwise noted, each function returns a pointer to its first string argument.

Function	Action
strcat(*s1*, *s2*)	Concatenates *s2* onto *s1*.
strcmp(*s1*, *s2*)	Compares strings and returns negative, 0, or positive, depending on whether *s1* is less than, equal to, or greater than *s2*. Comparison is alphabetical.
strcpy(*s1*, *s2*)	Copies *s2* to *s1*.
strlen(*s*)	Returns the length of *s*, not counting the terminating null.
strncat(*s1*, *s2*, *n*)	Concatenates *s2* onto *s1*, copying at most *n* characters plus a terminating null.
strncmp(*s1*, *s2*, *n*)	Performs same action as strcmp, comparing at most *n* characters.
strncpy(*s1*, *s2*, *n*)	Copies *s2* to *s1*, copying at most *n* characters. It then adds nulls until exactly *n* bytes have been written to.
strstr(*s1*, *s2*)	Returns pointer to first occurrence of *s2* in *s1* or NULL if *s2* is not found.

The string.h file also declares the following string functions.

Function	Action
strchr(*s*, *ch*)	Returns pointer to first occurrence of *ch* in *s* or NULL if *ch* is not found.
strcoll(*s1*, *s2*)	Performs same action as strcmp using locale settings. See "setlocale Function."
strcspn(*s1*, *s2*)	Returns index of first character in *s1* matching any in *s2*; returns *s1* length if none found.
strerror(*n*)	Returns string description for specified error number.
strpbrk(*s1*, *s2*)	Returns pointer to first character in *s1* matching any character in *s2* or NULL if none found.
strrchr(*s*, *ch*)	Returns pointer to last occurrence of *ch* in *s*. (This function searches in reverse.)
strspn(*s1*, *s2*)	Returns index of first character in *s1* not matching any character in *s2*.

Continued

Function	Action
strtok(*s1*, *s2*)	Returns next token in *s1*, using delimiters in *s2*. See "Remarks."
strxfrm(*s1*, *s2*, *n*)	Uses locale settings to transform *s2* and to place the results in *s1*. Only the first *n* characters are transformed. See `setlocale` on page 218.

Finally, the library supports the following functions that begin with the "str" prefix. These require a different include file.

Function	Action
strftime	Writes formatted time string. See page 228.
strtod	Converts string to `double`. See page 230.
strtol	Converts string to `long`. See page 231.
strtoul	Converts string to `unsigned long`. See page 232.

Remarks

The most heavily used string functions are `strcpy`, `strcat`, `strcmp`, and `strlen`. Care is needed when calling `strcpy` and `strcat`, because they can easily increase the length of a string, which causes dangerous errors unless the string has enough space allocated to hold all the data. Here is an example of code that avoids the problem:

```
#include <string.h>
//...
char name[30] = "";
strcpy(name, "John ");      // Copy "John"
strcat(name, "Q. ");        // Append "Q. "
strcat(name, "Public");     // Append "Public"
```

Because the first string, name, has 30 bytes allocated, it has enough storage space to hold the resulting string, "John Q. Public." In C and C++, ensuring that strings have enough space is often a problem. One approach is to use the alternative functions, `strncpy` and `strncat`, which specify a limit on the number of characters to be copied. For example:

```
char s1[30], *s2;
// ...
strncpy(s1, s2, 29);
```

Although s1 in this example has 30 bytes allocated, a limit of 29 should be specified, because otherwise `strncpy` could potentially overwrite the terminating null. Similarly, use of `strncat` should allow for the null, as well as the current length of s1:

```
strncat(s1, s2, 29 - strlen(s1));
```

All these functions — `strcat`, `strcpy`, `strncat`, and `strncpy` — copy the terminating null along with other string data.

● — NOTE

> Considering all the pitfalls in the use of C/C++ strings, the `cStr` class developed in Chapters 5 through 8 has many advantages over ordinary strings.

Among the other functions, `strstr` is particularly useful for searching and indexing. It returns a pointer to a substring inside the first string argument (*s1*). If you want to convert this result to an index, use pointer arithmetic. For example, the following code finds the index of the word "England":

```
#include <string.h>
//...
int index;
char aString[] = "This land, this realm, this England."
index = strstr(aString, "England") - aString;
```

All the searching and indexing functions are case sensitive because they do simple comparisons of binary values.

The `strtok` function returns tokens; these are substrings, often words, separated by delimiter characters. For example, you can parse a sentence for individual words by using spaces and punctuation as delimiters. The first call to `strtok` specifies a string to parse as the *s1* argument. To continue parsing the same string, call `strtok` again and specify NULL for *s1*. Every character in *s2* is a delimiter.

If no more tokens are left, `strtok` returns a null pointer. This enables you to write loops such as the following, which parses a sentence.

```
#include <string.h>
#include <iostream.h>
//...
char str[] = "This land, this realm, this England.";
char *p = strtok(str, " ,.");
while (p) {
   cout << p << '\n';
   p = strtok(NULL, " ,.");
}
```

When executed, this code prints these results:

```
This
land
this
realm
```

```
this
England
```

Types and return values

Several string functions take an integer as an argument. In each of these functions, *n* has type size_t. This is a type declared in stdlib.h that is large enough to store any string length. (It is typically unsigned long.) String functions that return an integer also have type size_t.

Except where otherwise noted, each string function returns a pointer to the first string argument. This enables you to pass along results in another function call. For example, the following statement concatenates two strings onto the string name:

```
strcat(strcat(name, s1), s2);
```

strftime   Write formatted time display

Purpose

STRing Format Time: writes a formatted time display to a string; this display can contain date and time information in any format, including names of months and days of the week.

Syntax

```
#include <time.h>   // OR #include <ctime>

size_t *strftime(char *str, size_t max_size,
    const char *fmt, const struct tm *time)
```

The first two arguments describe the string that strftime writes to; *str* specifies the address of the string and *max_size* specifies the maximum number of characters to write. The function returns the number of characters actually written.

The *time* argument is a pointer to a tm structure that contains time and date information. See "Time" (p. 235) for a description of this structure type.

The *fmt* argument is a string that contains time-format specifiers as well as other characters to be written to the target string, as described next.

Format specifiers

The format string (*fmt*) can optionally contain any of the specifiers listed in Table 4.

Table 4 *Format Specifiers for strftime*

Format Specifier	Description
%a	Name of the day of the week, abbreviated
%A	Name of the day of the week
%b	Name of the month, abbreviated
%B	Name of the month
%c	Standard date and time string
%d	Day of the month (1–31)
%H	Hour (0–23)
%I	Hour (0–12)
%j	Day of the year (1–366)
%m	Month (1–12)
%M	Minutes (0–59)
%p	AM/PM string for the current locale setting
%S	Seconds (0–61) — allows up to two leap seconds
%U	Week of the year, with Sunday the first day of each week (0–53)
%w	Day of the week, with Sunday the first day (0–6)
%W	Week of the year, with Monday the first day of each week (0–53)
%x	Locale-specific date string
%X	Locale-specific time string
%y	Two-digit year string (0–99)
%Y	Four-digit year string
%Z	Name of time zone
%%	Literal percent sign (%)

Because the percent sign (%) is an escape character, you must use two consecutive percent signs (%%) if you want to write a percent sign to the target string.

Example

This example prints the current time and date in several different formats:

```
#include <stdio.h>
#include <time.h>
```

```
void main()
{
   char s[100];
   time_t t = time(NULL);
   tm *tmp = localtime(&t);
   strftime(s, 99, "The month is %B.",tmp);
   puts(s);
   strftime(s, 99, "The day of the week is %A.", tmp);
   puts(s);
   strftime(s, 99, "The time is %H:%M %p", tmp);
   puts(s);
}
```

Here is sample output from this program:

```
The month is December.
The day of the week is Sunday.
The time is 12:59 PM.
```

strtod   Convert string to double

Purpose

Reads a floating-point expression from a string (similar to atof).

Syntax

```
#include <stdlib.h>   // OR #include <cstdlib>

double strtod(const char *str, char **end);
```

The function reads *str*, skipping past leading whitespace characters and reading characters as long as they form a valid floating-point expression. For example, " -24.56xy7" is interpreted as -24.56. The function reads "E" and "e" as exponent signs, so that "5E2" is interpreted as 50.0.

The *end* argument is the address of a char* pointer; the function sets this pointer so that it points to the first character that cannot be read. You can optionally pass NULL or 0, causing this argument to be ignored.

If a valid number can be read, the function returns that value. In the case of overflow, it returns HUGE_VAL or –HUGE_VAL, depending on whether the result is positive or negative. In the case of underflow (tiny value too close to zero for representation), the function returns 0. In either case, the global variable errno is set to ERANGE.

● NOTE

Underflow can occur when there is an attempt to read a tiny number that is very close to, but not precisely equal to, 0. For example, 5E-999 is too small to be represented as a `double`.

Example

This example reads a string from the keyboard:

```
#include <stdlib.h>
#include <stdio.h>
//...
char *p;
char str[100];
double x = strtod(gets(str), &p);
```

strtol   Convert string to long int

Purpose

"String to long"; uses a specified radix (base) to read an integer from a string.

Syntax

```
#include <stdlib.h>    // OR #include <cstdlib>

long strtol(const char *str, char **end, int radix);
```

The function reads the string *str* using the specified *radix* (base). For example, a radix of 16 causes the string to be read in hexadecimal. The function skips past leading whitespaces and stops reading at the first invalid character.

The *end* argument is the address of a char* pointer. The function sets this pointer so that it points to the first character that cannot be read. You can optionally pass NULL or 0, causing this argument to be ignored.

Example

This example reads the string "FF" in hexadecimal radix and returns the result 255:

```
#include <stdlib.h>
#include <stdio.h>
//...
long n = strtol("FF", 0, 16);
```

Related functions are atoi, atol, and atof. The strtoul function performs the same action as strtol, but returns an unsigned long.

strtoul — Convert string to unsigned long

Purpose

String to unsigned long; uses a specified radix (base) to read an unsigned integer from a string.

Syntax

```
#include <stdlib.h>   // OR #include <cstdlib>

unsigned long strtoul(const char *str, char **end,
    int radix);
```

The function reads the string *str* using the specified *radix* (base). For example, a radix of 16 causes the string to be read in hexadecimal. The function skips past leading whitespaces and stops reading at the first invalid character.

The *end* argument is the address of a char* pointer; the function sets this pointer so that it points to the first character that cannot be read. You can optionally pass NULL or 0, causing this argument to be ignored.

Example

This example reads the string "FF" in hexadecimal radix and returns the result 255:

```
#include <stdlib.h>
#include <stdio.h>
//...
unsigned long n = strtoul("FF", 0, 16);
```

swprintf — Write data to wide-character string

Purpose

Translates zero or more numeric values into wide-character representation; similar to printf but uses wide-character strings.

Syntax

```
#include <wchar.h>   // OR #include <cwchar>

int swprintf(wchar_t *buffer,
const wchar_t *format, ...);
```

As with the printf declaration, the ellipses (. . .) indicate that the *format* string can be followed by any number of arguments. For each format specifier (such as %s, %d, or %f) in the format string, there must be a corresponding data argument following *format*. The output is written to the string pointed to by *buffer*.

The swprintf function is similar to sprintf, which prints to standard char* strings. However, swprintf uses wide-character (wchar_t*) strings.

swprintf returns the number of characters actually written, not counting the terminating null.

Example

For example, the following code places an ASCII representation of the floating-point number x into the wide-character string buf, along with the characters "x = ":

```
#include <wchar.h>
//...
wchar_t buf[256];
double x = 2.50e3;
swprintf(buf, L"x = %f.", x);   // Write to buf.
wprintf(buf);                   // Print buf.
```

The output of this program is:

```
x = 2500.000000.
```

For a list of format specifiers and their meanings, see printf (p. 205).

swscanf	Read data from wide-character string

Purpose

Reads text from a string, interprets it, and places the results in one or more data fields; similar to scanf and sscanf, but uses wide-character strings.

Syntax

```
#include <wchar.h>   // OR #include <cwchar>

int swscanf(wchar_t *s, const wchar_t *format, ...);
```

The function reads characters from the string pointed to by s.

The format string contains zero or more placeholders called *format specifiers* such as %i or %lf. For each format specifier, there must be a data-address argument following format. The first specifier corresponds to the first data address, the second specifier corresponds to the second address, and so on. The function returns the number of data fields successfully read.

The swscanf function is similar to the standard-string version, sscanf, except that it uses wide-character (wchar_t*) strings.

Example

This example reads the characters "1.234" from a wide-character string and then stores the number 1.234 in a floating-point variable, x:

```
#include <wchar.h>
//...
wchar_t data[] = L"1.234";
double x;
swscanf(data, L"%lf", &x);  // Read from data into x.
```

Note that the characters "1.234" are represented in this code as L"1.234". The L prefix is the C/C++ notation that tells the compiler to store these characters as a wide-character string.

For a list of format specifiers and their meanings, see scanf (p. 214).

system   Execute system command

Purpose

Sends a string to the operating system's command processor.

Syntax

```
#include <stdlib.h>   // OR #include <cstdlib>

int system(const char *str);
```

The meaning of the return value is implementation defined, but 0 usually indicates success.

Example

```
#include <stdlib.h>
//...
system("DIR /W");
```

tan   Tangent

Purpose

Returns the tangent of its argument.

Syntax

```
#include <math.h>   // OR #include <cmath>

double tan(double x);
```

The function takes an angle in radians and returns the ratio of two sides of a triangle.

Example

This example prints the tangent of pi/4, which equals 1:

```
#include <math.h>
#include <iostream.h>
//...
double pi = atan(1) * 4;
cout << "tan(pi/4) = " << tan(pi / 4) << endl;
```

See also acos, asin, atan, atan2, cos, and sin.

tanh   Hyperbolic tangent

Purpose

Returns the hyperbolic tangent of its argument.

Syntax

```
#include <math.h>   // OR #include <cmath>

double tanh(double x);
```

The function returns an angle in radians. See also sinh and tanh.

Time   Time and date functions

This family includes time and date functions for getting the current time and
displaying it in different formats. It also includes related capabilities, such as
getting program running time.

Syntax

```
#include <time.h>  // OR #include <ctime>
```

The following table summarizes the time and date functions. The arguments
t, t1, and t2 all have type time_t, a numeric time value; and tm is a tm
structure.

Function	Action
asctime(tm)	Returns a string display of a tm structure.
clock()	Returns program running time as clock_t value; this can be converted to seconds by dividing by CLOCKS_PER_SEC.
ctime(t)	Returns a string display of a time_t value. (Uses local time.)

Continued

Function	Action
difftime($t2$, $t1$)	Returns difference between two time_t values ($t2 - t1$) in number of seconds.
gmtime(*p_t)	Returns a pointer to a temporary tm structure, initialized from time_t data pointed to by p_t; uses Greenwich Mean Time.
localtime(*p_t)	Returns a pointer to a temporary tm structure, initialized from time_t data pointed to by p_t. (Uses local time.)
mktime(*p_tm)	Sets weekday and day-of-year fields for the tm structure pointed to by p_tm. Also returns corresponding time_t value.
strftime(s, $size$, fmt, *p_tm)	Returns a formatted string for specified tm structure. For more information, see page 228.
time(*p_t)	Returns current time as a time_t value. If p_t is not NULL, the function sets the time_t value p_t points to.

The three special types, tm, time_t, and clock_t, are all declared in the time.h file. The time_t type is typically an integer large enough to hold any possible date/time value; clock_t is also a simple numeric type.

Remarks

Many date/time operations start by getting the current date and time by calling the time function. This returns a time_t value. You can pass a pointer of type *time_t, in which case the value pointed to is set to the current time, or you can pass a null pointer. In either case, the function returns the current time.

```
#include <time.h>
//...
time_t t;
t = time(NULL);
```

The simplest way to convert a time_t value into a description is to call the ctime function, which returns a pointer to a string having the following format:

weekday month dd hh:mm:ss yyyy\n

For example, the following code displays the current time:

```
time_t t = time(NULL);
cout << ctime(&t);    // Need pointer to time_t
```

Here is sample output displayed by this statement at 1:04 in the afternoon on a Monday:

```
Tue Oct 31 23:04:55 2000
```

Using a tm structure

Another way to use a time_t value is to convert it to a tm structure by calling the gmtime or localtime function. For example, the following code gets the system time and uses it to get a pointer (tmp) to a tm structure. After this code is executed, tmp points to a structure containing data for the current time.

```
time_t t = time(NULL);
tm *tmp = localtime(&t);
```

● **NOTE**

The structure returned by localtime or gmtime is temporary and gets overwritten each time one of these functions is called. To retain the data, copy it to your own tm structure:

```
tm tmNow = *tmp; // Copy from struct pointed to.
```

A tm structure divides a date/time value into data fields, including weekday (0 to 6) and day of the year (0 to 365). The time.h file declares the tm structure type as follows:

```
struct tm {
    int tm_sec;      // Seconds, 0-59
    int tm_min;      // Minutes, 0-59
    int tm_hour;     // Hours, 0-23
    int tm_mday;     // Day of the month, 1-31
    int tm_mon;      // Month, 0-11
    int tm_year;     // Years - 1900
    int tm_wday;     // Day of the week, 0-6
    int tm_yday;     // Day of the year, 0-365
    int tm_isdst;    // Daylight Savings Time indicator
}                    // > 0 if DST in effect, 0 if not
```

After converting to a tm structure, you can access individual fields to get specific parts of the date or time. For example, the following code prints the current day of the month:

```
time_t t = time(NULL);
tm *tmp = localtime(&t);

cout << "Today's day of month is: " << tmp->tm_mday;
```

The mktime function takes a pointer to a tm structure and sets some of its fields. Specifically, it sets the tm_wday and tm_yday fields of the structure, based on the settings of other fields. For example, you can use the following function to return the day of the week as a number from 0 to 6, given any month, date, and year values.

```
#include <time.h>

int get_weekday(int month, int day, int year) {
    tm t;

    t.tm_mon = month + 1;
    t.tm_day = day;
    t.tm_year = year - 1900;
    if (mktime(&t) == -1)
        return -1;
    else
        return t.tm_wday;
}
```

The mktime function returns –1 if it cannot use the data in the structure (in this case, t) to create a meaningful calendar date. This example tests for that condition. The tm_wday and tm_yday fields do not need to be set before calling mktime, because those fields are set by the function.

You can call the asctime function to get a quick string representation of a date/time value, given tm structure input. The asctime function uses the same format as the ctime function, described in the previous section.

Printing a formatted time string

Yet another way to use a tm structure is to call the strftime function and specify a format string. This function is roughly analogous to printf, but it formats parts of a time value. For example, the following code prints out the day of the week as a name ("Sunday," "Monday," "Tuesday," and so on):

```
time_t t = time(NULL);
tm *tmp = localtime(&t);
char s[100];
strftime(s, 99, "The day of the week is %A.",
        tmp->tm_wday);
puts(s);
```

For more information, see the topic strftime.

tmpfile   Open temporary file

Purpose

Opens a temporary file in binary read/write mode. This file is automatically deleted when the file is closed or when the program terminates.

Syntax

```
#include <stdio.h>   // OR #include <cstdio>

FILE *tmpfile(void);
```

As with fopen, tmpfile returns a valid file pointer if it is successful; otherwise, it returns NULL. For more information on file I/O, see "Files" (p. 178).

tolower   Convert letter to lowercase

Purpose

Takes a single character, converts it to lowercase, and returns the result. If the character is already lowercase, or is not a letter, it is returned as is.

Syntax

```
#include <ctype.h>   // OR #include <cctype>

int tolower(int ch);
```

The argument type is int, but only the low byte of ch (the byte that stores a single character) is significant.

Example

```
#include <ctype.h>
#include <string.h>

void convert_to_lower(char s[]) {
    int i;

    for (i = 0; i < strlen(s); i++) {
        s[i] = tolower(s[i]);
    }
}
```

This sample function converts an entire string, one character at a time. Here is a sample string before conversion to lowercase:

```
I used to work for the FBI.
```

Here is the same string after the convert_to_lower sample function is called. Note how characters that are already lowercase, as well as punctuation, are preserved.

```
i used to work for the fbi.
```

toupper | Convert letter to uppercase

Purpose

Takes a single character, converts it to uppercase, and returns the result. If the character is already uppercase, or is not a letter, it is returned as is.

Syntax

```
#include <ctype.h>   // OR #include <cctype>

int tolower(int ch);
```

The argument type is int, but only the low byte of *ch* (the byte that stores a single character) is significant.

Example

```
#include <ctype.h>
#include <string.h>

void convert_to_upper(char s[]) {
    int i;

    for (i = 0; i < strlen(s); i++) {
        s[i] = toupper(s[i]);
    }
}
```

This sample function converts an entire string, one character at a time. Here is a sample string before conversion to uppercase:

```
I used to work for the FBI.
```

Here is the same string after the convert_to_upper sample function is called. Note how characters that are already uppercase, as well as punctuation, are preserved.

```
I USED TO WORK FOR THE FBI.
```

towlower   Convert wide character to lowercase

Purpose
Takes a single character, converts to lowercase, and returns the result. If the character is already lowercase or is not a letter, it is returned as is. Similar to tolower except that it uses wide-character input.

Syntax
```
#include <wctype.h>   // OR #include <cwctype>

wint_t towlower(wint_t ch);
```
Although the argument and return types are wint_t, you should pass a character of type wchar_t. The wint_t type is guaranteed to accept all wchar_t values.

Example
```
#include <wctype.h>
#include <wchar.h>

void convert_to_lower(wchar_t s[]) {
    int i;

    for (i = 0; i < wcslen(s); i++) {
        s[i] = towlower(s[i]);
    }
}
```

towupper   Convert wide character to uppercase

Purpose
Takes a single character, converts it to uppercase, and returns the result. If the character is already uppercase or not a letter, it is returned as is. Similar to toupper, except that it uses wide-character input.

Syntax
```
#include <wctype.h>   // OR #include <cwctype>

wint_t towupper(wint_t ch);
```

Although the argument and return types are wint_t, you should pass a character of type wchar_t. The wint_t type is guaranteed to accept all wchar_t values.

Example

```
#include <wctype.h>
#include <wchar.h>

void convert_to_upper(wchar_t s[]) {
    int i;

    for (i = 0; i < wcslen(s); i++) {
        s[i] = towupper(s[i]);
    }
}
```

va_<op>   Handle variable-length arg list

Purpose

This family of macro functions supports variable-length argument lists, which are declared with ellipsis (|). These macros enable you to read as many arguments as you choose, one at a time. Consequently, you can handle any number of arguments.

Syntax

```
#include <stdarg.h>
```

Here are the three macro functions that are used to support variable-length argument lists. Your function must have at least one required argument, which can then be followed by any number of arguments.

Function	Action
va_start(*argptr*, *parm*)	Initializes argument list using *argptr* (a variable of type va_list, described below) and the name of the last required argument, *parm*.
va_arg(*argptr*, *type*)	Returns next argument in the list, which must have specified *type*.
va_end(*argptr*)	Terminates reading of arguments.

To read a variable-length argument list, first declare an argument pointer. This is a variable of type va_list, which is a type defined in stdarg.h. Once declared, the argument pointer can be used in the *argptr* field of the macros.

```
va_list argptr;
```

The following code defines a function that takes any number of integer arguments, prints each argument, and then prints the total. This code requires that all of the arguments be of integer (int) type.

```
#include <stdio.h>
#include <stdarg.h>

void print_ints(int num_of_args, ...) {
    int total = 0, i;
    va_list args;

    va_start(args, num_of_args);
    while(num_of_args--) {
        i = va_arg(args, int);
        printf("%d\n", i);
        total += i;
    }
    printf("Total is %d.\n", total);
    va_end(args);
}
```

If you call this function with this statement:

```
print_ints(3, 20, 35, 15);
```

you get this output:

```
20
35
15
Total is 70.
```

Although this example only takes integer arguments, you can use the va_arg macro to read any data type; this type can even be determined at runtime. printf is a good example of a function that does just that.

vprintf, etc.   Print variable-length arg list

Purpose

This family includes functions for printing a variable-length argument list; you can use them to write a wrapper around printf or related function. These functions assume that you're processing an argument list using macros from the previous topic (va_<op>).

Syntax

The first three functions in this family correspond to printf, fprintf, and sprintf. The *va* argument is produced by declaring a va_list variable and then initializing it (see "Examples").

```
#include <stdarg.h>
#include <stdio.h>

int vprintf(const char *format, va_list va);
int vfprintf(FILE *f, const char *format, va_list va);
int vsprintf(char *s, const char *format, va_list va);
```

The other three functions are similar to the first three, but use wide-character strings.

```
#include <stdarg.h>
#include <stdio.h>
#include <wchar.h>

int vwprintf(const wchar_t *format, va_list va);
int vfwprintf(FILE *f, const wchar_t *format,
    va_list va);
int vswprintf(wchar_t *s, const wchar_t *format,
    va_list va);
```

The return value, in each case, is the number of characters actually written.

Examples

This example function does essentially the same thing that printf does; however, after printing the arguments, it waits for the user to press Enter.

```
#include <stdarg.h>
#include <stdio.h>

void printfshell(const char *fmt,...) {
    va_list args;

    va_start(args, fmt);  // Init arg list.
    vprintf(fmt, args);   // Pass to printf.
    va_end(args);
    getchar();       // Wait for user.
}
```

After this function is defined, you call printfshell by passing exactly the same arguments that you would pass to printf. There is no limit on the number of arguments.

```
printfshell("Here is a simple string.");
```

Library Functions

```
printfshell("x = %f.\n", x);
printfshell("i = %d, j = %d, k = %d.\n", i, j, k);
```

Here is a version that prints all output to stderr:

```
#include <stdarg.h>
#include <stdio.h>

void printflog(const char *fmt,...) {
    va_list args;

    va_start(args, fmt);        // Init arg list.
    vfprintf(stderr, fmt, args); // Pass to fprintf.
    va_end(args);
    getchar();     // Wait for user.
}
```

One thing I didn't do in these examples is pass along the return value of vprintf or vfprintf. This is easy to do and is left as an exercise for the reader.

| **wcs<op>** | **Wide-character string functions** |

Purpose

This family includes a wide-character version of each function in the "str < op >" family (p. 224).

Syntax

```
#include <wchar.h>  // OR #include <cwchar>
```

Here are the wide-character versions of the most common string-handling functions. The arguments s, s1, and s2 are strings of type wchar_t*, and n is an integer of type size_t. Except where otherwise noted, each function returns a pointer to its first string argument.

Function	**Action**
wcscat(s1, s2)	Concatenates s2 onto s1.
wcscmp(s1, s2)	Compares strings and returns negative, 0, or positive, depending on whether s1 is less than, equal to, or greater than s2. The comparison is alphabetical.
wcscpy(s1, s2)	Copies s2 to s1.

Continued

Function	Action
wcslen(*s*)	Returns the length of string argument, not counting the terminating null.
wcsncat(*s1*, *s2*, *n*)	Concatenates *s2* onto *s1*, copying at most *n* characters plus a terminating null.
wcsncmp(*s1*, *s2*, *n*)	Performs same action as wcscmp, comparing at most *n* characters.
wcsncpy(*s1*, *s2*, *n*)	Copies *s2* to *s1*, copying at most *n* characters. It then adds nulls until exactly *n* characters have been written.
wcsstr(*s1*, *s2*)	Returns pointer to first occurrence of *s2* in *s1* or NULL if *s2* is not found.

Each of these functions corresponds to a similarly named char* string function. For example, wcscat is the wide-character version of strcat.

Here are the wide-character versions of the other functions described in the "str< op >" topic. The only "str" function that does not have a wide-character equivalent is strerror. In this table, *s*, *s1*, and *s2* are all strings of type wchar_t*; *ch* has type wchar_t.

Function	Action
wcschr(*s*, *ch*)	Returns pointer to first occurrence of *ch* in *s* or NULL if *ch* is not found.
wcscoll(*s1*, *s2*)	Performs same action as strcmp using locale settings. See "setlocale Function," page 218.
wcscspn(*s1*, *s2*)	Returns index of first character in *s1* matching any in *s2*; returns *s1* length if none found.
wcspbrk(*s1*, *s2*)	Returns pointer to first character in *s1* matching any character in *s2* or NULL if none found.
wcsrchr(*s*, *ch*)	Returns pointer to last occurrence of *ch* in *s*. (This function searches in reverse.)
wcsspn(*s1*, *s2*)	Returns index of first character in *s1* not matching any character in *s2*.
wcstok(*s1*, *s2*)	Returns next token in *s1*, using delimiters in *s2*. See "Remarks."
wcsxfrm(*s1*, *s2*, *n*)	Uses locale settings to transform *s2* and to place the results in *s1*. Only the first *n* characters are transformed. See setlocale, page 218.

The library also supports the following functions that begin with the "wcs" prefix.

Function	Action
wcsftime	Writes formatted time string. See page 248.
wcstod	Converts string to double. See page 249.
wcstol	Converts string to long. See page 250.
wcstoul	Converts string to unsigned long. See page 250.

Remarks

Nearly all the comments and examples for the "str" functions apply equally well to their "wcs" counterparts — but remember that wide-character string literals require the "L" prefix. For example, here is the string-building example using wide-character strings:

```
#include <wchar.h>
//...
wchar_t name[30] = '""';
wcscpy(name, L"John ");        // Copy "John "
wcscat(name, L"Q. ");          // Append "Q. "
wcscat(name, L"Public");       // Append "Public"
```

This example correctly builds the wide-character string "John Q. Public". Similarly, you can use functions such as wcsncpy and wcsncat for safer operations:

```
wchar_t s1[30], *s2, *s3;
// ...
wcsncpy(s1, s2, 29);
wcsncat(s1, s2, 29 - wcslen(s1));
```

The wcstok function returns a token from a target string. As with strtok, the first argument (*s1*) is the address of a string to operate on; you can specify a new string or NULL. If you specify NULL, the function continues reading the last string specified. Each character in the second string (*s2*) is a delimiter. The function returns a null pointer of no token was read.

For example:

```
#include <wchar.h>
#include <iostream.h>
//...
wchar_t str[] = L"This land, this realm, this England.";
wchar_t *next;
wchar_t *p = wcstok(str, L" ,.");
while (p) {
   wprintf(L"%s\n", p);
   p = wcstok(NULL, L" ,.");
}
```

When executed, this code prints these results:

```
This
land
this
realm
this
England
```

wcsftime — Write formatted time display (wchar_t)

Purpose

Wide-character string format time (wcsftime) writes a formatted time display to a string; similar to strftime, except that it uses wide-character strings.

Syntax

```
#include <wchar.h>   // OR #include <cwchar>

size_t *wcsftime(wchar_t *str, size_t max_size,
    const wchar_t *fmt, const struct tm *time)
```

The first two arguments describe the string that strftime writes to; str specifies the address of the string and max_size specifies the maximum number of characters to write. The function returns the number of characters actually written.

The fmt argument is a string that contains time-format specifiers as well as other characters to be written to the target string. See strftime (p. 228) for a description of the time-format specifiers.

The time argument is a pointer to a tm structure that contains time and date information. See "Time" (p. 235) for a description of this structure type.

Example

This example prints the current time and date in several different formats:

```
#include <wchar.h>
#include <time.h>

void main()
{
    wchar_t s[100];
    time_t t = time(NULL);
    tm *tmp = localtime(&t);
    wcsftime(s, 99, L"The month is %B.\n", tmp);
```

```
    wprintf(s);
    wcsftime(s, 99, L"The day of the week is %A.\n",
        tmp);
    wprintf(s);
    wcsftime(s, 99, L"The time is %H:%M %p.\n", tmp);
    wprintf(s);
}
```

Here is sample output from this program:

```
The month is December.
The day of the week is Sunday.
The time is 12:59 PM.
```

wcstod | Convert wide-character string to double

Purpose

Reads a floating-point expression from a wide-character string; similar to strtod (see p. 230).

Syntax

```
#include <wchar.h>   // OR #include <cwchar>

double wcstod(const wchar_t *s, wchar_t **end);
```

The function reads a floating-point expression from the string *s*. It skips past leading whitespaces and stops reading at the first invalid character. This function accepts the same characters that strtod does, as well as implementation-defined floating-point expressions.

The *end* argument is the address of a wchar_t* pointer. The function sets this pointer so that it points to the first character that cannot be read. You can optionally pass NULL or 0, causing this argument to be ignored.

If a valid number can be read, the function returns that value. In the case of overflow, it returns HUGE_VAL or −HUGE_VAL. In the case of underflow, it returns 0. In either case, the global variable errno is set to ERANGE.

● NOTE

Underflow can occur when there is an attempt to read a tiny number that is very close to, but not precisely equal to, 0. For example, 5E-999 is too small to be represented as a double.

Example

This example reads a string from the keyboard and translates the number entered (if any), storing it in x.

```
#include <wchar.h>
#include <stdio.h>
//...
wchar_t wcs[100];
double x = wcstod(fgetws(wcs, 99, stdin), 0);
```

wcstol	Convert wide-character string to long int

Purpose

Uses a specified radix (base) to read an integer from a wide-character string; similar to strtol.

Syntax

```
#include <wchar.h>    // OR #include <cwchar>

long wcstol(const wchar_t *s, wchar_t **end, int radix);
```

The function reads the string s using the specified *radix* (base). For example, a radix of 16 causes the string to be read in hexadecimal. The function skips past leading whitespaces and stops reading at the first invalid character.

The *end* argument is the address of a wchar_t* pointer; the function sets this pointer so that it points to the first character that cannot be read. You can optionally pass NULL or 0, causing this argument to be ignored.

Example

This example reads the string "FF" in hexadecimal radix and returns the result 255:

```
#include <wchar.h>
//...
long n = wcstol(L"FF", 0, 16);
```

wcstoul	Convert wide-character string to unsigned long

Purpose

Uses a specified radix (base) to read an unsigned integer from a wide-character string; similar to stroul.

Syntax

```
#include <wchar.h>    // OR #include <cwchar>

long wcstoul(const wchar_t *s, wchar_t **end, int radix);
```

The function reads the string *s* using the specified *radix* (base). For example, a radix of 16 causes the string to be read in hexadecimal. The function skips past leading whitespaces and stops reading at the first invalid character.

The *end* argument is the address of a wchar_t* pointer; the function sets this pointer so that it points to the first character that cannot be read. You can optionally pass NULL or 0, causing this argument to be ignored.

Example

This example reads the string "FF" in hexadecimal radix and returns the result 255:

```
#include <wchar.h>
//...
unsigned long n = wcstoul(L"FF", 0, 16);
```

wmem<op>	Wide-character memory-block functions

Purpose

This family includes wide-character versions of each of the memory-block functions described in mem<op> on page 202.

Syntax

```
#include <wchar.h>    // OR #include <cwchar>
```

Each of the functions in this table corresponds to a standard mem function; for example, wmemchr is similar to memchr. The major difference is that *p*, *p1*, and *p2* are pointers of type wchar_t* rather than void*, and the character *ch* has type wchar_t. These functions are suitable for efficiently operating on large wchar_t strings.

Function	Action
wmemchr(*p*, *ch*, *n*)	Returns pointer to first character in string that matches argument *ch*.
wmemcmp(*p1*, *p2*, *n*)	Compares two strings and returns negative, 0, or positive, depending on whether first is less than, equal to, or greater than second; these return values are similar to those provided by strcmp and wcscmp.

Continued

Function	Action
wmemcpy(*p1*, *p2*, *n*)	Copies up to *n* characters from string *p2* to *p1*.
wmemmove(*p1*, *p2*, *n*)	Copies up to *n* characters from string *p2* to *p1*; these may overlap.
wmemset(*p*, *ch*, *n*)	Sets each character in string to *ch*.

All the pointer arguments accept both const and non-const pointers, except the first argument in wmemcpy and in wmemmove. In each of these cases, the first argument is not const, because the function changes the data pointed to.

The wmemcpy, wmemmove, and wmemset functions all return a wchar_t* pointer to the first memory-block argument (*p* or *p1*); wmemchr returns a wchar_t* pointer to the individual character found. wmemcmp returns an int.

Remarks

The wmemchr functions work slightly differently from their memchr counterparts. They return wchar_t* pointers rather than void* pointers, so there is typically no need to cast the results. Remember to use the "wcs" functions on strings of wchar_t, rather than the "str" versions. For example, wcslen is used here.

```
#include <wchar.h>
//...
wchar_t *p, *buf = L"This is a character X array."
p = wmemchr(buf, L'X', wcslen(buf));
int index = p - buf;  // Use pointer arithmetic to
                      //  get index.
```

The wmemcpy and wmemmove functions are similar to each other. wmemcpy can be used to assign all the values in one string (wstr1) to another string (wstr2) and is generally faster than wmemmove.

```
wchar_t wstr1[100], wstr2[100];
//...
wmemcpy(wstr2, wstr1, 100);   // Copy wstr1 to wstr2.
```

But wmemmove, which is more versatile, can be used to shift values inside a string. Here it is used to shift 100 characters down by one position, so that string positions 1 to 100 are copied to string positions 0 to 99.

```
wchar_t arr1[500];
//...
wmemmove (arr1, arr1 + 1, 100); // Shift downward.
```

wprintf — Print formatted wide-character string

Purpose

Translates any number of numeric values and prints the results along with other characters; similar to `printf`, but uses a wide-character-format string.

Syntax

```
#include <wchar.h>    // OR #include <cwchar>

int wprintf(const wchar_t *format,...);
```

The format string contains zero or more placeholders called *format specifiers*; the ellipses (. . .) indicate that the *format* string can be followed by any number of arguments. For each format specifier, there must be a data-field argument. The first specifier corresponds to the first data field, the second specifier corresponds to the second data field, and so on.

`wprintf` returns the number of wide characters printed.

Example

The following function call contains one format string with two specifiers (`%d` and `%f`), along with two data-field arguments, `i` and `x`:

```
wprintf(L"i = %d and x = %f.\n", i, x);
```

If `i` and `x` have the values 6 and 25.5, respectively, this function call prints:

```
i = 6 and x = 25.500000.
```

For a list of format specifiers and their meanings, see `printf` (p. 205).

wscanf — Read data with wide-character-format string

Purpose

Reads text from the keyboard, interprets it, and places the results in one or more data fields. Similar to `scanf` except that it uses a wide-character-format string.

Syntax

```
#include <wchar.h>    // OR #include <cwchar>

int wscanf(const wchar_t *format,...);
```

The format string contains zero or more placeholders called *format specifiers*. For each format specifier (such as %i, %d, or %lf), there must be a data-address argument following *format*. The first specifier corresponds to the first data address, the second specifier corresponds to the second address, and so on.

The value returned by wscanf is the number of data fields successfully read.

Example

This call to wscanf has one format specifier (%d) and one data-address argument (&i, the address of an integer). Note the use of the "L" prefix to specify a wide-character string literal.

```
wscanf(L"%d", &i);    // Place decimal integer in i.
```

For a list of format specifiers and their meanings, see scanf (p. 214).

in plain english in p
sh in plain english i
glish in plain englis
in plain english in p
sh in plain english i
glish in plain englis
in plain english in p
glish in plain englis
in plain english in p
sh in plain english i
glish in plain englis
in plain english in p
sh in plain english i
glish in plain englis
in plain english in p
lish in plain englis
in plain english in p
sh in plain english i
glish in plain englis
in plain english in p
sh in plain english i
lish in plain englis
in plain english in p
lish in plain englis

I/O Stream Classes

One of the areas of emphasis in this edition of *C++ In Plain English* is the I/O stream class family. For an introduction to, as well as special features of, the I/O stream, see Chapters 4 and 10 in Part II, "C++ Tutorial."

The C++ library supports `printf` and `scanf`, which is reassuring for those who have C legacy code. If you're writing programs from scratch, however, the I/O classes offer some advantages. In particular, they are *extensible* to all data types: they not only work with all of the primitive types that the compilers support, but you can also make them work with your own classes, as explained in Chapter 10.

One challenge in describing the I/O classes is that they use inheritance. For example, most of the important functions of the `ifstream` class are inherited from `istream`, its base class. Figure 10-1 (p. 494) summarizes the inheritance tree of the I/O classes.

The root class, `ios`, is not described in this chapter, because you never use it directly, but its member functions are described. There is also another class in the I/O hierarchy called `streambuf`, which is only of interest if you want to replace the default buffering system for input and output. These are omitted due to space considerations.

The rest of the chapter describes each individual class, object, and member function.

bad   Detect fatal error

Purpose

Function. Returns a nonzero value if any fatal I/O errors have occurred.

Syntax

```
#include <iostream.h>

int stream.bad() const;
```

Example

This example assumes that `infile` is a previously created file input stream.

```
if (infile.bad()) {
    cout << "Fatal error occurred with input file."
    return -1
}
```

cerr   Console error object

Purpose

Object. Provides access to standard error — usually the monitor. This stream is nearly the same as standard output, except that the two streams can be redirected separately.

Syntax

```
#include <iostream.h>

cerr
```

The `cerr` object is an instance of the `ostream` class.

Example

This example prints a message to standard error output.

```
cerr << "Invalid data." << endl;
```

cin
Console input object

Purpose
Object. Provides access to standard input, usually the keyboard.

Syntax
```
#include <iostream.h>

cin
```

The cin object is an instance of the istream class.

Example
This example gets input and assigns it to the variables i and j.

```
cin >> i >> j;
```

clear
Clear or set error flags

Purpose
Function. Clears error flags, if no argument is specified; otherwise, it sets error flags to the argument.

Syntax
```
#include <iostream.h>

int stream.clear(flags = 0) const;
```

For a list of error flags, see rdstate page 282.

Example
This statement clears all error flags of the standard output stream (cout).

```
cout.clear();
```

clog
Console error object

Purpose
Object. Provides access to standard error — usually the monitor — but uses buffered output. Writing to this object is nearly the same as writing to cerr.

Syntax
```
#include <iostream.h>

clog
```

I/O Stream Classes

The clog object is an instance of the ostream class.

Example

This example prints a message to standard error output.

```
clog << "Invalid data." << endl;
```

close   Close file stream

Purpose

Function. Closes the file associated with a file-stream object.

Syntax

```
#include <fstream.h>

void filestream.close();
```

filestream is an object of type fstream, ifstream, or ofstream.

If you don't call close yourself, the associated file is automatically closed as soon as the object is destroyed. However, if the object will be around for awhile, you should close a file as soon as you're done with it.

After the associated file is closed, you cannot use the stream object again until you call open.

Example

The following code opens file junk.txt, closes it, and then reopens the stream with another file.

```
fstream fs("c:\\junk.txt", ios::in);
//...
fs.close();
fs.open("c:\\morejunk.txt", ios::in);
```

cout   Console output object

Purpose

Object. Provides access to standard output, usually the monitor.

Syntax

```
#include <iostream.h>

cout
```

The cout object is an instance of the ostream class.

Example

This example prints a message to standard output.

```
cout << "Hello, C++." << endl;
```

---

eatwhite   Gobble up leading spaces

Purpose

Function. Reads and ignores characters, up to the next character that is not whitespace.

Syntax

```
#include <iostream.h>

void inputstream.eatwhite();
```

inputstream is an object of istream or any of its derived classes: fstream, ifstream, istrstream, or strstream.

The function reads and ignores every whitespace (space, tab, or newline) that it finds. The first nonwhitespace character stops the function and remains in the input stream, so that it will be the next character read.

Example

```
cin.eatwhite();
```

---

eof   Detect end-of-file condition

Purpose

Function. Returns nonzero if no more characters are available; otherwise, returns zero.

Syntax

```
#include <iostream.h>

int stream.eof() const;
```

Example

The following code reads and prints lines of text from file stream inf, until no more characters are available.

```
char str[256];
while (!inf.eof()) {
    inf.getline(str, 256);
    cout << str << endl;
}
```

I/O Stream Classes

fail Detect fatal error

Purpose
Function. Returns a nonzero value if a nonfatal I/O error has occurred.

Syntax
```
#include <iostream.h>

int stream.fail() const;
```

Example
This example assumes that infile is a previously created file input stream.

```
if (infile.fail()) {
    cout << "Error occurred with input file."
    return -1
}
```

fill Set or get fill character

Purpose
Function. Sets the fill character for a particular stream, or returns the stream's current fill character. This character is used to pad numeric fields.

Syntax
```
#include <iostream.h>

char stream.fill() const;
char stream.fill(char ch);
```

The first version of the function returns the current fill character. The second version sets a new fill character and returns the previous value.

Although supported by all stream classes, the fill function is used mainly with output steams. If a stream's width attribute (see the width function, p. 293) is larger than the width of a numeral to be displayed, the extra space is padded with the fill character. Typically, this is set to a blank space (the default), or to '0'.

Example
This code demonstrates the effect of the fill function by printing leading zeroes for each number printed.

```
char c = cout.fill('0');
cout.width(5);
cout << 4 << 5 << endl;
cout.fill(c);
```

flags   Set or get format flags

Purpose

Function. Replaces all format flags of a stream with a new set of flag values, or returns the current flag settings.

Syntax

```
#include <iostream.h>


long stream.flags() const;
long stream.flags(long f);
```

The first version of the function returns the current flag settings as a long. The second version specifies a new set of flags and returns the previous settings. Unlike the setf function, a call to the second version of flags replaces *all* format flag settings of a stream, so that it may have the effect of turning some flags off.

You can use the bitwise OR operator (|) to combine flags and the bitwise AND (&) to test values.

Examples

The first example turns on the ios::hex (hexadecimal) and ios::right (right justify) flags, and turns all other format flags off.

```
long saved_flags;
saved_flags = cout.flags(ios::hex | ios::right);
```

The next example gets the current flag settings of cout and tests whether ios::hex is on.

```
long current_flags;
current_flags = cout.flags();
if (current_flags & ios::hex)
    cout << "Output is in hex.";
```

flush   Force it through

Purpose

Function. Flushes a buffer associated with a stream; this causes all the data in the buffer to be written to the device.

Syntax

```
#include <iostream.h>

ostream& stream.flush();
```

I/O Stream Classes

The function returns a reference to the stream object through which the function was called, enabling you to reuse the stream object in a larger expression, although there is no requirement that you do so.

Although supported by all stream classes, the flush function is used mainly with output streams.

Examples

Here is a simple use of flush to force immediate printing of text, even though it does not contain a newline.

```
int n;
cout << "Enter a number: ";
cout.flush();
cin >> n;
```

In this next example, the reference to the stream (cout) is used in the larger expression. The effect is to flush the buffer and then print some text.

```
(cout.flush()) << "More text" << endl;
```

| freeze | Freeze or unfreeze string buffer |

Purpose

Function. Freezes or unfreezes an internal string buffer for an array-based stream.

Syntax

```
#include <strstrea.h>  // Brings in iostream.h

void arraystream.freeze(bool frz = true);
```

arraystream is an object of type ostrstream or strstream.

If *frz* is true, the string buffer is frozen, and further output to the string is ignored. This is the default. If *frz* is false, the string buffer is unfrozen and output can resume.

This function is used with streams that have a dynamic string buffer. (See ostrstream and strstream constructors, pp. 278 and 289, respectively.) Such a buffer can grow without limit and is moved around in memory as needed. Freezing the buffer fixes its address, but causes further output to be ignored. Calling the str function, which gets the address, automatically freezes the buffer.

Unfreezing the buffer enables you to write to the stream, but makes the string address invalid until you call str again.

Example

```
#include <strstrea.h>
//...
ostrstream oss;
oss << "Here is some output." << endl;
oss << "Here is some more." << endl;
char *p = oss.str();  // This freezes string.
cout << p << endl;

// Unfreeze and write more output
oss.freeze(false);
oss << "Still more output.";
p = oss.str();
cout << p;
```

fstream   File input/output class

Purpose

Class. Defines functions for reading and writing to a file. Inherits from both istream and ostream. See also ifstream and ofstream, pages 269 and 274, respectively.

Constructors

```
#include <fstream.h>  // Brings in iostream.h

fstream();
fstream(char *filename, int mode, int
    access=filebuf::openprot);
fstream(filedesc fd);
fstream(filedesc fd, char *pch, int nLength);
```

The first constructor creates an empty stream object that must be explicitly initialized later by calling the object's open function (p. 275).

The second constructor opens a named file, which can include a path specification. The second argument, mode, must be set to a combination of one or more mode flags. At a minimum, you should use ios::in, ios::out, or ios:in|ios::out. Text mode is assumed unless you specify ios::binary. For more information on mode flags, see the open function (p. 275). The last argument, access, defaults to filebuf::openprot, which is the normal access mode for files (see your compiler documentation for other access modes).

If you want to ensure that the file already exists, add ios::nocreate to the mode argument and compare the resulting object to 0 or NULL. (See "Example.") If you do not use ios::nocreate, the constructor always creates an object as long as the filename is valid and there are no other errors. New files start out as 0 bytes long.

The third and fourth constructors specify a *file descriptor*, a low-level handle used by the operating system. In the fourth constructor, *pch* points to a buffer; a NULL value that prevents buffering.

Member Functions

The fstream class supports the following member functions. Functions specific to file operations are in bold. read and write are especially useful with binary files.

bad	flush	precision	**setmode**
clear	gcount	put	sync_with_stdio
close	get	putback	**tellg**
eatwhite	getline	rdstate	**tellp**
eof	good	**read**	unsetf
fail	ignore	**seekg**	width
fill	**open**	**seekp**	**write**
flags	peek	setf	

Operations

This class inherits both the insertion operator (<<) from the istream class and the extraction (>>) operator from the ostream class.

Example

This code provides an example of writing and reading text to the same file. The nocreate mode ensures that the file previously exists. If it doesn't exist, the constructor sets the object iofile to 0. If you *do* want to be able to create a new file, then remove nocreate from the code.

```
#include <fstream.h>
//...
char str[500];
fstream iofile("c:\\junk.txt",
     ios::in | ios::out | ios::nocreate);
if (!iofile) {
     cout << "File does not exist.";
     return -1;
}
iofile << "Here is some text.";
iofile.seekg(0, ios::beg); // Move back to start.
iofile >> str;             // Read the first word.
cout << str << endl;
iofile.close();
```

gcount   Get count of characters written

Purpose

Function. Returns the number of characters actually read by the last input operation; this is particularly useful with binary operations.

Syntax

```
#include <iostream.h>

int inputstream.gcount() counst;
```

inputstream is an object of istream or any of its derived classes: fstream, ifstream, istrstream, or strstream.

Example

This example reads 16 bytes of a file at a time. After any attempt to read a file, if fewer than 16 bytes were read, the end of the file has been reached and the loop ends. This example assumes that fin is a previously opened input stream.

```
int n;
do {
    fin.read(dat, 16);
    n = fin.gcount();

    // Print the data read...

} while (n == 16);
```

get   Get character

Purpose

Function. Reads a single character or a line of text from an input stream.

Syntax

```
#include <iostream.h>

int inputstream.get();
istream& inputstream.get(char &ch);
istream& inputstream.get(char *buf, int num,
    char delim='\n');
```

inputstream is an object of istream or one of its derived classes: fstream, ifstream, istrstream, and strstream.

The first version returns the next character, or EOF if no more characters are available. The second version gets a character but places the result in the character argument, which must be an lvalue. (See "Examples" for clarification.)

The third version reads characters until it reads either *num* characters or the *delim* character. The characters read are copied to the address pointed to by *buf* and then null terminated. (Note that *buf* may also have type signed char* or unsigned char*.) If the delimiter character is read, it is not copied. This performs the same action as getline.

Both the second and third versions return a reference to the input stream itself — that is, the object through which get was called.

Examples

This example reads a character and places it in the variable c:

```
char c;
c = cin.get();
```

This next example does the same thing, but passes c as an argument:

```
cin.get(c);  // Place next character in c.
```

getline   Read a line of text

Purpose

Function. Reads the remaining line of text from an input stream.

Syntax

```
istream& inputstream.getline(char *buf, int num,
    char delim='\n');
```

inputstream is an object of istream or any of its derived classes: fstream, ifstream, istrstream, and strstream.

The function reads characters until it reads either *num* characters or the *delim* character. The characters are copied to the address pointed to by *buf* and then null terminated. (Note that *buf* may also have type signed char* or unsigned char*.) If the delimiter character is read, it is not copied to the string.

The function returns a reference to the input stream itself — that is, the object through which getline was called.

Remarks

The behavior of the function is identical to the third version of get. The advantage of getline is that the name is more self-documenting. These functions are similar, but not identical to, the fgets function, although get and getline do not copy a newline, and fgets does.

Example

This example places the current line of input from the keyboard into input_string. The newline is not copied.

```
char input_string[256];
cin.getline(input_string, 255);
```

good   Sanity check

Purpose

Function. Returns a nonzero value if no I/O errors have occurred.

Syntax

```
#include <iostream.h>

int stream.good() const;
```

Example

This example assumes that infile is a file input stream.

```
if (!infile.good()) {
    cout << "Error occurred with input file.";
    return -1;
}
```

ifstream   Input file class

Purpose

Class. Defines functions for reading input from a file. Derived from istream.

Constructors

```
#include <fstream.h>  // Brings in iostream.h

ifstream();
ifstream(char *filename, int mode=ios::in, int
    access=filebuf::openprot);
ifstream(filedesc fd);
ifstream(filedesc fd, char *pch, int nLength);
```

The constructors are nearly the same as for the fstream class. For more information, see fstream (p. 265). See open (p. 275) for information on file modes.

I/O Stream Classes

The only difference is that with the ifstream class, the mode defaults to ios::in, which opens the file for input. If you specify any other mode flags, they are combined with ios::in. For example, the following code creates a file stream for an existing file (it will not create a new one) in binary mode. Input mode is assumed.

```
ifstream inf("my.dat", ios::binary | ios::nocreate);
```

If you want to ensure that the file previously exists, use ios::nocreate and then compare the resulting object to 0. Otherwise, the program always succeeds in creating an input stream (as long as the file name is valid and there are no other errors), although it is 0 bytes long in the case of a new file. See "Example."

Member Functions

The ifstream class supports the following functions. Functions specific to file operations are in bold; read is especially useful with binary files.

bad	flags	peek	**setmode**
clear	gcount	precision	sync_with_stdio
close	get	putback	**tellg**
eatwhite	getline	rdstate	unsetf
eof	good	**read**	width
fail	ignore	**seekg**	
fill	**open**	setf	

Operators

This class inherits the extraction operator (>>) from the istream class.

Example

This program prints out the contents of autoexec.bat, reading one line at a time. The code will not create this file if it does not already exist.

```
#include <fstream.h>

int main() {
    ifstream inf("c:\\autoexec.bat", ios::nocreate);
    if (!inf) {
        cout << "Could not open file.\n";
        return −1;
    }
    char str[256];
```

```
    while (!inf.eof()) {
        inf.getline(str, 256);
        cout << str << endl;
    }
    inf.close();
    return 0;
}
```

ignore   Skip characters

Purpose
Function. Reads and ignores the specified number of characters.

Syntax
```
#include <iostream.h>

istream& inputstream.ignore(int num=1, int delim=EOF);
```

inputstream is an object of istream or any of its derived classes: fstream, ifstream, istrstream, or strstream.

The function reads the input stream until *num* characters or the delimiter has been read. Every character read in this way is ignored, so that it is not read again (unless you use the seekg function to move the file pointer back). If the delimiter is read, then the next get operation will read the character right *after* the delimiter.

The function returns a reference to the input stream itself, which is the object through which ignore was called.

Examples
These examples assume that infile is a previously created file input stream.

```
infile.ignore();      // Skip next character.
infile.ignore(5);     // Skip next five characters.
```

istream   Input class

Purpose
Class. Defines functions for reading an input stream such as cin.

Constructors
You cannot call an istream constructor directly. See cin (p. 259). Also see ifstream (p. 269) and istrstream (p. 273), which let you create an input stream around a file or string.

I/O Stream Classes

Member Functions

The istream class supports the following functions. Names of functions originating in this class are in bold. Although read, seekg, and tellg are declared here, they are most likely to be used in derived classes such as ifstream and istrstream.

bad	flags	**peek**	setf
clear	**gcount**	precision	sync_with_stdio
eatwhite	**get**	putback	**tellg**
eof	**getline**	rdstate	unsetf
fail	good	**read**	width
fill	**ignore**	seekg	

Operators

The istream class defines an *extraction* operator (>>), which reads text, interprets it, and stores the result in an lvalue (typically a variable). The variable's type determines data format. Note that when you read into a string, the operator stops reading at the first whitespace.

```
cin >> input_string;  // Read to first whitespace
```

The operation reads as many characters as are valid for the particular type. For example, for an integer variable, the operation inputs characters until it reads a non-digit character. The first character not input is left in the input stream, so that this character will be the first to be read by the next operation.

The first thing the operation does is read and discard leading whitespace characters.

Examples

Among the input functions, getline is particularly useful. It gets an entire line of input, not stopping until it reads a newline or the maximum number of characters specified.

```
#include <iostream.h>
//...
char str[100];
int c, n;
cin.getline(str, 99);
cin.setf(ios::hex);
cin >> n;
c = cin.peek();
cin.getline(str, 99);
```

istrstream

Input-from-string class

Purpose

Class. Defines functions for reading input from an array. Derived from istream.

Constructors

```
#include <strstrea.h>  // Brings in iostream.h

istrstream(char* buf);
istrstream(char* buf, int length);
```

The first constructor uses the specified string as the input source; the string must be null terminated, and the stream uses all the characters up to but not including the null. The second constructor uses the number of bytes indicated by *length*.

Member Functions

The class supports the following functions. The only function originating in this class, str, is in bold.

bad	flags	peek	setf
clear	gcouint	precision	**str**
eatwhite	get	putback	sync_with_stdio
eof	getline	rdstate	tellg
fail	good	read	unsetf
fill	ignore	seekg	width

Operators

This class inherits the extraction operator (>>) from the istream class.

Example

```
#include <strstrea.h>
//...
char str = "25.5 1 2 3";
double x;
int i, j, k;
istrstream iss(str, strlen(str));
iss >> x;
iss >> i >> j >> k;
cout << "The value of x is " << x << endl;
```

I/O Stream Classes

ofstream	Output file class

Purpose

Class. Defines functions for sending output to a file. Derived from ostream.

Constructors

```
#include <fstream.h>  // Brings in iostream.h

ofstream();
ofstream(char *filename, int mode=ios::out, int
    access=filebuf::openprot);
ofstream(filedesc fd);
ofstream(filedesc fd, char *pch, int nLength);
```

The constructors are nearly the same as for the fstream class. For more information, see fstream (p. 265).

The only difference is that with the ofstream class, the mode defaults to ios::out, which opens the file for output. If you specify any other mode flags, they are combined with ios::out. For example, the following code creates a file stream in binary mode, as well as opening the file for output.

```
ofstream outf("c:\\junk.dat", ios::binary);
```

Opening a file for output automatically truncates the file, unless you also open it in append or input mode. See open (p. 275) for more information on modes.

Member Functions

The ofstream class supports the following functions. Functions specific to file operations are in bold; write is especially useful with binary files.

bad	flags	rdstate	unsetf
clear	flush	**seekp**	width
close	good	setf	**write**
eof	**open**	**setmode**	
fail	precision	sync_with_stdio	
fill	put	**tellp**	

Operations

The class inherits the insertion operator (<<) from the ostream class.

Example

In this example, c:\junk.txt is opened for output. This file does not have to previously exist. Opening the file fails only if the system rejects the name as invalid, or if it can't create the file for some reason.

```
#include <fstream.h>
//...
double x = 2.7172;
ofstream outf("c:\\junk.txt");
if (!outf) {
    cout << "Could not open file.";
    return -1;
}
outf << "Here is a string.\n";
outf << "The value of x is: " << x << endl;
outf.close();
```

open   Associate file with stream

Purpose

Function. Opens a file and attaches it to a file-stream object. Not necessary if the stream is already associated with a file.

Syntax

```
#include <fstream.h>    // Brings in iostream.h

void filestream.open(char *filename, int mode,
     int access = ios::protmode);
```

filestream is an object of type fstream, ifstream, or ofstream.

The *filename* argument can contain optionally contain a relative or absolute directory path.

If *filestream* has type ifstream or ofstream, the *mode* argument is not required; it defaults to ios::in or ios::out, respectively. In any case, input mode is always assumed for ifstream objects and output mode is assumed for ofstream objects. The *mode* argument is required for objects of type fstream. If you want read/write mode, you must specify ios::in| ios::out.

The following are the flag values for *mode*. Note that text mode is assumed unless you specify binary.

Flag	Description
ios::app	All output is appended to the end of the file, which must also be opened for output.
ios::ate	When file is opened, the file pointer moves to the end of the file; but this doesn't prevent I/O operations elsewhere in the file.
ios::binary	Binary mode. No data translation is performed.
ios::in	File is opened for input.
ios::nocreate	Open fails if file does not already exist.
ios::noreplace	Open fails if file *does* already exist (unless ios::app or ios::ate is specified).
ios::out	File is opened for output. This mode implies ios::trunc unless ios::app, ios::ate, or ios::in is also specified.
ios::trunc	Existing file, if any, is truncated to 0 bytes upon being opened.

Binary mode avoids data translation, so you see bytes exactly as they are in the file. In particular, binary mode does not write newlines as carriage-return/linefeed pairs, or read those pairs as newlines. This is the main difference between binary and text mode.

You can specify any number of mode flags, by combining them through bitwise OR (|). For example:

```
ios::app|ios::out|ios::binary
```

If the open function fails, the value of *filestream* is set to 0. You can specify ios::nocreate to ensure that open succeeds only if it finds an existing file. (This usually makes sense for input files.) Conversely, you can specify ios::noreplace to prevent an existing file from being overwritten.

Examples

This example creates an output file stream and later opens it for binary write operations. You don't have to specify ios::out explicitly.

```
ofstream outfile;
//...
ofstream.open("c:\\junk.dat", ios::binary);
```

This next example uses an fstream object, which must be explicitly opened for input or output. The ios::nocreate flag is set, so the open fails — leaving fs set to zero — unless the file already exists.

```
fstream fs;
//...
fs.open("stuff.txt", ios::in | ios::nocreate);
```

```
if (!fs) {
    cout << "File not found.";
    return -1;
}
```

ostream   Output class

Purpose

Class. Defines functions for writing output through an output stream such as cout.

Constructors

You cannot call an ostream constructor directly. See cout, cerr, and clog. See also ofstream and ostrstream, which let you create an input stream around a file or string.

Member Functions

The class supports the following functions. Names of functions originating in this class are in bold. Although seekp, tellp, and write are declared here, they are most likely to be used in derived classes such as ofstream and ostrstream.

bad	flags	rdstate	unsetf
clear	**flush**	**seekp**	width
eof	good	setf	**write**
fail	precision	sync_with_stdio	
fill	**put**	**tellp**	

Operators

The ostream class defines an *insertion* operator (<<) that takes an expression and prints out its value in a text-string display. The data type of the operand determines format.

```
cout << "The value of n is " << n << endl;
```

Note that the insertion operator does not automatically print spaces around numeric output. You have to specify any spaces yourself.

Examples

```
#include <iostream.h>
//...
int x = 2.71;

cout.precision(5);   // Set print field to 5 digits
                     //  of precision.
```

```
cout << x;     // Print value of x.
cout.flush;    // Force immediate output.

// Print flag values
cout.setf(ios::hex);
cout << "Flag values are" << cout.flags() << endl;
```

ostrstream   Output string class

Purpose
Class. Defines functions for sending output to an array. Derived from ostream.

Constructors
```
#include <strstrea.h>

ostrstream();
ostrstream(char* pch, int length, int mode=ios::out);
```

The first constructor creates a stream using an internal string buffer that is empty at first, but dynamically expanded and moved as needed. The second constructor uses a string buffer of fixed length. The third argument defaults to a value of ios::out.

If you use the first constructor, then at some point, you need to call the str function to get a pointer to the data. Calling this function freezes the internal string buffer; all further output is ignored until you call the freeze function with a false argument to unfreeze the buffer. See "Examples."

Member Functions
The ostrstream class supports the following functions. Names of functions originating in this class are in bold. str gets a pointer to the string data, and pcount returns the number of characters written.

bad	flush	rdstate	unsetf
clear	**freeze**	seekp	width
eof	good	setf	write
fail	**pcount**	**str**	
fill	precision	sync_with_stdio	
flags	put	tellp	

Operations
This class inherits the insertion operator (<<) from the ostream class.

Examples

The first example creates an output stream around a fixed-length string of 500 characters, to which it then writes. Finally, it prints the string.

```
#include <strstrea.h>
//...
char str[500];
int n = 5;
ostrstream oss(str, 500);
oss << "The value of n is" << n;
cout << oss.str();
```

This next example uses the internal string buffer. The advantage of this buffer is that it grows as needed, and you don't have to worry about running out of space.

```
ostrstream oss2;
oss2 << "Here is some string data.";
char *p = oss.str();        // This freezes buffer.
puts(p);                    // Display string data.
oss.freeze(false);          // UNFREEZE.
oss2 << " more data."       // Write some more data.
```

After you unfreeze the internal string buffer, you can resume writing to the stream.

I/O Stream Classes

| pcount | Get number of characters written |

Purpose

Function. Returns the number of characters written to an internal string buffer.

Syntax

```
#include <strstrea.h>   // Brings in iostream.h
```

```
streamsize arraystream.pcount() const;
```

arraystream is an object of type ostrstream or strstream.

The function returns the number of characters written so far to the string buffer. (See ostrstream (p. 278) or strstream (p. 289) constructor for more information.) The streamsize type is an integer large enough to contain the size of any stream.

Example

```
#include <strstrea.h>
//...
ostrstream oss;
oss << "Here is some output." << endl;
oss << "Here is some more." << endl;
cout << oss.pcount() << " characters written.\n";
```

peek   Look at next character

Purpose

Function. Reads the next character without storing it; the character remains in the input stream.

Syntax

```
#include <iostream.h>


int inputstream.peek();
```

inputstream is an object of istream or any of its derived classes: fstream, ifstream, istrstream, or strstream.

The function returns the next character or EOF, if no more characters are available. The value returned is what the next call to get will retrieve.

Example

```
int c;
c = cin.peek();
```

precision   Get or set number of digits

Purpose

Function. Gets or sets the stream's precision — that is, the number of digits past the decimal point displayed for a floating-point value.

Syntax

```
#include <iostream.h>


int stream.precision() const;
int stream.precision(int p);
```

The first version gets the stream's current precision. The second version sets a new value and returns the old. By default, the precision of a stream is six digits.

Although supported by all stream objects, this function is mainly used with output streams.

Example

```
double pi = 3.141592;
cout.precision(4);
cout << "To 4 decimal points, pi is: " << pi << endl;
```

put   Write a character

Purpose

Function. Writes a single character to an output stream.

Syntax

```
#include <iostream.h>

ostream& outputstream.put(char ch);
```

The function writes the character *ch* and returns a reference to the stream — that is, the object through which the function was called.

Example

This example prints the contents of a file. The code assumes that infile is a previously opened stream.

```
char c;
while (!infile.eof()) {
    c = infile.get();
    outfile.put(c);
}
```

putback   Put back last character

Purpose

Function. Places the last character read back onto an input stream.

Syntax

```
#include <iostream.h>

istream& inputstream.putback(char ch);
```

inputstream is an object of type istream or any of its derived classes: fstream, ifstream, istrstream, and strstream.

This function places *ch* back onto the input stream; it is assumed that a character was read and that this character was *ch*. The library definition guarantees that you can put back one character. There is no guarantee that you can put back any more than one. You can think of putback as working with a one-character buffer. Once this buffer is emptied, you should not call putback again until you have read at least one character.

The function returns a reference to the stream — that is, the object through which putback was called.

Example

The following example reads a character; if it is the delimiter character, the code terminates the token string and puts the delimiter character back onto the stream.

```
char c, delim = '\n';
char token[256];
char *p = token;
//....
c = infile.get();
if (c == delim) {
    *p = '\0';
    infile.putback(c);
} else
    *p++ = c;
```

rdstate   Return error flags

Purpose

Function. Returns an integer containing a set of status flags.

Syntax

```
#include <iostream.h>

int stream.rdstate() const;
```

The value returned by rdstate contains several status flags. You can use the bitwise AND operator (&), along with bit masks (as is done in "Example"), to test for the presence of an error flag, but you test for ios::goodbit by comparing the value directly to 0.

Flag	Description
ios::goodbit	No errors. (This is equal to 0.)
ios::eofbit	No more characters available; end-of-file condition has occurred.
ios::failbit	Nonfatal I/O error.
ios::badbit	Fatal I/O error.

Example

This example (which assumes that inf is a previously open stream) prints out all the text in the stream, one line at a time, stopping only when the end-of-file condition is flagged.

```
char str[256];
while (!(inf.rdstate() & ios::eofbit)) {
    inf.getline(str, 256);
    cout << str << endl;
}
```

Note the eof, good, fail, and bad functions provide other, more direct ways to get the same status information provided by rdstate.

read	**Read data in binary format**

Purpose

Function. Performs a binary read on an input stream; this reads binary values exactly as they are found rather than interpreting them as text.

Syntax

```
#include <iostream.h>

istream& inputstream.read(char *buf, int num);
```

inputstream is an object of type istream or one of its derived classes: fstream, ifstream, istrstream, or strstream.

The function reads exactly *num* bytes into the char* array pointed to by *buf* (which may also have type unsigned char* or signed char*). Null termination is not a factor in the behavior of read. The function returns a reference to the stream — that is, the object through which the function was called.

To determine how many bytes were actually read, call the gcount function. If fewer bytes were read than requested, this means that the end of the stream has been reached.

Remarks

Although read uses a char* buffer, you should not assume that you are limited to text. A char* buffer is used because it's convenient to think of the data as a series of raw bytes.

After you read the data, you need to extract it from a char buffer. Of course, you don't want the bits to change. The solution is to recast pointer types. This does not alter data, but makes the compiler treat the buffer address as a pointer to a different type. This way, you can use that address to get any kind of data you want. For example, this code reads a long. (It assumes that a long was previously written to the file.)

I/O Stream Classes

```
char buffer[256];
long amount;

// Read into char array.
infile.read(buffer, sizeof(long));

// Copy long data from char array. Use ptr cast.
amount = *(long*) buffer;
```

Example

This example is a complete hex-dump program. It prints out the numeric value of every byte in the file.

```
#include <fstream.h>   // Brings in iostream.h

void print_data(char *bytes, int num);

int main() {
    char name[81], dat[16];
    int n;
    cout << "Enter the name of the file: ";
    cin >> name;
    ifstream fin(name, ios::in | ios::nocreate);
    if (!fin) {
        cout << "File could not be opened.";
        return 1;
    }
    do {
        fin.read(dat, 16);
        n = fin.gcount();
        print_data(dat, n);
    } while (n == 16);   // If < 16 bytes read, quit.
    return 0;
}


// Print up to 16 bytes in hex code.
void print_data(char *p, int num){
    int i;
    for (i = 1; i <= num; i++, p++)
        cout << hex << *p << ' ';
    cout << endl;
}
```

The key lines of the program are:

```
do {
    fin.read(dat, 16);
    n = fin.gcount();
    print_data(dat, n);
} while (n == 16);
```

The read function attempts to read 16 bytes; the gcount function returns the number of bytes actually read. When this number is less than 16, you know that the end of the file has been reached. At that point, the program prints as many bytes as it has and then stops.

It is possible to refine the code so that print_data displays a prettier line of output, including ASCII equivalents for printable characters. This is left as an exercise.

seekg — Move "get" pointer

Purpose
Function. Moves the *get pointer*, which determines the next byte to read.

Syntax
```
#include <iostream.h>

istream& inputstream.seekg(streamoff offset,
    ios::seek_dir origin);
istream& inputstream.seekg(streampos position);
```

inputstream is an object of type istream or any of its derived classes: fstream, ifstream, istrstream, or strstream. However, this function does not work with standard input.

The first version of the function takes an integer and one of three reference points. This is the easiest and most versatile to use. The *offset* argument has type streamoff defined in iostream.h; this is actually an integer type large enough to hold any valid offset. The *origin* argument is passed one of three values:

Flag	Description
ios::beg	Seek from beginning of the file.
ios::cur	Seek from current position, forward.
ios::end	Seek from end of file, forward. This is useful when you are appending to a file, but it is not especially useful with "get" operations.

The second version of seekg syntax takes an argument of type streampos, which must be previously returned by a call to tellg or tellp. This version is useful for moving to a "bookmark" set with one of those functions.

Both versions return a reference to the stream itself.

Examples

These examples assume that infile is a previously opened file stream, and that the file consists of structures of type employee_rec. The second operation moves to record n + 1, because the first record is at offset 0.

```
// Move to beginning of the file.
infile.seekg(0, ios::beg);

// Move to record #n+1.
infile.seekg(n * sizeof(employee_rec), ios::beg);
```

seekp · Move "put" pointer

Purpose

Function. Moves the *put pointer*, which determines the next byte to write to.

Syntax

```
#include <iostream.h>

ostream& outputstream.seekp(streamoff offset,
    ios::seek_dir origin);
ostream& outputstream.seekp(streampos position);
```

outputstream is an object of type ostream or any of its derived classes: fstream, ofstream, ostrstream, or strstream. However, this function does not work with standard output.

In almost every other respect, this function is identical to the seekg function. See seekg (p. 285) for more information on arguments. There is some redundancy here; with input streams, you use seekg; with output streams, you use seekp. In the case of read/write streams, you can use either. On most systems, there is actually only one file pointer per file.

Examples

These examples assume that outfile is a previously opened file stream, and that the file consists of structures of type employee_rec. The second operation moves to record n + 1, because the first record is at offset 0.

```
// Move to beginning of the file.
outfile.seekp(0, ios::beg);

// Move to record #n+1.
outfile.seekp(n * sizeof(employee_rec), ios::beg);
```

setf   Turn on format flags

Purpose

Function. Sets one or more format flags for a stream; this function only
affects the flags specified.

Syntax

```
#include <iostream.h>

long stream.setf(long flags);
long stream.setf(long flags1, long flags2);
```

The first version sets the flags contained in the *flags* argument by perform-
ing a bitwise OR (|). Consequently, all flags specified in the argument are
turned on; any existing flags that are on stay on as well. Here is the action
in terms of bitwise operators:

```
new_flags = old_flags | flags
```

The second version clears all the flags specified in *flags2*. It then turns on
flag values specified in *flags1*, but only if they are also specified in *flags2*.
In other words, "If a flag is set in *flags2*, give the flag the same value it has
in *flags1*. Otherwise, leave it alone." Here is the action in terms of bitwise
operators:

```
new_flags = (old_flags & ~flags2) | (flags1 & flags2)
```

Both versions of the function return the previous value of the flag settings,
contained in a long integer. Remember that the function always acts on a
particular stream. Each stream maintains its own format flags.

Examples

This example turns on hexadecimal display for the standard output stream
cout, leaving other flags unaffected. This flag affects all subsequent integer
output.

```
cout.setf(ios::hex);
```

This next example turns on two flags for cout, leaving other flags unaffected.

```
cout.setf(ios::hex | ios::showbase);
```

I/O Stream Classes

setmode   Set binary or text mode

Purpose
Function. Switches a file to binary or text mode.

Syntax
```
#include <fstream.h>   // Brings in iostream.h

int filestream.setmode(int mode=filebuf::text);
```

filestream is an object of type fstream, ifstream, or ofstream. The *mode* argument, if specified, must be one of these values:

- filebuf::text, which specifies text mode
- filebuf::binary, which specifies binary mode

If no argument is specified, the default value filebuf::text is used.

Remarks
There is rarely any reason to call this function, because text mode (the default) or binary mode is specified when the file is opened.

Example
This example opens a file in binary mode and then switches to text mode.
```
fstream fs("c::\\junk.txt", ios::in | ios::binary);
//...
fs.setmode();  // Switch to text mode.
```

str   Get address of string buffer

Purpose
Function. Gets the address of string buffer used by an array-based stream.

Syntax
```
#include <strstrea.h>  // Brings in iostream.h

char* arraystream.str();
```

arraystream is an object of type istrstream, ostrrstream, or strstream.

If the stream was created with a fixed-length buffer, the str function simply returns the address of that buffer. If the stream was created with a dynamic string buffer (see ostrstream or strstream), the function returns the address of the buffer and freezes the data; this causes further write operations to be ignored. The stream can be unfrozen again by calling *arraystream*.freeze(false).

This freezing is necessary, because a dynamic buffer needs to be moved around in memory from time to time if it is to accommodate unlimited growth. Once the stream commits to a fixed string location, it's no longer able to grow safely; therefore, write operations are ignored. Unfreezing solves the growth problem, but invalidates the fixed address.

Example

```
#include <strstrea.h>

strstream ss;    // Use dynamic buffer.
ss << "The value of n is: ";
ss << n << endl;
ss << "Some more data." << endl;
cout << ss.str();   // Print contents of ss.
                    // Contents of ss now frozen, until
                    //  freeze(false) called.
```

strstream   String I/O class

Purpose

Class. Defines functions for both reading and writing to an array. Inherits from both istream and ostream. See also istrstream (p. 273) and ostrstream (p. 278), which are more specific.

Constructors

```
#include <strstrea.h>

strstream();
strstream(char* pch, int length, int mode);
```

The first constructor creates a stream using an internal string buffer that is empty at first, but dynamically expanded and moved as needed. The stream is opened for read/write operations.

The second constructor uses a string buffer of fixed length. The mode argument must be explicitly set; acceptable values are ios::in, ios::out, and ios::in|ios::out, which enables both read and write operations.

If you use the first constructor, then at some point, you need to call the str function to get a pointer to the data. Calling this function freezes the internal string buffer; all further output is ignored until you call the freeze function with a false argument, to unfreeze the buffer. See "Examples" under ostrstream (p. 279).

Member Functions

The strstream class supports the following member functions. Functions originating in this class are in bold.

bad	**freeze**	precision	**str**
clear	gcount	put	sync_with_stdio
eatwhite	get	putback	tellg
eof	getline	rdstate	tellp
fail	good	read	unsetf
fill	ignore	seekg	width
flags	**pcount**	seekp	write
flush	peek	setf	

Operations

This class inherits both the insertion operator (<<) from the istream class and the extraction (>>) operator from the ostream class.

Example

The following example writes and reads from the same string. Note that after writing, you need to seek to the position you want to read from.

```
#include <strstrea.h>
//...
char str[500];
int n;
strstream ss(str, 500, ios::in | ios::out);
ss << "25 35 50";
ss.seekg(0, ios::beg);   // Move to beginning of file.
ss >> n;                 // Read value of n from ss.
cout << n << endl;       // Print value of n.
```

sync_with_stdio — Sync with global I/O functions

Purpose

Function. Coordinates I/O classes with stdio.h functions, so that you can use both in the same program.

Syntax

```
#include <iostream.h>


static void stream.sync_with_stdio();
```

This function can be called through any stream object. The effect is to coordinate all I/O functions and classes. If you do not call this function and attempt to use both kinds of I/O operations, the use of separate buffers for the same device (such as the monitor) can cause baffling results for the end user.

I/O Stream Classes

Example

```
cin.sync_with_stdio();
```

tellg — Tell position of "get" pointer

Purpose

Function. Returns the position of the *get pointer*, which determines which byte to read.

Syntax

```
#include <iostreaam.h>

streampos inputstream.tellg();
```

inputstream is an object of type istream or any of its derived classes: fstream, ifstream, istrstream, or strstream. However, this function does not work with standard input.

The function returns the current position in the stream as a value of type streampos. This value, in turn, can be passed later to the seekg function to jump back to where you are now.

There is little difference between this function and tellp, except that tellp works with output streams.

Example

This example assumes that infile is a previously opened file stream.

```
streampos saved_pos = infile.tellg();
//...
infile.seekg(saved_pos);    // Jump back!
```

tellp — Tell position of "put" pointer

Purpose

Function. Returns the position of the *put pointer*, which determines which byte to write to.

Syntax

```
#include <iostreaam.h>

streampos outputstream.tellp();
```

outputstream is an object of type ostream or any of its derived classes: fstream, ofstream, ostrstream, or strstream. However, this function does not work with standard output.

The function returns the current position in the stream as a value of type streampos. This value, in turn, can be passed later to the seekp function to jump back to where you are now.

There is little difference between this function and tellg, except that tellg works with input streams.

Example

This example assumes that outfile is a previously opened file stream.

```
streampos saved_pos = outfile.tellp();
//...
outfile.seekp(saved_pos);    // Jump back!
```

unsetf   Turn off format flags

Purpose

Function. Turns off one or more flags; this function only affects the flags specified.

Syntax

```
#include <iostream.h>

long stream.unsetf(long flags);
```

This function clears all the flags specified in *flags*. In other words, it reverses the bit values of *flags2* and performs a bitwise AND (&). Here is the action in terms of bitwise operators:

```
new_flags = old_flags & ~flags
```

The function returns the previous value of the flag settings, contained in a single long integer. Remember that this function is always relative to a particular stream. Each stream maintains its own format flags.

Examples

This example turns off the ios::showbase flag for the standard output stream, cout. This does not affect any other flags.

```
cout.unsetf(ios::showbase);
```

This next example turns off two flags.

```
cout.setf(ios::showbase | ios::scientific);
```

width   Get or set field width

Purpose
Function. Gets or sets the print-field width of a stream; this determines the
minimum space a number display occupies.

Syntax
```
#include <iostream.h>

int stream.width() const;
int stream.width(int w);
```

The first version returns the stream's current width attribute. The second
version sets a new value and returns the old.

Although all stream objects support this function, it is mainly useful with output streams. Each number is printed into a field this size or wider. If the number display is smaller, it is left-justified (or right-justified if the ios::right flag
is turned on) and padded with the fill character.

You can use this function to help make a column of numbers line up.

Example
```
cout.width(7);
cout.precision(1);
cout << 1.0 << endl;
cout << 22.53 << endl;
cout << 100.2 << endl;
```

The output of this code is:

```
    1.0
   22.5
  100.2
```

write   Write data in binary format

Purpose
Function. Performs a binary write to an input stream; this writes binary values exactly as they are rather than translating them into text.

Syntax
```
#include <iostream.h>

ostream& outputstream.write(char *buf, int num);
```

I/O Stream Classes

outputstream is an object of type ostream or any of its derived classes: fstream, ofstream, ostrstream, or strstream.

The function writes exactly *num* bytes from the char* array pointed to by *buf* (which may also have type unsigned char* or signed char*). Null termination is not a factor in the behavior of write. The function returns a reference to the stream — that is, the object through which the function was called.

Remarks

Although write uses a char* buffer, you should not assume that you are limited to text. A char* buffer is used because it's convenient to think of the data as a series of raw bytes.

Before you write the data, you need to coerce it into the char buffer. Of course, you don't want the bits to change. The solution is to recast pointer types. This does not alter data, but it does make the compiler treat the buffer address as a pointer to a different type. This way, you can use that address to hold any data you want. For example, this code writes a long to a file:

```
char buffer[256];
long amount = 1999;

// Copy long data into char array. Use ptr cast.
*(long*)buffer = amount;

// Write out 4 bytes of the char array.
outfile.write(buffer, sizeof(long));
```

Example

This program example writes out a record containing a floating-point number, two integers, and a string. Then it seeks to the twentieth record and writes these same values again.

```
#include <fstream.h>  // Brings in iostream.h
#include <string.h>

struct funny_rec {
    double x;
    int i, j;
    char name[40];
};

int main() {
    ifstream outfile("c:\\junk.dat", ios::out);
    if (!outfile) {
        cout << "File could not be opened.";
        return 1;
```

I/O Stream Classes

```
        }
        char buffer[1000];
        funny_rec rek;
        rek.x = 27.5;
        rek.i = 1;
        rek.j = 2;
        strcpy(rek.text, "Janet the Enforcer");
        *(funny_rec*) buffer = rek;
        outfile.write(buffer, sizeof(rek));
        outfile.seekp(19 * sizeof(rek), ios::beg);
        outfile.write(buffer, sizeof(rek));
        return 0;
}
```

C++ Tutorial

english in plain english in p
ain english in plain english in
plain english in plain english
english in plain english in p
plain english in plain english
english in plain english in p
ain english in plain english in
plain english in plain english
english in plain english in p
ain english in plain english in
plain english in plain english
english in plain english in p

This part provides general background on C++ and object orientation. If you are new to the C and C++ languages, you should start with Chapter 1. If you are familiar with C but new to C++, start with Chapters 4 and 5. (In that case, you still might want to look at Chapter 1 for an overview of the general concepts of object orientation.) Later chapters focus on advanced areas such as operator overloading (Chapter 7) and virtual functions (Chapter 9).

IN THIS PART

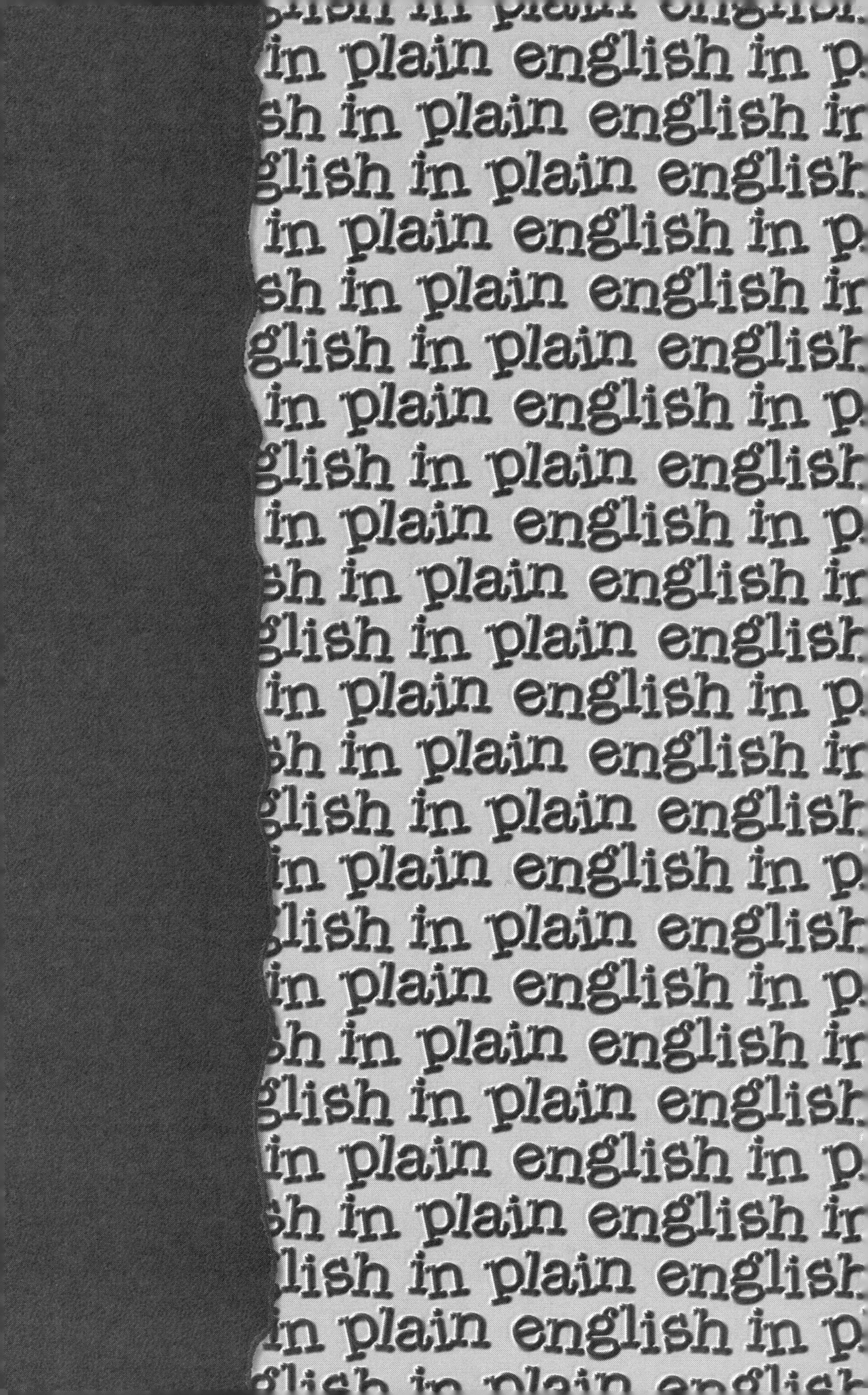

What C++ Will Do for You

1

In the Dark Ages of computers, programmers were slaves to the machine. Developers had to write all their instructions in binary codes (representing 1s and 0s), the computer's native language. As time went on, newer programming languages gave programmers better ways to express program logic and data structures. Improvements in computer languages meant that programmers could be less concerned with the internal structure of the computer and more focused on the purpose of the program.

Object-oriented programming takes the evolution of software a little further. Although its benefits have perhaps been over-sold, the object-oriented approach does improve programmer efficiency. In traditional, pre-object-oriented programming, the most significant structural element is the division between code and data. This division accurately reflects the internal workings of a computer, but it is not a realistic way of representing the world in general.

Object-oriented programming, however, is analogous to the human brain. This organ is a colossal set of individual brain cells. To borrow computer terminology, each cell is an *object*,

1

having both its own underlying material (data) and programmed behavior (code). It would be nonsensical to try to separate these different aspects of a brain cell, asking where its code is and where its data is. It would be more nonsensical to ask where all the code of the brain is and where all its data is.

This analogy summarizes what object orientation is all about: it replaces the traditional approach with an approach that makes *objects* the fundamental units. Objects are units that combine state information and behavior, and each object can send signals and respond to stimuli just as cells in the brain do.

Programs written with object-oriented languages don't automatically model reality better than other programs do. A successful program is more the result of careful thought, planning, and diligence than of the choice of language. Still, if you're going to adopt the object-oriented approach (and more and more system software requires it), many features of an object-oriented language such as C++ are extremely convenient and helpful.

Why C++? C++ probably isn't the most widely used object-oriented language; more people probably use Visual Basic, and, arguably, Visual Basic is object-oriented. However, C++ is a close contender. More significantly, most programmers view C++ as the most comprehensive object-oriented language. One can argue that Smalltalk or Eiffel is a purer implementation of object orientation, but C++ certainly sets the standard by which other languages are measured. Knowing C++ has become important to a programmer's career, almost as important today as knowing C was a few years ago. Any large, serious development project started today is likely to be written in C++. To development managers, C++ is the state of the art.

To some, Java is the emerging language of the future, at least in the area of applications for the Internet. It's instructive to note, however, how much of Java's syntax is taken from C++. In fact, if you learn C++ first, Java is extremely easy to learn.

In any case, it's worth asking, why use C++? As with C, the answer has a great deal to do with the need for both power and efficiency.

The Origins of C++

C++ has its origins in, of all things, the Norwegian armed forces. From Norway came a language called *Simula*, one of the first languages to use classes (a *class* being a program unit containing both data and associated functions). Classes, as you learn in this book, are closely linked to the idea of objects, a class being an object type.

Simula was developed to model events. Although the two concepts are not identical, an *event-driven* model of program organization has much in common with an object-oriented model. This is why Visual Basic, Windows, OS/2 Presentation Manager, and many other event-driven architectures are object oriented, or at least object based. Because of its concept of independent objects responding to messages, object orientation is a natural way to implement an event-driven system.

Enter Bjarne Stroustrup who, in 1978, was writing a simulator for distributed computer systems as part of his doctoral program at the Computing Laboratory at Cambridge University. Stroustrup found Simula's use of classes a perfect way to express the interaction of different machines on a network. The problem was that Simula was inefficient for the large-scale systems programming he was doing. He needed the object-oriented features of Simula combined with the power and efficiency of a language such as . . . well, such as C.

C++ was born of this marriage. Stroustrup created C++ as a C language with classes and added Simula's stronger sense of data types. "C with classes" went through a few iterations before it became the C++ accepted as standard today. But the language is still a realization of Stroustrup's original vision of C married to Simula classes.

Making the Transition from C to C++

You may have heard that C++ is a "better C than C." What people mean by this is that C++ has a superset of the features found in C. They claim that you can compile the same program in C++ that you can in C, and that, in addition, C++ provides some nice refinements that you can add to your program without going all the way to object orientation.

The first part of the preceding statement is only approximately true. Many C programs can be compiled as C++ programs without change, but an occasional nagging difference crops up in some programs. A goal of this book is to point out these differences as clearly as possible. (For the most complete help here, see Appendix A [p. 498].)

The important point is that C++ does not *impose* object orientation on you. It may come as a relief to know that if you are a C programmer, you can switch to C++, observe the few additional restrictions that C++ imposes, and keep right on going. You don't have to rewrite anything as an object. As you spend more time with C++, you can gradually introduce more of the C++ extensions into your programming.

Classes: Organization by Objects

If you're going to take the time and trouble to bother with C++, though, you probably want to pierce to the heart of what C++ is all about — object orientation. Conceptually, an object is simply a data structure that may have built-in functions associated with it. (A *class*, a topic that comes up often in this book, is an object type.) It may seem as if C++ has quite a few operators, keywords, and rules — mostly to handle special cases; yet the idea of objects itself is elegant and simple.

Traditional program organization represents how things work in computer software and not how things work in life. Technically, all the contents of a computer memory constitute data, but a significant portion of what's stored in memory is a special kind of data called *code*. The code comprises instructions to the processor: add two numbers, jump to a new address, and so on. Other memory contents make up *data* as people normally use the term: information for you or the computer to use.

Code and data are well segregated inside computer memory because (unlike a human brain) a computer has only one central processor, and this processor treats code and data differently. Large chunks of code have to be organized together into code segments because the processor executes them sequentially, only occasionally jumping to a new location. Program organization reflects this fact. Typically, code is organized into a hierarchy of *functions*, each function being a collection of instructions executed as a block. Data is organized into records (structures), arrays, and tables.

Despite all this nice structure, the resulting program is a hierarchy of functions alongside a collection of unrelated data structures. The traditional programming language does not enforce any connection between the two groups (see Figure 1-1).

Is this segregation of code and data a problem? It's usually fine for simpler programs, but a programmer has to remember which functions are supposed to use which data structures, or errors occur.

Even the computer's own hardware doesn't fit the traditional model of software, as you'll see if you open your computer. The structure of the computer itself doesn't reflect the code/data distinction! Instead, the board consists of a number of independent chips that are wired to send signals back and forth to each other (Figure 1-2).

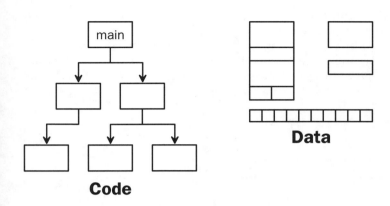

Figure 1-1   *Traditional program organization segregates code and data.*

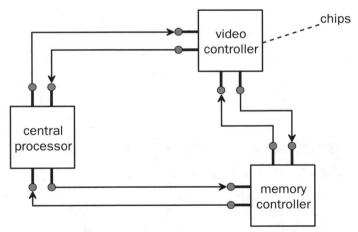

Figure 1-2   *Life inside the system box.*

   In the object-oriented approach, the chips become objects. In C++ terminology, the make and model of a chip (for example, Pentium) is a *class*; an individual chip is an *object*. A software emulation of a chip is neither pure code nor pure data. Like a brain cell, a chip has both code (behavior) and data (state information).

If you set out to write a program to emulate the internals of computer hardware, you will find that design and programming will be greatly aided by representing each chip as an object. This is where the object-oriented side of C++ most clearly differs from C: the fundamental unit of program organization becomes not code or data, but the object's *class* — which is a type containing both code and data (Figure 1-3).

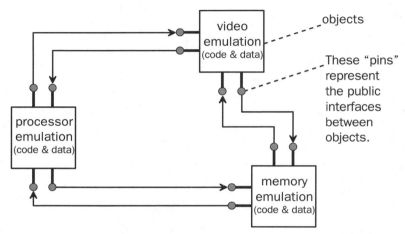

Figure 1-3 *Object organization.*

Encapsulation: Cure for a Programming Headache

One of the most important ideas in Figure 1-3 is the *black box* concept. Chips communicate with each other only through specific pins; except for these interfaces, each chip is a mystery to all the others. No chip can reach in and interfere with the internal workings of another chip. Moreover, people who design computers need know nothing about the internal circuitry of a chip as long as the chip's input and output do precisely what the manufacturer says they do.

The benefits of this black box feature are substantial. The system works because each chip has a functional specification that states exactly how the chip behaves. As long as you can find another chip that adheres to the same specification, you can pop out an old chip and replace it with a new one and the whole system will continue to work as it did before. It may be that the internal circuitry of the new chip is completely different — but you don't care. As long as a chip interacts the same way with the rest of the system, any two chips are interchangeable.

Nowhere is there a greater need for interchangeable parts than in software development. In a typical project, a software team constantly rewrites the internals of every part of the program. To make an analogy, the programmers are continually popping out old chips and replacing them with new ones to fix bugs, improve efficiency, or add new features. In the traditional approach, different parts of the program are not cleanly divided, with often-disastrous results. A change to any part of a program can potentially affect every other part. The work that programmer Pete is doing, for example, can reach in and refer to the internals of the part that programmer Camille is writing. But as soon as Camille makes any changes, all of Pete's assumptions become invalid, and errors happen.

To some extent, the features of the C language can be used to mitigate this problem. The connecting links between different modules — the *interfaces* — can be managed at the file level. Specifically, you have programmers Pete and Camille stick to working on different files and then show restraint in declaring data as shared. Certain facilities of the C language (such as the `extern` and `static` keywords) can be used to control which data and functions in one file are visible to other files.

C++ provides much finer control over the sharing of data and functions between parts of the program. The unit of data protection is no longer limited to the file level; it can be as large or as small a unit as you want — a class. With C++, you can make any functions or data (members) private at the class level. These private members become invisible to the rest of the program; they cannot be accessed. The public members of an object make up its interface. These public members constitute the "pins" that are visible outside an object. The rest of the program can refer to these members, and the assumption is that they will not change. Meanwhile, you can rewrite the internals of a class to your heart's content.

The clean division between interface and internals is called *encapsulation*, which is a fancy name for "protecting the insides of something." C++'s approach to encapsulation provides more control over *scope* — the visibility of variables within the program. Encapsulation also makes the public/private distinction explicit in the source code. The language is a great aid to documenting which part of a class is its interface and which part is internal.

1

● **NOTE**

When you're first learning about C++ and object orientation, you may be tempted to use the terms *object* and *class* interchangeably. The distinction, however, is important: a class is a type and an object is an instance of that type. I have a lot more to say about that distinction in Chapter 5.

Polymorphism: Decentralized Control

An ideal of an object-oriented system is that each object be as independent as possible. I should be able to send a generalized signal to an object and have it respond appropriately; I shouldn't have to know how it carries out the response, or even what precise type the object is.

To use another hardware analogy, I should be able to send out a general `print` command without knowing the make and model of the printer ahead of time. As long as everyone observes the same protocol for communication, my `print` command should always work. I know, in a general way, what the command should do: print my document. A dot-matrix printer will respond to the `print` command very differently than a laser printer.

The point with object orientation is that I want my main function or main loop to know as little as possible. Decisions as to how to carry out a command should reside in the objects themselves. At times, it is much better for the main function to send only a general signal.

Chapter 9 has a simple example of how this might work. The example uses a series of menu commands. When a user selects a command, the main function sends a message, `Do_Command`, to the appropriate menu object, which then responds in a completely different way, depending on which command it represents (Figure 1-4).

This approach is superior because the program is never limited to a particular set of commands. All the main function does is send a `Do_Command` message to the appropriate menu object, and then the right thing happens. This approach supports future development of new menu commands without the need to rewrite the main function. It also opens the possibility of dynamically changing menu items. The menu can grow or change at runtime, which is impossible with a traditional approach.

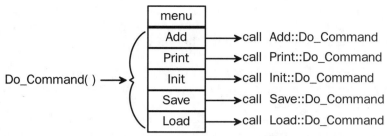

Figure 1-4   *A polymorphic menu system sends a general command to a menu object.*

Object-oriented theorists refer to this mechanism as *polymorphism* ("many forms," from the Greek). This is a long word, but all it really means is decentralized control. Different objects respond to the same message (function call) in different ways. Fewer decisions have to be centralized in the main loop.

This kind of design, by the way, is a crucial part of any graphical user interface system, such as the Macintosh or Microsoft Windows. The operating system cannot know ahead of time how all windows might work; otherwise, application development would be extremely limited. Instead, the operating system must rely on the individual windows to respond in their own ways to general messages (such as "Initialize your display").

This same kind of mechanism can be implemented in C by callback functions; callback functions, however, are wild and unregulated. To control how objects respond to messages, C++ uses a more structured approach involving inheritance hierarchies and virtual functions. You learn more about these terms in Chapters 8 and 9. In practical terms, the important thing to know is that the C++ approach is more reliable and convenient, and is self-documenting.

C++ and Strengthened Types

Object orientation is what's most interesting about C++. The most fundamental theme in C++, however, is that it has a much stronger concept of *types* than C does. (A variable's type determines what kind of data it can store and how it stores that data.) Even object orientation can be seen as an extension of the idea of stronger types: C++ strengthens types to the extent that they can contain code as well as data.

C++'s emphasis on types is an aid to safer, more reliable programming, whether or not you use objects. In C, it is easy to accidentally use a variable declared as a 4-byte floating-point number in one module and as an 8-byte number in another module. The result is a large error at runtime. C++ prevents such errors through *type-safe linkage*, which prevents the linker from equating two symbols having different type information.

Overloading is another concept that runs through C++. Overloading uses type information to distinguish how functions and operators should work. It reflects the importance of types in the language.

Function overloading

Overloading means reusing a name. In C++, one of the most common examples of this is *function overloading*, which means writing two different versions of the same function. In actuality, overloaded functions are completely distinct and have separate function definitions as well as separate declarations. From the programmer's perspective, function overloading is a convenient way of providing multiple variations on the same theme.

For example, you can write two versions of the GetNum function. One version takes a pointer to an integer, and the other version takes a pointer to a floating-point number. Each version has a separate function definition. C++ uses the type information in the argument list to differentiate the functions. When a call to GetNum appears in source code, C++ looks at the data type of the argument to determine which of these two functions to call:

```
void GetNum(int *pn);
void GetNum(double *pf);
```

Operator overloading

Operator overloading is similar to function overloading. When C++ encounters an operator (such as +, - , /, or *), it examines the types of the operands to determine how to evaluate them. Implicit in this last statement is that operators can be applied to any type. In C++, you can apply addition (+), subtraction (-), or any of the other standard operators to a type — provided that the type declaration defines how the operator works. In other words, you can write a function that defines how the addition operator (+) works when applied to your type. For example, in Chapters 5, 6, and 7, I build a CStr class that uses addition (+) to concatenate strings, just as in Visual Basic:

```
CStr name, first("Bernie"), last("Schwartz");

name = first + last;
```

Operator overloading, in effect, lets you create types (that is, classes) that look like true extensions to the C++ language. These types become as fundamental as int (integer) or long (long integer). You can apply any operator to your own types, just as you can to primitive types.

C++: Future Directions

Over the last few years, the position of C++ as the definitive object-oriented language has strengthened. Although C++ is not the purest flavor of object-orientation available, it is now so widely used as to become almost a requirement for serious programmers.

During these last few years, the proposed American National Standards Institute (ANSI) standard for C++ has become more stable, although it has added some new areas for C++ compilers to support. In particular, Amendment 1 to the ANSI specification includes substantial support for wide-character strings.

This, in turn, reflects the changing nature of software. Wide-character strings are important for international applications, which have to be able to support any natural language — including languages such as Chinese and Japanese. These languages have large character sets that cannot be accommodated by the 1-byte ASCII format.

The software world is changing in other ways. A few years ago, the standard processor width was 16 bits for most platforms, and the standard int type in C and C++ was implemented as 16 bits. Now, a processor width of 32 bits is almost universal. Consequently, the int type is 32-bits wide on nearly all C and C++ compilers.

But even 32 bits is not the ultimate size. In 1999, the ISO C-language standard added the long long type to support 64-bit integers, and most C++ compilers have followed suit.

A further development is the ANSI specification for a Standard Template Library. This is a large, complex subject that requires its own book — or at least a larger book than this.

In short, C++ has become stable while keeping pace with the world in which we live. If you are serious about programming, it's definitely the language to know in the new millennium. Although it is challenging, at least at first, you will find your effort well rewarded.

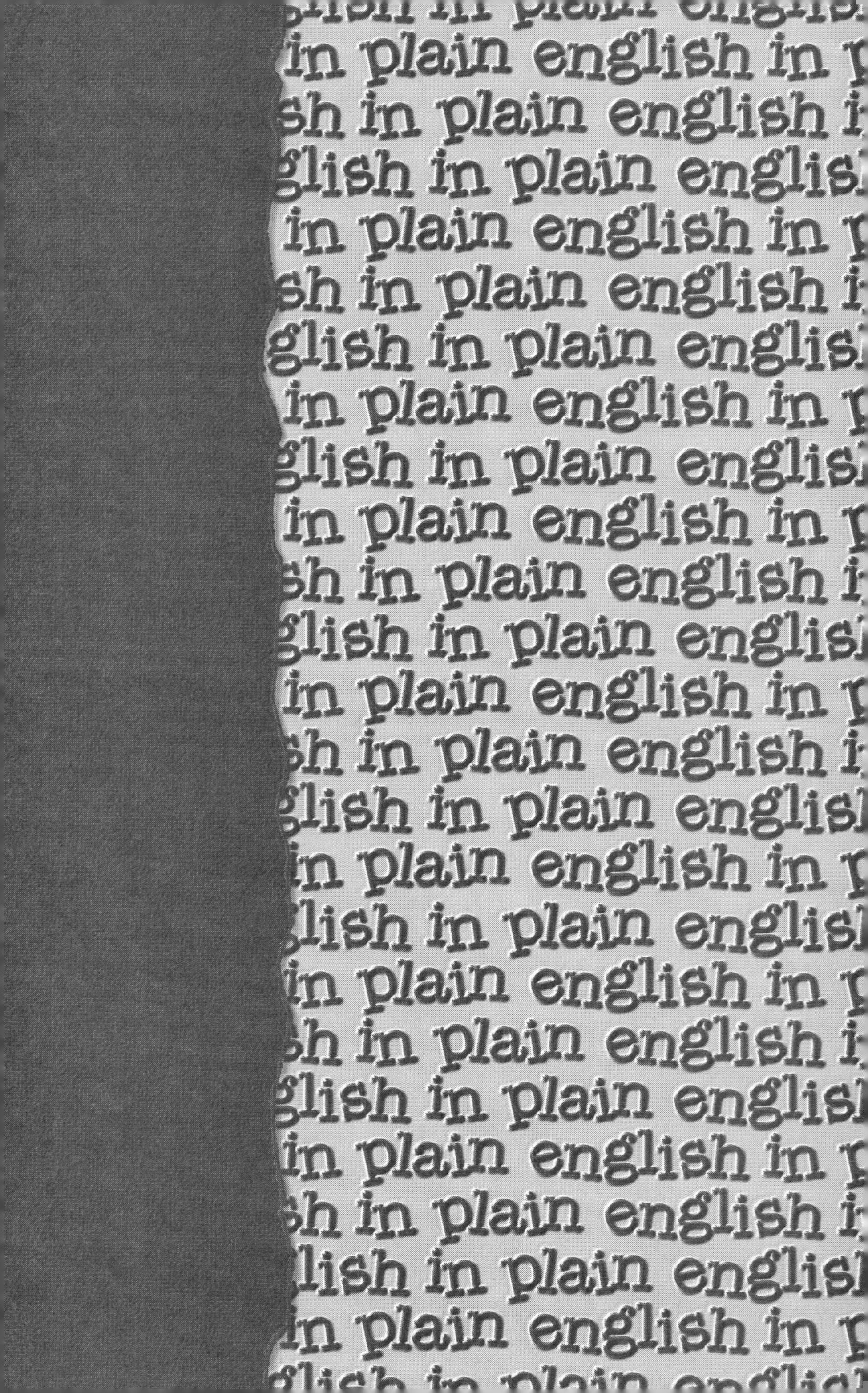

Basic Features of
C++ Programs

2

The core features of C and C++ are more complex — but not *that* much more complex — than core features of some other popular languages. At first, you have to spend a little time thinking about semicolons (;) and operator precedence. But this additional complexity buys you a lot more power and flexibility, as well as the ability to write compact code.

Most of the features that intimidate programmers new to C and C++ have to do with pointers — sharp, scary items that access data indirectly. This topic is sufficiently important that it's relegated to its own chapter (see Chapter 3). In the meantime, you can relax. I won't jab you with pointers just yet.

C and C++ are two distinct languages, but they share the same basic structure. For simplicity's sake, this chapter refers just to C++, pointing out places where the rules for C are different from those of C++.

Your First C++ Program

The first test of a programming system is to print a simple string of text characters. Such a program in C++ is not quite as simple as in BASIC, but neither is it very long:

```
#include <stdio.h>

void main () {
    printf("Can you C++ now?");
}
```

As you type this program, you should notice several things. First, capitalization counts in C++, in contrast to other languages such as FORTRAN and BASIC. When you enter keywords and names, C++ expects you to match uppercase and lowercase letters precisely, and it gets upset if you don't match them. Another thing to watch for is the punctuation: the semicolon (;) and the braces ({}). You must enter these characters as indicated.

However, in some ways C++ gives you more freedom than other languages. On any given line, you can space things many different ways, and you can even put syntax elements on different lines. C++ doesn't care.

```
#include <stdio.h>

void
main ()
{
    printf
        ("Can you C++ now?");
}
```

This version works because C++ uses the semicolon (;) to determine where the printf statement ends; it usually ignores the end of the physical line (except in the case of directives — we discuss those later [see p. 317] — and comments). On the one hand, you have to do a little more typing, but on the other hand, the C++ syntax grants you more freedom than BASIC does.

●—**NOTE** ———————————————————————————————

After typing the previous code into a source file, you use a compiler or development environment to *compile* it, which is the process of translating the code into an executable program. For information on how to build a program, see your compiler documentation.

● **C/C++**

Everything in this section applies equally well to the C language, except for one detail: in C, the `void` keyword in front of `main` is optional. In C++, it is required. Here, `void` means that the function (`main`) does not have a `return` statement. More about `void` later.

You can, of course, print your own string instead of "Can you C++ now?" Here's the general pattern for the program:

```
#include <stdio.h>

void main () {
    printf("enter-your-string-here");
}
```

Enter any text you want in place of *enter-your-string-here*.

Adding Data Declarations

Programs start to become interesting and useful at the point where they can store and manipulate information. Such programs need a place to put the data variables.

The C++ variable declaration consists of a type name followed by a variable name and a semicolon. The type tells the compiler what kind of information to store in the variable. Examples of types include `int`, `short`, `long`, `float`, and `double`, among others. This example declares two variables of type `int` (an `int` stores an integer, which is a positive or negative whole number):

```
int variable_name1;
int variable_name2;
```

The C++ variable-declaration syntax is simple. It doesn't involve any extra keyword, such as `Dim` or `var`.

You can create multiple data declarations on the same line. Separate each variable with a comma. The following example declares three variables of type `short` (i, j, k) and three variables of type `float` (x, y, z). These types are short integer and floating point, respectively.

```
short i, j, k;
float x, y, z;
```

The keywords `int`, `short`, and `float` are all different data types in C++. `short` is similar to `int` but is 16 bits wide, unlike `int`, which is 32 bits wide on most current systems. `float` stores floating-point numbers. I'll have more to say about these data types later.

The basic syntax for data declarations in C++ has another interesting twist. You can initialize variables as they are declared. Doing so gives a variable a starting value but does not prevent you from changing it later.

To initialize a variable, use the equals sign followed by a value. For example:

```
int my_var = 0;          // my_var initialized to 0
int your_var = 1;        // your_var initialized to 1
int a, b = 10, c = 12;   // b and c are initialized,
                         //  a is not
```

Before proceeding, we need to discuss comments. In C++, a comment consists of all the text starting with the double slashes (//) forward to the end of the line. The compiler ignores anything in a comment. In theory, you can put any text in a comment, but people usually add comments to explain how the program works.

● C/C++

C++ also supports the begin- and end-comment symbols from the C language (/* and */, respectively). Not all C compilers support the C++ comment-to-end-of-line symbol (//), although some do.

Armed with the ability to declare and initialize data, you can now create a more interesting program:

```
#include <stdio.h>

void main () {
    int x = 1;
    int y = 2;

    printf("The sum of x + y is %d", x + y);
}
```

The printf function supports formatted output. It can take a numeric argument such as x+y and print the value of this number along with other characters. The format character %d means "Print the next argument as a decimal integer." Here, d stands for decimal integer. Floating-point values are printed with %f.

The types defined for you in C++ (as opposed to data types you create yourself as explained in later chapters) are called *primitive data types*. All the primitive types are variations on just two kinds of data: integer and floating-point. Floating-point numbers can hold fractions, and integers can't. Floating-point numbers are more flexible, but integers are more efficient. If you know that a certain variable will never need to hold a fraction, declare it as an integer.

The basic characteristics of the `int`, `short`, `long`, `float`, and double data types are summarized in Table 2-1. The `scanf` function is a data-entry function described later in this chapter.

Table 2-1 *Characteristics of Common Data Types*

Type	Kind of data	Typical size	printf format symbol	scanf format symbol
short	integer	2 bytes	%d	%hd
long	integer	4 bytes	%d	%ld
int	integer	2 or 4 bytes	%d	%d
float	floating point	4 bytes	%f	%f
double	floating point	8 bytes	%f	%lf

● **NOTE**

You can use `i` (integer) as well as `d` (decimal integer). The difference is explained later, in the section on `scanf`, "Getting Input" (see p. 321).

The size of a data type determines its range. For example, the range of a short is –32,768 to 32,767 because that's the range of signed integers you can represent using 16 binary digits (2 bytes). The range of a long is approximately plus or minus 2 billion. For a more comprehensive list of data types and their ranges, see Section 4, page 68.

More About #include

At this point, you may be wondering, "Why do I have to use #include?"
    In C++, every function except main must be *declared* before being used. Declaring a function is a way of telling the compiler how the function will be used: in particular, what kinds of arguments it takes and what value, if any, it returns. Declarations are required for functions you write as well as for standard library functions, such as printf. Rather than declare printf yourself, it's easier to include a special file for this purpose (called a *header file*) that has all the needed declarations. The file stdio.h has declarations for all the standard input/output functions, such as printf.
    #include is a directive rather than a statement. A *directive* is a special command in your source code that is executed before the program is actually compiled. Directives are different from ordinary

lines of code: they begin with a pound sign (#) and are terminated by the end of the line rather than a semicolon (;). In addition, they must begin in column 1. The #include directive tells the compiler to read in a particular header file.

Once you're familiar with the C++ standard library, you can usually figure out which header file(s) are needed without having to look them up. The most common library functions fall into one of the general categories shown in Table 2-2.

Table 2-2 *Common C++ include Files*

Header file	Include directive	Declares these functions
stdio.h	#include <stdio.h>	Standard input and output functions, including functions that perform file operations.
iostream.h	#include <iostream.h>	Stream operators (C++ only), which can be used to replace printf and scanf. Chapter 4 (p. 367) explains the use of the stream operators.
string.h	#include <string.h>	String-manipulation functions; for example, copy one string to another.
ctype.h	#include <ctype.h>	Functions for testing and changing the type of individual characters in a string.
math.h	#include <math.h>	Trigonometric, logarithmic, exponential, and other fun things that engineers love to play with.
malloc.h	#include <malloc.h>	C functions for dynamically getting and freeing blocks of memory from the operating system. (C++ also provides the built-in operators new and delete for this purpose.)

The following syntax display summarizes the general pattern for a simple C program. It doesn't involve any functions except main, but later in the chapter (see p. 325), we add functions to the syntax. All the #include directives should come before anything else in the program; although this is not an absolute rule, it is usually a good idea.

```
include_directives

void main() {
    data_declarations_and_other_statements
}
```

The placeholder *data_declarations_and_other_statements* includes both data declarations, to which you were introduced in the previous section, and other statements, which are often called *executable statements*. This last category is a large one, and I break it down somewhat in the next section.

●—C/C++——————————————————————

With C, all data declarations must appear before all other statements. C++ relaxes this restriction, letting you place declarations almost anywhere.

What Can I Do with a Statement?

After declaring variables, you can use statements to perform a number of actions. These actions usually manipulate or use the variables in some way. In C++, you can mix declarations and other statements in any order. (You can't do that in C.) However, it usually makes sense to declare variables first, because in both C and C++ you must explicitly declare a variable before using it.

Aside from control structures and functions, which I discuss later, all of the actions that you can perform boil down to these three:

- Assign a value (optionally involving a calculation)
- Print output
- Get input

The next three sections discuss how to do each of these actions in C++.

Assigning values

Assignment statements in C++ look similar to those in other languages, especially BASIC. The main difference from BASIC is that C++ statements are terminated by semicolons.

Before assigning data to a variable, make sure that you declare the variable:

```
int amount, a, b, c;
```

To assign a value to one of these four variables, place the variable name on the left side of an equals sign (=). On the right side, place a variable, a constant (such as 1 or –240), or a compound expression (such as 2 * c).

```
a = 1;
amount = -240;
b = 2 * c;
amount = a + 10 * b * -1;
```

In C++, the asterisk (*) represents multiplication.

These statements look very similar to initialization inside a data declaration. In fact, in C++ there is very little difference between initialization and assignment, except that initialization creates a variable and assigns it an initial value.

●—C/C++

Initialization of variables is more restricted in the C language; only constant values can be used to initialize in a data declaration. In C++, this restriction is relaxed; any valid expression can be used to initialize.

Printing output

You can use the `printf` function to print simple strings or to print formatted output displaying any number of numeric values. For example, the following lines of code print two lines, each displaying the value of certain variables. You must first include stdio.h and declare each variable before using it.

```
#include <stdio.h>

void main() {
    int date = 10, d2 = 15;
    float temp = 45.0, t2 = 33.5;

    printf("On Dec. %d, the temperature was %f.\n", date,
        temp);
    printf("On Jan. %d, the temperature was %f.\n", d2,
        t2);
}
```

Note that %d should correspond to an integer argument and %f should correspond to a floating-point argument. These lines of code print these results:

```
On Dec. 10, temperature was 45.000000.
On Jan. 15, temperature was 33.500000.
```

This example introduces another aspect of printing in C++: in a C++ string, the special character \n causes printing to start on a new line. (Not surprisingly, this character is named *newline*.) If this character were omitted from the example, all the output would run together as shown in the following output. The printf function does not automatically append a newline.

```
On Dec. 10, the temperature was 45.000000.On Jan. 15,
the temperature was 33.500000.
```

The newline character is an example of a C++ escape sequence that begins with a backslash. Other sequences include \t, which prints a tab; and \", which prints a double-quotation mark. To print an actual backslash, use two backslashes: \\. See page 360 for a complete list of all the C/C++ escape characters.

●—C/C++

C++, but not C, supports the cin and cout objects as an alternative to printf and scanf. These objects are introduced in Chapter 3, Table 3-2.

Getting input

The scanf function reads data. Although it uses format characters as printf does, it has these differences: First, all the arguments to scanf are memory addresses, so you must place the address operator (&) in front of each variable unless it is a pointer. Second, scanf is stricter about types. A long argument must correspond to the %ld (long decimal) symbol, and a double argument must correspond to the %lf (long floating-point) symbol.

The following lines of code show how you can prompt for and retrieve four different kinds of data. You cannot print a prompt string using scanf; you must use printf to print the string. The format symbols used here are %d, %hd, %ld, %f, and %lf.

```
#include <stdio.h>

void main() {
    int i;
    short sho;
    long lng;
    float flt;
    double dbl;

    printf("Enter a value for i: ");
    scanf("%d", &i);
```

2

```
    printf("Enter a value for sho: ");
    scanf("%hd", &sho);

    printf("Enter a value for lng: ");
    scanf("%ld", &lng);

    printf("Enter a value for flt: ");
    scanf("%f", &flt);

    printf("Enter a value for dbl: ");
    scanf("%lf", &dbl);
}
```

Instead of using the %d symbol, which specifies decimal-integer format, you can use %i, which just specifies integer format. These have the same effect, except that %i permits the user to specify octal or hexadecimal format by using the appropriate prefix (0 or 0x, respectively). For example:

```
printf("Enter a value for i: ");
scanf("%i", &i);

printf("Enter a value for sho: ");
scanf("%hi", &sho);
```

Some C++ Quirks

C++ and C have some quirks — syntax features that are not especially difficult, but may throw you if your background is in another
programming language.

Watch out for that semi!

Probably the most common error encountered by beginning C and
C++ programmers is omitting the semicolon (;). It's also possible
to type a semicolon where C++ doesn't expect one.

The rule for using semicolons is this: Terminate every statement
with a semicolon unless one of the following is true:

- The statement is not really a statement but a directive, such
  as #include or #define, or

- The statement is a compound statement. In practice, this
  means that you don't place a semicolon after a terminating
  brace (}) unless it is the end of a class or variable declaration.

You learn more about classes in Chapter 5. (A semicolon also appears after an initialization list as part of a declaration, but don't worry about that for now.)

The simple program shown in Figure 2-1 demonstrates the rule and the two exceptions.

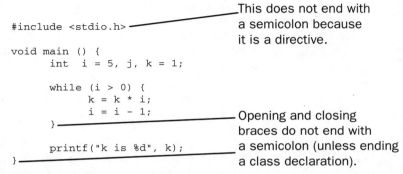

```
#include <stdio.h>                    This does not end with
                                      a semicolon because
                                      it is a directive.
void main () {
      int   i = 5, j, k = 1;

      while (i > 0) {
            k = k * i;
            i = i - 1;                Opening and closing
      }                              braces do not end with
                                      a semicolon (unless ending
      printf("k is %d", k);         a class declaration.
}
```

Figure 2-1   *Using semicolons in C++.*

C++ uses a semicolon to indicate the end of a statement rather than relying on the end of a physical line. Whenever a statement threatens to grow wider than the physical screen, you can simply spread the statement across multiple lines. For example:

```
printf("On %d/%d/%d, the temperature was %f.\n",
      date,
      month,
      year,
      temp);
```

Another consequence of C++ syntax is that you can place several statements on one line, as in the following four assignments. Remember that a semicolon terminates each statement, including the last one.

```
a = 0; b = 0; c = 0; d = 0;
```

The next section shows an even more compact way to write this code.

Assignments are expressions, too

One of the most fundamental units of grammar in the C++ language is an *expression*. With very few exceptions, an expression evaluates to a value. An expression is a variable, a constant, a function call, or a compound expression made up of smaller expressions connected by operators such as +, −, *, /, and so on.

A surprising thing about C and C++ is that the assignment operator (=) is an operator just like any other, and an assignment expression is an expression just like any other. This means that you can assign the same value to several variables using a single, compact statement:

```
a = b = c = d = 0;  // Initialize variables to 0.
```

An assignment evaluates to the value that was assigned. So an expression such as d = 0 first assigns 0 to d and then evaluates to 0. This value is then reused in the next expression to be evaluated. The assignment operator (=) associates right to left, so the rightmost assignments are evaluated first. Figure 2-2 shows how the complete statement performs each assignment, each time reusing the value 0 in the next assignment.

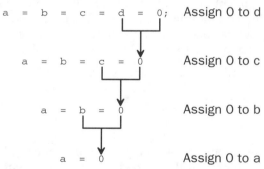

Figure 2-2 *Multiple assignments in C++.*

But be careful. When an assignment appears inside an if condition, it is still an assignment even though it looks like a test for equality. The problem is that assignment does not evaluate to true and false. For example, in the following code, the assignment n = 5 evaluates unconditionally to 5, which means true (as do all nonzero values).

```
if (n = 5)                      // ERROR! n gets 5.
    printf("n is equal to 5.\n"); // Always executes!
```

Here, the string is always printed no matter what value is in n, because n = 5 puts 5 into n and then returns 5. C++ does not assume that you want to test for equality. C and C++ provide a separate operator to test for equality (==). This operator performs a comparison and evaluates to true (1) or false (0) just as you would expect.

```
if (n == 5)                    // Test n against 5.
    printf("n is equal to 5.\n"); // Print if n eq. 5.
```

In the history of C and C++, thousands of programmers have bashed their heads against their desks, trying to find an elusive bug that turned out to be the use of assignment (=) rather than test for equality (==). This is one of the most common mistakes made by people learning C or C++. Assignment (=) inside a conditional is usually wrong. Most other programming languages don't let you do it in the first place. With the greater freedom of C and C++ comes the flexibility to step on your own foot.

Adding Functions to Your Program

In C++, there is just one kind of subroutine: the function. Those functions that don't return a value are declared void; those that do return a value have a return type such as int, double, or float. This keeps C++ syntax streamlined. There is no separate Sub or Function keyword as in Visual Basic.

You've almost certainly encountered functions before. A function takes zero or more arguments — depending on how it's declared — and evaluates to a single value that can be reused in a larger expression. Figure 2-3 illustrates how a call to the Pythagoras function might work.

```
#include <math.h>
...

c = Pythagoras(3.0, 4.0)
```

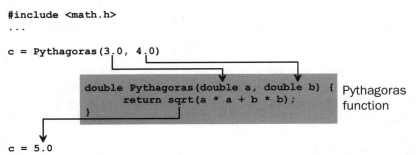

```
double Pythagoras(double a, double b) {   Pythagoras
    return sqrt(a * a + b * b);           function
}
```

```
c = 5.0
```

Figure 2-3 *A function call in action.*

In Figure 2-3, the expression `Pythagoras(3.0, 4.0)` results in a call to the `Pythagoras` function, passing the values `3.0` and `4.0` to the two parameters. The function uses the `return` statement to transfer control back to the caller and return the value `5.0`.

General syntax for functions

When functions are taken into account, the general syntax for a C++ program follows the pattern shown in Figure 2-4.

```
include_directives

function_prototypes

void main(){
     data_declarations_and_other_statements
}

return_type function_name(argument_list){
     data_declarations_and_other_statements
}
```

Repeat for each function defined

Figure 2-4   *General syntax of a C++ program.*

Before you can call a function, you must declare it; *function_ prototypes* serves this purpose. A function prototype provides type information to the compiler so that it knows what type of arguments to expect. The format of a function prototype looks almost identical to that of the first line (the heading) of a function definition:

```
return_type function_name(argument_list);
```

However, a function *prototype* ends with a semicolon (;). Do not — repeat, do not — place a semicolon after the terminating brace (}) of a function *definition*. Because prototypes end with semicolons and function definitions do not, it is easier to tell them apart.

● **TIP**

Prototypes and headings for a function definition are so similar that you can copy the first line of a function definition to get a prototype and vice versa. Remember to insert or delete the semicolon, as appropriate.

Function example

Function syntax makes more sense in the context of an example. Figure 2-5 illustrates each part of the function syntax, including the prototype, function call, and function definition. The prototype prepares for the function call (by letting the compiler know what types to check for), the function call executes the function, and the function definition tells the program how to execute the function.

```
#include <studio.h>
#include <math.h>                              ──── Include directives

double Pythagoras(double a, double b);  ──────Function prototype

void main() {
     double a, b, c; ──────────── Data declarations

     printf("Enter Length 1: ");
     scanf("%lf", &a);
     printf("Enter Length 2: ");
     scanf("%lf", &b);
     c = Pythagoras(a, b);
     printf("The hypotenuse is %f.", c);
}                                                    Function
                                                     definition
double Pythagoras(double a, double b) {
     double c;

     c = sqrt(a * a + b * b);
     return c;
}
```

Figure 2-5 *An example program that calls a function.*

For this example, you must include two header files (stdio.h and math.h), because the program uses I/O functions (printf and scanf), as well as a math function (sqrt), which returns the square root of a number. The header files provide prototypes for these functions.

Figure 2-6 analyzes the syntax of the Pythagoras function definition. The return type is double, which indicates that the function evaluates to a double-precision floating-point number.

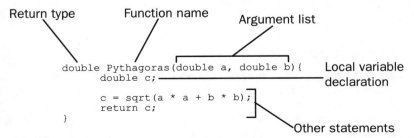

Figure 2-6 *Breakdown of function definition syntax.*

Functions in the void

If a function does not need to return a value, declare it with the void return type. Unlike functions with other return types, a void function does not need a return statement. The function can use return to exit early, but it can also let execution terminate naturally at the end of the function definition. See page 104 for more information on return.

The following example calls a void function named print_vars.

```
#include <stdio.h>

void print_vars(int i1, int i2, int i3);

void main() {
    int a, b, c;

    a = b = c = 1;
    print_vars(a, b, c);
    a = b = c = 2;
    print_vars(a, b, c);
}

void print_vars(int i1, int i2, int i3) {
    printf("The value of param1 is %d.\n", i1);
    printf("The value of param2 is %d.\n", i2);
    printf("The value of param3 is %d.\n\n", i3);
}
```

Local, Global, and Other Variables

One of the attributes of a variable is its scope, which determines where it is visible in the program. Four principal kinds of scope are inherited from C: local, global, static, and external. To these, C++ adds class scope, which attaches a variable to an object of a particular class.

Local variables

A local variable is private to a function definition. Each function can have its own variable named i for example, and can modify this variable without affecting the variable named i in any other function.

To declare a local variable, simply place the declaration inside a function definition. For example, the variable c is local in the following

Pythagoras function definition. Changes to this variable do not affect the value of c in any other function.

```
#include <math.h>
...
double Pythagoras(double a, double b) {
    double c;

    c = sqrt(a * a + b * b);
    return c;
}
```

One of the differences between C++ and other languages is that in C++, main is a function just like any other. It has two unique features: it is the program entry point, and it doesn't need a prototype. main can have its own local variables. For example, in the following code, the variables a, b, c, and h are all local to main.

```
void main() {
    double a, b, c, h;

    a = b = c = 1;
    print_vars(a, b, c);
    h = Pythagoras(a, b);
    print_vars(a, b, c);
}
```

Global variables

It's usually preferable to make a variable local because you can then control exactly what code can change the variable. Sometimes, however, you need scope that extends beyond a single function. Global variables have scope and lifetime that extend to the entire source file — that is, they retain their values as long as the program runs. Global variables enable functions to communicate by sharing information.

To make a variable global, define it outside all function definitions.

The example program in Figure 2-7 uses three global variables. All the functions in the program share access to the variables a, b, and c.

●—**NOTE**——————————————————————————————

Global variables are visible from the point where they are declared to the end of the source file. It's common to declare them near the top of the file.

```
#include <studio.h>
#include <math.h>            ──────── Include directives

void Pythagoras(void);       ╱────── Global variable
void Setvars(void);                  declarations
                                     (Note that these are
double a, b, c;                      declared before main.)
void main() {
     Setvars();
     Pythagoras();
     printf("\nThe hypotenuse is %f.", c);
}

void Pythagoras(void) {
     c = sqrt(a * a + b * b);
}

void Setvars(void) {
     printf("Enter value of Length 1: ");
     scanf("%lf", &a);
     printf("Enter value of Length 2: ");
     scanf("%lf", &b);
}
```

Figure 2-7 *Global variable example.*

Static variables

A static variable combines the visibility of a local variable with the extended lifetime of a global variable. This is useful when you want a local variable that retains its value between function calls. For example:

```
void print_vars(int i1, int i2, int i3) {
     static int count = 0;

     printf("The value of param1 is %d.\n", i1);
     printf("The value of param2 is %d.\n", i2);
     printf("The value of param3 is %d.\n", I3);

     count = count + 1;
     printf("I've been called %d time(s).\n\n",
          count);}
```

The variable count is initialized to zero just once — the first time the function is called. (In contrast, ordinary local variables are initialized each time the function is called.) After each call to print_vars, the value of count increases by 1. At the same time, count is private to this function and is not affected by what happens to count variables in other functions.

External variables

As a program grows in size, it's common to divide the code into multiple modules, compile them, and link them. A module corresponds to one C++ source file.

Each function is automatically visible to all other modules in the project unless you declare it static (by placing the static keyword at the beginning of the prototype and the function-definition heading); in that case, the function is visible only within the module.

Variables are visible only in the module where they're declared unless you make them external. To make a variable external, first define it as a global variable in exactly one module:

```
int global_count;
```

All other modules that use this same variable need to include an extern declaration:

```
extern int global_count;
```

This declaration says to the compiler, "Recognize global_count as an external variable. It may be defined here or in another module."

Another way to use external variables is to place all the extern declarations in a header file, and then include that header in every source file. For example:

```
// ----------------------------------------------
// MYPROG.H - Extern declarations and function
// prototypes for myprog.

extern int global_count;
extern int current_checkno;
extern double accumulator;
//...
```

Each of these variables must be defined in one — and only one — source file. For example, module A defines the first two variables:

```
// ----------------------------------------------
// A.CPP

#include "myprog.h"

int global_count;
int current_checkno;
//...
```

Module B defines the third external variable:

```
// ----------------------------------------------------
// B.CPP

#include "myprog.h"

double current_accumulator;
//...
```

No matter where they are defined, these three variables are shared by all functions in the program because of the extern declarations in the header file. The extern declarations do not create the data; that must be done with standard variable declarations, which are also called *definitions*.

Fun with Control Structures

Control structures let you express decisions and loops in a readable way. This arrangement frees you from having to use the spaghetti-code style of programming seen in old versions of BASIC and assembly language.

This section introduces two of the most frequently used control structures: if and while. C++ also supports the do, for, and switch control structures, which are described in Chapter 13.

The if statement

Here's the syntax for the C++ if statement:

```
if (expression)
    statement
[ else
    statement ]
```

Here, the brackets indicate that the else clause is optional. An if statement can appear without else, as in this example:

```
if (age < 21 )
    printf(What do you think you're doing?\n);
```

An if statement can also include an else clause, as in this example:

```
if (age < 21 )
  printf("What do you think you're doing?\n");
```

```
else
   printf("Eat, drink, and be computer literate.\n");
```

Technically, there is no C++ "elseif" keyword as in Visual Basic. However, the statement following `else` can itself be another `if` statement. This is a common example of nesting one control structure inside another:

```
if (age < 21 )
   printf("What do you think you're doing?\n");
else
   if (age == 21)
      printf("Okay, just one drink.\n");
   else
      printf("Eat, drink, and be computer literate.\n");
```

Because C++ doesn't care about spacing, you can rewrite the code this way:

```
if (age < 21 )
     printf("What do you think you're doing?\n");
else if (age == 21)
     printf("Okay, just one drink.\n");
else
     printf("Eat, drink, and be computer literate.\n");
```

Control structures, such as `if`, are frequently used with compound statements. A compound statement consists of any number of statements placed between braces ({}). A compound statement can be used anywhere a single statement can be used.

```
if (age < 21 ) {
    printf("Hey! What do you think you're doing?\n");
    printf("Serve minors? Just what kind of place ");
    printf("do you\nthink we run?\n");
}
else if (age == 21)
     printf("Okay, just one drink.\n");
else {
    printf("Eat, drink, and be computer literate.\n");
    printf("But we suggest that you be careful \n");
    printf("driving home on the information super-\n");
    printf("highway tonight...");
}
```

NOTE

Remember to use double equals signs (==) to test for equality.

The while statement

The while statement is another control structure that is frequently used with compound statements. The syntax for while is:

```
while (expression)
    statement
```

As with if statements, the conditional expression in the while statement can be any valid integer expression. All nonzero values are interpreted as true. Comparison operators (<, >, ==, <=, =>, and !=) return true (1) or false (0).

For example, the following code counts down from 5 to 1. The while statement executes the statement block repeatedly until the condition, n > 0, is false.

```
int n = 5;

while (n > 0) {
    printf("%d\n", n);
    n = n - 1;
}
```

This next example, which is slightly more compact, does the same thing:

```
int n = 5;

while (n) {
    printf("%d\n", n);
    n = n - 1;
}
```

The next section shows you how to make this example even more compact.

Impress Your Friends with Fancy C++ Operators

C++ has a number of fancy operators that are generally not found in any other language (except C). These operators include increment and decrement operators, assignment operators, and bitwise operators.

Increment and decrement operators

Among the most useful of the fancy C++ operators are increment and decrement. These operators simply add or subtract one from a variable. For example:

```
n++;    // Add 1 to n.
n--;    // Subtract 1 from n.
```

You can certainly use these operators inside a larger expression. For example, the decrement operator can be used to make the count-down-from-five example in the previous section even more compact:

```
#include <stdio.h>
//...
int n = 5;
while (n)
    printf("%d\n", n--);
```

This code uses the *postfix* version of the decrement operator (where the operator follows the variable, as in n--), which performs the side effect — doing the subtraction — only after getting the value of the variable. In this case, the operator causes the code to print the value of n and then subtract 1. Consequently, this example prints the numbers 5, 4, 3, 2, and 1, as desired.

When the operator is used by itself in a statement, there is no difference between postfix and prefix. For example, each of these statements does the same thing:

```
n--;
--n;
```

But in many cases, the difference between the prefix and postfix versions is important. To summarize, here is how the two versions of the increment operator (++) work:

Operator	Action
++n (prefix)	Increment n and then pass along the result to the larger expression, if any.
n++ (postfix)	Pass along the value of n and *then* increment n.

The postfix version is potentially the trickiest if you're not used to it. Notice how the change is not reflected in the following statements until after the operator is applied:

```
int count = 3;
printf("%d\n", count);    // Print 3.
```

```
printf("%d\n", count++);   // Print 3, then increment.
printf("%d\n", count);     // Print 4.
```

In the prefix version, however, the change is reflected right away:

```
int count = 3;
printf("%d\n", count);     // Print 3.
printf("%d\n", ++count);   // Print 4.
printf("%d\n", count);     // Print 4.
```

The decrement operator works similarly.

Operator	Action
--n (prefix)	Decrement n and then pass along the result to the larger expression, if any.
n-- (postfix)	Pass along the value of n and *then* decrement n.

Assignment operators

C++ assignment operators include not only the standard assignment operator (=) but also a range of other operators that combine assignment with another operation. These operators are similar to the increment and decrement operators because they modify a variable by performing an operation.

For example, addition-assignment (+=) performs both an addition and an assignment. The statement:

```
n += 10;
```

is equivalent to the longer statement:

```
n = n + 10;
```

You can think of prefix increment and decrement as special cases of addition-assignment and subtraction-assignment. For example, these expressions are equivalent:

```
(--n)        // Subtract 1 from n, return result.
(n -= 1)     // Subtract 1 from n, return result.
```

C++ supports a large set of assignment operators that work in a similar way, performing an operation and assigning the result to the variable on the left. These operators include *= (multiplication-assignment), /= (division-assignment), and many others. For more information, see Chapter 11.

Bitwise, logical, and shift operators

To programmers new to C and C++, bitwise operators are often the most interesting part of the language. These operators let you test and modify individual bits.

Table 2-3 summarizes bit-testing operations along with logical operators. *Logical* operators are similar to bitwise operators except that they do not test individual bits. The logical operators treat all nonzero operands the same way, and therefore ignore individual bit values.

Table 2-3   *Logical and bitwise operators*

Operator	Description
&	Bitwise AND. Sets a bit in the result if both of the corresponding bits in the two operands are set.
|	Bitwise OR. Sets a bit in the result if either of the corresponding bits in the two operands is set.
~	Bitwise NOT (one's complement). Sets a bit in the result if the corresponding bit in the single operand is not set.
&&	Logical AND. If both operands are nonzero, evaluates to true (1); otherwise evaluates to false (0). Combines Boolean conditions, as you would expect.
||	Logical OR. If either operand is nonzero, evaluates to true (1); otherwise evaluates to false (0). Combines Boolean conditions, as you would expect.
!	Logical NOT. Evaluates to true (1) if operand is zero, and to false (0) if the operand is nonzero. Reverses the true/false value of a Boolean condition, as you would expect.

C++ also supports right-shift and left-shift operators, as shown in Table 2-4.

Table 2-4   *Right-shift and left-shift operators*

Operator	Description
val >> *n*	Shifts bits within *val* right by *n* places and returns the result.
val << *n*	Shifts bits within *val* left by *n* places and returns the result.

All bitwise and shift operators work on the binary representation of their operands regardless of what notation is used. The binary representation consists of a series of 1s and 0s (Figure 2-8).

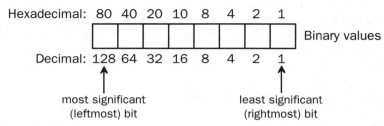

Figure 2-8 *Binary representation.*

For example, the number 18 is stored as 00010010, and the number 6 is stored as 00000110. Using binary AND tests each bit position, setting a bit in the result to 1 only if both corresponding bits in the operands are 1. The result in this case is 00000010 binary, or 2.

The following program uses the left-shift operator (<<) and bitwise AND (&) to print the binary representation of an integer. Note that the "0x" in 0x8000 is C++'s notation for hexadecimal representation. 0x8000 has 1 set in the leftmost position and 0 in every other position.

```
#include <stdio.h>

void print_binary(short input_field);

void main() {
    short n;

    do {
        printf("\nEnter a short integer ");
        printf("(0 to quit): ");
        scanf("%hd", &n);
            print_binary(n);
    } while (n);
}

void print_binary(short input_field) {
    int i = 1, bit_set;

    while (i <= 16) {
        bit_set = ((0x8000 & input_field) > 0);
        printf("%d", bit_set);
```

```
                    input_field = input_field << 1;
                    i++;
            }
    }
```

Inside the while loop, 0x8000 is ANDed with the argument. The result is either 0x8000 or zero. The result is compared to zero, and the comparison expression evaluates to either 1 or 0, which is then printed:

```
(0x8000 & input_field) > 0
```

C++ supports a left-shift-and-assignment operator (<<=) that combines left shift with assignment. You can make the program more compact by using this operator and applying it to input_field near the bottom of the loop.

Bit Fields: Extreme Compaction

An alternative way to store and retrieve information in individual bits is to use *bit fields*, a feature unique to C and C++. Bit fields do not do anything that you couldn't do with bitwise and shift operators, but in some cases, they are much easier to use.

To declare a data structure using bit fields, declare a structure with unsigned members as follows (the brackets indicate optional items):

```
struct [struct_name] {
    unsigned field1 : width1;
    unsigned field2 : width2;
    ...
    unsigned fieldN : widthN;
} [struct_vars];
```

For example, the following declaration declares a type, card, that contains a rank value (1 to 13) as well as a suit value (1 to 4):

```
struct card {
    unsigned int rank : 4;
    unsigned int suit : 2;
};
```

Now, why are rank and suit assigned the widths 4 and 2, respectively? This question is important. The answer is that 4 bits stores up to 16 values, and 2 bits stores up to 4 values. This makes the fields large enough to store 13 and 4 values, respectively, as needed. When deciding on the width of a bit field, remember that for a width n, the maximum number of values is 2 to the power of n.

You can now declare card structures and assign values to the fields. This example assumes that clubs, diamonds, hearts, and spades are represented as 0, 1, 2, and 3:

```
card cd1, cd2, cd3, deck[52];

cd1.rank = 1;  // Assign ace=1.
cd1.suit = 3;  // Assign spades=3.
```

Figure 2-9 shows how these values would be stored in the lower 8 bytes. This scheme enables rank and suit to be stored in 1 byte rather than in 2 bytes or more.

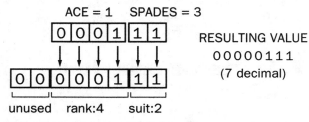

Figure 2-9 *Assigning bit-field values.*

Whew! This chapter has introduced a whirlwind of C/C++ grammar and operators. If all this is new to you, don't despair. Feel free to refer back to this chapter whenever you need to. If you already understand most of it, give yourself a big pat on the back!

Pointers, Strings, and Things

3

One thing that distinguishes C and C++ from most other computer languages is their use of pointers. At first, pointers may seem difficult or exotic, but other languages use pointers all the time. The difference is that these other languages carry out pointer operations under the covers — you just don't see them. C and C++ provide more control over pointers.

In general, pointers store addresses, which are relatively small units of data (4 bytes on 32-bit systems) that give the *location* of another piece of data. (I provide a more detailed description of pointers in the next section.) The beauty of pointers is that you can access data of any size simply by knowing its location.

C++ encourages the dynamic creation of objects by using the new operator, which returns a pointer. Moreover, certain operator functions (described in Chapter 7) require understanding of pointers. This chapter focuses on the use of pointers with parameters, strings, and arrays.

A More Efficient Way to Pass Data

Simply stated, a pointer is a variable or an argument that stores an address. A pointer gives the *location* of another variable; a function can use that location to manipulate data of any size.

Suppose you and I are two different functions (okay, I know that sounds silly, but stay with me on this). Suppose, further, that you have a large piece of data that you need to share with me. For example, you might need to pass me a long string of characters so I can display it on the screen.

Unless the data is global (and remember that it is poor design to have too many globals) there are two possibilities:

- You can pass the data structure by giving me a copy of the entire data structure. This approach is fine in the case of small data types, but can be inefficient when you start dealing with arrays, strings, and other large objects.

- You can give me the *address* of the data structure. An address looks just like an integer but it has a special meaning to the computer — an address tells the processor where to find something in memory.

To visualize these scenarios, try to picture the computer's stack, which is the area of memory reserved for passing data between functions. Passing a data structure directly causes an entire copy of the data to be placed on the stack. Passing an address, however, causes a relatively small amount of data to be placed on the stack (typically, either 2 or 4 bytes, depending on the computer's address size). As the function being called, I need only the location of the data structure — its address — to gain access to all the data. Figure 3-1 illustrates these two approaches to passing data.

In the second scenario, I have only the address of the data; but this is all I need to access or modify the original data. Manipulating data through its address is called *indirection*. Modern processors are designed with a great deal of support for indirection.

The usefulness of pointers is not limited to saving memory on the stack. Among other things, pointers enable passing by reference, which is discussed next.

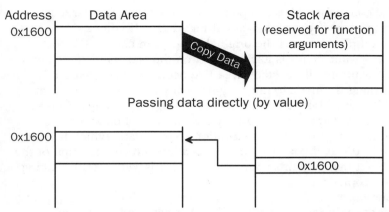

Passing data by passing its address (passing by reference)

Figure 3-1 *Passing data directly and passing its address (a pointer).*

Pointers and Passing by Reference

If you've used BASIC, FORTRAN, Pascal, or most any other computer language, you're probably familiar with passing by reference and passing by value: A function can permanently change the value of an argument only if you pass by reference.

With languages such as BASIC and FORTRAN, passing by reference is automatic or easily controlled by a simple keyword (such as var in Pascal). You may not have realized it, but these languages pass a pointer when you pass by reference. The language hides this fact from you, so you don't have to learn pointer syntax, which C requires that you learn. (Pascal has pointer syntax but restricts its use to memory allocation.)

●─**NOTE**────────────────────────────────

C++, but not C, lets you declare *reference arguments* by declaring them with the address operator (&). This technique is introduced in Chapter 6 (see p. 413). However, it's best to learn first how to pass by reference the hard way—with pointers. Even with C++, eventually you have to use pointers, and the best way to learn is to start with passing by reference.

The connection between pointers and passing by reference should be clear if you look again at Figure 3-1. If you pass by value, I get a complete copy of the original data. I can change the copy as much as I want, but this has no effect on the original data. When I finish execution, all the stack area I've been using is released. None of the changes I made to my copy have any effect on the program.

If, however, I get a pointer to your data, then changes I make affect you. A pointer is not exactly a new piece of data; instead, it is something that tells me the location of your data, which lets me change it. It's as if you gave me the location and combination of the file cabinet that contains your original records, rather than making separate copies for me.

Therefore, passing a pointer (an address) is the same as passing by reference. In fact, that's literally what passing by reference means: a pointer refers to the original copy of the data.

Steps for passing by reference

To use pointers to pass by reference, you need to perform three steps:

1. In the prototype and function-definition argument list, declare the parameter using the pointer-indirection operator (*).

2. When passing an argument, make sure to pass an address. Typically, this means applying the address operator (&) to your argument.

3. Within the function definition, apply the pointer-indirection operator (*) when you want to access the data pointed to.

The rest of this section discusses each of these steps in detail.

First, you must apply the indirection operator (*) to declare your intention to use a pointer argument. The declaration is the same as it would be if the argument were not a pointer, except that the indirection operator (*) is placed to the immediate left of the argument name. For example, the following prototype declares a function taking one argument: a pointer to an int:

```
void double_it(int *n);
```

Second, you must pass an address argument. To pass the address of a variable of primitive type, apply the address operator (&) to that variable. For example:

```
int amount;
//...
double_it(&amount);  // Pass address of amount.
```

Finally, within the function definition, use the indirection operator (again) to access the data pointed to. For example:

```
*p = *p * 2;
```

By using multiplication assignment (*=), you could instead write:

```
*p *= 2;
```

The two operators (* and &) are inverses of each other. The pointer-indirection operator (*) means "the object pointed to by," and the address operator means, "get the address of." The first operator, *, gets contents from an address (for example, it converts a pointer to an int into an actual int); the second operator, &, gets an address.

●─NOTE

Using p without the indirection operator (*) affects the pointer itself and not the thing pointed to. For example, (*p)++ increments the data pointed to, whereas p++ advances the pointer to the next address. The compiler won't tell you that this is a problem, so you have to be very careful; use the indirection operator (*) to modify data, and only modify the pointer itself if you want to change the address that it contains.

Two complete pass-by-reference examples

Both the indirection (*) and the address (&) operators are necessary for working with pointers, as the examples in this section demonstrate. To pass by reference, you first have to put an address on the stack (which involves &); later, in the function definition, you use that address to access the data pointed to (which involves *).

Figure 3-2 is the complete context for the example code from the previous section. The example first defines the variable amount and sets it to 5. After calling the double_it function and passing the address of amount, the variable contains the value 10. If double_it were passed the normal way (by value), the double_it function would have no effect.

Figure 3-3 is an example that passes two arguments by reference. (Incidentally, you can mix pointers and simple data types in the same argument list.) Here, the function switches the value of variables a and b. The function can modify both a and b because the address of each is passed, enabling the function to access a and b themselves rather than copies of a and b.

```
#include <stdio.h>

void double_it(int *p);

main () {
    int amount = 5;

    printf("The value of amount is %d.\n", amount);

    double_it(&amount);

    printf("The value of amount is %d.\n", amount);
}

void double_it(int *p) {
    *p = *p * 2;
}
```

Address of amount is passed to the parameter, *p.

Figure 3-2 *Passing the address of amount to the double_it function.*

```
#include <stdio.h>

void swap(double *x, double *y);

main () {
    double a = 1.5, b = 3.9;

    printf("a = %lf, b = %lf\n", a, b);

    swap(&a, &b);

    printf("a = %lf, b = %lf\n", a, b);
}

void swap(double *x, double *y) {
    double temp;

    temp = *x;
    *x = *y;
    *y = temp;
}
```

Addresses of a and b are passed to the parameters *x and *y.

Figure 3-3 *Passing addresses of variables a and b.*

Pointers and Arrays

In C++, pointers have a close connection to arrays. Arrays can often be processed more efficiently using pointers.

Arrays are an important element of almost every computer language. Arrays are essential in serious programming projects for two reasons:

- They provide a convenient way to allocate arbitrarily large chunks of data in program memory.

- They can be used to perform a large number of operations with a few lines of code. By combining an array with a loop, you can perform a series of statements and then repeat the operations on an arbitrarily large chunk of memory.

The importance of arrays and loop processing cannot be overestimated. Computer programming, and computers themselves, would be far less powerful without this single aspect of programming. C++ enhances this capability by providing pointer operations.

Array basics

This is the C++ syntax for declaring arrays:

```
type   name[length];
```

Multidimensional arrays have the following syntax, in which the ellipses (. . .) indicate that [length] may be repeated any number of times:

```
type   name[length1][length2]...[lengthN];
```

In both cases, the brackets are intended literally. In the multidimensional case, the number of dimensions can be two, three, or *n*, where *n* is as high a number as you want. Bear in mind, though, that an array with an unreasonably high number of dimensions is likely to eat up all your computer's memory. A 1000 by 1000 array of 256-byte character strings requires over 250 megabytes (MB)!

The rest of this example discusses a single-dimension case, although multiple dimensions follow similar rules. The length in the declaration indicates the number of elements in the array. (For multiple arrays, the number of elements is *length1* * *length2* * ... *lengthN*.) The lowest index is always 0, and the highest is always *length* - 1.

A couple of examples should help make this clear. Consider this declaration:

```
int   a[5];
```

This declaration creates five integers. The variables are referred to as:

```
a[0]
a[1]
a[2]
a[3]
a[4]
```

The highest index value supported here is 4, which is 1 less than the length (5). Similarly, a 10-element long array can be declared:

```
int  b[10];
```

This declaration creates 10 integers. Again, the highest index, 9, is 1 less than the length (10).

```
b[0]
b[1]
b[2]
b[3]
b[4]
b[5]
b[6]
b[7]
b[8]
b[9]
```

●—**TIP**————————————————————————————

I'm emphasizing that the highest index used is *length* -1 because a common source of bugs when working with arrays is to incorrectly set the initial and terminating conditions of a loop. Even experienced programmers occasionally set the terminating condition wrong because they forget that the highest index is *length* -1. So check your loop conditions carefully.

When I say that a declaration such as int a[5] creates five integers, I mean that literally. Figure 3-4 shows how the integers are laid out sequentially in memory for 16-bit systems. Each element is 2 bytes wide. (On 32-bit systems, each int element is 4 bytes wide.)

Declaring an array of five integers is similar in many ways to declaring each integer separately. You could declare five integers this way:

```
int a0;
int a1;
int a2;
int a3;
int a4;
```

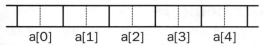

a[0]   a[1]   a[2]   a[3]   a[4]

Figure 3-4   *An array with five integers.*

How is this different from declaring the five-element integer
array a, which generates the elements a[0], a[1], a[2], a[3], and
a[4]?

Well, most obviously, the array declaration saves effort.
Declaring integers individually is not so tedious when there are only
5 integers, but think of how many lines of code are saved when there
are 1000 integers:

```
int a[1000];
```

And there's another reason: You can use a variable to index an
array, as well as a constant (for example, an index can be n). For
example:

```
int a[5];

a[0] = 10;
a[1] = a[0] + 1;

int n = 2;
a[n] = a[1];    // Assign a[1] to a[2]
```

Using variable indexes with arrays is a powerful technique. It
enables loop processing of arrays, as in this example:

```
// Initialize all 1000 elements of the array to
//   contain the value 100.

int a[1000];
int i = 0;
while (i < 1000)
     a[i++] = 100;
```

Here, the increment operator (++) is used to increment the value
of i *after* the value of a[i] is taken. This works because the *postfix*
increment is used. (The postfix operator grabs the current value of i,
passes it along, and increments i as an additional effect.) For clarity,
the last two lines could be rewritten as:

```
while (i < 1000) {
     a[i] = 100;
     i++;
}
```

Loop processing with pointers

Pointers provide another way to perform loop processing. The pointer version is generally more efficient than a version using array indexes. (This is particularly true with multidimensional arrays.) For instance, the example at the end of the last section could be written this way:

```
// Initialize all 1000 elements of the array to 100

int a[1000];
int i = 0;
int *p = a;
while (i++ < 1000)
    *p++ = 100;
```

Some of these statements require a closer look. The third statement declares a pointer, p, and initializes it to the starting address of the array, a. In C and C++, array names have a special property; in code, an array name evaluates to the address of the first element. (You don't use &.) Therefore, the code initializes the pointer to the starting address by using the array name by itself.

```
int *p = a;
```

This statement is equivalent to the longer, but more obvious, statement below. These statements are the same because an array name is equivalent to the address of its first element.

```
int *p = &a[0];
```

The loop statement relies on C++ rules of associativity to do things in a certain order.

```
while (i++ < 1000)
    *p++ = 100;
```

Tables 1 (p. 44) and 2 (p. 44) in Section 3 show that indirection (*) and increment (++) have the same level of precedence, but as unary operators, they associate right-to-left. (Most other operators associate left-to-right.) The increment operator is applied first. Therefore, it is the pointer that is incremented, not what the pointer refers to. Parentheses help clarify the statement:

```
while (i++ < 1000)
    *(p++) = 100;
```

Because it is a *postfix* increment, the increment is applied after the expression is evaluated. Remember that the *postfix* increment gets the value of its operand and changes the operand later. The expression *(p++) does the following:

1. Gets the value of the pointer p.

2. Increments the value of p. (Postfix operation.)

3. Accesses the data pointed to by p *before* it was incremented (in Step 2).

Thus, the expression *(p++) has the same meaning as *p, except that, as an additional effect, it also increments p by 1.

The loop could have been made even more self-evident, but less compact, by writing it this way:

```
while (i++ < 1000) {
        *p = 100;    // Assign 100 to element pointed to
        p++;         // Point to next element
}
```

The first statement inside the loop (*p = 100) is an operation on the data pointed to. However, the second statement (p++) is an operation on the pointer itself. Adding 1 to a pointer always advances it to point to the next element regardless of the size of the base type. C and C++ use *scaling* during pointer arithmetic: when you add an integer to a pointer, the integer is multiplied by the size of the base type.

Figure 3-5 illustrates how this loop processes the array by assigning a value and then advancing to the next element.

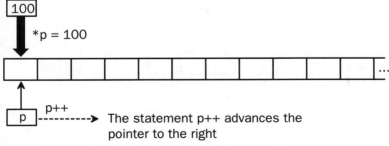

Figure 3-5   *Using a pointer for loop processing on an array.*

Similar code can be used to copy all the members of one array, b, to all the members of another array, a:

```
int a[1000], b[1000];
//...
int i = 0;
int *pa = a;
```

```
int *pb = b;
while (i++ < 1000)
    *pa++ = *pb++;
```

Again, the postfix increment (++) is applied before indirection (*), because these operators associate right to left. The loop therefore has the same effect as the following, less compact, version. And because the postfix increment is used, the values of pa and pb are incremented only after their values are taken. The code therefore behaves like the following:

```
while (i++ < 1000) {
    *pa = *pb;    // Copy element from b to a
    pa++;         // Point to next element in a
    pb++;         // Point to next element in b
}
```

In this code, the name "pa" stands for "pointer to variable a"; the name "pb" stands for "pointer to b." It's always a good idea to name variables in a way that helps you understand what they do.

Figure 3-6 illustrates how this loop processes the array by assigning a value and then advancing to the next element.

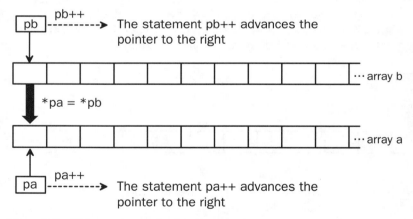

Figure 3-6 *Using pointers for loop processing on two arrays.*

C++ Strings

Array-handling techniques, especially those involving pointers, are useful in handling C++ character strings. If you are not well versed in how pointers can be used to process array elements, you should review the preceding section.

In C++, a character string is an array of char. Technically, a char is an integer 1 byte in length. (However, there is no necessary connection between strings and 1 byte; the wide-character format, used in products intended for international distribution, uses 2 bytes per character.) When printed on screen, each char value is mapped to a printable character. The mapping system most widely in use today is the ASCII (American Standard Code for Information Interchange) coding convention.

Simply stated, a character string is implemented as an array of 1-byte integers in which each integer represents an ASCII character code. (See Appendix D, p. 514, for a table of the first 127 ASCII codes.)

● — **NOTE** ——————————————————————————————

If you are used to string handling in BASIC, you may at first find it more difficult in C++. For example, you have to call a library function (strcpy) to copy one string to another. In Chapters 5, 6, and 7, I use object-oriented features to create a string class as easy to use as BASIC strings. To understand the code for Chapters 5, 6, and 7, however, it's important to first understand the underlying mechanics of C++ strings.

C++ strings have one special characteristic in addition to being arrays. This is the first cardinal rule of string handling: A string is terminated with a null byte ('\0'), which is a value of zero (as opposed to a printable character "0").

The location of the null-terminator byte determines the effective length of the string. This is a potential point of confusion for people who are new to C/C++ strings. You can allocate as many bytes for a string as you want, but the current length depends on the location of the first null byte. If you pass a string to the printf function, for example, only the characters up to the first null are printed; everything past that character is ignored. This can be stated as the second cardinal rule of string handling: The array dimension of a string determines its maximum length (minus 1 for the null–terminator byte) and not its current length.

The following simple example should clarify this matter. Suppose you declare this string:

```
char str[10] = "Hello";
```

The name str is declared as a char array. It is, therefore, a string with a maximum length of 9 (10 minus 1 for the null-terminating byte). The declaration initializes the string with the value "Hello," so it is represented in memory as shown in Figure 3-7.

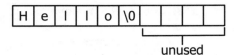

Figure 3-7 *A string with unused bytes.*

The last 4 bytes are not currently in use. But they could be used if a new set of characters were copied into the string (by using the strcpy function, as you learn later). In no case, however, should more than 10 bytes (including the null-terminator byte) be copied to this string location. Doing so would overwrite data areas reserved for other variables or even other programs, with potentially grave consequences. This is another way in which C++ differs from languages such as BASIC. You need to pay attention to the maximum lengths you have set.

An alternative technique for creating a string is to omit an explicit array dimension. In that case, C++ allocates just enough bytes to store the initial string, and no more. This approach is fine as long as the string will never grow in length.

```
char str[] = "Hello";
```

Figure 3-8 shows the resulting byte layout in memory.

Figure 3-8 *This string has no unused bytes.*

When creating C++ strings, you can initialize them with any string constant, as was done in the last two examples. This use of the equals sign (=) is initialization and not assignment; it is limited to the same statement that declares and defines the string.

After a string is declared, you must use the strcpy function to copy a new string value (or write a strcpy function yourself, which is easy). You can't simply assign one string to another as if they were numbers or simple objects. This can be stated as the third cardinal rule of C++ string handling: Because strings are arrays, they can't be directly assigned to each other. You must call a function or use a loop to copy one character at a time.

This is where string handling in C++ seems more difficult than in other languages. Statements such as A$ = B$ cannot be written as they can in BASIC. This code produces an error:

```
char string1[10] = "One";
char string2[10] = "Two";
```

```
string2 = string1;        // ERROR! Cannot assign to
                          //  string
```

Your compiler would probably give you an unhelpful, unfriendly message such as "Cannot assign to a constant." Such a message makes sense only when you consider that C++ array names are actually constants — a string name is equivalent to the address of the first byte.

To copy the contents of one string to another, use the strcpy function:

```
#include <string.h>

char string1[10] = "One";
char string2[10] = "Two";
strcpy(string2, string1);   // Correct way to copy
                            //  string1 to string2
```

The #include directive needs to be present to support string functions such as strcpy. The string.h file contains declarations for the string-handling functions. Remember that in C++, you must declare a function before using it. By including string.h, you get the declarations you need for these string functions so that you don't have to declare them individually.

Table 3-1 summarizes some of the other common string functions. In this table, s, s1, and s2 are string arguments. Each of these is passed the name of a string (such as string1 and string2 in the previous example) or a pointer to a string.

Table 3-1 *C++ string-handling functions*

Function	Description
strlen(s)	Returns the number of characters up to, but not including, the first null byte.
strncpy(s1, s2, n)	Copies at most n characters from s2 to s1. Then copies terminating nulls until exactly n bytes are written.
strcat(s1, s2)	Concatenates the contents of s2 onto the end of s1.

This code uses the strcpy and strcat functions from the standard library:

```
#include <stdio.h>
```

```
#include <string.h>
...
char *name[81];     // Max. length is 80 characters,
                    //  plus 1 for the null
strcpy(name, "Archie");
strcat(name, " ");
strcat(name, "Leach");
printf("%s, he is my friend.\n", name);
```

The %s format character specifies that the corresponding argument is the address of a string. Remember that an array name (in this case, an array of characters) translates into the starting address. This code prints this string:

```
Archie Leach, he is my friend.
```

Pointers are convenient for writing string-handling functions. For example, you could write your own version of the strcpy function. In practice, this is not necessary because the standard library provides this function. However, it is useful to see how easy such a function is to write in C++.

```
char *strcpy(char *dest, char *src) {
    while (*src != '\0') {
        *dest = *src;
        dest++;
        src++;
    }
    *dest = '\0';   // Add terminating null
    return dest;
}
```

There are several ways to make this code more compact, although this version is probably the easiest to understand. (As an exercise, however, you can apply some of the techniques found in the previous section to reduce the example's size by several lines.) In any case, Figure 3-9 illustrates how the function works.

String literals

The examples in the previous section made ample use of *string literals*. These are constants formed by placing text between quotation marks. In the following example, "Hello" is a string literal.

```
char s[] = "Hello";
```

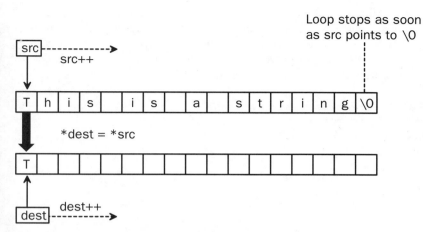

Figure 3-9 *How the strcpy function works.*

When you place a quoted string in a program, C/C++ does two things: (a) it stores the character data in program memory; and (b) it passes along the string's address. Therefore, the effect of the preceding code is:

```
char s[] = address-of-"Hello"
```

String literals come in two varieties. Text enclosed in double quotation marks creates a string — that is, *an array of* char — and passes along its address. A double-quoted string can be passed to any argument taking an address of type char*.

A character enclosed in single quotation marks is different. Such an expression represents a single byte value, not a string. Note the difference between these two statements.

```
char c = 'A';     // Assign char value to c.
char s[] = "A";   // Assign string address to s.
```

The second statement here, but not the first, creates an array. This array has two bytes. A second byte is allocated for the terminating null. You can create an even smaller array:

```
char s[] = "";
```

Here, s is assigned the address of an array with exactly one byte, holding a terminating null.

All string literals, whether string or single-character, recognize escape sequences. These are special codes preceded by a backslash (\). Because backslashes have special meaning, you have to use double backslashes (\\) whenever you want to represent an actual backslash. Table 3-2 lists the escape sequences.

Table 3-2 *Escape sequences for characters*

Character	Meaning
\a	Bell (alert)
\b	Backspace
\f	Formfeed (advance page)
\n	Newline
\r	Carriage return
\t	Tab
\v	Vertical tab
\'	Single quotation mark
\"	Double quotation mark
\\	Literal backslash
\0	Null value (0)
\ddd	ASCII character, octal notation
\xdd	ASCII character, hex notation

The last two lines of Table 3-2 show the syntax for embedding an ASCII value inside a string. For example, you can embed the char value 255 (hex FF) inside an otherwise normal string:

```
char s[] = "This has a funny\xFF character inside.";
```

Wide-character strings

In the mid-1990s, Amendment 1 to the ANSI specification mandated support for wide-character strings. These strings are the same as standard (char) strings except for one difference: 2 bytes, rather than 1 byte, represent each character. This makes it possible for a program to handle natural languages such as Chinese and Japanese. These languages have many more characters than can be represented by a single byte.

The wide-character set — which is implementation-dependent — is a superset of ASCII codes. A wide character can contain an ASCII code in its lower byte and zeroes in the high byte. For this reason, ASCII characters are used in wide-character examples throughout this book.

To create a string literal in wide-character format, use an "L" prefix. Otherwise, rules for string literals are the same as for standard char strings. For example:

```
wchar_t wcs[] = L"This is a sample string.";
```

This declaration looks similar to a standard string declaration, with two differences: first, the wchar_t (wide-character) type is used rather than char. Second, the "L" prefix is used. This causes each of the individual characters ("T," "h," "i," and so on) to be stored in 2 bytes each.

Library support for wide-character strings is extensive. Each of the "str" functions, for example, has a "wcs" (Wide Character String) counterpart. The following example concatenates two strings:

```
wchar_t wcs[256];
wcscpy(wcs, "Joe ");
wcscat(wcs, "Bloe ");
```

For a list of all the wide-character functions, see page 184 in Section 6.

Using new and delete Operators

Another one of the uses of pointers is to help create objects on demand. This technique is called *dynamic memory*, which means that you can determine, at runtime, how much memory you need for a particular item — or whether you need that item at all.

In C, this capability was supported by the malloc, free, and related functions. These are still fully supported for backward compatibility. However, the new and delete operators in C++ offer many advantages, including:

- A header file isn't needed to support new and delete. They are part of the language.

- new and delete are intelligent about types; the return value of new, unlike malloc, doesn't need to be cast to a different type.

- Objects receive special support; new and delete call constructors and destructors. As described in Chapters 5 through 7, these are initialization and destruction functions. new and delete are also fully usable with primitive types.

To allocate memory using new, place the type of the object after new. You can optionally allocate an array of objects by using the second syntax that follows. In this syntax, the brackets are intended literally.

```
pointer = new type;
pointer = new type[n];
pointer = new type(args);        // Objects only
```

Here is a simple use of new to create a single integer:

```
int *p1;
p1 = new int;
```

You must always assign the value returned by new to a pointer. The pointer provides access to the data. Typically, new is used to create an array. The return value is still a simple pointer to the type. For example:

```
int *p1, *p2, *p3;
int num;
//...
p1 = new int;           // p1 points to a single integer
p2 = new int[500];      // p2 points to the first of 500
                        //   integers
num = 75;
p3 = new int[num];      // Allocate 75 int's.
```

The array dimensions can either be a constant or a variable expression such as *num* above. This enables you to determine memory requirements at runtime.

To free memory allocated with new, use the delete operator followed by a pointer name. If new was used with the array form, place empty brackets ([ ]) before the pointer name, as shown here:

```
delete pointer;     // if one object created with new
delete [] pointer;  // if array was created with new []
```

This following example allocates 500 integers, assigns values to 2 of the integers, and prints a value:

```
#include <stdio.h>
//...
int *p = new int[500];

if (p) {
    p[0] = 5;           // Assign 5 to first element
    p[50] = -33;        // Assign -33 to 51st element
    printf("The 51st element is %d.\n", p[50]);
```

```
    //...
    delete [] p;
}
```

The new operator returns a null value if there is insufficient memory. For safest results, test this value before attempting to use or delete the allocated data.

4

Input, Output, and C++

Chapter 2 introduced input/output (I/O) techniques to help you write simple programs. But there's a good deal more to input and output in C++.

C++ provides an object-oriented approach to input and output. The C++ library provides I/O destinations as *stream objects* cin and cout. As streams, these objects represent data flows in which you can send or receive data. This may sound abstract, but these objects are easy to use. Moreover, as you'll learn, the C++ approach has some advantages.

Not all input and output involves the keyboard and screen. The object-oriented approach can be applied to file-stream destinations as well as to the console, as described later in the section "File and Stream Operators" in this chapter.

Going with the Flow: Introduction to Streams

The term *stream* is frequently used in this chapter. It is often used in systems programming generally. What is a stream?

In everyday usage, a stream is a flow of water. In computer programming, a stream is a flow of data. A chief characteristic of a stream is that it is a one-directional flow. Although you might argue that this isn't absolutely true (even a small stream can have whirlpools and backflows), it's true enough to hang a metaphor on. An input/output stream is a sequence of bytes continually flowing in one direction or another, either as input or output.

Another characteristic of a stream is that it is nearly inexhaustible. Streams sometimes run dry, but you don't expect this to happen often. An output stream, in particular, will always accept another byte, except under error conditions such as a full disk.

The two most commonly used streams in programming are standard input and standard output, and they do not run dry. You can always ask standard input to provide another ASCII character from the keyboard, and you can always print another character on the screen (see Figure 4-1).

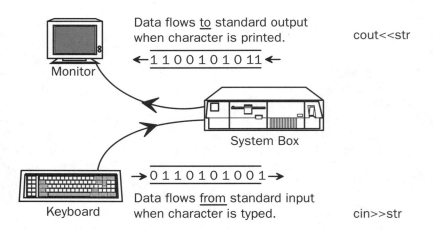

Figure 4-1 *Input and output streams.*

Files are also considered streams. When performing file input or output, you can always put or get the next byte. "The next byte" is always valid, except under error conditions. An example of something that holds data but is usually not considered a stream is an array or structure. An array, for example, always has a specific size and cannot grow as an output file can. (The C++ library, however, makes it possible to treat arrays as streams, although these streams can run out of space. See `strstream` in Section 7, page 289, for more information.)

To some extent, the concept of streams is a fiction created by computer scientists. An area of random access memory (RAM), for example, can be treated as a large array, or it can be used as virtual disk memory. It's the same hardware in either case. As with many other concepts in programming, what makes something a stream is how it is treated. In the final analysis, a stream is a context in which the idea of "the next byte" makes sense.

A stream is either an input or an output stream. Barring error conditions such as end-of-file or disk full, these statements are true:

- With an input stream, you can always read the next byte.

- With an output stream, you can always write another byte.

The capability to read or write the next byte implies the capability to read or write any number of bytes. Writing a 2-byte field, for example, is the same as writing one byte and then writing another byte. Of course, the bytes must be read and written in a consistent order.

Stream Operators (<< and >>): A First Look

Stream operators (<< and >>) in C++ provide an alternative to using printf, scanf, and the other functions defined in stdio.h. Stream operators provide two advantages: first, you don't have to use format specifiers if you are happy with the default formats; and second, it's possible to extend the operators so that they work with your own classes. (Chapter 5 introduces the subject of classes.) For information on how to extend the operators, see Chapter 10.

●—NOTE ─────────────────────────────

This chapter presents several input/output techniques: printf and scanf, stream operators, and line-based input. The C++ standard library uses different I/O buffers for each technique; mixing them causes unpredictable results. If you must mix them, you should take special action; the C++ I/O classes provide the sync_with_stdio function for coordinating printf and scanf with I/O stream data. See page 290 in Section 7.

The following is a simple program that gets two floating-point numbers and prints their sum:

```
#include <iostream.h>void main() {
    double a, b;
```

```
    cout << "Enter the first number: ";
    cin >> a;
    cout << "Enter the second number: ";
    cin >> b;
    cout << "The total is ";
    cout << a + b << endl;
}
```

The previous program behaves the same way as the following program, which uses printf and scanf:

```
#include <stdio.h>

void main() {
    double a, b;

    printf("Enter the first number: ");
    scanf("%lf", &a);
    printf("Enter the second number: ");
    scanf("%lf", &b);
    printf("The total is %lf\n", a + b);
}
```

Note these important points about the version that uses the stream operators cin and cout:

- The file iostream.h, rather than stdio.h, is included.

- No format specifiers are needed. C++ uses the type of the object (a and b in the example) to determine how to perform the data transfer. In this respect, the stream operators are like the BASIC PRINT statement and are a little easier to use than printf and scanf.

- The address operator (&) isn't applied to operands with cin, as it is with scanf. (Here, input streams act more like BASIC by using reference arguments, which you learn more about in Chapter 6.)

- Data flows toward standard output (cout), which usually represents the display screen:

  ```
  cout << "Enter the first number: ";
  ```

- Data flows from standard input (cin), which usually represents the keyboard:

  ```
  cin >> a;
  ```

- The C++ stream objects print a carriage return by using endl, while C uses a \n (although C++ supports this as well).

The direction of the arrows may seem arbitrary at first, but if you think about the direction in which data flows, you'll remember which way the arrows should go. Refer to Figure 4-1 for an illustration.

● NOTE

The stream operators look suspiciously like the left- and right-bit shift operators. In fact, that's exactly what they are! This is an example of *operator overloading*, a technique described in Chapter 7. The behavior of the shift operators is redefined for `istream` and `ostream` classes so that the shift operators become `put` and `get` operators.

When overloading operators, it's a good idea to maintain the operator's general meaning. For example, you'd want the plus sign (+) to perform an operation similar to addition. The use of << and >> as stream operators is an exception to this principle. The << and >> operators were overloaded for stream operations because they had syntactic advantages as well as being visually appropriate.

In the example at the beginning of this section, the last two lines can be rewritten as one. These two lines print two pieces of data — a string and a number:

```
cout << "The total is ";
cout << a + b;
```

The following more compact statement can replace the previous two lines:

```
cout << "The total is " << a + b;
```

The associativity of the shift operators is left-to-right, which means that the following expression is evaluated first:

```
cout << "The total is "
```

As is common in C and C++, this expression does two things: It sends the string to cout (this is its side effect, if you will), and then it evaluates to a value. It so happens that expressions of the form cout << item evaluate to cout itself. Therefore, cout << "The total is" is replaced by cout. Consequently, C++ evaluates the expression as follows:

```
cout << "The total is " << a + b;
(cout << "The total is ") << a + b;    // Print string.
cout << a + b;                         // Print a + b
```

In effect, this is a trick in C++ that enables you to reuse cout repeatedly within one large, complex expression. This case first prints the string and then prints a + b.

Similarly, you can perform the same trick to input several numbers in one statement, because each expression of the form `cin >> item` evaluates to `cin`. For example:

```
cin >> a >> b >> c >> n;
```

Figure 4-2 shows how C++ breaks down this statement, each time performing an input operation as the expression's side effect.

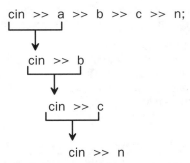

Figure 4-2 *How C++ evaluates multiple input to cin.*

The Joy of Formatting

One attraction of using `cin` and `cout`, especially for beginners, is that you don't have to use the funny symbols that you use with `printf` and `scanf`. The operator recognizes each data type, and each data type has a reasonable default behavior. For example, by default the following statement prints the decimal representation of n, which is the most common format.

```
cout << n;
```

But what if you want to print in hexadecimal or octal format? For example, you can do the following with the `printf` statement:

```
int n = 16;
printf("n is %x hex, %o octal, and %d decimal.\n",
    n, n, n);
```

This code prints this text:

```
n is 10 hex, 20 octal, and 16 decimal.
```

The next example, which uses the C++ stream operators, prints the same results:

```
int n = 16;
cout << "n is " << hex << n << " hex, ";
```

```
cout << oct << n << " octal, and ";
cout << dec << n << " decimal." << endl;
```

hex, oct, and dec are special kinds of objects (which you learn more about in Chapter 5). When sent as output to cout or as input from cin, they change the format of the next integer read or written to the stream.

Line-Based Input with stdio.h

Some C++ programmers prefer to use the I/O library functions declared in stdio.h and inherited from C. If you have a C-programming background and are accustomed to using these functions, or if you are maintaining legacy code written in C, it may make sense to continue using them. You'll probably encounter problems if you mix different input or output techniques. Therefore, if you have existing code, it may be best to continue using stdio.h functions throughout the program.

There is more to the input and output functions than I described in Chapter 2. For one thing, printf and scanf support a variety of format specifiers that are particularly useful with printf. For example, you can use %x to print integers in hexadecimal format. You can also control the spacing and precision of floating-point numbers as well as left or right justify your output fields. See the topics printf (p. 205) and scanf (p. 214).

Some of the most useful functions declared in stdio.h support line-oriented input and output. You can use puts, for example, as a more efficient way of printing strings. The statement

```
printf("%s\n", string);
```

behaves the same as

```
puts(string);
```

The latter version is more efficient, however, because it avoids the overhead of the more elaborate printf function. At the same time, the puts function is less flexible, because it prints a newline whether or not you want one.

One of the most useful functions declared in stdio.h is gets ("get string"). When you call this function, it waits until the user types something and presses Enter. Then the function places the entire line of input — spaces and all — into the string argument. For example:

```
#include <stdio.h>
//...
```

```
char str[81]; // Allow for max. chars on screen.
gets(str);   // Get line of input and place in str.
```

I have found using gets preferable to using scanf in all but the simplest programs. Once you read a line of input into a string, you are free to analyze it or interpret its contents any way that you choose. This capability is useful in writing a compiler or other sophisticated tool, because you can lexically analyze the input as you wish. In plain terms, this means that you have total control over which characters divide different fields and how sequences of spaces should be interpreted. When you use scanf or cin, you have no control over how a numeric or string field is defined. The scanf function gives you input when and if it decides that the user has typed something valid.

As a simple example of line input, you might decide that your program will accept input delineated by the at sign (@):

```
Here is some input@1234@More input@34.0005
```

The following code uses gets to input this entire line. The code then assigns each input field — delineated by @ — to a different string. This example demonstrates how you can input embedded spaces in strings, something that scanf and the cin input operator (>>) don't support. Each of the individual strings is read into a different row of the two-dimensional array sarray.

```
#include <stdio.h>
char str[81]; // Allow for max. chars on screen.
char sarray[50][81];

void main() {

    int i = 0;
    char *p = str;
    char *s;

    gets(str); // Get line of input and place in str.

    while(*p != '\0') {

    // Set s equal to next string in array.
        s = sarray[i++];

    // Read chars into string, up to next @.
        while (*p != '\0' && *p != '@')
            *s++ = *p++;
```

```
    // Stop reading - terminate string and advance
    //   pointer past the @.
        *s = '\0';
        p++;
    }
}
```

When you have isolated a numeric field (for example, "1234") as input to one of these strings, you can optionally convert it to a numeric value by calling the `atoi` or `atof` function. See Section 6 for more information on these functions. Section 6 also provides information on the string-tokenizing function `strtok`, which you can use to automate some of this work.

By itself, the previous program doesn't do anything. You can, however, print the contents of all the strings that were read in by adding this code just before the end — that is, the last closing brace — of `main`:

```
i = 0;
s = sarray[0];
while (*s != '\0') {
    s = sarray[i++];
    puts(s);
}
```

It is possible to read in strings of length zero. This happens, for example, if the user enters a line of input such as "@This is a @@@string." If a zero-length string is read, this code will still work fine.

File Operations with stdio.h

The line-oriented I/O functions of the previous section — `gets` and `puts` — are put to good use in the next example, which demonstrates sequential file I/O. This example prompts the user for a file name, but the user has the option of just pressing Enter. The `gets` function responds in a reasonable way by inputting an empty string.

File input and output is almost as easy in C++ as it is in any other language. If you use the standard library functions declared in stdio.h, follow these four basic steps:

1. Include the stdio.h header file and declare a file pointer of type `FILE*`. (Repeat this last part for each file that you want to open.)

2. Open the file by calling the `fopen` function. This function returns a value that you assign to the file pointer.

3. Read or write to the file as appropriate using file I/O functions such as `fprintf`, `fscanf`, `fputs`, and `fgets`, and so on. These functions work almost the same way as their counterparts `printf`, `scanf`, `puts`, and `gets`, except that they take a file pointer as an additional argument.

4. Close the file by calling the `fclose` function.

Figure 4-3 illustrates the first three steps. This figure is a bit over-simplified. In step 2, the `fopen` function actively checks the file system. (The function does more than associate a file with a name.) If the requested file is not found, or for some reason cannot be opened, the program must stop and respond to the error condition.

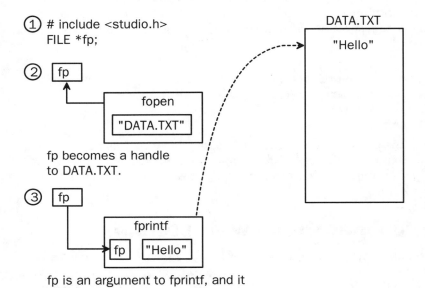

① # include <studio.h>
FILE *fp;

② fp

fopen
"DATA.TXT"

fp becomes a handle
to DATA.TXT.

③ fp

fprintf
fp "Hello"

fp is an argument to fprintf, and it
directs output to the file.

DATA.TXT

"Hello"

Figure 4-3 *Summary of file I/O programming.*

The following example program illustrates each of these steps, although it calls `fgetc` rather than `fprintf`. Note that `main` has a return value in this program. This technique enables `main` to return a code to the operating system: 0 (for success) or –1 (for error).

```
// Sample program to print out the contents of a text
//   file, converting all lowercase to uppercase.
//   The program prompts for the filename.
```

```
#include <stdio.h>
#include <ctype.h>

int main()
{
    int c;
    FILE *fp;
    char filename[81];

    printf("Enter file name, please: ");
    gets(filename);
    if ((*filename) == '\0') { // Is string empty?
        puts("No file name entered.\n");
        return -1;
    }

/* Open for reading; "r" specifies read mode. */

    fp = fopen(filename, "r");
    if (!fp) {
        puts("Error: file name not found.\n");
        return -1;
    }
    while ((c = fgetc(fp)) != EOF)
        putchar(toupper(c));

    fclose(fp);
    return 0;
}
```

In the example, the file is treated as an input file, so it is opened for read mode in line 23 (reprinted below). The second argument is a string containing "r," for read mode. Write mode is "w," and read-write mode is "rw."

```
fp = fopen(filename, "r");
```

The example program calls the fgetc function to read from the file. This function reads a single character from the input stream and is the file-input version of getchar, which reads a single character from standard input. The character read is compared to EOF, a constant defined in stdio.h, that indicates the end-of-file condition.

Line 28 (reprinted below) calls fgetc. This complex line of code calls fgetc to get a character; assigns the result to the integer variable, c; and compares that value to EOF. As long as the value returned is not EOF (the end of file has not yet been reached), the loop continues.

```
while ((c = fgetc(fp)) != EOF)
    //...
```

All the file operations in this chapter assume *sequential* access with text-based I/O. Such access techniques treat files as streams similar to the screen and keyboard. This access mode is often easiest to program, because it grows out of the standard I/O techniques (`printf`, `scanf`, and so on) that most beginners start with.

However, you can just as easily use stdio.h functions to read and write to binary files. You can also perform random access by moving the file pointer. For more information on file I/O functions in stdio.h, see page 178 in Section 6.

Files and Stream Operators

The stream concept can be applied to disk files as much as to the screen and keyboard. C++ supports objects of type `ifstream` (input-file stream) and `ofstream` (output-file stream). You create these objects by specifying the name during initialization. First, however, include the file fstream.h. This file automatically includes all the contents of iostream.h.

```
#include <fstream.h>
```

To create file-stream objects, specify the name in parentheses when you define the object. For example:

```
ifstream inf("C:\\TXT\\DATA.TXT");
ofstream outf("C:\\TXT\\OUTPUT.TXT");
```

As always when specifying full pathnames, remember to use double backslashes inside C-quoted strings whenever you're indicating a single backslash. Once the objects are defined and initialized with full or relative pathnames, you can use them just as you can `cin` and `cout`.

```
outf << "Here is a string written to a file.";

long n;
inf >> n;
```

Stream objects evaluate to null values if an error condition, such as end-of-file, is present. Thus, you can write loops, such as the following, that stop after text has been exhausted.

```
char string[81];
while (inf)
    inf.getline(string, 80);
```

The getline function is a member function of the inf object; getline provides the same functionality that gets and fgets do. The first argument is a character string in which the characters read are stored; the second argument is the maximum number of characters to read.

This program prints the contents of the file DATA.TXT:

```
#include <fstream.h>

void main() {
    char buffer[81];

// Open input file C:\STUFF.TXT.

    ifstream inf("C:\\STUFF.TXT");

// While end of file not reached, get and print
//   a line of text, appending a newline each time.

    while (inf) {
        inf.getline(buffer, 80);
        cout << buffer << "\n";
    }
}
```

You can also use the I/O stream classes to read and to write to binary files, as well as to perform random access. See Section 7 for more information on all the I/O stream classes, including the file-stream classes ifstream, ofstream, and frstream.

To Stream or Not to Stream

At this point, you may be wondering: With so many ways to get input and print output, which way should I use?

Some C++ authors only use the stream objects cin and cout, and do so for a good reason. These objects, along with their related classes, functions, and operators, make use of object orientation. For many people, the stream objects represent the "new, better" way of doing things. At the same time, printf and scanf work perfectly well, and if you're maintaining C legacy code, you may be living with them for a long time.

If you have printf and scanf legacy code, but want to introduce the stream objects into the same application, you can do so, although it can get messy. If you must mix them, make sure that you use the sync_with_stdio function (p. 290) to avoid conflicts.

Here are the specific, practical advantages of the stream objects:

- They are easier to use. You never have to look up format specifiers. When you send an expression to cout, the expression's own type determines how it should be printed. At the same time, you can modify the format as needed.

- Because they use the object-oriented approach, the stream objects are *extensible,* in that they can accommodate new data. This may sound esoteric, but it has concrete benefits. printf and scanf are written to support a specific set of formats. If a new data type comes along, there is no way to make printf and scanf accommodate it. However, you can always make cin and cout work directly with new types. Chapter 10 describes exactly how.

- Because of this extensibility, you can assume that the stream objects support any primitive data type the compiler supports, including long long and long double. printf and scanf lack this support, because they support only the specific formats described for those two functions (p. 205 and p. 214).

In short, cin and cout beautifully illustrate two distinctive features of C++. First, C++ is more sensitive to type information. You don't use format specifiers with cin and cout, because the language is smart enough to recognize the types of the operands and respond appropriately.

Second, cin and cout illustrate object orientation. In traditional programming, a facility like printf is frozen: it works with a fixed set of types. In theory, you could rewrite printf to work with a larger set of data formats — but you would need to have access to the original source and then recompile. Regardless of the number of formats printf supports, it is still a finite set. If someone comes up with a new type later, printf won't support it. This limitation doesn't apply to cin and cout.

What's beautiful is that you can see the benefits in a few lines of code. Most situations illustrating object-oriented benefits involve entire systems. With cin and cout, however, you can see much of the point of object orientation: it lets you create flexible entities that work easily with new situations and new types. The next chapter begins a much fuller exploration of this world of objects.

A Touch of Class

A key concept in C++ is active types: a type is defined in terms of what can be *done* with it, as well as by its internal structure. This is what classes are all about.

If you create your own string type, for example, what would it mean to add two strings? If you have a mathematical bent, you could define a complex-number type; what would it mean to add or multiply them? In C++, you can define any new type and any operations on that type.

Class describes any kind of user-defined type. Once a class is defined, it becomes part of the language itself for all practical purposes. Classes, in short, extend C++.

Developing Class: A Better String Type

When people first learn C, they often complain that character strings are cumbersome. In BASIC, for example, you can do this:

```
str1 = "My name is "
str2 = "Bill."
str3 = str1 + str2
```

Now str3 contains the message "My name is Bill." In standard C, this operation takes more work:

```
strcpy(str1, "My name is ");
strcpy(str2, "Bill.");
strcpy(str3, str1);
strcat(str3, str2);
```

In this chapter, and in the two chapters that follow, we'll build a new string type that is every bit as good as the string type in BASIC. In many ways, the new string type will be better than anything in BASIC because it will give you the ability to customize the type. When you work with classes in C++, you can add new capabilities to them at any time.

From now on, whenever I talk about a user-defined type, I'll follow C++ terminology in my use of the term class. This term applies to structures and unions, as well as to anything created with the class keyword.

To create a class, use the class keyword with this syntax:

```
class class_name {
    declarations
};
```

In C++, the declarations can include function declarations as well as data declarations. (Functions and variables in a class are called *member functions* and *data members*, respectively.) First, let's look at the simplest possible string class:

```
class CStr {
    char    sData[256];
};
```

The name CStr is the class name, and sData is a data member that holds the contents of the class. This simple class stores the string data. Now let's add some member functions:

```
class CStr {
private:
    char sData[256];
public:
    char *get(void);
    int  getlength(void);
    void cpy(char *s);
    void cat(char *s);
};
```

The string data, sData, is declared private to the class. No one can touch it except the class's own functions. The last half of this chapter rewrites the internals of the class, but code that uses the old version of the class will still work. This is a big advantage of classes.

When you declare classes with the class keyword, all declarations are private by default. It is a good idea to explicitly declare items private by using the private keyword; however, you can save a little work by omitting the keyword. The previous declaration is exactly equivalent to this:

```
class CStr {
    char sData[256];
public:
    char *get(void);
    int  getlength(void);
    void cpy(char *s);
    void cat(char *s);
};
```

Member Functions: A Class Act

You can write definitions for member functions just as you would for any other function, with one difference: the function name must be preceded by a special prefix.

class_name::

The two colons (::) form a single operator, called the *scope-resolution operator*. This operator, combined with the class name, clarifies which function you're referring to. More than one class can have a function with the same name. For example, a class named CMyclass can also have a function named get. Outside the class declarations,

CMyclass::get

refers to the version of the get function belonging to CMyclass, and

CStr::get

refers to the version of the get function belonging to CStr. The syntax for a class-member function definition is:

return_type class_name::*function_name* (*arguments*) {
    statements
}

In this case, the class name is CStr. In the function definitions that follow, remember that "CStr::" is simply part of the function name. Aside from this *class_name* prefix, these function definitions look just like those you might write for ordinary functions.

```
#include <string.h>
char* CStr::get(void) {   // Return ptr to string data.
     return sData;
}

int CStr::getlength(void) { // Return length.
     return strlen(sData);
}

void CStr::cpy(char *s) {     // Copy from string arg.
     strcpy(sData, s);
}

void CStr::cat(char *s) {     // Concatenate string arg
     strcat(sData, s);        //   onto object.
}
```

Figure 5-1 summarizes how declarations and function definitions are linked by the class name, which in this case is CStr.

```
class CStr (
     char sData[256];
public:
     char *get(void);
     int getlength(void);
     void cpy(char *s);
     void cat(char *s);
};

#include <string.h>
char *CStr::get(void) {   // Return ptr to string data.
     return sData;
}

int CStr::getlength(void) {   // Return length.
     return strlen(sData);
}

void CStr::cpy(char *s) { // Copy string arg to object.
     strcpy(sData, s);
}

void CStr::cat(char *s) { // Concatenate string arg
     strcat(sData, s);    //   onto object.
}
```

Figure 5-1   *CStr class declaration and function definitions.*

Organizing the code into files

Declarations should be placed in a header file. Function code should be placed in a C++ source file that is compiled and linked into the current project or a library. With this approach, CStr code is organized this way:

```
//------------------------------------------------------
// cstr.h
// This file declares the CStr class.
// Every module that refers to CStr must include
//  this file.

class CStr {
    char sData[256];
public:
    char *get(void);
    int  getlength(void);
    void cpy(char *s);
    void cat(char *s);
};

//------------------------------------------------------
// cstr.cpp
// This file contains definitions of CStr functions.
// Compile this file and link to the project.

#include "cstr.h"
#include <string.h>

char* CStr::get(void) {  // Return ptr to string data.
    return sData;
}

int CStr::getlength(void) { // Return length.
    return strlen(sData);
}

void CStr::cpy(char *s) {    // Copy from string arg.
    strcpy(sData, s);
}

void CStr::cat(char *s) {    // Concatenate string arg
    strcat(sData, s);        //  onto object.
}
```

Alternatively, if you want to declare a class used only within a single module of a single project, you can place all the code in a single .cpp file, including the declaration. The approach described earlier — using separate header and implementation files — is appropriate for classes that will see a lot of use in different projects.

Another approach is to place all the class declarations for a project in a single header file. In any case, function definitions that are not part of a class declaration *must* be placed in one or more .cpp files and compiled.

The deadly semi: Watch out for that syntax!

One syntax error you're sure to make a few times — unless you're careful — is to use too many or too few semicolons. Class declarations end with them; function definitions do not.

As a general rule, C and C++ statements do not follow a terminating brace (}) with a semicolon. All function definitions follow this rule:

```
char *CStr::get(void) {
    return sData;
}
```

However, class, struct, and union declarations require a semicolon after the terminating brace.

```
class CStr {
    char sData[256];
public:
    char *get(void);
    int  getlength(void);
    void cpy(char *s);
    void cat(char *s);
};
```

This rule may seem one of the more arbitrary rules in C and C++, but it does have the benefit of helping the compiler distinguish between declarations and function definitions. All declarations, except function definitions, require the terminating semicolon. This includes function prototypes, whether or not they're inside a class:

```
char *get(void);
```

What's an object, anyway?

Together, a class declaration and function definitions define how the string type works. The next step is to use the CStr declaration to create some strings:

```
#include "cstr.h."

CStr  str1, str2, str3;
```

In C++, as soon as you have successfully declared a class, you can use the class name to declare variables, just as you can with int, long, float, double, and so on. The class name takes on the same status in the language that data-type keywords have.

●—C/C++———————————————————————

The capability to define variables extends to the struct and union keywords. In C++, as soon as you declare a structure Mystruct, you can use it to declare variables:

```
Mystruct a, b, c, d;
```

In C, you have to use the struct keyword:

```
struct Mystruct a, b, c, d;
```

Alternatively, you could use a typedef declaration to skip this step. In either case, C requires extra work. For the sake of compatibility with C, C++ supports this same use of struct and typedef. After you start using C++, you can adopt the practice of declaring variables directly.

After you have declared the strings, what do you call them? What are the entities a, b, c, and d in this declaration?

```
CStr a, b, c, d;
```

These variables are all objects. If you have been listening to the dogma of object orientation, this may be an exciting moment for you — you finally have objects!

Before you celebrate, however, you should realize that you've been using objects all along. An object in C++ is just a variable or other piece of data. What's exciting about objects in C++ is that some objects — through their class declaration — can support function calls and other operations.

Calling a member function

Without further ado, let's look at behavior in the string objects. These objects know how to respond to the get, getlength, cpy, and cat functions:

```
#include "cstr.h"

CStr string1, string2;

string1.cpy("My name is ");  // Copy string to string1
string2.cpy("Bill.");        // Copy string to string2
string1.cat(string2.get());  // Concat string2 onto
                             //   string1

puts(string1.get());         // Get string1 data and
                             //   print
```

Each of the last four lines involves a call to a member function. Note the use of the dot (.) in a function call:

```
object.member_function(arguments)
```

If you've used structures in C, this syntax should look familiar. It's a natural extension of the syntax used to refer to a structure member:

```
object.member
```

Let's look more closely at one function call. This first function call gives a command to the string1 object, in effect saying, "Copy the given string to yourself."

```
string1.cpy("My name is ");  // Copy string to string1
```

This function call tells string1 to copy the data "My name is " to itself. The string1 object knows how to copy other strings this way because it has a built-in cpy function. Figuratively, you can say that cpy is part of the object's behavior.

In actuality, what happens is this: The compiler recognizes string1.cpy() as a function call. It knows that string1 is an object of the class CStr. The function call is therefore resolved as a call to CStr::cpy (see Figure 5-2).

Earlier in the program, string1 and string2 were defined as objects of class CStr. So calls to string2.cpy() also result in calls to CStr::cpy. Objects of the same class share all their function code, and in this sense, have the same behavior.

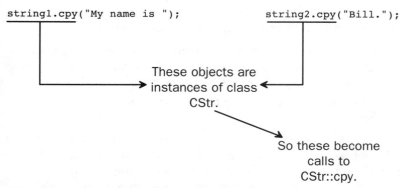

Figure 5-2   *Resolving calls to member functions.*

What happens in the `CStr::cpy` function call? Control passes to the `CStr::cpy` function, just as it would with any normal function call.

But something interesting is going on here, as Figure 5-3 shows: the variable `sData` is a `CStr` data member. This data member belongs to the object `string1`.

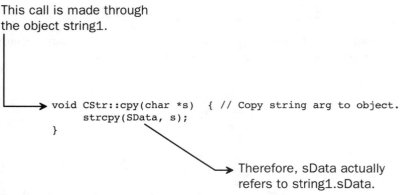

Figure 5-3   *Member function access to data members.*

Each object of class `CStr` has its own copy of the data member `sData`. In this example, the statement calls `CStr::cpy` through the string object `string1`. Thus, when the function refers to `sData`, it is `string1`'s copy of `sData` that is referenced. Figure 5-3 illustrates this connection.

Code and data work differently in objects. The following rules hold true regardless of what's public and what's private:

- Objects of the same class share function code. C++ resolves a call to a member function by determining the object's class and then calling *class*::*member_function*.

- But each individual object has its own copy of the data members.

One way to understand this difference is to remember that objects are just packets of data. If you've worked with structures in C, the fact that C++ objects have data members is nothing new. Because these packets are collections of variables, they can vary from each other. Each C++ object has its own copy of the data members.

The concept of member functions is what's new. But member functions are just functions restricted to working on data of a particular class. A member function works equally well on any object in its class. Functions, therefore, exist at the class level.

Figure 5-4 illustrates the class/object relationship and how it involves code and data. Assume that you define four string objects: str1, str2, str3, and str4:

```
CStr   str1, str2, str3, str4;
```

Each of these objects shares code created for the CStr class while also having its own copy of the CStr data member sData.

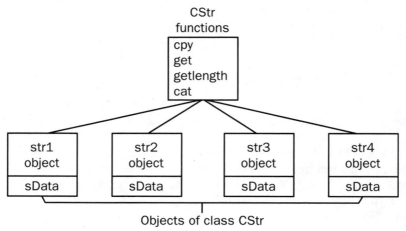

Figure 5-4   *Code and data in the CStr class.*

In this case, there is only one data member, but most classes have more than one. For example, you might create a class CTemp_point, which locates a point in three-dimensional space and a temperature value:

```
class CTemp_point {
    int    x, y, z;
    double temp;
public:
    void   set_point(int x, y, z);
    void   get_point(int *x, *y, *z);
    void   set_temp(double new_temp);
    double get_temp(void);
};
```

Assume, also, that you define four objects of this class:

```
CTemp_point  pntA, pntB, pntC, pntD;
```

Here, all the instances of this class — that is, the individual points — share the CTemp_point function code just as string objects share the CStr function code. However, each point has its own copy of the four data members: x, y, z, and temp (see Figure 5-5).

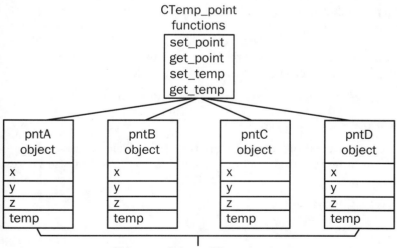

Figure 5-5 *Code and data in the CTemp_point class.*

Member functions: A walk-through

If it's clear to you how member functions work, you can skip to the next section. This section gives an additional perspective on the working of member functions by walking through a series of function calls. Consider this code:

```
#include "cstr.h"

CStr  string1, string2;

string1.cpy("My name is "); // Call CStr::cpy.
string2.cpy("Bill.");       // Call CStr::cpy.
string1.cat(string2.get()); // Call CStr::cat and
                            //  CStr::get.
puts(string1.get());        // Call CStr::get.
```

The first function call results in a call to CStr::cpy, because string1 is an object of type CStr. The result of this call is to set string1's copy of the data member:

```
string1.cpy("My name is "); // Call CStr::cpy.
```

The next line of code results in a call to the same function, CStr::cpy. This time, however, the call is made through the object string2, so that it is string2's data member that is changed:

```
string2.cpy("Bill.");       // Call CStr::cpy.
```

The next two statements result in calls to CStr::cat and CStr::get (the latter is called twice in this code).

```
string1.cat(string2.get()); // Call CStr::cat and
                            //  CStr::get.
puts(string1.get());        // Call CStr::get.
```

As a final example, consider another class declaration, CTemp_point. Assume that the function definitions are provided elsewhere in the program.

```
class CTemp_point {
    int    x, y, z;
    double temp;
public:
    void  set_point(int x, y, z);
    void  get_point(int *x, *y, *z);
    void   set_temp(double new_temp);
    double get_temp(void);
};
```

With this declaration, you might declare two objects:

```
CTemp_point  mypoint, point_break;
```

The following function call results in a call to `CTemp_point::set_point`. If any data members are affected, they will be `mypoint`'s copy of these members.

```
mypoint.set_point(0, 0, 0);
```

Pointers to Objects

Just as you can have pointers to structures and pointers to variables, you can have pointers to objects in C++.

To create objects dynamically, you have to use pointers. This means creating objects on the fly and allocating and freeing them at will, without necessarily giving them the lifetime of a program or even the lifetime of a function call.

C++ supports the `new` and `delete` operators for dynamic object creation. (These were introduced in Chapter 3.) The `new` operator returns a pointer. When you use it, you follow it with a type or class name.

```
CStr *pString;
pString = new CStr;
//...
delete pString;            // Free allocated memory
```

Although you could use the `malloc` and `free` functions to allocate memory for objects, `new` and `delete` are much better because they automatically call constructors and destructors. You learn about constructors and destructors later in this chapter.

The syntax for using pointers to objects in C++ is a natural extension of that for pointers to structures in C. To refer to a data member, use the `->` operator:

ptr->member

Not surprisingly, you can use a similar syntax to call member functions for the object pointed to:

ptr->member_function(args)

Reaping the Benefits of Private Data

You may be wondering what's so wonderful about classes and member functions. After all, isn't the member-function technology just so much syntactic sugar? What is the difference between these two function calls?

```
strcpy(string1, "hello");
string1.cpy("hello");
```

There's at least one major benefit to member-function technology. In the standard approach, rewriting a module is always risky and prone to cause problems in any code using the module. With classes, however, you can rewrite the function definitions, as well as private data members, without causing errors.

A pressing problem in software development is this: How do you fix, update, or alter one part of a program without disrupting the parts that interact with it? Object orientation helps solve this problem. As long you leave the public members alone, you can change all the private members. You can also rewrite public function definitions as long as you don't change the argument or return types.

The original class declaration of CStr was far from optimal. It can be improved for efficiency and flexibility. One problem is that the current implementation of CStr fixes its maximum size at 256 bytes. This may be too small in some cases, and overkill in other cases.

```
class CStr {
    char sData[256];
public:
    char *get(void);
    int  getlength(void);
    void cpy(char *s);
    void cat(char *s);
};
```

Enough of this inefficiency. A better implementation uses a pointer that can be set to any address. It also stores length as an integer for more efficient reporting of length.

```
class CStr {
    char *pData;
    int  nLength;
public:
    char *get(void);
    int  getlength(void);
```

```
        void cpy(char *s);
        void cat(char *s);
};
```

The internal members of CStr have changed. But because the public declarations haven't changed, the rest of the program isn't affected.

Because sData is gone, all the function definitions must be rewritten. In this implementation, strings are created and re-created as needed through dynamic memory allocation.

```
#include <string.h>

char *CStr::get(void) {  // Return ptr to string data.
    return pData;
}

int  CStr::getlength(void) { // Return length.
    return nLength;
}

void CStr::cpy(char *s) {    // Copy string arg.
    int n;

    n = strlen(s);
    if (nLength != n) {
        if (pData)
            delete [] pData;
        pData = new char[n + 1];
        nLength = n;
    }
    strcpy(pData, s);
}

void CStr::cat(char *s) {    // Concatenate string arg.
    int n;
    char *pTemp;

    n = strlen(s);
    if (n == 0)
        return;
    pTemp = new char[n + nLength + 1];
    if (pData) {
        strcpy(pTemp, pData);
        delete [] pData;
    }
    strcat(pTemp, s);
```

```
        pData = pTemp;
        nLength += n;
}
```

Even though many changes were made, all the code that uses the `CStr` class still works. For example, the following code, used with the previous version of `CStr`, continues to work correctly without any change:

```
CStr string1, string2;

string1.cpy("My name is ");  // Copy string to string1.
string2.cpy("Bill.");         // Copy string to string2.
string1.cat(string2.get());   // Concat string2 onto
                              //   string1.
puts(string1.get());          // Get string1 data and
                              //   print.
```

Even though the externals of `CStr` haven't changed, the change to the class has been profound. `CStr` behaves the same way as before and looks the same to the outside world, but the way it goes about doing things is much more efficient. The `CStr` implementation now uses the `new` operator to allocate exactly the amount of bytes needed for the data at any given time. The next section walks through how these functions work.

You've had a taste of object-oriented magic — you can alter large parts of the class-definition code all you want without worrying about introducing unforeseen errors into the rest of the program.

This magic is called *encapsulation*. It means that certain parts of the object are encapsulated, or protected, from the outside (Figure 5-6). There must be some interaction with the outside world, of course, or the class is useless. This external part is usually called the *interface*.

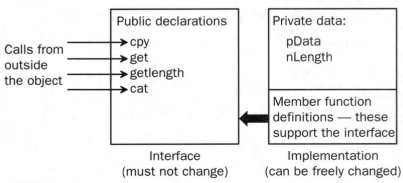

Figure 5-6 *Encapsulation in the CStr class.*

In standard C, any statement can reach into the internals of a data structure and access any part of it. That's fine until you rewrite the data structure in some way. At that point, your debugging nightmares begin, because all the code anywhere that refers to the structure must be rewritten — and in a big program, you've probably forgotten all the places that refer to your data structure! Encapsulation prevents these nightmares.

The Dynamic-Memory Implementation: A Walk-Through

In the last section, I claimed that the new implementation for CStr is much more efficient. This is true even though there is more code to execute.

The new class is more efficient in its use of string memory. Every string occupies exactly the memory it needs at any time. This memory management is not free: more statements are needed to manage the memory. Yet overall, the result is a better string class. Best of all, there is no arbitrary limit of 256 bytes of storage.

The cpy and cat functions make use of the new and delete operators. As described in Chapter 3, the new operator returns a requested block of memory just as the malloc function does. However, new is a little easier to use and doesn't require a header file. The use of new takes this general form:

```
pointer = new type[num_elements];
```

After the memory is no longer needed, you can free this same block by calling the delete operator:

```
delete [] pointer;
```

● **NOTE** ───────────────────────────────

All the memory allocation for CStr can be done by using malloc and free rather than new and delete. However, make sure that you always use free with malloc and delete with new. Don't attempt to cross-pollinate the operators and functions.

Under this new implementation, the cpy member function copies a new string into the current string data area. However, it has an important side effect. If the new string data is longer or shorter than the current string, the current string must grow or expand in size. This is crucial if the new string is longer, because there are no unused bytes in this implementation. Strings cannot grow without corrupting other data.

The solution is to allocate a new block of memory and copy the new data there. The steps are:

1. Get the length of new string data.

2. If the new length is different from the current length, then free the current memory block and allocate a new memory block of the same size as the new string.

3. Copy the new string data into this memory block.

First, the function gets the length of the new string data and stores it in the local variable n:

```
n = strlen(s);
```

Next, this length is compared to the current length, and, if they are not equal, the current string data must grow or shrink to the new size — plus one for the null terminator. The easiest way to do that is to release the current block and then allocate a new block of the correct size. Finally, the class variable nLength is updated to the new length.

Remember that one additional byte must be allocated for the terminating null.

```
if (nLength != n) {
    if (pData)
        delete [] pData;
    pData = new char[n + 1];
    nLength = n;
}
```

The rest of the function copies the new string data to the object's current string data (pointed to by class variable pData).

```
strcpy(pData, s);
```

The cat (concatenate) member function is more complex. It must create a new memory block but also copy data from the current string data, all before finally concatenating the new string. Without this preliminary work, there would be no room for the object's string data to grow without corrupting other data. The concatenation steps are:

1. Get the length of the new string data. Return immediately if this string is zero length, because there's nothing more to do.

2. Allocate a memory block large enough to hold the combined strings, plus 1 byte for the terminating null.

3. If there is current string data, copy this data to the new memory block and then delete the old memory block.

4. Finally, concatenate the new string and update pData to point to the new memory block. Update nLength as well.

The first three lines get the length of the new string data and return immediately if the length is zero:

```
n = strlen(s);
if (n == 0)
    return;
```

The function then allocates a memory block large enough for the combined strings plus 1 byte for the terminating null.

```
pTemp = new char[n + nLength + 1];
```

You now have a new memory block, pointed to by pTemp, that is big enough to hold the combined strings. The next thing to do is to copy the current string data into this block and then free the memory block that held that data:

```
if (pData) {
    strcpy(pTemp, pData);
    delete [] pData;
}
```

At this point, there is a memory block containing the current string, and it has the extra room needed to concatenate the new string data onto the end. After performing the concatenation, the function ends by updating pData and nLength:

```
strcat(pTemp, s);
pData = pTemp;
nLength += n;
```

Life and Death of an Object: Constructors

The CStr class has a couple of problems. First, until string data is assigned, the pData member doesn't point to anything. This is risky, because the user may expect to always get a meaningful address even if it is only the address of an empty string. But the get function simply returns pData, which might be a null pointer.

```
char *CStr::get(void) {  // Return ptr to string data.
    return pData;
}
```

The best solution is to initialize pData when an object is created. I've been relying on the fact that, by default, member variables are initialized to zero or (in the case of pointers) to NULL. However, this is not good programming practice.

There's a worse problem. Nothing frees the current memory block when the string is destroyed. The result is a *memory leak;* every time a string is created, initialized, and destroyed, it leaves behind a hole in memory. If you don't have infinite memory, this could be a problem.

● **NOTE**

When an object is defined as local to a function, it's destroyed as soon as the function terminates. Global objects terminate when the program ends.

The general problem is that there's a need to take certain actions when the object is created, and certain actions later when it's destroyed. Fortunately, C++ makes object initialization and cleanup easy by providing constructors and destructors. These special member functions control how an object is created or destroyed. The naming syntax is unusual: for a given class,

- the name of a constructor is *class*, and
- the name of a destructor is ~ *class*.

The string class is named CStr, so the constructor and destructor are named CStr and ~CStr, respectively:

```
class CStr {
    char *pData;
    int  nLength;
public:
    CStr();          // Constructor
    ~CStr();         // Destructor

    char *get(void);
    int  getlength(void);
    void cpy(char *s);
    void cat(char *s);
};
```

Constructors and destructors have some quirks. One quirk is that they have no return type of any kind — not even void. This is an exception to the rule that every C++ function must have a return type. Another quirk is that instead of using void, the argument lists are left blank.

The function definition for the constructor initializes the two class variables as well as allocating a 1-byte string. The string contains a null terminator:

```
CStr::CStr() {
    pData = new char[1];
    *pData = '\0';
    nLength = 0;
}
```

Odd, isn't it? The name CStr appears twice in the function heading. The first occurrence of CStr should be taken together with the scope-resolution operator (::) as an indicator that this function is a member of the CStr class. So CStr:: is a prefix. The second occurrence of CStr is the name of the function itself.

The destructor is simpler. All it does is release the current memory block by using delete. Remember that the name of the function is ~CStr.

```
CStr::~CStr() {
    delete [] pData;
}
```

Destructors tend to be limited. All a destructor does is free any loose system resources hanging around. Constructors, however, have more interesting possibilities. You learn more about them in Chapter 6.

Function Inlining for Fun and Profit

OK, you say, encapsulation sounds wonderful, but it's too inefficient. (Remember that encapsulation is the concept that internals, such as pData and nLength, cannot be accessed from outside. The user of an object has to call public functions to get at the values.) Encapsulation has many benefits, but it also means that you often end up with one-line functions such as these:

```
char *CStr::get(void) {  // Return ptr to string data.
    return pData;
}

int  CStr::getlength(void) { // Return length.
    return nLength;
}
```

There's a certain overhead associated with each function call, so calling a function rather than just getting a value slows performance.

Fortunately, C++ provides an optimal solution: inline functions. *Inline* refers to expanding something directly into the body of the code (that is, placing it inline) instead of executing a jump via the processor's CALL instruction. For extremely short functions, the inline approach is ideal. In this case, if `getlength` were an inline function, then the compiler would, in effect, replace this statement:

```
x = string1.getlength();
```

with this:

```
x = string1.nLength;
```

This arrangement eliminates function-call overhead and preserves execution speed.

Normally, this second C++ statement is illegal (nLength is private and can't be accessed), but because nLength is accessed through getlength, a public member, there is no problem. The inline function approach preserves both encapsulation and efficiency.

In C++, functions are automatically inlined when you place them inside the class declaration. Here, it is done for get and getlength:

```
class CStr {
    char *pData;
    int  nLength;
public:
    CStr();             // Constructor
    ~CStr();            // Destructor

    char *get(void) {return pData;}
    int  getlength(void) {return nLength;}
    void cpy(char *s);
    void cat(char *s);
};
```

Despite their brevity, get and getlength are functions and obey the same syntax rules that normal functions do. Each can have more than one statement if you choose, although most inline functions are very short. As with standard function definitions, the closing brace in these function definitions is not followed by a semicolon.

C++ also supports an `inline` keyword so that you can selectively make any function an inline function. But as I said, inlining is automatic inside a class declaration.

Structures as a Special Case of Classes

How is a class different from a structure? If you've used structures in C, you'll recall that they're collections of data that can be of varying types. How is this different from a class?

In C++, you can add member functions to struct declarations as well as to class declarations. The only difference between struct and class is that all members are public by default in a struct declaration, and private by default in a class declaration. The struct behavior, incidentally, is necessary to make it backward compatible with C.

The situation is potentially confusing because the word "class" refers not just to types created with the class keyword, but also to types created with struct and union. Think of structures and unions as special cases of classes in which everything is public by default. When you use the class keyword, everything is private by default — which is the preferred way to do things, because C++ encourages encapsulation.

Classes in Perspective

Classes are a simple and elegant concept. A class is a user-defined type in which part of the definition of that type can include the operations (functions) that it supports. In other words, you tell me what something is by what it can do.

Encapsulation

An important feature of C++ classes is encapsulation. This means a clean separation between the interface of a class, which is public to the world, and the internals, which cannot be accessed by anything outside the class. Such a separation is immensely useful, because it means that you can rewrite the internals of the class without messing up the rest of the program. (The revisions themselves should be error-free, but that goes without saying.) In the old world of C, intricate connections between internals throughout a program meant that any revisions at any time — no matter how correct they were in and of themselves — could wreck the entire system.

I'd like to report that object orientation has eliminated all causes of bugs, but you'd know I was kidding or given to delusions. Commitment to and use of encapsulation, however, does prevent a major cause of bugs.

Classes, objects, and instantiation

Another key concept is the distinction between classes and objects. A class is a user-defined type; an object is a thing of that type. This is not as abstract as it sounds. The class is the general mold or assembly line for a set of objects. The class determines the size, shape, properties, and built-in behavior of each object. Once the class is defined, any number of objects of that class may then be created.

For each class, there are zero or more objects. Each object belongs only to a single class — except when *multiple inheritance* is used. (Multiple inheritance is an advanced feature described in the glossary.) For the most part, the class-to-object relationship is a one-to-many relationship.

The process of creating an object of a certain class is referred to as *instantiation*. A class with zero objects has not been instantiated. Some classes — called *abstract* classes — can have an effect even though they are never instantiated. Chapter 9 discusses these kinds of classes further.

Classes: Reusing and publishing

Before concluding this chapter, I want to emphasize the true power of classes. The usefulness of a class becomes clear when it's versatile enough to be used in many programs.

You're on your way to creating just such a useful class with CStr. Once it's finished, it will become a useful language extension that you can use in many programs. There is still work to do, however.

A class is most useful when you can give it to someone else and say, "Here, use this in your own programs." To enable this class distribution, you should organize your code as follows:

- Place your class declaration in a header file. Header files traditionally contain type information that is needed by every module in a program, so programmers use an #include directive to read this type information into each module.

- Place your function definitions (except those that are inline) into a separate source file, which you compile and then give to the class user to link into his or her project. For an example of how code can be divided into header and source files, see the section "Organizing the Code into Files," earlier in this chapter.

The beauty of this division is that you need not share most of your source code with people who use your class if you choose not to. You need only provide the header file and object files containing compiled code. Class users include the header file with each of their modules and then add your object file to the linker command line. They can automate the latter step by the use of "make" files, projects, or batch files.

With this introduction to classes, you know almost enough to write useful classes that you can reuse in your programs. But even a mildly sophisticated class such as CStr needs a way to make copies of itself; it also ought to respond to operators. These two topics — copy constructors and operator functions — are the subject of the next two chapters.

5

Another Look at Constructors

6

The name *constructor* is apt: A constructor is a function that manufactures an object. You may think of constructors simply as initialization functions, but they have some important subtleties.

To write your classes correctly, you often need special constructors. One of the most important functions is the copy constructor, which tells the class how to pass an instance of itself as an argument or to return a value. As discussed in the next chapter, a class such as CStr is likely to cause errors without a correctly written copy constructor.

This chapter is shorter than Chapter 5. There are only a few key facts that you have to remember about constructors, but these facts are vital to your C++ health.

Overloading: Constructors and More Constructors

When you define a string object, you may want to initialize it in a variety of ways. For example, wouldn't it be nice to be able to place any and all of the following in your programs?

```
CStr a, b, c;                // Define with no initial
                             //   value.
CStr name("Joe Bloe");       // Initialize from char*.
CStr name2(name);            // Initialize from another
                             //   CStr.
```

Or even to combine them on the same line:

```
CStr title("The Big Show");
CStr a, name("Joe"), b(title);
```

Each of these declarations invokes a different constructor. C++ lets you write any number of constructors for the same class, in which each constructor takes a different type of argument or arguments. This is an example of the technique of *function overloading*, which means that the same function name can be reused in different contexts.

Remember that the name of the constructor is always the same as the name of the class itself. Here are the prototypes for the three constructors you need:

```
CStr();                  // No initializer.
CStr(char *s);           // Initialize from char*.
CStr(CStr &str);         // Initialize from another CStr.
```

Let's look at the first two constructors first. The third introduces a new use for the ampersand (&), which is discussed later in this chapter, in the section "The Copy Constructor and References."

●—NOTE

The term *overloading* occurs a good deal in C++ literature. In general, almost any C++ function — not just class functions — can be overloaded. Overloading means that you can reuse the same name and rely on differences in the argument list to distinguish one function from another. Either the number of arguments or the types of arguments (or both) must differ. (Argument names are irrelevant in this case.) For example, C++ considers the following two functions to be different, and each must have its own definition:

```
Display(int);
Display(char*);
```

C++ calls a different function — Display(int) or Display(char*) — depending on which type of argument it finds in the source code at compile time.

A Tale of Two Constructors

The first constructor is the one originally shown in Chapter 5. This constructor has the task of initializing an empty string:

```
CStr::CStr() {
    pData = new char[1];
    *pData = '\0';
    nLength = 0;
}
```

The CStr(char*) constructor, which initializes from a standard C string, is roughly the same length. The basic requirements for CStr constructors are always the same: allocate memory to hold string data, initialize the data, and initialize the nLength data member.

```
CStr::CStr(char *s) {
    pData = new char[strlen(s) + 1];
    strcpy(pData, s);
    nLength = strlen(s);
}
```

In both cases, the scope-resolution operator (CStr::) is used to prefix the constructor name, because these are function definitions and occur outside the CStr declaration.

These constructors are invoked in these example definitions:

```
CStr string1;                // Invoke CStr()
CStr string2("Hello, C++."); // Invoke CStr(char*)
```

Interlude with the Default Constructor

Before moving on to the third constructor, CStr(CStr&), let's look at a special kind of constructor, the default constructor. Surprise! This is actually the first constructor you looked at — the constructor with no arguments:

```
CStr::CStr() {
    pData = new char[1];
    *pData = '\0';
    nLength = 0;
}
```

Every class has, or should have, a default constructor. In every class, the default constructor is simply the constructor with no arguments. C++ has an interesting quirk concerning its handling of constructors:

- If a class declares no constructors of any kind, the compiler supplies a default constructor. This is a hidden constructor. This function is not sophisticated; it simply initializes all data members to zero. In the case of CStr, this behavior is inadequate, but it might be sufficient for simpler classes.

- However, if you go back and add any constructors to the class declaration, the compiler-supplied default constructor goes away. It simply vanishes!

The moral of the story should be clear: You should always include a default constructor, even if that constructor doesn't do anything. This is a form of defensive programming. It ensures that if you go back later and add other constructors, the default constructor won't vanish. (It will vanish if you rely on the compiler-supplied default constructor, but it won't vanish if you write your own, no matter how simple.)

●—NOTE ——————————————————————

Remember that the default constructor is simply the constructor with no arguments. For the CStr class, the default constructor is CStr( ).

Such a default constructor might well do nothing. For example:

```
class CHorse {
    BREED horse_breed;
    char *name;
public:
    CHorse();
};

CHorse::CHorse() {
}
```

The importance of having a default constructor cannot be over-emphasized. It so happens that the default constructor is invoked in two situations: when defining variables with no initial values (already mentioned), as well as when declaring an array of objects with uninitialized members.

```
CHorse  posse[30];
```

Default constructors are also invoked when you use the new operator without arguments — this operator (discussed in the previous chapter) is important in C++ and occurs frequently. If the default constructor is missing, all these situations result in an error.

Given the way I've described the behavior of C++ (making the hidden default constructor vanish as soon as you add your own constructors), it may sound as though the compiler is trying to play a nasty trick on you. Yet, the behavior makes sense if you think about it. C++ is designed to be as compatible as possible with C, which includes porting structures from C and considering them classes.

C has no notion of member functions or constructors, but simplistic classes (namely, C `struct` types) must be ported to C++ and work correctly. This is why the compiler supplies a hidden default constructor: to handle backward-compatibility cases in which there are no member functions at all. Once you start defining new classes and writing member functions, however, you should supply your own default constructor.

The Copy Constructor and References

The copy constructor `CStr(CStr&)` is another constructor that's difficult to live without. As mentioned earlier, the copy constructor is invoked when you use one object to initialize another of the same class:

```
CStr name("Joe Bloe");
CStr name2(name);        // Call copy constructor.
```

In the first line of code, `name` is defined and initialized from the string "Joe Bloe". C++ calls the constructor `CStr(char*)` to initialize this string. Then in the second line, `name2` is initialized as a copy of `name`. The object `name2` is the same type of object as `name` and should be assigned the same contents.

The constructor that tells how to make a copy from another object of the same type is the class's copy constructor. This constructor is very important, because, in addition to variable definition, it is automatically invoked in these situations:

- When an object of the class is passed by value. C++ calls the class's copy constructor to create a copy of the argument, which is then placed on the stack:

```
void Print_string(CStr str);
```

- When a function returns an object of the class — that is, the class is the return value type. C++ calls the copy constructor to create an object that is handed back to the function caller:

```
CStr Func1(void);
```

Because these situations are so common, the compiler supplies a hidden copy constructor if you don't provide one explicitly. However, this compiler-supplied constructor is simplistic. All it does is perform a simple member-by-member copy. In some cases, this is fine.

But CStr is a good example of a class in which a simple member-by-member copy is inadequate, and the results can be disastrous. Figure 6-1 shows what happens when this approach is used to copy one CStr object to another.

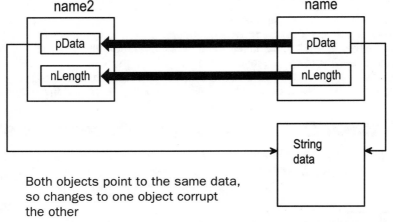

Figure 6-1   *Effects of simple a member-by-member copy on CStr objects.*

After the member-by-member copying is performed, the second object (name2) has a pointer to the same memory block that the first object points to. Such a situation works for now, but any change to either object could invalidate the other object's data. There are many ways this could happen, but the most obvious way occurs if one object is deleted. The string data is removed and now name2 has a pointer to nothing.

```
pString = new CStr;
pString->cpy("John Q. Public");
CStr name2(*pString);
//...
delete pString;        // String data removed.
puts(name2.get());     // Error! name2 has invalid ptr.
```

The basic idea of copying is that if you lose or destroy the original, the copy should live on and be fully usable. But that's not what happens here. When the copy constructor is invoked (in the third line of this example), it initializes the pointer name2.pData to the same address

as pString->pData. Deleting *pString frees the memory block, but
name2.pData still points to this same memory block, which is now
invalid.

Clearly, the copy constructor should do what the CStr(char*)
constructor does: allocate a new memory block and then make a
physical copy of the string data. This copy constructor is easy to
write because it should look almost exactly like CStr(char*). First,
however, you need to understand what references are and how they
are used in copy construction.

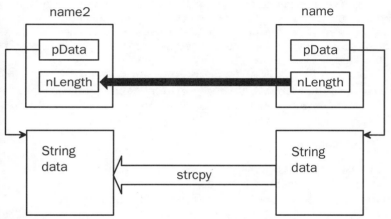

Figure 6-2 *Correct implementation of copy construction for CStr.*

References: The address operator (&) used in a new way

To write a copy constructor, you must use reference types. This
requires the use of the address operator (&) in a declaration.

In a simple variable definition, the ampersand indicates that
one variable is to be used as an alias for another variable.

```
int a;
int &b = a;  // b is an alias for a
a = 10;
b++;         // This increments a
```

In the preceding example, the ampersand is used to make b an
alias for a. The preceding code is functionally equivalent to the following code, which uses pointers:

```
int a, *b;
b = &a;      // *b is an alias for a
```

```
a = 10;
(*b)++;      // This increments a
```

A careful comparison of the two code examples highlights one critical difference: when b is defined as a reference (&b) in the first example, it is not treated as a pointer in the source code. The compiler may implement b as a pointer, but this fact is hidden by the C++ syntax; b looks like a normal integer.

●—**NOTE**

Declaring a reference and getting an address are two different actions, even though both use the ampersand (&). C++ may be confusing here because there are three or four different uses for the ampersand. In addition to declaring references and getting addresses, the ampersand is also used for bitwise AND, a binary operation.

You can use the ampersand simply to create aliases for variables, but the most important uses tend to occur in function calls. Look at the prototype for CStr's copy constructor:

```
CStr(CStr &str);
```

This constructor takes one argument, str, which is a reference type for CStr. This indicates to the compiler that the argument can actually be passed as a pointer, which is very efficient, but subsequent references to str avoid pointer syntax.

In simple terms, to make a copy of an object, the copy constructor gets a pointer to the original object and accesses members through that pointer. The source object is passed by reference, without explicit pointer syntax, just as you might do in BASIC, Pascal, or FORTRAN.

If you think about it, passing by reference is required here, so that the copy constructor gets a pointer rather than making a copy of its argument (str). If the copy constructor had to get a copy of an object before it could *create* a copy, then it would have to invoke itself before it ever got started! The result would be a self-defeating infinite loop.

Writing the copy constructor

At this point, all you need to remember about the address operator is this: treat the argument as a value and not a pointer, even though you know it's being passed by reference. A correct copy constructor for CStr is:

```
CStr::CStr(CStr &s) {
    char* sz = s.get();
    int n = s.getlength();
```

```
        pData = new char[n + 1];
        strcpy(pData, sz);
        nLength = n;
}
```

This function is similar to the CStr(char*) constructor. The principal difference is that the copy constructor must first extract the string and string-length data.

The header of the function definition may seem confusing at first because the class name, CStr, is used three times, although each time in a slightly different way. Figure 6-3 analyzes and explains each occurrence. The three uses are closely related, but each fulfills a different role in the syntax — scope qualifier, name, or argument type.

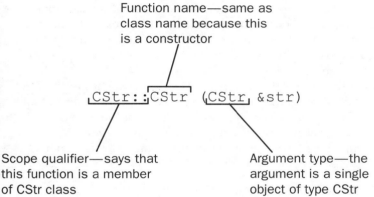

Figure 6-3 *Syntax of a copy constructor definition.*

The finishing touch: The const keyword

One reason for passing by reference is to enable the function to change the argument's value. If you've studied BASIC, FORTRAN, or Pascal, you've no doubt learned that this is the main reason for passing an argument by reference.

But the last thing the copy constructor should ever do is change its argument. Here, passing by reference is for efficiency's sake. One would like to pass by reference, but prevent the possibility of ever changing the argument.

Fortunately, C++ provides such a technique — place the const keyword in front of the argument declaration:

```
class CStr {

    CStr(const CStr &s);
```

```
    //...
};

// Copy constructor with const arg.
// All code is the same except for arg declaration.

CStr::CStr(const CStr &s) {
    char* sz = s.get();
    int n = s.getlength();
    pData = new char[n + 1];
    strcpy(pData, sz);
    nLength = n;
}
```

Now the copy constructor cannot change the value of any member of s. Any attempt to assign values to s or any of its data members would be flagged as an error by the compiler. Nor can s be passed to any other function unless that function also takes a const argument. Using a const argument is the preferred way to write a copy constructor, because it prevents errors.

But now there's another problem: The first two lines of the function make calls through the argument s. How does the compiler know that these function calls won't corrupt s? The solution is to declare the get and getlength functions as const functions. Doing so means that these functions have a contract to not change any data members, making them safe to call for a const object:

```
int getlength(void) const {return nLength;}
char *get(void) const {return pData;}
```

Whew! This extra work may make const seem like more trouble than it's worth, but all the rules make sense, if you think about them. For more information on the fine points of the const keyword, see page 76 in Section 4.

Other Constructor Examples

As another example, consider the CTemp_point class introduced in Chapter 5. This class produces objects that record a point on a three-dimensional grid and a temperature at that point. In the following code, several constructors are added to the code from Chapter 5:

```
class CTemp_point {
    int     x, y, z;
    double temp;
public:
```

```
CTemp_point();
CTemp_point(int xx, yy, zz);
CTemp_point(const CTemp_point& pt);

void set_point(int xx, yy, zz);
void get_point(int *xx, *yy, *zz);
void set_temp(double new_temp);
double get_temp(void);
};
```

The first and third constructors in this declaration are, respectively, the default constructor and the copy constructor. The CTemp_point class is much simpler than the CStr class — there is no dynamic memory to allocate, reallocate, or clean up — so, in this case, there is nothing for the default constructor to do. However, for reasons explained earlier, you must include the default constructor. Otherwise, C++ assumes that there is no default constructor and prevents you from (for example) using the new operator or declaring uninitialized objects for that class.

The default constructor is easy to write:

```
CTemp_point::CTemp_point() {
}
```

The next constructor is slightly more interesting. It has three arguments. Constructors may have any number of arguments. The temp data member remains set to zero in this case.

```
CTemp_point::CTemp_point(int xx, int yy, int zz) {
    x = xx;
    y = yy;
    z = zz;
}
```

Finally, the copy constructor initializes an object by copying the data members of its argument pt. This argument is another object of type CTemp_point. This constructor could be omitted from the program code with no effect because it performs the same actions (member-by-member copy) as the compiler-supplied copy constructor:

```
CTemp_point::CTemp_point(const CTemp_point& pt) {
    x = pt.x;
    y = pt.y;
    z = pt.z;
    temp = pt.temp;
}
```

Each of the following three statements makes a call to one of the three constructors:

```
CTemp_point pt1;
CTemp_point pt2(100, 101, 200);
CTemp_point pt3(pt2);
```

How C++ Calls Constructors (Conversion)

C++ calls constructors in ways that you might not expect. Consider these declarations:

```
CStr name1("John Doe");
CStr name2 = name1;
CStr name3 = "Jane Doe";
```

Clearly, the first declaration results in a call to the constructor CStr(char*). More surprisingly, the second declaration also calls the copy constructor. This is not obvious. You might think that the second statement creates name2 by calling the default constructor and then performs an assignment from name1 to name2. However, it doesn't do either of these things. The following declarations are exactly equivalent, in ultimate effect as well as in the way the constructors are called:

```
CStr name2 = name1;
CStr name2(name1);
```

In C++, assignment and initialization are sharply distinguished (there is no overlap) even though they look much the same. Except in a variable definition, the equals sign (=) always indicates assignment. In a variable definition, however, the equals sign always indicates initialization, which results in a call to the appropriate constructor, and not to the assignment operator.

As you'll discover in Chapter 7, assignment is an operator whose behavior you can define. It is not the same as the copy constructor. One would expect the copy constructor and the assignment operator to do the same thing, but this is not always true. (The main difference is that a copy constructor cannot assume that an object was previously initialized and may, therefore, have to do a little more work.)

Similarly, the final declaration calls the constructor CStr(char*):

```
CStr name3 = "Jane Doe";
```

There's another case in which constructors are called: conversion from other data types (in this case, char*) to the class in question (in this case, CStr). A constructor does double-duty as a conversion function whenever this condition is true: there is exactly one argument and that argument has a different type from the class. In other words, a constructor of the form *class(type)* tells how to convert from *type*.

The constructor CStr(char*) tells the compiler how to convert a char* string into a CStr object. Consequently, you can use a char* string wherever a CStr object is expected, and the compiler will convert it for you. For example:

```
CStr make_uppercase(CStr s);   // prototype

CStr string1;
string1 = make_uppercase("cia/fbi");
```

The last line of this code sequence makes a call to the constructor CStr(char*) to create a CStr object from the string "cia/fbi". The resulting object is then passed to the function make_uppercase.

Summary: The Key Points of Construction

In the simplest case, a constructor is just a convenient initialization function; however, constructors have many subtleties. The major points are summarized in the next few sections.

Overloaded constructors

The name of a constructor is always that of the class itself. So, for the CStr class, every constructor is named CStr. There is no return type, not even void.

As with most C++ functions, constructors can be overloaded. This means that you can reuse the same name with different argument lists (in which either the number or types of arguments must differ). The significance of overloading in this chapter is that you can create a number of constructors in which each initializes from different kinds of arguments.

The default constructor

```
class();
```

One of the most important constructors is the default constructor — which for any given class is the constructor that has no arguments. This constructor is called when you define an object without initialization, create an uninitialized array of objects, or use the new operator with no arguments. The compiler is a little deceptive because it creates a hidden default constructor for you, but if you add any constructors of your own, the hidden constructor goes away. This is why you should write your own default constructor, even if it doesn't do much.

The copy constructor

```
class(class&);
```

The copy constructor is another constructor of great importance for each class. Its most obvious use is to initialize one object from another object of the same type. This constructor is also called when you pass the type by value as an argument to a function or when you use the type as the return value in a function call. The compiler always supplies a hidden copy constructor if you don't supply a copy constructor. Remember, though, that this compiler-supplied constructor performs a simple member-by-member copy, which, for a class such as CStr, is inadequate.

The argument to a copy constructor uses the address operator (&), which means to pass by reference, as in BASIC or FORTRAN — without pointer syntax.

Initialization and conversion

Object definition and initialization always invoke constructors, even when they use the equals sign (=). In this context, the equals sign does not mean exactly the same thing as assignment.

```
CStr string1 = "Hi world!";   // Call CStr(char*)
```

Another case in which constructors are automatically invoked is in type conversion. Given the constructor CStr(char*), you can pass a char* argument to a function where CStr is expected, and the compiler performs the conversion for you.

With preliminaries such as classes and constructors out of the way, let's move on to one of the most interesting, time-saving, aspects of C++: operator overloading.

7

Class Operations (Operator Overloading)

An interesting feature of C++ is *operator overloading* — defining what a particular operator does when applied to your own classes. With very few exceptions, you can customize the meaning of any C++ operator. (The limitations are described in the last section of this chapter.)

Operator overloading enables you to extend C++ in a way that is possible in very few languages. For example, you can define a string type and then define what it means to "add" the strings:

```
CStr first("Norma"), last("Jean");
CStr str = first + " " + last;
```

The process of defining operator behavior is straightforward. For each operator and combination of types, there is a function that gets called to evaluate expressions in which that operator is used.

Operator overloading is some of the most fun you can have with C++.

The Basic Syntax

There are a number of subtle twists and turns when it comes to operator functions, but the basic syntax is simple. For a given operator @, the name of the operator function is:

operator@

So, for example, operator functions for +, -, *, and / have these names:

```
operator+
operator-
operator*
operator/
```

This looks deceptively simple, and you probably suspect that there's more to this operator business. To begin with, what are the arguments? The answer depends on several factors:

- Is the operation binary or unary? (Some operators, such as the minus sign, can go both ways.)

- If the operation is binary, do you want to support the occurrence of objects on either side of the operator? For example, do you want to support both string + cstr_object and cstr_object + string? If you do, you need to use friend functions. (These global functions are given access to the class through use of the friend keyword.)

It's beginning to get more complicated, but this chapter explains such esoteric concepts as friend functions. In any case, here is the proper syntax for the addition functions:

```
class CStr {
//...
    friend CStr operator+(CStr str1, CStr str2);
    friend CStr operator+(CStr str, char *s);
    friend CStr operator+(char *s, CStr str);
};

// Note that the friend keyword isn't needed in the
//   definitions below
CStr operator+(CStr str1, CStr str2) {
//...
}

CStr operator+(CStr str, char *s) {
//...
```

```
}

CStr operator+(char *s, CStr str) {
//...
}
```

You should see the strong connection between function overloading and operator overloading in this code. There can be many functions named operator+. What differentiates these functions are their argument lists. The operator+ functions that have one or more CStr arguments are those that define how addition works with CStr objects.

Writing the Addition (+) Operator Function

The following definition successfully implements the addition of two CStr objects. Each argument represents an operand in the expression str1+str2.

```
CStr operator+(CStr str1, CStr str2) {
    CStr new_string(str1);
    new_string.cat(str2.get());
    return new_string;
}
```

CStr appears at the beginning of the function heading as the return-value type. To return a CStr result, the operator+ function definition creates an entirely new CStr object in the first line:

```
CStr new_string(str1);
```

This statement calls the copy constructor to initialize new_string as an exact copy of str1, the first operand. The next statement concatenates the second operand, str2, onto the end of new_string. This process produces the appropriate string.

```
new_string.cat(str2.get());
```

The final task is to pass the new string as the return value.

```
return new_string;
```

This statement makes a copy of new_string before it goes out of scope and is destroyed. As explained in Chapter 6, the compiler automatically invokes the copy constructor CStr(CStr&) to create the return-value copy. This same return-value object is placed on the stack, so that the caller can access it.

With a sophisticated class such as CStr, returning a value would fail without a correctly written copy constructor. The hidden copy constructor supplied by the compiler would perform a straight member-by-member copy that would result in errors. That's why I introduced the subject of copy construction first (in Chapter 6) before describing how operator overloading works.

The mechanics of calling an operator function

When C++ sees an expression such as str1 + str2, it translates the expression into the appropriate function call. Figure 7-1 illustrates how this works. If the function did not exist, C++ would report an error at compile time saying that the operation was not defined.

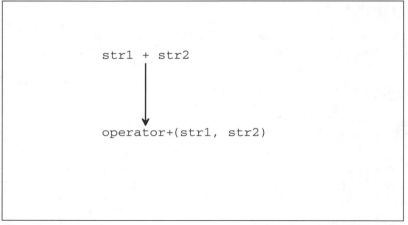

```
str1 + str2

    |
    |
    v

operator+(str1, str2)
```

Figure 7-1 *Translation of an expression into a function call.*

The following code is an example of how string addition might be used. Each statement is an object definition. The last statement carries out an addition operation (calling the operator+ function) to produce a CStr value. That value is then used to initialize the object name by means of the copy constructor.

```
CStr first("Archie ");
CStr last("Leach");
CStr name(first + last);
```

Figure 7-2 illustrates how the addition operation works. The value of the expression first + last is stored in a separate CStr object. The operator+ function creates this object and then returns it as a CStr object containing "Archie Leach". This is a temporary object, and the compiler will destroy it when it is no longer needed.

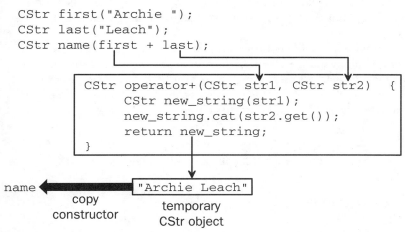

Figure 7-2 *Mechanics of a call to operator +.*

And the rest. . . (other addition functions)

The other operator+ functions for the CStr class look similar to the first operator+ function shown in the previous two sections.

```
CStr operator+(CStr str, char *s) {
    CStr new_string(str);
    new_string.cat(s);
    return new_string;
}

CStr operator+(char *s, CStr str) {
    CStr new_string(s);
    new_string.cat(str.get());
    return new_string;
}
```

All operator+ functions look similar. In every case, the general procedure for evaluating string addition is the same:

1. Create a new CStr object, initialized with the contents of the first operand.

2. Concatenate the contents of the second operand.

3. Return the resulting CStr object.

Who needs friends?

When writing binary operator functions, you often need to make use of the friend keyword. (In this context, a *binary operator* is simply an operator that works on two operands, such as + in the expression X + Y.)

Normally, global functions have no access to private members of a class. The friend keyword offers a way around this restriction by granting access to all members. For example, the function setbk is a friend of the class CBook; this enables setbk to access private members of the class (a, b, and c in this case).

```
class CBook {
     int a, b, c;
     friend void setbk(CBook bk, int x, int y, int z);
};

void setbk(CBook bk, int x, int y, int z) {
     bk.a = x;
     bk.b = y;
     bk.c = z;
}
```

The friend keyword makes it possible to write functions such as operator+(char*, CStr). You can implement operator functions as member functions without using the friend keyword, but such functions assume that an object of the class appears on the left side of the operator. For example, the function operator+(CStr, char*) could have been written as a member function.

```
class CStr {
//...
     CStr operator+(char *s);
}

CStr CStr::operator+(char *s){
     CStr new_string(*this);
     new_string.cat(s);
     return new_string;
}
```

The first statement in the body of the definition initializes the new string with an object referred to as *this. The value of *this is the left operand. To understand how the code works, remember that this approach to defining addition translates an expression as shown in Figure 7-3.

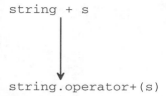

```
string + s
```

```
string.operator+(s)
```

Figure 7-3 *Translation of operation into a member function call.*

With this approach, addition is translated into a member function called through the left operand, which is a CStr object. In C++, the this keyword is a pointer to the current object, and *this refers to the object itself. So, the first statement initializes new_string to the contents of the left operand by referring to *this.

```
CStr new_string(*this);
```

I have more to say about the this keyword later in this chapter and on page 120 of Section 4.

In any case, the problem with writing operator functions this way is that it restricts you to always having your class object on the left side of the operator. Only with nonmember functions is it possible to write a function that tells how to evaluate

```
s + string
```

which reverses the operands shown earlier. For this reason, binary operators are usually implemented as friend functions and not member functions. (Because they are not member functions, they must be friend functions so that they can access private data as needed.) That's the approach I adopted at the beginning of the chapter:

```
class CStr {
//...
     friend CStr operator+(CStr str1, CStr str2);
     friend CStr operator+(CStr str, char *s);
     friend CStr operator+(char *s, CStr str);
};
```

However, the assignment operator is a special case. It must be implemented as a member function and not as a friend, as discussed in the next section.

Writing the Assignment Function

Assignment (=) is a special operation for which the compiler supplies
a default, hidden function if you don't write your own assignment
function. As a general rule, assignment between objects of the same
type is always supported in C++, just as direct assignment between
structures is supported in standard C. Therefore, statements such as
these are valid:

```
CStr string1, string2;
//...
string1 = string2;     // Assign value of string2 to
                       //  string1
```

●─NOTE ──

It's possible to prevent assignment altogether if you want to define an
assignment operator function and then make it private to the class.

However, as with the copy constructor, the compiler-supplied
assignment behavior is inadequate for a class such as CStr, which
uses dynamic-memory allocation. This default behavior is a simple
member-by-member copying. As pointed out in Chapter 6, this
behavior can lead to errors.

Therefore, when writing a class such as CStr, you need to carefully define the behavior of the assignment operator. The assignment
operator function must be a member of the class, with the following
prototype within the class declaration:

```
class& operator=(const class &arg);
```

The argument name (arg) is optional in the declaration. The corresponding function definition has this syntax:

```
class& class::operator=(const class &arg) {
    statements
}
```

In the CStr class, the assignment operator function could have
the following prototype. The only aspect of this declaration that you
have a choice about is the argument name.

```
class CStr {
//...
    CStr& operator=(const CStr &source);
};
```

The assignment operator declaration can be intimidating to C++ beginners because so much of it uses syntax elements that are not found in C. All the syntax elements have been introduced in this and previous chapters. Nevertheless, it may help to review them. Figure 7-4 analyzes the syntax of the CStr-to-CStr assignment function.

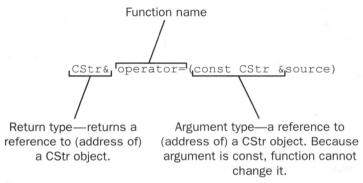

Figure 7-4 *Analysis of an assignment operator declaration.*

The assignment function definition

The assignment function turns out to be easy to write once you understand all the syntax. The following is the shortest version of this function:

```
CStr& CStr::operator=(const CStr &source) {
    cpy(source.get());
    return *this;
}
```

The function doesn't need to be any longer than this; it works perfectly well. In fact, this function is so short that it is a good candidate for function inlining. The definition can be given in the CStr declaration.

```
class CStr {
//...
    CStr& operator=(const CStr &source)
        {cpy(source.get()); return *this;}
};
```

In either case, the two statements in the body of the function definition are short and do simple things. The first statement calls the cpy function, which already exists, to do the copying. (Chapter 5 showed how to write the cpy function.) The second statement returns the object itself—that is, the same CStr object that is the target of the assignment. In effect, the statement return *this says:

```
Return myself!
```

Figure 7-5 illustrates how C++ translates an assignment expression. This function is called through str1, the left operand. This becomes important in the next section, when you look more closely at the this keyword.

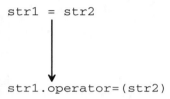

```
str1.operator=(str2)
```

Figure 7-5 *Translation of an assignment expression.*

The "this" pointer and its uses

Within a member function, the this keyword is a pointer to the current object. (*Current object* means the object through which the function was called.) Each time you call a member function, C++ passes a hidden this pointer as an argument (see Figure 7-6).

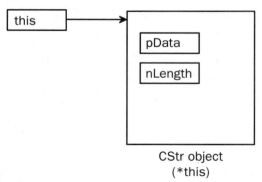

CStr object
(*this)

Figure 7-6 *The "this" pointer as used with the CStr class.*

Within the member-function definition, references to a data member are automatically translated into object-member references using the this pointer, as shown in Table 7-1. Many member functions never use the this pointer because its use within the function is implicit.

Table 7-1 *Implicit use of "this" pointer*

Data member reference	Equivalent to
pData	this->pData
nLength	this->nLength

Sometimes you need to refer explicitly to the object, making it necessary to use this. Such is the case with assignment functions. Assignment expressions in C and C++ return a value — that of the left operand. That assignments return a value makes possible the following kinds of statements:

```
int     x, y, z;
CString stringA, stringB, stringC;

x = y = z = 0;
stringA = stringB = stringC = "hello!";
```

After "hello!" is assigned to stringC, the expression stringC = "hello" returns the resulting value of the stringC, which is then assigned to stringB. To support this syntactical convention, an assignment function must return the value of the left operand as its last action.

Remember that the assignment function is called as a member function of the left operand. The left operand is the current object (the object through which the function was called). Therefore — if you still follow me — in implementing assignment, the final task of an object is to return itself. Here's how you express this idea in C++:

```
return *this;
```

The this keyword is a pointer to the current object. Therefore, *this refers to the object itself.

Assignments and reference types (&)

The use of reference types is necessary in the syntax of assignment operators. References let you transfer data between objects without making extra copies and without using pointer syntax.

Figure 7-7 illustrates how assignment between two CStr objects should work. The return value is a pointer to the object on the left. (In source code, a reference is returned, and the compiler actually implements this by returning a pointer.) This object, in turn, becomes the argument for the next assignment to be performed.

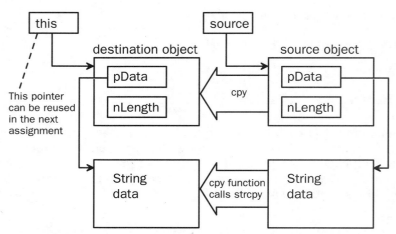

Figure 7-7   *Mechanics of a CStr assignment.*

Writing a Conversion Function

The CStr class is now extremely flexible and easy to use. You can, for example, use it to concatenate and assign expressions, just as with strings in BASIC.

```
CStr first = "Norma";
CStr middle = "Jean";
CStr last = "Baker";
CStr name;

name = first + " " + middle + " " + last;
```

Before leaving the CStr example, there's another capability that would be useful for CStr to have. In the best of all worlds, you should to be able to use the class wherever char* is expected. For example, puts is one of many standard library functions that takes a char* argument. It would be convenient to pass a CStr object to this function and have it print the contents, just as it would with a char* argument.

```
#include <stdio.h>

CStr warn = "This is your final warning";
puts(warn);              // puts takes a char* argument
```

In C++, you can get this functionality by writing a conversion function. This function tells the compiler how to convert an object of the class to another type. As Chapter 6 pointed out, constructors also perform conversion. Whether the compiler calls a conversion function or a constructor depends on the direction of the conversion (see Figure 7-8). For any given class, conversion functions handle outgoing conversions (convert *to* another type). Constructors handle incoming conversions (convert *from* another type).

Remember that *to* and *from*, as used previously, are relative to where you are in the code. If you are writing code for the CStr class, for example, an incoming conversion is the one converting from another type to CStr.

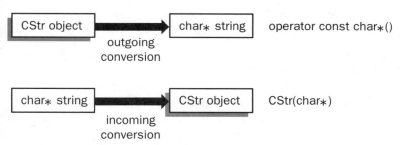

Figure 7-8   *Conversion and constructor functions compared.*

The conversion function is a member function that is declared as follows within the class declaration. The declaration has no return type and no arguments.

operator *type* ()

Converting from a CStr object to char* is easy because all the function has to do is extract the data pointer. The following code declares a conversion function within the CStr class declaration. Function inlining is used because the definition is so short.

```
class CStr {
    //...
    operator const char*() {return get();}
};
```

I used const char* as the conversion type here rather than char*. This is the same as an ordinary char* type, except that const protects the string data from modification. You can, if you choose, remove const, but if you do, be careful about corrupting the data.

Most string-handling functions in the standard C++ library (including puts) take a const char* argument unless they write to the string, in which case they take a char* argument. Because of the way memory allocation works in CStr, it is dangerous to allow direct modification of the string data through the pointer.

The CStr Class in Summary

You've come a long way with the CStr class, gradually building it up over the course of three chapters. I've used the CStr class to introduce many of C++'s core concepts.

You might question whether writing such a class is worth the work. If you were going to create only a few instances of this class and never use it again, it might not be worth it. But once you've successfully created and debugged the class, you can use it in many programs. As an extension to the C++ language, CStr is very cost-effective. You can define CStr objects in any program, as long as you:

- Include the header file cstr.h in each source module that refers to the CStr class.

- During a build, link in cstr.obj, which should contain the implementations for CStr member functions in compiled form. You can even add cstr.obj to the standard library.

Here are the final contents of the cstr.h file, which declares all the members of the CStr class presented until now:

```
// CSTR.H - Declaration of the CStr class

class CStr {
    char *pData;
    int  nLength;
public:
    CStr();             // Constructors
    CStr(char *s);
    CStr(const CStr &str);
    ~CStr();            // Destructor

    char *get(void) const {return pData;}
    int  getlength(void) const {return nLength;}
    void cpy(char *s);
    void cat(char *s);

    friend CStr operator+(CStr str1, CStr str2);
    friend CStr operator+(CStr str, char *s);
    friend CStr operator+(char *s, CStr str);

    CStr& operator=(const CStr &source)
        {cpy(source.get()); return *this;}
    operator const char*() {return get();}

};
```

Three of the member functions are defined in the CStr declaration as inline functions. Because they are defined in the class declaration, they don't need to be defined in cstr.cpp, the implementation file for the class. The file cstr.cpp contains the remaining definitions. You simply compile this code and link the resulting object file to any project that needed to use the class.

```cpp
// CSTR.CPP - implementation of CStr class

#include "cstr.h"
#include <string.h>

CStr::CStr() {
    pData = new char[1];
    *pData = '\0';
    nLength = 0;
}

CStr::CStr(char *s) {
    pData = new char[strlen(s) + 1];
    strcpy(pData, s);
    nLength = strlen(s);
}

CStr::CStr(const CStr &s) {
    char* sz = s.get();
    int n = s.getlength();
    pData = new char[n + 1];
    strcpy(pData, sz);
    nLength = n;
}

CStr::~CStr() {
    delete [] pData;
}

void CStr::cpy(char *s) {   // Copy string arg.
    int n;

    n = strlen(s);
    if (nLength != n) {
        if (pData)
            delete [] pData;
        pData = new char[n + 1];
        nLength = n;
    }
    strcpy(pData, s);
```

```
        }

        void CStr::cat(char *s) {    // Concatenate string arg.
            int n;
            char *pTemp;

            n = strlen(s);
            if (n == 0)
                return;
            pTemp = new char[n + nLength + 1];
            if (pData) {
                strcpy(pTemp, pData);
                delete [] pData;
            }
            strcat(pTemp, s);
            pData = pTemp;
            nLength += n;
        }

        CStr operator+(CStr str1, CStr str2) {
            CStr new_string(str1);
            new_string.cat(str2.get());
            return new_string;
        }

        CStr operator+(CStr str, char *s) {
            CStr new_string(str);
            new_string.cat(s);
            return new_string;
        }

        CStr operator+(char *s, CStr str) {
            CStr new_string(s);
            new_string.cat(str.get());
            return new_string;
        }
```

Another Class Operator Example

Before leaving the subject of operator overloading, let's look at
another example that uses operator functions: the CTemp_point class
first introduced in Chapter 5 (p. 380). This class specifies a point on a
three-dimensional grid and a temperature value. Some of the member
functions are much easier to implement than CStr is, because the
CTemp_point class does not involve memory allocation.

```
class CTemp_point {
    int    x, y, z;
    double temp;
public:
    CTemp_point();
    CTemp_point(int xx, int yy, int zz);
    CTemp_point(CTemp_point &pt);

    void set_point(int xx, int yy, int zz);
    void get_point(int *xx, int *yy, int *zz);
    void set_temp(double new_temp);
    double get_temp(void);

    CTemp_point operator+(double temp_diff);
    CTemp_point operator-(double temp_diff);
    CTemp_point& operator=(const CTemp_point &pt);
};
```

When you design a class, an important task is deciding which operations to support. In the case of the CStr class, it made sense to define addition as an operation between two strings that produce a third string. In the case of the CTemp_point class, it isn't so clear what addition should do. What would it mean to add together two points on a grid?

The CTemp_point class supports only two simple operations. These add or subtract from the temperature data member (temp) and leave the grid coordinates untouched. There's no operation defined for adding two points to each other.

```
pt1 = pt2 + 33.3;    // Ok; addition to flt pt defined.
pt2 = pt2 + 1;       // Ok; 1 can be converted to
                     //  floating pt.
pt2 = pt1 + pt3;     // ERROR! Operation not defined.
```

Like the CStr addition functions, these operator functions return an object by value. Consequently, they follow the same basic steps: create a new object, set some values, and return the object as a value. (The last step implicitly calls the class's copy constructor.)

```
CTemp_point CTemp_point::operator+(double temp_diff) {
    CTemp_point new_pt(*this);
    new_pt.temp += temp_diff;
    return new_pt;
}

CTemp_point CTemp_point::operator-(double temp_diff) {
    CTemp_point new_pt(*this);
```

```
       new_pt.temp -= temp_diff;
       return new_pt;
}
```

The last task to add is the assignment-operator function. In this case, the function is not really necessary because it implements assignment in the same way that the compiler would do it anyway. However, it's still useful as an example. This approach uses a simple member-by-member copy from the right operand (translated into the argument, pt) to the left operand (the object through which the function is called). As with nearly all assignment functions, the last line of the function returns *this.

```
CTemp_point& CTemp_point::operator= (
   const CTemp_point &pt) {
      x = pt.x;
      y = pt.y;
      z = pt.z;
      temp = pt.temp;
      return *this;
}
```

Forging Ahead with Operator Overloading

Believe it or not, I've only begun to discuss the subject of operator overloading. The remainder of this chapter summarizes the points discussed so far, and provides an overview of features not yet covered.

Naming an operator function

Operator functions follow a simple naming scheme. For any given operator @, the name of the function is operator@. The exception is conversion functions, for which the name is:

```
operator type ()
```

Binary operators

When the compiler evaluates an expression of the form *obj1@obj2*, it translates the expression into the function call:

```
obj1.operator@(obj2)
```

if this function is defined within *obj1*'s class. The function may also
be defined outside the class, in which case the compiler translates
the expression into this function call:

operator@(*obj1, obj2*)

Declaring this function as a friend of a class gives the function
access to all class members.

The advantage of using the latter form is that it makes it possible
to implement the same operation regardless of whether *obj1* appears
to the right or to the left of the operator. To support the reverse order,
write a separate function:

operator@(*obj2, obj1*)

If the declaration of *obj2*'s class is supplied by someone else (for
example, if obj2 has a standard type such as int or char*), this is the
only way to define this operation.

Unary operators

When the compiler evaluates an expression of the form @*obj1*, it
translates the expression into the function call:

obj1.**operator@**()

if this function is defined within *obj1*'s class. The function may also
be defined outside the class, in which case the compiler translates
the expression into this function call:

operator@(*obj1*)

Declaring this function as a friend of a class gives the function
access to all class members.

As an example, unary minus (-) can be defined for the CTemp_
point class, in which the effect is to reverse the sign of the temp data
member:

```
class CTemp_point {
    //...
    CTemp_point operator-();
};

CTemp_point CTemp_point::operator-() {
    CTemp_point new_point(*this);
    new_point.temp *= -1;
    return new_point;
}
```

As with all operator functions (except conversion), the return type must be declared explicitly. The compiler can make no assumptions about the return type. You can define an operation on class A, for example, so that it returns an object of any type you wish.

The assignment operator

The assignment operator defines how to assign an object from another object of the same class. Although assignment is a binary operator like any other, it has some special restrictions. The assignment function must be defined as a member function with this declaration:

```
class& operator=(const class &arg)
```

The function is called as a member function of the left operand of an assignment, and the right operand is the argument *arg*. The final task of an assignment function is to return the left operand, which it does by using the this pointer:

```
return *this;
```

Assignment from other types

An assignment function determines how the compiler assigns a value to an object from another object of the same class. There is no valid assignment function that involves assignment from another type. Instead, the compiler calls the appropriate constructor or conversion function, if available, to convert from one data type to another.

```
CHorse stacy, sugar;

stacy = sugar;        // Calls CHorse::operator=
stacy = "fast";       // Calls CHorse::CHorse(char*)
char *name = sugar;   // Calls CHorse::operator char*()
```

Other assignment operators (+=, -=, and so on)

You might think that if you define both addition (+) and assignment (=) for a given class, the addition-assignment operator (+=) is automatically defined, but this is not the case. Each assignment operator (such as +=, -=, *=, and so on) is considered a separate operator, and to support it you need to write another function. For example, the following code implements += for the CStr class. (Because of its small size, it is a good candidate for function inlining.)

```
class CStr {
    //...
    CStr& operator+=(CStr &str);
};

CStr& CStr::operator+=(CStr &str) {
    cat(str.get());
    return *this;
}
```

The last statement of all assignment-operator functions (as well as straight assignment) should be return *this.

Increment and decrement operators

Although increment (++) and decrement (--) operators are unary operators and follow most of the rules for unary operators, they come in both prefix and postfix versions. Note these special differences between prefix and postfix versions:

- The prefix version alters the operand and then returns its value. The function returns a reference to the current object.

- The postfix version returns a copy of the old value of the object. (See the following example.) This version has a dummy argument of type int, which is passed the value 0 during a call. The only purpose of this argument is to differentiate the function definitions.

This example illustrates postfix and prefix versions for the increment operator (++).

```
class CPoint {
private:
    double x, y;
public:
    CPoint& operator++();    // prefix
    CPoint  operator++(int); // postfix
};

// Prefix ++. For efficiency's sake, returns
//   a reference (&).

CPoint& operator++() { // Prefix version
    x++;
    y++;
    return *this;
}
```

```
// Postfix ++. Must include dummy arg.
//
CPoint operator++(int dummy) {
    CPoint point(*this);   // Make a copy.
    x++;                   // Change original.
    y++;
    return point;          // Return the copy.
}
```

The subscript operator ([])

You implement the subscript operator when you write your own
array collection class. The operator[] function takes one integer
argument giving a zero-based array position. You should return a reference; this enables subscript expressions to appear on either side of
an assignment.

The new and delete operators

You can implement these operators to control how a class manages
memory. To write the operator functions, include the file stddef.h
and use the following declarations, replacing myclass with your own
class name.

```
#include <stddef.h>

class myclass {
//...
    void* operator new(size_t);
    void  operator delete(void*, size_t);
```

The operator new function always returns a void* pointer, and
the operator delete function always gets a void* argument. (The
pointers will automatically be recast as needed.) The operator new
function can include additional arguments that can correspond to one
or more values used to initialize the object. This function can be
overloaded as needed.

Most of the time there is no need to write operator new and
operator delete functions. The standard compiler behavior is usually more than adequate.

The function call operator ()

This operator enables objects of your class to be used like function names. You can overload this operator with multiple definitions. In the following example, the object print_it can be used as if it were a function name.

```
class Print_class {
public:
    int operator()(long a);
    int operator()(char *s, int n);
    //...
};

Print_class print_it;

// This next statement calls
// Print_class::operator()(char*, int)
print_it("cat", 3);
```

Summary of Syntax Rules

These rules generally apply to operator functions:

- You can only define behavior for existing C++ operators. Furthermore, the following operators cannot be overloaded: member access (.), scope resolution (::), pointer to member (.*), and conditional (?:).

- No matter which classes they are applied to, operators retain their normal associativity and precedence.

- All operator functions are inherited by derived classes, except for the assignment operator (=).

- Each operator is defined separately. For example, the addition-assignment operator (+=) is not automatically defined just because you wrote a function for assignment (=) and for addition (+).

- You cannot use default argument values in an operator function.

- You cannot implement any operator as a static member function.

Inheritance: C++ and Good Genes

Inheritance is all about software reuse, C++'s greatest promise. Never write the same piece of code twice! Make exponential gains in productivity! Of course, it's not quite that easy. But inheritance does provide a convenient way of extending all of one class's features to another. Consequently, you don't have to repeat features common to both classes.

Beyond that, inheritance provides the underlying structure for virtual functions, which are discussed in Chapter 9.

As much as any C++ buzzword, inheritance seems to metaphorically endow objects with life. After all, isn't inheritance a property of living things? That would be going too far, but inheritance, as you'll see, does let you develop a useful hierarchy that goes from the general to the specific — much like a deity or Darwin (take your pick).

Return to CStr: A Software Dilemma

If you've read the chapters of this book sequentially, you know about the CStr class and how to write it. Let's assume for a moment, though, that someone else developed the CStr class and then sold you the right to use the software. Typically, you are provided with:

- A header file containing the class declaration; and
- An object-file (.obj file) containing the implementations of member functions of the class in compiled form.

Most of the source code is not provided to the class user with this approach. What happens, then, if you want to extend or customize the CStr class in some way? One approach is to rewrite CStr from scratch. A better alternative is to create a class that contains a CStr object as a member; in such an approach, you're essentially building an outer class around the CStr class.

However, an even better alternative, considering the amount of work required, is to use inheritance. This means creating a new class and *deriving it* from CStr. In deriving one class from another, you get all the members of the base class (in this case, CStr). You can then add or change any members that you want.

Son of CStr (Or Is It "Daughter"?)

The final version of the CStr class — which is summarized in Chapter 7 — supports a number of useful functions and operations, including those shown in Table 8-1.

Table 8-1 *Functions and Operations of the CStr Class*

Function or operation	Description
get	Returns pointer to null-terminated string data.
getlength	Returns length of string data.
cpy	Copies string from char* argument.
cat	Concatenates char* argument onto current string data.
+	Concatenates two strings, of which at least one is a CStr object. The other may be a CStr object or a char* pointer.
=	Copies string data from another CStr object.

The class also supports a number of useful constructors. Let's assume that you'd like to retain all this functionality as well as add the following:

- output, which would print string data to standard output; and
- input, which would input a string from standard input.

Deriving a class through inheritance makes it easy to add this functionality, even if you don't have access to the original CStr code other than the header file. The next section introduces the syntax.

Derived class syntax

Assume that *Base_class* has already been declared. The following syntax derives *Derived_class* from *Base_class* with the result that *Derived_class* automatically has all the members defined in *Base_class* in addition to any declarations of its own.

```
class Derived_class : public Base_class {
     declarations
};
```

The only part that is new here is the colon (:) and the syntax that follows:

```
public Base_class
```

In this context, public is the base-class access specifier. Alternatively, you can specify either private or protected. In almost all cases, however, public is the best choice. For more information on private and protected used as base-class access specifiers, see pages 100 and 101 in Section 4.

The declarations for *Derived_class* include new members to be added to the declarations in *Base_class*. For example, the following code derives CIoStr from CStr and then adds two functions of its own. It's necessary to include the file cstr.h so that the declaration of CStr is read in. CStr must be fully declared before it is used as a base class.

```
// CIOSTR.H - declaration of the CIOStr class

#include "cstr.h"

class CIoStr : public CStr {
public:
    void input(void);
    void output(void);
};
```

Once CIoStr is declared, you can use it to define objects. These objects support all the CStr members (because CStr is the base class) as well as the input and output functions.

```
CIoStr iostring1, iostring2, iostring3;

iostring1 = "This is a new string";
iostring2 = iostring1 + ".";
iostring2.output();
iostring1.input();
iostring3.cpy(iostring1);
```

Writing functions for the new class

CIoStr follows the same rules that any class follows for implementing member functions: For each member function, you can either define the function inside the class declaration (in which case it is automatically an inline function), or you can define the function outside the declaration (in a file named, for example, ciostr.cpp). In the latter case, you use CIoStr:: to prefix the name.

The definitions of the new CIoStr functions are simple.

```
#include <stdio.h>
#include "ciostr.h"

void CIoStr::output(void) {
    printf("%s", get());
}

void CIoStr::input(void) {
    char buffer[256];

    gets(buffer);
    cpy(buffer);
}
```

Only two functions (input and output) are defined here and they are defined with the CIoStr:: prefix. Many other functions are inherited from the base class CStr, all of which were defined with the CStr:: prefix in the file cstr.cpp. For example:

```
void CStr::cpy(char *s) {    // Copy string arg.
    int n;

    n = strlen(s);
    if (nLength != n) {
        if (pData)
```

```
            delete [] pData;
        pData = new char[n + 1];
        nLength = n;
    }
    strcpy(pData, s);
}
```

Thus, CIoStr supports two kinds of functions: those contributed by the base class CStr, and those added by CIoStr itself. The prefix used in the definition varies depending on where the member function is declared and defined — in the base class or in the derived class.

Overriding functions and clarifying scope

You've already seen inheritance at work, whether or not you've noticed it. The definitions of the CIoStr functions use functions from the base class. Take another look at the input function:

```
void CIoStr::input(void) {
    char buffer[256];

    gets(buffer);
    cpy(buffer);
}
```

The last statement in the definition calls the CStr::cpy function. As in other member-function definitions, the function can be referred to as cpy, because it is a member of CIoStr (by virtue of inheritance from CStr).

The situation gets more complex, though, if the derived class CIoStr overrides one or more functions in the base class. In this example, there is little motivation to override any of the CStr functions, but it is still perfectly valid to do so. For example:

```
class CIoStr : public CStr {
public:
    void input(void);
    void output(void);

// Overridden from base class CStr
    void cpy(char *s);
};

void CIoStr::cpy(char *s) {
  // Alternative implementation of cpy function
}
```

Now there are two versions of cpy: one defined in the CIoStr class and a second defined in its base class CStr. Member functions of CIoStr can call either of these functions. But to call the original version of cpy now, you must use the scope-resolution operator (::) to specify that the CStr version should be called. Otherwise, the new version (CIoStr::cpy) is assumed.

```
void CIoStr::input(void) {
    char buffer[256];

    gets(buffer);
    CStr::cpy(buffer);    // Call base-class version
                          //  of cpy.
}
```

In general, when the compiler sees a name, it attempts to resolve the scope in this order:

1. If the context is within a member-function definition, the compiler checks whether the name is declared within the same class. If it is, the compiler uses that version.

2. Next, the compiler checks the declaration of the base class. (This is done recursively; if the base class has its own base class, then all the base classes are checked.)

3. Finally, if the name is not declared within the class hierarchy, the compiler checks whether the name is declared globally.

● **NOTE**

If a member function is intended to be overridden by derived classes, the function should usually be declared virtual for reasons explained at the end of the chapter. For now, however, you can ignore virtual functions.

Inheritance hierarchies

As the last section hinted, base classes can have their own base classes, and derived classes can have their own derived classes. Because this arrangement may seem complex, let's consider a simple example. Suppose you want to declare a class that has even more functions available than CIoStr has. You can derive a class from CIoStr even though CIoStr itself was derived from CStr.

```
#include "ciostr.h"

class CFontIoStr : public CIoStr {
    int     ptsize;
```

```
public:
    void clr(void) { cpy(""); }
    void setchar(int c, int n);
    void set_font(int size);
};
```

This new class, CFontIoStr, inherits all the members of CStr and CIoStr, because each successive generation adds or overrides members from the previous class. Nothing is ever lost. CFontIoStr has one new data member (ptsize) and three new member functions that the other classes do not have.

The three classes — CStr, CIoStr, and CFontIoStr — create a class hierarchy, albeit a simple one. The original string class, CStr, is indirectly a base class of CFontIoStr, the most recent class. Through inheritance, CStr passes its contents all the way down to CFontIoStr, much as grandparents pass genes to a grandchild. Figure 8-1 illustrates this simple class hierarchy.

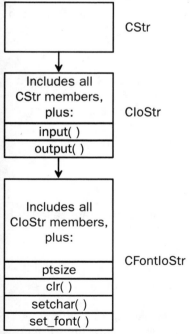

Figure 8-1 *A class hierarchy.*

Much more complex class hierarchies are possible. You can derive several classes from any given base class, and the result can be a family tree of classes as elaborate as you like.

Without Inheritance: Doing It the Hard Way

Although inheritance is not the only technique for creating reusable software (nor is it automatically the best technique in all cases), it's useful to see how inheritance can save you work.

Suppose you don't have access to the original CStr source code except for the class declaration (consequently, you don't have access to source code for function definitions), but you want to write a new class, CIoStr, with all the capabilities of CStr plus a couple more. How would you create a CIoStr class without using inheritance and without rewriting all the CStr functions from scratch?

You could write such a class without inheritance by writing a new class that forms, in effect, a shell around a CStr object and then translating calls to the outer class into calls to the CStr object. Figure 8-2 illustrates this scheme conceptually.

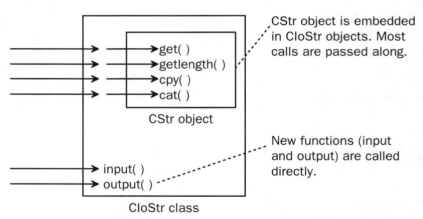

Figure 8-2 *Object containment that simulates inheritance.*

The difficulty of this approach is that every call to a CStr function must be explicitly translated into a call to the CStr object. Here's what the code looks like:

```
#include "cstr.h"

class CIoStr {
```

```
    CStr   str;
public:
// New functions
    void input(void);
    void output(void);

// Old functions, simulating CStr inheritance
    char   *get(void) const {return str.get(); }
    int    getlength(void) const
           {return str.getlength(); }
    void   cpy(char *s) {str.cpy(s);}
    void   cat(char *s) {str.cat(s);}
//...
```

In addition to these functions, a complete implementation also creates pass-through functions in CIoStr for the operator functions, the conversion functions, and the constructors of the CStr class.

Now compare the version of CIoStr developed in this section to the earlier one:

```
#include "cstr.h"

class CIoStr : public CStr {
public:
    void input(void);
    void output(void);
};
```

The effect is the same with either approach: the CIoStr class supports all the same member functions that CStr does and then adds two new functions (input and output). Clearly, the version that uses inheritance has a simpler, cleaner, and more elegant syntax.

In theory, you can think of inheritance and object containment — declaring one object inside another — as being different. Inheritance, according to object-oriented theory, should be used in situations of the form "A is a kind of B." A, the derived class, is simply a more specialized version of B, the base class. Adopting this approach, you would say that CIoStr is a more specialized kind of string than CStr and that it adds new functions. But both are strings.

With object containment, on the other hand, one class uses — or is a client of — the other class. For example, you might create a CAddress class that contains several strings (CStr objects), among other data.

```
class CAddress {
    CStr   name;
    CStr   line1;
    CStr   line2;
```

```
    int    months_at_residence;
};
```

CAddress isn't simply a more specialized type of string; it is a fundamentally different type from CStr.

These cases are fairly clear-cut. In some cases, however, it can be more difficult to decide whether one class should be derived from another (inheritance) or whether one class should contain the other (object containment). The best policy is to remember that inheritance is a convenient bit of syntax for including all the members of one class in another, and is, therefore, not very different from containment. (Inheritance also has a critical role in virtual functions, which are discussed in Chapter 9.)

Another way to simulate inheritance is to use object containment and rely on the user of the object to adjust function calls.

```
#include "cstr.h"

class CIoStr {
public:
    CStr    str;

    void input(void);
    void output(void);
};
```

It's easy to write this class, but it's not as convenient to use. Most functions have to be called through the data member str. For example, this code fragment calls the cpy function:

```
CIoStr    Iostring;
//...
iostring.str.cpy("Let's go to the Oscars.");
```

If you had used inheritance, the call to cpy would be made more directly. The moral of the story is that in situations such as this one, inheritance can be more convenient than other techniques.

Public, Private, and Protected Access

So far I have introduced one member-access keyword—public. In certain respects, this keyword is the most useful. However, C++ has three member-access keywords: public, private, and protected.

Within class declarations, private is the default member-access level. Because it is the default, you can usually get away with not using it. However, making private access explicit is a good idea because it makes the class declarations easier to read. For example, here is the CFontIoStr declaration with the private keyword used to clarify the access level of ptsize:

```
#include "CIoStr.h"

class CFontIoStr : public CIoStr {
private:
     int ptsize;
public:
     void clr(void) { cpy(""); }
     void setchar(int c, int n);
     void set_font(int size);
};
```

The third access level, protected, is an intermediate level between private and public. A member with protected access can be accessed within the scope of the class and its derived classes, but is private in any other scope.

Look at the CIoStr declaration again. This class inherits from CStr, the original class, and adds two new functions.

```
#include "cstr.h"

class CIoStr : public CStr {
public:
     void input(void);
     void output(void);
};
```

In the declaration of CStr, the two data members (pData and nLength) were declared private. This was done by default, because they were not declared with the public keyword. This is fine unless you want the new functions in CIoStr to be able to refer to the data members. At that point, there is a problem:

```
void CIoStr::print(void) {
     printf("%s", pData);  // ERROR! No access to pData
}
```

Earlier, I said that a derived class inherits all the members of its base class. This is true, even here. The data member pData is present in every instance of CIoStr and can be accessed indirectly through a CStr member function such as get or cpy. Although it is present, pData is not *visible* in derived classes.

If pData and nLength had been declared with the protected keyword in the CStr declaration, then they could be accessed in CStr function definitions and in CIoStr function definitions.

```
class CStr {
protected:
    char *pData;
    int  nLength;
public:
    CStr();              // Constructors
    CStr(char *s);
    CStr(const CStr &str);
    ~CStr();             // Destructor
//...
```

Figure 8-3 summarizes the three levels of member-access rights — public, protected, and private.

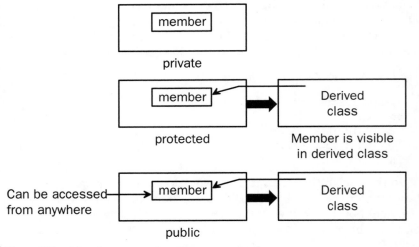

Figure 8-3 *Member-access levels summarized.*

Is it better to declare data members as protected or as private? The answer depends on the purpose of the members. In the case of the CStr class, it probably isn't necessary to declare pData and nLength as protected, because a series of public functions — get, getlength, cpy, and cat — provide complete access to the data.

In this case, the interface (the set of public functions) completely encapsulates the data. If you were to give the class to other programmers, there would probably be no reason to let them directly alter nLength in their derived classes. Instead, they should set data properly by using the cpy function. Providing direct access to pData or nLength could result in errors.

Yet, in other cases, it might be useful to make members visible to derived classes. Declaring members as protected provides maximum flexibility to derived classes while retaining most of the advantages of private access.

● **NOTE**

Member functions can be declared public, private, or protected, just as data members can. You can also declare data members as public. Remember, however, that public data members become part of the interface; if the class is already being used, changing the interface can introduce errors in the rest of the program.

Another Example: Fast Cars and Inheritance Trees

A central idea of inheritance is that you can declare a general type and then derive any number of more specific types from it. These types can be the basis for even more specific types; thus, a family tree of classes can be as elaborate as you like.

For example, you might define a general class to store information about various cars:

```
class CAuto {
public:
    char  make[20];
    char  model[20];
    int   year;
    int   color_selection;

// Constructors
    CAuto() {}
    CAuto(char mak[], char mod[], int y, int c);
};


#include <string.h>

CAuto::CAuto(char mak[], char mod[], int y, int c) {
    strcpy(make, mak);
    strcpy(model, mod);
    year = y;
    color_selection = c;
}
```

●—**TIP**

Here, I've included two arrays of char (make and model) to store character strings. I used the char type so that the example can be entered easily from scratch. However, if you have declared and compiled the code for the string class CStr, this would be an ideal place to use it. The declarations of the first two CAuto members could be replaced by:

```
CStr make;
CStr model;
```

Assignments to make and model then could be made through simple assignments rather than a call to strcpy. To use the CStr class, remember to include the cstr.h header file in your source code and to link in cstr.obj.

For cars in general, this information might be adequate, but for certain kinds of cars, you might want to store more information. With a sports car, you are interested in everything in the CAuto class (make, model, year, and color), but you might also want to keep track of horsepower and acceleration time from 0 to 60 mph. The following CSportsCar definition inherits CAuto members and adds some members of its own.

```
class CSportsCar : public CAuto {
public:
    double horse_power;
    double accel_0_60;

// Constructor
    CSportsCar() {}
};
```

You can say that sports cars (CSportsCar) are one subspecies of cars in general (CAuto). Another subspecies of CAuto might be station wagons (CWagon). With this class, other information might be appropriate, such as storage capacity and maximum number of passengers.

```
CWagon : public CAuto {
public:
    double storage;
    int passengers;

// Constructor
    CWagon() {}
};
```

So far, you have one base class (CAuto) with two derived classes (CSportsCar and CWagon). To make things more interesting, let's add another class: CRaceCar.

The first thing to do when designing the CRaceCar class is to decide where it fits in the inheritance hierarchy. You can consider racecars, for the sake of this example, a subspecies of sports car. For a racecar, you want to store all the information that you would for sports cars in general, as well as one other piece of information — the number of racing competitions won.

```
CRaceCar : public CSportsCar {
public:
      int   races_won;
};
```

Because the class is designed as part of an existing inheritance hierarchy, the amount of code to write is quite small. However, CRaceCar is a simple class, so adding a default constructor is not important.

You may have noticed that I didn't include a constructor here, although I did for the other classes. As I pointed out in Chapter 6 (see the section entitled "Interlude with the Default Constructor," p. 409), it is usually a good idea to add a default constructor, particularly if there is any chance that you will add other constructors later. However, CRaceCar is a simple class.

Figure 8-4 shows the resulting inheritance hierarchy.

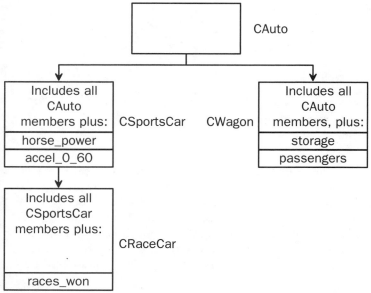

Figure 8-4 *A class hierarchy for automobiles.*

Base-Class Constructors

Inheritance is a way of including class members (both data and functions) previously declared in another class. C++ supports a special feature — base-class constructors — to support efficient initialization of these inherited members.

The previous section introduced a sports-car class, CSportsCar, which inherits members from the CAuto class and adds its own. To this declaration, it would be nice to add a second constructor to initialize all the data members, including those inherited from CAuto.

```
CSportsCar : public CAuto {
public:
    double horse_power;
    double accel_0_60;

// Constructors
    CSportsCar() {}
    CSportsCar(char mak[], char mod[], int y, int c,
        double hp, double a);

};
```

The new constructor initializes all the data members, one by one.

```
#include <string.h>

CSportsCar::CSportsCar(char mak[], char mod[], int y,
    int c,double hp, double a)        {
strcpy(make, mak);
    strcpy(model, mod);
    year = y;
    color_selection = c;
    horse_power = hp;
    accel_0_60 = a;
}
```

There are several problems with this function. First, it is inefficient. It is not obvious here, but C++ always constructs an object by first calling the constructor for the base class, if any. Because no base-class constructor is specified, the compiler generates a call to the CAuto default constructor. Consequently, all the original members of CAuto are already initialized — in this case, to zero — before the first statement in this function starts executing. The function initializes all CAuto members twice.

The second problem is potentially much worse. The CAuto members were declared public, but had they been declared as private, this CSportsCar constructor would be impossible to write.

The solution is to specify the appropriate base-class constructor in the CSportsCar constructor function definition. Here is the syntax:

```
class::class(arglist1) : Base_class(arglist2) {
    statements}
```

In this syntax, *arglist2* can optionally use any arguments from *arglist1*. These arguments are passed through to the base-class constructor. This base-class constructor must match, by number and type of arguments, a constructor defined in *Base_class*.

In the following function definition, a colon (:) follows the CSportsCar argument list and the appropriate CAuto constructor. The first four arguments are passed through to the base CAuto class constructor, which takes four arguments. If you review the CAuto declaration, you'll see that CAuto has just such a constructor.

```
CSportsCar::CSportsCar(char mak[], char mod[], int y,
    int c, double hp, double a) :
    CAuto(mak, mod, y, c) {
        horse_power = hp;
        accel_0_60 = a;}
```

Now the four data members inherited from CAuto are initialized only once. There is also a fringe benefit: the resulting CSportsCar constructor is shorter and easier to write.

Base Classes and Pointers

This final look at inheritance sets up much of the rationale behind virtual functions, the subject of Chapter 9. Many programmers consider the virtual-function capability to be at the heart of object orientation, so it's worth taking a few minutes to understand the problem it addresses.

Inheritance creates a kind of one-sided relationship between types in C++. Generally, C++ does not let you assign pointers of one type to pointers of a different type without using a data cast. (A cast is a way of explicitly changing an expression's type.) However, you can assign an object of a derived type to a pointer of base-class type-without using a cast. Figure 8-5 illustrates this rule.

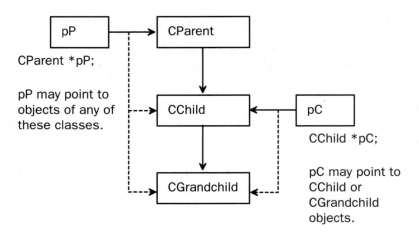

Figure 8-5 *Pointer assignment between base and derived types.*

Interestingly, this pointer assignment is allowed in only one direction: a base-type pointer can point to a derived type. This arrangement makes sense if you think about it. Consider this case:

```
CStr    *pBase;
CIoStr DerivedObj;

pBase = &DerivedObj;    // Assignment to base-class
                        //  pointer is allowed.
```

When the pointer pBase is declared, the compiler assumes that it will point to an object of type CStr. Errors could arise if pBase is made to point to an int variable, for example, because the int type does not support CStr members. There is no problem, however, in making pBase point to an object of a derived type (in this case, CIoStr), because the derived type must include *at least the same members* that CStr does. The following statement works equally well whether pBase points to a CStr object or to a CIoStr object:

```
pBase->cat(" blah blah blah");
```

Yet, the converse does not hold. Consider what would happen if C++ let you freely assign the address of an object of base type (CStr) to a pointer to the derived type (CIoStr):

```
CStr    BaseObj;
CIoStr *pDerived;

pDerived = &BaseObj;    // ERROR! Cannot assign to
                        //  derived type without cast
```

The problem is that the base type CStr is a subset, and not a superset, of the type pointed to by pDerived. The object pointed to by pDerived should include at least all the members that CIoStr does, but CStr does not include everything in CIoStr. For example, what happens when this function call is made?

```
pDerived->input();
```

In the CIoStr declaration, the input function is a new member beyond those declared by CStr. This operation would be invalid if pDerived points to a CStr object.

In summary, a pointer to a class can be assigned the address of something in the same class or a derived class. The pointer's type controls which members can be accessed. You could declare an array of pointers to CStr, for example, and each pointer could point to a different type — CStr, CIoStr, or CFontIoStr. Despite this fact, you can use the pointer to refer only to members, such as the cpy function, that are declared in CStr itself.

```
CStr *pStr[10];
pStr[0] = new CStr;
pStr[1] = new CIoStr;
pStr[2] = new CFontIoStr;
```

An interesting question arises when one of the member functions is overridden. Suppose that CIoStr overrides the cpy function with its own implementation, as described earlier in this chapter. This operation creates two versions of the function: CStr::cpy and CIoStr::cpy. Which version of cpy do these statements call?

```
CIoStr iostr;
CStr *pStr = &iostr;
pStr->cpy("Initialize me.");
```

The last statement calls CStr::cpy (the base-class version) and not CIoStr::cpy. When the compiler scans the code and attempts to resolve this function call to an address, the compiler must use the type information it has. In this case, all it knows is that pStr points to something of type CStr. It therefore calls CStr::cpy.

```
pStr->cpy("Initialize me.");
```

But wait a minute, you say, that can't be right! The object knows that it is an object of type CIoStr and not CStr. The object should be able to call the version of the function found in the CIoStr class.

That determination cannot be made until runtime. The problem is that at compile time, the compiler cannot know the precise type pointed to, yet it must make a determination of the function's address. Its only choice is to use the type information given and assume CStr scope.

For example, in the following code, the expression pStr[n] could point to any object of type CStr, CIoStr, or CFontIoStr, but the compiler has to assume CStr as the type.

```
CStr *pStr[10];
//...
pStr[n]->cpy("hi!");
```

During running of the program, the precise type pointed to by pStr[n] is finally determined. If the decision of which function to call could be delayed until runtime, then the expression pStr [n]->cpy("hi!") could call the right function, either CStr::cpy or CIoStr::cpy, as appropriate.

This is just what happens with *virtual* functions, which are the subject of the next chapter. Virtual functions use *late binding*, which means that a reference to a function, such as pStr[n]->cpy, is not bound to an actual function address in memory until runtime.

8

Virtual Functions and Why They're Good

An object-oriented program can be thought of as a set of objects that communicate by sending each other messages. Ideally, the messages should have a good deal of independence. I should be able to send the message "Hello" or "What is your name?" without necessarily knowing the identity of the recipient.

This is what virtual functions are all about. I can call a virtual function without necessarily knowing the exact type of the object through which I'm calling the function. In fact, the object's class *may not even exist* at the time the code that calls the function is written. New types of objects can be added in the future, along with new function code, all without my having to recompile the main module. This gives programs greater decentralization. The decision about how to resolve a function call is relegated entirely to the objects themselves.

When you start programming in C++, it's not always obvious why this is so useful. In this chapter, I use a menu command example to help make the concepts more concrete.

●─**NOTE**───────────────────────────

The term *virtual* usually describes something that isn't quite real but works as if it were. In the case of functions, *virtual* describes a function call that can be translated to any number of different function addresses. In some ways, the name is misleading, because a virtual function is entirely real. It is simply executed as an indirect function call rather than as a fixed function address.

Applying the virtual Keyword

To make a member function into a virtual function, precede the function declaration with the virtual keyword. The keyword must appear at the beginning of the declaration, before the return-value type.

```
virtual   return_type   name(arguments);
```

The result is that the function is declared virtual, which means that it is *late bound*. In late binding, the address of the function does not have to be determined until runtime. (Most of this chapter is devoted to explaining why this is useful.)

Once the virtual keyword is used in the function declaration, you don't need to use it again in the function definition, in derived class declarations, or in derived class function definitions. The function remains virtual in all derived-class declarations using the same name and type.

For example, suppose you have a class CTimePiece that has a ShowTime function. This function is declared virtual.

```
class CTimePiece {
public:
    virtual void ShowTime(void);
    //...
};
```

The function definition for ShowTime does not need to include the virtual keyword.

```
#include <iostream.h>

void CTimePiece::ShowTime(void) {
    cout << hours << ":" << minutes;
};
```

In any classes derived, directly or indirectly, from CTimePiece, the ShowTime function is virtual — including the following class, which overrides the ShowTime function.

```
class CClock : public CTimePiece {
public:
    void ShowTime(void); // Override function
    //...
};

void CClock::ShowTime(void) {
    paint_clock_face(hours, minutes);
}
```

There is no requirement that a virtual function be overridden by derived classes or that it be called through a pointer. A virtual function can be called in the same ways that any other member function can be called. There is no difference in the syntax, either in declaration or in usage. (This is to say that the syntax in the C++ source code looks the same as for normal member functions, even though there are differences under the covers.)

```
CTimePiece time;
CClock clock;

time.ShowTime();
clock.ShowTime();
```

Virtual functions obey all the normal syntax rules for member functions. They cannot, however, be inlined.

The effect of making a function virtual most often shows up when you access objects through base-class pointers. (I suggest that you review the section entitled "Base Classes and Pointers" on page 463 of Chapter 8, if you haven't read it.) With the ShowTime function, you could use the same line of code to call different function implementations. In this example, assume that CClock and CDigital are both derived classes of CTimePiece.

```
CTimePiece *pTime;

pTime = new CClock;
pTime->ShowTime();  // Calls CClock::ShowTime

pTime = new CDigital;
pTime->ShowTime();  // Calls CDigital::ShowTime
```

When Should You Make a Function Virtual?

There is no difference in syntax between virtual and nonvirtual functions except for the one-time use of the virtual keyword in a declaration. This is true even though C++ handles them differently. Consequently, it's easy to introduce virtual functions into existing C++ projects.

But should you make all your functions virtual just because it's easy to do so? Except for inline functions, you could make almost all your functions virtual simply by putting the keyword everywhere the functions are first declared. However, not all functions should be virtual functions.

If there's no chance that a derived class will override a function, then the function should not be declared virtual. Each time you call a virtual function, you pay a slight performance penalty. In addition, each virtual function takes up slightly more space in program memory than it would if it were not virtual. The point is that there's no reason to make a function virtual unless doing so might make a difference.

If you write a function in a base class and it is clear that the function is intended to be overridden in derived classes, then it is wise to declare the function virtual. You can override a function in a derived class even though it is not virtual, but then in certain situations the wrong function might be called.

In the example at the end of the last chapter, this code calls the function CStr::cpy (the base-class version) even though it looks as if it should call CIoStr::cpy (the derived-class version):

```
CIoStr iostr;
CStr *pStr = &iostr;
pStr->cpy("Initialize me.");   // Call CStr::cpy or
                               //   CIoStr::cpy?
```

If the cpy function were originally declared as virtual (as shown next), the code would call CIoStr::cpy, as expected.

```
class CStr {
//...
    virtual void cpy(char *s);
//...
```

Admittedly, this example is not very realistic. There isn't much need to override the cpy implementation (except for the purpose of illustration). Consequently, because cpy is not likely to be overridden, there isn't much point in its being virtual.

The next section presents a member function that is a perfect candidate to be made virtual because it is designed to be overridden.

Menu Command Example

A simple scenario for object-oriented design is a program menu system. The program displays a series of menus from which the user makes a selection. The program then responds by carrying out the indicated command.

This system is easy enough to implement using traditional, procedure-oriented programming techniques, but object-oriented design offers some advantages. If each menu command is coded as a separate object, then the individual menu commands can manage themselves to a certain extent. This arrangement removes the need for the main program to maintain a look-up table or `switch` statement, which would have to be continually revised as new commands are added.

The result is a program that is easier to write, less error-prone, and much more flexible.

Declaring and defining the base class

The base class CMenuItem is a prototype for all the menu commands. The program doesn't instantiate this class. In other words, it doesn't define any object of class CMenuItem; it defines only classes derived from CMenuItem.

CMenuItem is a simple class. It contains only two members, as the class declaration in cmenu.h shows.

```
// CMENU.H - declaration of the CMenuItem base class

class CMenuItem {
public:
    char title[81];
    virtual void Do_Command(void) = 0;
};
```

This example introduces a new bit of syntax. The characters =0 at the end of the Do_Command declaration indicate that it is a *pure virtual function*. This is the same as any other virtual function except that it has no implementation in the base class; it is implemented only in classes derived from CMenuItem. The Do_Command function is not defined at all in this class; Do_Command becomes a kind of placeholder for functions to be defined later.

These strange functions are discussed further in the section "Functions with No Implementation (Pure Virtual Functions)," later in this chapter.

Each menu-command object implements its own version of Do_Command. The main program calls Do_Command for the selected object to execute a command. This is all the main program has to do. In effect, calling Do_Command sends a message to the object saying, "Execute your command."

Declaring and defining the menu objects

Each menu command is represented as a CMenuItem object that implements the CMenuItem function Do_Command. This example program uses three menu commands. When printed, they appear as follows:

1. Sound a bell.
2. Print a wise saying.
3. Add two numbers.

The declarations for all the menu commands are identical except for the class name. Each declaration must declare Do_Command to indicate that it is overriding the definition in the base class.

```
// CMDS.CPP - Defines and initializes menu commands

#include <stdio.h>
#include "cmenu.h"

class CMenuBell : public CMenuItem {
    void Do_Command(void);
};

class CMenuSaying : public CMenuItem {
    void Do_Command(void);
};

class CMenuAdd : public CMenuItem {
    void Do_Command(void);
};
```

Each of the Do_Command implementations carries out an actual command. These functions can be of any length. The first two are short, the last is longer.

```
// CMDS.CPP (continued)
void CMenuBell::Do_Command(void) {
    putc('\007', stdout);  // "\007" rings a bell
}
```

```
void CMenuSaying::Do_Command(void) {
    puts("If you know the meaning of the universe,");
    puts("make the sound of one hand clapping.");
}

void CMenuAdd::Do_Command(void) {
    double    x, y;

    printf("Enter a number: ");
    scanf("%lf", &x);
    printf("Enter a number: ");
    scanf("%lf", &y);
    printf("The total of the numbers is %f.", x + y);
}
```

Finally, the cmds.cpp file declares an array of pointers to CMenuItem objects, an integer storing the number of commands, and an initialization function. The main program uses all of these.

```
int num_commands;
CMenuItem *commands[20];

void Init_Commands(void) {
    commands[0] = new CMenuBell;
    strcpy(commands[0]->title, "Sound a bell.");
    commands[1] = new CMenuSaying;
    strcpy(commands[1]->title, "Print a message.");
    commands[2] = new CMenuAdd;
    strcpy(commands[2]->title, "Add two numbers.");
    num_commands = 3;
}
```

Using the objects

The main program is easy to write, because the menu objects do almost all the work. This is consistent with the basic theme of object orientation, which tends to decentralize decision-making and resources in favor of objects rather than the main program loop.

The main program must first gain access to the two pieces of global data — num_commands and the commands array — by declaring them with the extern keyword. This keyword is necessary if you want to use variables declared in another module.

```
// MAIN.CPP - Uses the menu objects to manage a menu

#include <stdio.h>
#include "menu.h"
```

```
extern int num_commands;
extern CMenuItem *commands[];
```

The main function first calls `Init_Commands` to initialize the menu. Then it sets up a loop that displays the menu and responds to commands. If the user enters any number not corresponding to a menu command, the loop ends.

```
void main(void) {
    int i, sel;

    Init_Commands();
    do {
        puts("\nMENU:\n");
        for (i = 0; i < num_commands; i++)
            printf("%d. %s", i+1, commands[i]->title);
        printf("\nEnter a selection: ");
        scanf("%d", &sel);
        if (sel > 0 && sel <= num_commands)
            commands[sel]->Do_Command();
    } while (sel <= num_commands);
}
```

This is the entire program. It shows the effect of the virtual keyword clearly. Suppose that the program were the same except that the `Do_Command` was not declared virtual. In that case, this next line of code would always execute the same command no matter what the user's selection was:

```
commands[sel]->Do_Command();
```

If `Do_Command` were not virtual, then, during compilation, C++ would resolve the function call based on the class that `commands[sel]` points to. The variable `commands` is an array of pointers to `CMenuItem` objects. Because `Do_Command` isn't virtual, the compiler would resolve this as a call to `CMenuItem::Do_Command`.

In this case, `CMenuItem` doesn't provide any implementation of `Do_Command` at all, because in `CMenuItem`, `Do_Command` is a pure virtual function. But if `Do_Command` were not virtual, the base class would have to provide some implementation, which we could call the default implementation. Without virtual functions, the main program would always execute this default implementation and the actual menu commands would never execute.

The advantage of virtual menu commands

Given the way this code is written, the use of virtual functions is clearly required, but does it have to be written this way? What was gained by designing a program-menu system based on virtual functions?

Certainly, you can write this menu program using traditional programming techniques. But in the traditional approach, more control must be placed in the main loop. For example, rather than call Do_Command through the current object, code inside the main loop would have to test the value of the selection and then take a different action depending on the value:

```
switch (sel) {
    case 1:
        Bell_Do_Command();
        break;
    case 2:
        Saying_Do_Command();
        break;
    case 3:
        Add_Do_Command();
        break;
};
```

Each time the menu structure of the program changed, this code would have to be revised, as would any place in the program that activated a menu command. The program is easier to maintain using the virtual-function approach, which requires only one statement to activate a selected menu command:

```
commands[sel]->Do_Command();
```

The main point is not that the traditional approach necessarily requires much more coding overall or even that it is less elegant (although it is). The point is that the traditional approach centralizes all control inside the main loop. With the virtual-function approach, the code in main.cpp never needs to be recompiled. Future menu commands can be added without having to rewrite or rebuild the main program.

And there are other advantages to the virtual-function approach. The menu has to be initialized somewhere; in this case, it is initialized in the Init_Commands function. Once the virtual-function framework is in place, however, you can use any initialization technique. For example, you could initialize the menu from a data file. (In Windows programming, the build process does something similar by using the resource compiler to build menus.)

With the virtual-function approach, the menu can even change during runtime. For example, because of a condition determined during running, some menu items may no longer apply, or new ones may be needed. (Look at how the File menu of Microsoft Word and other popular applications changes during runtime.) The virtual-function approach is more dynamic. It can revise the menu structure at any time. With the switch statement used in the traditional approach, the menu structure is hard-coded; in other words, it is firmly fixed in the flow of control of the program and cannot be changed after the program is compiled.

●—C/C++

Most object-oriented aspects of C++ can be simulated in C, although the C implementation is usually clumsier and requires additional work. This is true in the case of virtual functions. You can simulate the virtual-function capability by using *callback functions*. A callback is a function whose address you pass to the main program or to a specialized routine, which then calls the function you have written, as needed.

You could use callbacks instead of virtual functions, but you would need to write a callback function for each menu command and then initialize an array of structures specifying menu titles and callback function addresses. The virtual-function approach involves less work and provides a more coherent, easy-to-read structure for this same program mechanism.

The later section "How Virtual Functions Are Implemented" further describes the similarities between virtual functions and callback functions.

Functions with No Implementation (Pure Virtual Functions)

The Do_Command function is an example of a pure virtual function. In cmenu.h, the characters =0 in the declaration of the Do_Command member function indicate that it has no implementation in this class — that is, there is no function definition for CMenuItem::Do_Command. However, classes derived from CMenuItem must implement Do_Command before they can be used.

```
class CMenuItem {
public:
    char title[81];
    virtual void Do_Command(void) = 0;
};
```

Any class that has at least one pure virtual function is an *abstract class*. The CMenuItem class is such a class, because it declares Do_Command, which is a pure virtual function. As an abstract class, CMenuItem has an important limitation: it cannot be directly used to create an object. You can, however, declare pointers to CMenuItem.

```
CMenuItem *pMenu;        // OK
CMenuItem menu_thing;    // Error! Cannot instantiate
```

If abstract classes cannot be instantiated, what good are they? Abstract classes are useful in laying the foundation for families of classes. The CMenuItem class is a good, albeit simple, example of this approach.

The CMenuItem class could have implemented Do_Command by having it do nothing:

```
// CMENU.H - declaration of the CMenuItem base class

class CMenuItem {
public:
     char title[81];
     virtual void Do_Command(void);
};


// MENU.CPP - implementation of CMenuItem

void CMenuItem::Do_Command(void) {
}
```

However, this involves needless extra work, because there was never any intention of instantiating CMenuItem directly or calling CMenuItem::Do_Command. In addition, making the function a pure virtual function ensures that derived classes must define it; otherwise, the compiler will complain as soon as you try to create objects from the class.

How Virtual Functions Are Implemented

For the most part, this book doesn't focus on how C++ is implemented. Sometimes there is more than one way for a compiler to implement a specific feature of C++, and you don't usually need to understand underlying compiler implementation to understand object orientation and C++.

However, C programmers do tend to worry about program efficiency and trade-offs between speed and size — and C++ programmers tend to have the same mindset. The speed and size penalties involved with virtual functions are worth understanding. In the simple case (no multiple inheritance), the implementation of virtual functions is relatively straightforward and standard from one C++ compiler to the next.

Virtual functions are closely related to callback functions. Both mechanisms take advantage of the processor's capability to make indirect calls, which are function calls through a pointer. For example, this code uses C syntax to call the function Hello indirectly:

```c
void Hello(int n) {
    printf("Hello, your lucky number is %d.\n", n);
}

void (*pFunction)(int);

pFunction = &Hello;
(*pFunction)(5);    // Call Hello through pFunction
```

The virtual-function capability adds several things to this indirect-call capability: It expresses indirect calls in terms of member functions, it builds tables of function pointers for each class, and it hides the indirect-call syntax so that calls to virtual functions look just like calls to any member function. In some cases, if you are writing a derived class, you may even have forgotten that a particular function is virtual. Making a function virtual creates no difference in the way you write it or call it.

All these things are ultimately programming conveniences, but that's not to say that they aren't important. By making indirect function calls easier to use, the virtual-function capability encourages you to use them. It also provides a framework (class hierarchies) that gives indirect function calls meaningful structure and context.

For each class that has at least one virtual function, the compiler builds a table of function pointers. Each entry in the table contains the address of a virtual function. For example, consider this class:

```cpp
class CShape {
public:
    virtual int SetPoints(double ptArray[]);
    virtual void DrawMe(void);
    virtual void Move(double x, double y);
};
```

In the CShape class, the three functions SetPoints, DrawMe, and Move are good candidates for being made virtual, because they are likely to be overridden in classes derived from CShape.

The C++ compiler constructs a table of function pointers for the CShape class. Notably, it does not construct such a table for each individual CShape object; one table for the entire class is enough because all objects of the same class share all member functions.

This table is the virtual function table, or *vtable*, for the class. It has a pointer to the definition of each virtual function. If there are any nonvirtual functions in the class declaration, they do not appear in this table. There is no reason that they should; nonvirtual functions can be handled as normal function calls.

Figure 9-1 shows what the function table for CShape looks like.

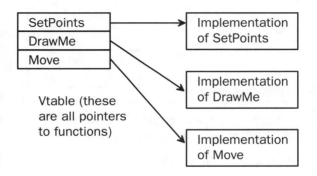

Figure 9-1 *Virtual function table for CShape.*

Any number of other classes can be derived from CShape, and all these classes implement their own versions of these three functions. (Such classes can also add other virtual functions, but those functions are added to the end of the vtable.) At runtime, how does an object "know" that it is an object of type CShape, for example, as opposed to some other class derived from CShape?

The answer is that each individual object has a hidden data member that points to the vtable for the class. (If the object's class has no virtual functions, however, then the compiler does not need to add this member.) This hidden pointer, which we can name pVtable, is placed at the beginning of the object. In reality, the object doesn't know its type and doesn't need to. The program code simply makes an indirect function call through the pointer, and the appropriate function code is called automatically. Each object's pVtable member points to the vtable for its class (CCircle and CSquare, for example, would each have its own vtable), so the object is linked to all the function code for that class.

Figure 9-2 illustrates the structure of a CShape object. You can see how an indirect function call through pVtable results in a call to function implementations for the class.

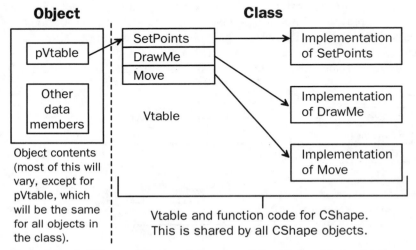

Figure 9-2 *A CShape object and the virtual function table (vtable).*

Consider a call to a virtual function through the object myshape:

```
CShape myshape, *pShape;
pShape = &myshape;
pShape->DrawMe();
```

The C++ compiler translates the call to DrawMe into this indirect function call:

```
(*(pShape->pVtable->DrawMe))();
```

This entire virtual-function mechanism can certainly be done in standard C if these steps are carried out:

1. For each class, declare a structure consisting of a function pointer for each virtual function.

2. Initialize each member of this structure so that it points to the appropriate function.

3. Alter the class declaration so that it includes an additional member, pVtable.

4. Initialize pVtable to point to the class virtual function table.

5. Translate all virtual-function calls, as shown in the previous code fragment.

None of this is impossible to do in standard C, but C++ is much more convenient because it automates all this work for you. C++'s capability to implement virtual functions under the covers without ever altering the source code used to call these functions is a central feature of C++ in relation to C. If you understand the essence of virtual functions, you've pierced to the heart of what object orientation is all about.

9

Advanced Use of Stream Classes

The I/O stream classes have some special features. Perhaps the most interesting is that you can extend your own classes to work with them when doing text operations << and >>. You can define what it means to display or read an object of your class.

Other advanced features include the I/O manipulators and stream flags. The manipulators change the format of the next item printed or read. The flags specify changes that are more permanent. For example, this statement causes the standard output stream to use hexadecimal number format until told to do otherwise:

```
cout.setf(ios::hex);
```

Again, it should be emphasized that the capabilities of stdio.h functions (printf, scanf, fopen, and related functions) correspond to those of the I/O stream classes. You can do the same kinds of operations with both. The biggest advantage of the stream classes is their extensibility, which is where this chapter starts.

Interacting with I/O Classes

This section explains how to get your own classes to work with the insertion (<<) and extraction (>>) operators.

The strategy of this section is to write operator functions combining your class with the two major stream classes istream and ostream. Doing so provides support for working with cin and cout, which are instances of these classes. In addition, the operator functions are inherited by the derived stream classes, including the file I/O classes, ifstream and ofstream.

The stream-class operators (<< and >>) support text operations, which translate values to their text-character representations. To directly transfer values to and from files, you would use binary operations. (To perform binary I/O, see the read and write functions in Section 7, pages 283 and 293, respectively.)

Extending the ostream insertion operator (<<)

To work with objects such as cout or cerr, you need to write an operator<< function that defines how your class interacts with the ostream class. Such a function has the following prototype, which you add to your class declaration:

```
friend ostream& operator<<(ostream&, class&);
```

As the syntax implies, everything should be entered as shown except *class*, which you replace with the name of your own class. Because the left operand is not the class itself, the function must be added as a friend function. (This is why the friend keyword exists — to support operator functions such as this one.)

The function definition has the following form. You can use any names that you want for *arg1* and *arg2*.

```
ostream& operator<<(ostream& arg1, class& arg2) {
    statements
    return arg1;
}
```

The function returns *arg1*. The function should always return a reference to the ostream object that was passed to it (that is, the left operand). This enables the following expression to return a reference to cout itself:

```
cout << obj
```

which, in turn, makes possible statements such as this:

```
cout << obj << endl;
```

The following is an example of a simple class that interacts with ostream.

```
#include <iostream.h>

class CPnt {
public:
    long x, y;
    CPnt(){x=y=0;}          // default constructor
    CPnt(long newx, long newy) {x = newx; y = newy; }
    friend ostream& operator<<(ostream&, CPnt&);
};

ostream& operator<<(ostream& os, CPnt& pnt) {
    os << pnt.x << " " << pnt.y;
    return os;
}
```

Given these declarations, you can now write code such as this:

```
CPnt p1(2, 5);
cout << p1 << endl;
```

Extending the istream extraction operator (>>)

If you want your class to support text operations with the istream classes (this includes cin as well as input file objects), include the following declaration inside your class:

friend istream& operator>>(istream&, *class*&);

As with the operator<< function prototype for the ostream class, you should enter everything exactly as shown except for the *class* placeholder, which should contain the name of your own class.

The function definition has the following form. You can use any names that you want for *arg1* and *arg2*.

```
istream& operator>>(istream& arg1, class& arg2) {
    statements
    return arg1;
}
```

The function returns *arg1*. The function should always return a reference to the istream object that was passed to it (that is, the left operand). This enables the following expression to return a reference to cin itself:

```
cin >> obj1
```

which, in turn, makes possible statements such as this:

```
cin >> obj1 >> obj2;
```

The following code provides a complete example of a class that supports text operations with ostream and istream classes:

```
#include <iostream.h>

class CPnt {
public:
    long x, y;
    CPnt(){x=y=0;}        // default constructor
    CPnt(long newx, long newy) {x = newx; y = newy; }
    friend ostream& operator<<(ostream&, CPnt&);
    friend istream& operator>>(istream&, CPnt&);
};

ostream& operator<<(ostream& os, CPnt& pnt) {
    os << pnt.x << " " << pnt.y;
    return os;
}

istream& operator>>(istream& is, CPnt& pnt) {
    is >> pnt.x >> pnt.y;
    return is;
}
```

Given this code for the extraction operator (>>), you can read in values for CPnt objects by writing statements such as this:

```
CPnt pnt;
cout << "Enter two coordinates: " << endl;
cin >> pnt;
```

The last statement in the preceding code causes the program to wait while the user enters two integers, which can be separated by a space or a newline.

An important aspect of this example is that the << and >> operators are, in fact, compatible. This is important because the istream and ostream operators are inherited by the file-stream classes (ifstream and ofstream). Consequently, data written by the output function must be in a format readable by the input function.

The code in this section provides compatibility. During output, pnt.x and pnt.y are separated by a space. For example, the insertion function (<<) would write the point 25, 1025 as:

```
25 1025
```

Assume that this output is placed in a file and is then read into a CPnt object. The extraction function (>>) reads two fields of integer data, one after another. It therefore reads the data correctly.

● **NOTE** ───

Reading and writing text strings poses a difficulty, because they need to be delimited. If you use >> to input to a string variable, characters are read only up to the first white space. An easy solution is to read and write each string as a separate line of text. See the getline function in Section 7 (p. 268).

Improving the display format

The display format used in the previous sections printed a pair of numbers, using only a single space to separate them. For example, CPnt(35, 10) would be printed as:

```
35 10
```

Many display formats are possible, of course, but one obvious improvement would be to place a comma between the numbers:

```
35, 10
```

The problem in inserting a comma is that the input and output formats need to be compatible. Text that is written by the insertion operator (<<) should be read correctly by the extraction operator (>>).

Let's take a closer look at how text-based input works. Assume that extraction (>>) is used to read a number:

```
is >> pnt.x;
```

After skipping leading white spaces, if any, this operation reads characters as long as they form a valid number. As soon as it reads a character that doesn't form part of a number, it stops reading. That character is the next to be read.

Consequently, if the input line is 35, 10, the first extraction operation reads up to the comma (,). The comma is then the next character to be read. The second extraction operation then reads the comma, which the operation does not recognize as a valid number and therefore reads as 0.

```
is >> pnt.y;
```

The solution is to skip one character after the first number is read. This way, the operation skips over the comma. The ignore function skips the specified number of characters. Here is the revised code, which supports the comma format:

```
ostream& operator<<(ostream& os, CPnt& pnt) {
// Print display with comma.
    os << pnt.x << ", " << pnt.y;
    return os;
}

istream& operator>>(istream& is, CPnt& pnt) {
    is >> pnt.x;
    is.ignore(1);    // Skip the comma.
    is >> pnt.y;
    return is;
}
```

I/O Manipulators

The I/O manipulators are predefined objects that affect data streams either by changing data formats or by appending a terminator. You use these manipulators by combining them with the insertion (<<) and extraction (>>) operators. For example:

```
cout << endl;    // Print a newline.
```

Each manipulator affects the next item to be printed or read. For example:

```
cout << hex << n;  // Print n in hex.
```

Unlike the I/O flags (discussed in the next section), the manipulators do not permanently affect a stream. Notably, however, they can be used to override the stream's current default format.

Table 10-1 lists the I/O manipulators.

Table 10-1 *I/O Manipulators*

I/O manipulator	Description
dec	Turns integer format to decimal.
endl	Appends a newline.
ends	Appends a null.
flush	Flushes the stream, forwarding buffered data to the physical device.
hex	Turns integer format to hexadecimal.
oct	Turns integer format to octal.

This example prints h as a hexadecimal number and o as an octal number, and then prints a newline:

```
#include <iostream.h>
int h, o;
//...
cout << hex << h << " " << oct << o << endl;
```

Remember that the insertion operator is really the left-shift operator (<<), which associates left to right and returns a reference to the stream object — in this case, cout. The last line of code above is, therefore, equivalent to the following:

```
cout << hex;    // Switch to hex format.
cout << h;      // Print h.
cout << " ";    // Print " ".
cout << oct;    // Switch to oct format.
cout << o;      // Print o.
cout << endl;   // Print newline.
```

The I/O manipulators work in a similar way with input objects. For example, the following statement uses keyboard input to assign values to h and o, assuming hex and octal formats:

```
cin >> hex >> h >> oct >> o;
```

Format Flags

Each stream has its own internal format-flag settings. (A *flag* is just a bit that has a predefined meaning.) Any of these flags can be turned on or off by calling the setf and unsetf member functions. The flags determine the default format of the stream — how the stream displays or reads data unless overridden.

Table 10-2 lists the format flags.

Table 10-2 *Format Flags*

Flag	Description
dec	Uses decimal radix for integers.
fixed	Displays floating-point numbers in standard notation; for example, 123.5.
hex	Uses hexadecimal radix for integers.
internal	If field width is larger than size of output, pads characters between sign or base prefix and data.
left	If field width is larger than size of output, left-justifies characters.
oct	Uses octal radix for integers.
right	If field width is larger than size of output, right-justifies characters.
scientific	Displays floating-point numbers in scientific notation; for example, 1.235e2.
showbase	Shows prefix (OX or O) when printing hex and octal numbers.
showpoint	Displays all floating-point numbers with decimal point and trailing zeros.
showpos	Shows positive sign (+) with positive numbers.
skipws	Skips leading white space characters during input.
stdio	Flushes stdout and stderr after each output.
unitbuf	Flushes buffer after each output.
uppercase	Prints hex digits in uppercase, as well as hex prefix X and exponent symbol E.

All of the flags are members of the ios class. To set a flag, use the ios:: prefix and call the setf function of any stream object. For example:

```
#include <iostream.h>
//...
cout.setf(ios::scientific); // Use scientific notation
```

```
cout.setf(ios::showpos);      // Show pos. number sign
cout << 1234.5 << endl;
```

This example prints the following result. Note that the output stream prints the plus sign (+), as well as using scientific notation.

```
+1.234500e003
```

Because the flags represent individual bits, you can use the bit-wise OR operator (|) to combine them. For example:

```
cout.setf(ios::scientific | ios::showpos);
```

You can turn off any condition by calling the unsetf member function. For example:

```
cout.unsetf(ios::showpos);   // Cancel showpos.
```

Every stream class and object supports the three functions for setting flags: setf, unsetf, and flags. flags can be used to get current flag settings, as well as to set all the flags at once. For more information on setf, unsetf, and flags, see pages 287, 292, and 263, respectively.

Remember that settings on a given stream are persistent until you change them; if you use hex to print a number in a hexadecimal format to cout, subsequent numbers will print in hexadecimal format until you reset the format to oct or dec.

Overview of the Stream Classes

So far, your use of the stream class has probably been limited to the stream objects cin and cout. Because these objects are instances of istream and ostream, respectively, they support all the functions defined by those classes.

You can also use the stream classes to create new objects based around classes derived from istream and ostream. You cannot use these two classes to create new objects directly, but you can use their derived classes.

The fstream, ifstream, and ofstream classes let you create stream objects based on a file. The strstream, istrstream, and ostrstream classes let you create stream objects based on arrays of char in memory.

Figure 10-1 summarizes the standard I/O stream classes and their inheritance relationships.

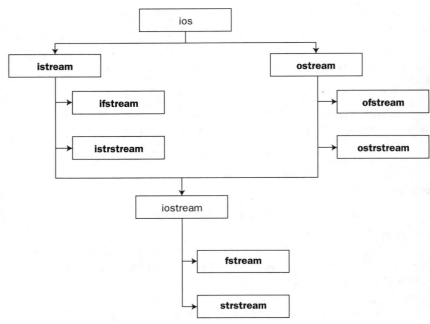

Figure 10-1 *I/O stream class hierarchy.*

The class hierarchy also contains another class, streambuf, which I have omitted for the sake of simplicity. It controls the buffering used by the stream classes.

The rest of this chapter summarizes the stream classes, which can be grouped into three major categories: input classes, output classes, and input/output classes.

Input classes

These classes include istream and its derived classes.

istream

This is the principal input class; it defines most input functions. You cannot use this class to create objects directly, but you can use the pre-defined object cin, which supports the istream functions. (See p. 271.)

ifstream

This class builds an input stream around a file. It is derived from istream and supports all istream operations. (See p. 271.)

```
ifstream infile("c:\\data.txt");
infile >> n;   // Read value of n from file.
```

istrstream

This class builds an input stream around an array of char in memory. It is derived from istream and supports all istream operations. (See p. 273.)

```
char buffer[500] = "10 25 35";
istrstream iss(buffer, 500);
iss >> n;   // Read value of n from string.
```

Output classes

These classes include ostream and its derived classes.

ostream

This is the principal output class, and it defines most output functions. You cannot use this class to create objects directly, but you can use the predefined objects cout, cerr, and clog, which all support the ostream functions. cerr and clog are the standard error and buffered error output streams, respectively. By default, they send output to the monitor just as cout does, but they can be redirected separately. (See p. 277.)

ofstream

This class builds an output stream around a file. It is derived from ostream and supports all ostream operations. (See p. 274.)

```
ofstream outfile("c:\\data.txt");
outfile << n;    // Write value of n to file.
```

ostrstream

This class builds an output stream around an array of char in memory. It is derived from ostream and supports all ostream operations. (See p. 278.)

```
char buffer[500];
ostrstream oss(buffer, 500);
oss << n;        // Write value of n to string.
```

Input/output classes

These classes include two usable classes — ofstream and ostrstream — as well as the class iostream, which is part of the hierarchy but can't be used to create objects. These classes inherit capabilities from *both* istream and ostream.

fstream

This class builds a stream around a file. You must specify which modes to open it with. (See p. 265.)

```
fstream outfile("c:\\data.txt", ios::in|ios::out);
```

ostrstream

This class builds a stream around an array of char in memory. You must specify which modes to open it with. (See p. 278.)

```
char buffer[500];
strstream ss(buffer, 500, ios::in|ios::out);
```

10

in plain english in plain english

Summary of C/C++ Differences

In porting C code to C++, look for these areas in which C++ does not compile C code and make the appropriate corrections:

- C++ functions that are declared with a return type other than void must return a value. Failing to do so might get you off with a warning in C; in C++, this error is a more egregious sin.

- C++ requires that function-definition headings use prototype style rather than old-fashioned C function syntax (the only form supported in the first versions of C). For example, this heading of a function definition is valid in C:

```
void swap(a, b)
double *a;
double *b;
{
//...
```

This syntax is invalid in C++ and would have to be rewritten as follows:

```
void swap(double *a, double *b) {//...
```

A

- C++ imposes stronger type checking. In particular, you cannot assign an address or pointer to a pointer of a different base type unless you use a type cast or are assigning to a void* pointer. Assignment between pointers of different types does not merely generate a warning as in C; instead, it is an out-and-out error. Type casts solve the problem:

```
void *vp;
int *ip;

ip = (int*) vp; // Data cast required
vp = ip;        // Ok: you can assign int * to void*
```

- C++ requires that functions be declared before being used. With C, you can get away without declaring the function first; the result is that C assumes an int return type and an indeterminate argument list. This is sloppy programming and never recommended, but you can slip it into your C code as long as you're happy with the default int return type. C++ is less permissive in this instance.

- It's possible to have name conflicts in your C++ code that did not arise in C code. In C, for example, you can recycle a global name by using it once to name a structure or union type (a "tag name" as opposed to a name defined by typedef) and using it again to name a function or variable. You cannot do this in C++, because C++ places all these identifiers in the same namespace. Fortunately, this kind of name conflict is rare.

There is another pitfall to watch for if you are mixing C and C++ source modules. Given the same symbol, C++ generates a different name when it generates .OBJ code. The C++ naming convention decorates each name so that type information is embedded into the .OBJ code. Then the linker won't recognize MyVar declared as int and MyVar declared as float as the same symbol. (This is called *type-safe linkage*.) By the way, the decoration scheme is implementation specific, so avoid making assumptions about it.

The result is that when linked together, C and C++ modules won't recognize each other's symbols. Fortunately, C++ provides an easy workaround: use extern "C" declarations in the C++ module to import symbols defined in C. An extern "C" declaration suppresses the usual name decoration performed by C++.

```
extern "C" {
    long way_home; // way_home defined in a C module
};
```

A

Going in the reverse direction — from C++ to C — is potentially much more difficult because C++ supports so many more features. You will probably never want to go in that direction. If you did, you might need to rewrite a lot of code. Although C++ is stricter when it comes to the use of types, it provides more freedom than C in these ways:

- You can place variable declarations and other statements (executable statements, if you will) in any order. In C, you have to put all local declarations at the beginning of a function or statement block.

- You can use any valid expression to initialize a variable or object. You are not limited to initializing with constants, as in C.

- When you declare a class (including a structure or union), the class name automatically becomes a fully usable type name. You do not have to qualify the class name with the class, struct, or union keyword to make it a type. In C, you would need to qualify a structure named Record as struct Record to use it in declarations and casts, or else use typedef to create a true type name. For the sake of backward compatibility, C++ supports syntax such as struct Record and class Record, although this is never necessary in C++ code written from scratch.

If you write code to be compiled in both C and C++ (for example, you're writing a source-code library for a variety of customers), you must observe the strongest restrictions of both C and C++.

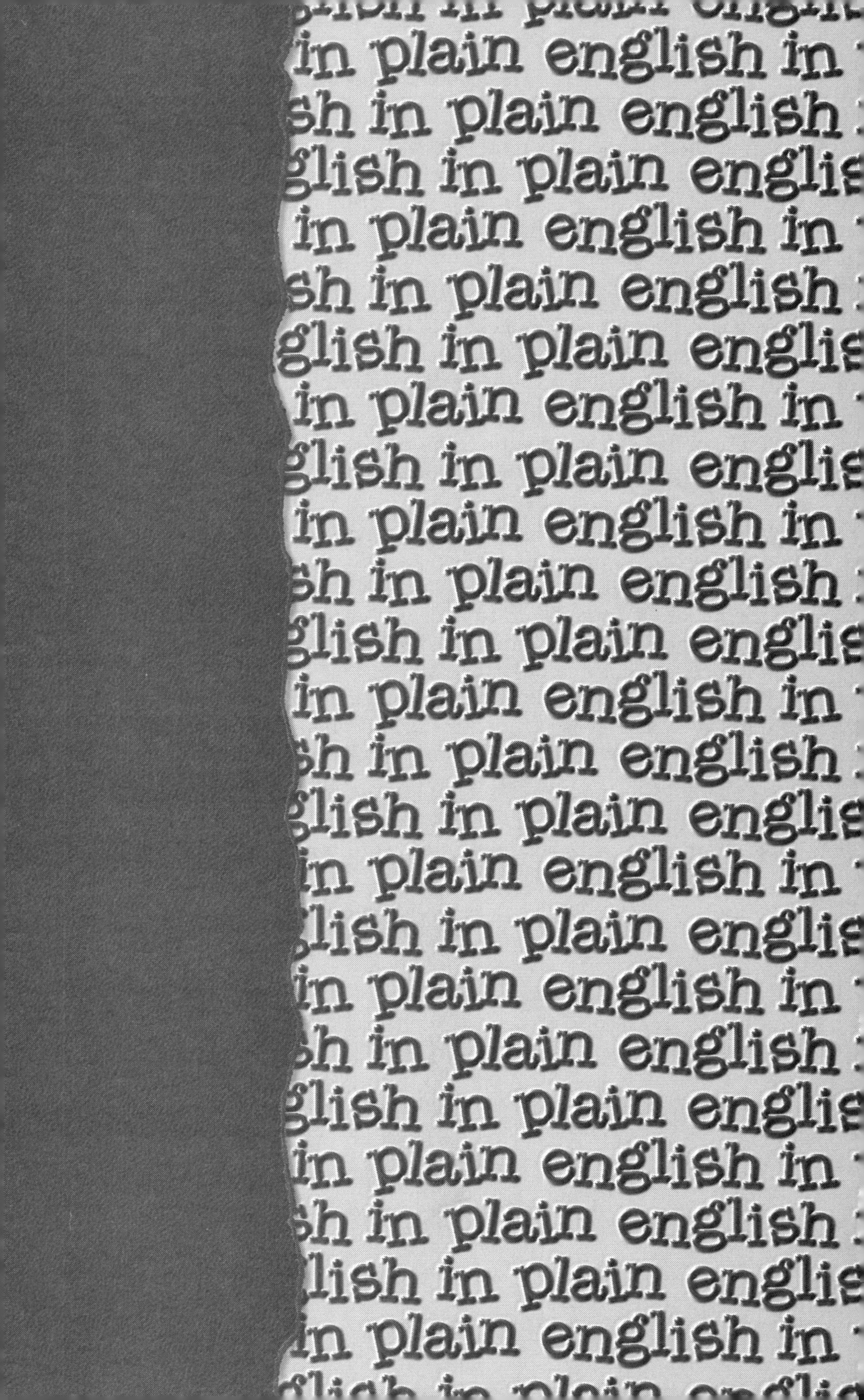

in plain english in
in plain english
in plain
in plain english in
in plain english
in plain
in plain english in
in plain
in plain english in
in plain english
in plain
in plain english in
in plain english
in plain
in plain english in
in plain
in plain english in
in plain english
in plain
in plain english in
in plain english
in plain
in plain english in

Overview of ANSI C++ Features

After years of changes, the ANSI specification for C++ is now considered stable. This means that there is a widely accepted standard version of C++ that is unlikely to change much in years to come. Compiler vendors should support this version of C++, and programmers should move toward using it more frequently.

Many of the new features in the ANSI specification represent extensions to the original language. Use of these is optional. This includes the mutable and explicit keywords.

Some of the changes are potentially more significant. The ANSI specification now encourages certain new programming practices and discourages others. Although the old ways of doing things will probably be supported for some time to come, some of the old ways will eventually be *deprecated* — meaning that the compiler will issue warnings suggesting that you change your ways. Someday, support may be dropped altogether for some of the old language features.

The major new areas of the ANSI specification include:

- New-style header files
- ANSI type cast operators

B

- Templates and exception handling
- Other new keywords
- Scope inside an if statement
- Overloading functions with enum types
- Forward references to nested classes
- Amendment 1 and C99

The first two areas — header files and cast operators — represent changes to the preferred way of doing things.

New-Style Header Files

Traditionally, the #include directive has a simple function: to read in a header file. Such a file has always been a normal, physical disk file that can be read just like any other file.

The new approach is to include virtual header files for the standard library. With this approach, the #include directive pulls in declarations for standard library functions by specifying a namespace, such as cstdlib, cstdio, or cmath, in the library. The compiler can respond by reading in the appropriate disk file or by loading the declarations through other means. This change was made to enable possible efficiencies in the future.

In practical terms, this means that instead of using this directive:

```
#include <math.h>
```

you can now use this:

```
#include <cmath>
```

In this book, I have stuck to using the old approach in example code because it is more familiar to C++ programmers. Section 4, however, lists both kinds of declarations for each library function. At some point in the future, everyone will be encouraged to switch to the new approach.

ANSI Type Cast Operators

The C language supports one style of cast operator for all occasions, and early versions of C++ supported this same operator with few changes. (The main change was that the rule requiring pointer casts became stricter.) Here is an example of a char* cast using the old-style C operator:

```
char *p = (char*) malloc(n);
```

Although this operator is still supported and even used a few times in this book, its use is now officially discouraged. In its place, ANSI C++ now provides four new cast operators:

```
const_cast
dynamic_cast
reinterpret_cast
static_cast
```

Only one of these — dynamic_cast — represents a truly new capability. If support for runtime type information (RTTI) is turned on (see your compiler documentation for details), dynamic_cast can help determine the exact type of an object pointed to at runtime. Its use is related to the typeid operator, which is also a relatively new feature that requires RTTI support to be turned on.

The other three operators perform the same operations supported by the old-style cast, but each has a different purpose. The advantage of these operators is that they stand out much more in source code, and because each one is different, they make the purpose of each line of code clearer. In particular, const_cast and reinterpret_cast represent potentially dangerous recasting of types. By using these keywords, you flag the critical lines of code that engage in the risky practices.

For example, you always need to be careful when recasting a pointer type. The statement at the beginning of this section recasts a pointer type and can be written as follows:

```
char *p = reinterpret_cast<char*>(malloc(n));
```

See Section 4 for in-depth description of each cast operator.

Templates and Exception Handling

Templates and exception handling are two major features of C++ that have been around for a while in some compilers but are not in all the early versions of C++. Many people asked that template support be added to C++ when it first came out. Templates are a technique for potentially making your code more reusable because you can write a general class or function into which you can plug a specific type. Microsoft, surprisingly, was slow to add this feature but eventually bowed to public demand. They were quicker to add other features, such as exception handling, as well as greater support for DOS and Windows-specific features. Platform-specific features, however, have largely not made it into the ANSI specification.

Exception handling is a superior technique for responding to runtime errors and other events. Its use is greatly preferred over the old

C library functions, `raise` and `signal`, which provide a way to handle only a limited set of events.

The ANSI specification now officially requires full support for both templates and exception handling. For more information on these features, see the `template` keyword, as well as the `try`, `throw`, and `catch` keywords, which support exception handling. You can read about all these keywords in Section 4 (pp. 122, 121, and 74 respectively).

In addition to supporting the `template` keyword for defining new templates, the ANSI specification also outlines a Standard Template Library that contains generalized collection classes. (You can use these classes to generate collections of any type you want.) Space limitations prevent this book from covering the Standard Template Library, which is a large subject unto itself.

Other New Keywords

In addition to the keywords already mentioned, the ANSI specification supports the `mutable`, `explicit`, and `bool` keywords:

- The `mutable` keyword modifies a member declaration, enabling a member to be changed even if it is part of a `const` object.

- The `explicit` keyword prevents a constructor from supplying a conversion.

- The `bool` keyword defines a data type that has only two values: `true` and `false`.

Use of `mutable` and `explicit` is optional. See pages 96 and 85 in Section 4 for more information.

Use of `bool` is a little different: It represents a better, and therefore preferred, approach to handling true/false values. For many years, if you wanted to store a true/false value in C or C++, you had to store it in a plain-vanilla integer variable. There are problems with doing this, however: Any nonzero value is considered "true," even though it's possible to combine two nonzero values with bitwise AND (&) and get zero, which is "false." With the `bool` data type, all nonzero values get converted to 1 (true); consequently, any AND or OR operation on two true values — whether bitwise or logical — produces a true result.

Along with support for the `bool` type, ANSI C++ adds the predefined constants `true` and `false`, which equate to 1 and 0, respectively. See pages 72, 122, and 86 in Section 4 for more information.

Another ANSI data type that was not present in all the early versions of C++ is the `wchar_t` type, the wide-character data format.

(See p. 135 in Section 4.) Because this format allocates an extra byte for each character, it makes possible the use of non-European character sets. The acceptance of this type in the C++ standard recognizes the growing importance of international marketing. It's a new world out there!

Scope Inside an if Statement

In ANSI C++, you can declare a variable inside an if condition. Such a variable has scope throughout the body of the if statement, but not outside it. For example:

```
if (int j = 1) {
    cout << j << endl;  // This is ok: j defined.
}

j = 2;                  // ERROR! j out of scope.
```

What is new here is that j is declared in the condition, not in the statement block itself. A single equals sign (=) means that j is assigned the value 1, not that it is tested for equality to 1.

The most obvious practical use for this technique is controlling the scope of pointers returned by dynamic_cast. In the following code, pd can only be used within the if statement; therefore, it can only be used if the dynamic_cast succeeds.

```
if (D *pd = dynamic_cast<arg>) {
    // This succeeds only if arg points to a D object.
    // pd can be safely referred to here.
}

pd->func2();  // ERROR! pd out of scope.
```

Inside the if statement, use of pd is safe because the cast succeeded (and therefore returned a non-null value to pd). Outside of the if statement, use of pd generates a compile-time error, requiring you to correct the error before releasing the program. The net result is that if this is the only place pd is declared, the compiler automatically prevents all use of pd except valid uses, thereby preventing a source of runtime errors.

See page 82 in Section 4 for more information on the dynamic_ cast operator.

Overloading Functions with enum Types

B

ANSI C++ strengthens the status of types declared with enum; specifically, you can differentiate between an enum type and other integer types when you overload functions. In older versions of C and C++, enum types are interchangeable with the int type in a function signature. Here is an example of code supported by the new capability:

```
enum suit {
    clubs, diamonds, hearts, spades
};

void func1(int n) {
    cout << "Inside func1(int)" << endl;
}

void func1(suit card) {
    cout << "Inside func1(suit)" << endl;
}
```

The function call:

```
func1(spades);
```

prints:

```
Inside func1(suit)
```

Forward References to Nested Classes

A long-standing feature of C and C++ lets you refer to a class (or in C, a structure type) without fully declaring it first. (See the glossary topic "forward reference," page 542, for more background on this subject.) ANSI C++ extends this capability to nested classes. For example:

```
class Chicken {

    class Egg;     // Enable forward reference to Egg.

    int a, b;
    Egg *p;        // Forward reference.
```

```
        class Egg {  // Nested class declared here.
            int n;
        };
};
```

You can also declare the nested class outside the enclosing class, but to do so you must use the scope operator (::) to qualify the declaration.

```
class Chicken {

        class Egg;    // Enable forward reference to Egg.

        int a, b;
        Egg *p;       // Forward reference.
};

class Chicken::Egg { // Nested class declared here.
        int n;
};
```

Amendment 1 and C99

These are the latest areas of change to C++.

Amendment 1 to the ANSI specification mandates the wchar_t type, as well as a large set of standard-library functions to support this type. These functions enable you to perform any operation on wide-character strings that you can perform on standard char* strings using the function library. For a list of all the wide-character functions, see page 160 near the beginning of Section 6.

C99 mandates support for the long long int, and long double types. For descriptions of these types, see page 94 in Section 4.

Standard Exceptions

A s explained in Section 4, you can throw and catch exceptions of any type. You can also catch the standard exceptions defined in C++ itself. These exceptions are automatically raised in response to certain situations — you don't have to use the throw keyword to raise them yourself.

The base class for C++ standard exceptions is named, appropriately enough, exception. This class declares constructors and a destructor, but no data members. (See your compiler documentation for the exact declaration.) This class, in turn, has two direct subclasses, each of which corresponds to a general category of exceptions.

Exception class	Description
logic_error	Reports an action that cannot be carried out. The conditions at runtime make the action unreasonable.
runtime_error	Reports invalid or incorrect results of an action. Such an exception results from an action that meets initial conditions (such as valid arguments), but has invalid results.

In a sense, all the standard exceptions represent run time errors. (They were errors that got past the compiler and were not the result of bad syntax.) However, the logic_error exceptions result from an attempt to do something that — given conditions known at runtime — is unreasonable even before attempted; for example, calling a function with invalid arguments. The runtime_error category includes actions that failed only after being duly attempted.

This table lists the specific exception classes by general type.

Exception class	Base class	Description
domain_error	logic_error	Violation of a domain condition just prior to an action
invalid_argument	logic_error	Attempt to call a function with a bad argument
length_error	logic_error	Attempt to create an object longer than maximum size of size_t
out_of_range	logic_error	Attempt to call a function with an out-of-range argument
bad_cast	logic_error	Invalid use of dynamic_ cast; reported for references (see p. 82)
bad_typeid	logic_error	Bad value used in an expression identifying type (type_info)
range_error	runtime_error	Operation had an invalid result
overflow_error	runtime_error	Operation resulted in arithmetic overflow (result was too big for the appropriate data type)
bad_alloc	runtime_error	Dynamic memory allocation failed

ASCII Character Codes

The following table lists the first 128 ASCII character codes, along with their decimal values. Values 127 and 0 through 25 are nonprintable characters that have special meaning on most personal computers and networks, including IBM compatibles. The common special codes are listed, including ACK (acknowledge), BS (backspace), LF (linefeed), FF (form feed) and CR (carriage return).

00	NUL	26		52	4	78	N	104	h
01		27		53	5	79	O	105	i
02		28	FS	54	6	80	P	106	j
03		29	GS	55	7	81	Q	107	k
04		30	RS	56	8	82	R	108	l
05		31	US	57	9	83	S	109	m
06	ACK	32	(space)	58	:	84	T	110	n
07	BEL	33	!	59	;	85	U	111	o
08	BS	34	"	60	<	86	V	112	p
09	TAB	35	#	61	=	87	W	113	q
10	LF	36	$	62	>	88	X	114	r
11		37	%	63	?	89	Y	115	s
12	FF	38	&	64	@	90	Z	116	t
13	CR	39	,	65	A	91	[	117	u
14		40	(	66	B	92	\	118	v
15		41	)	67	C	93	]	119	w
16		42	*	68	D	94	^	120	x
17		43	+	69	E	95	_	121	y
18		44	-	70	F	96	`	122	z
19		45		71	G	97	a	123	{
20		46	'	72	H	98	b	124		
21	NAK	47	/	73	I	99	c	125	}
22	SYN	48	0	74	J	100	d	126	~
23		49	1	75	K	101	e	127	DEL
24		50	2	76	L	102	f		
25		51	3	77	M	103	g		

D

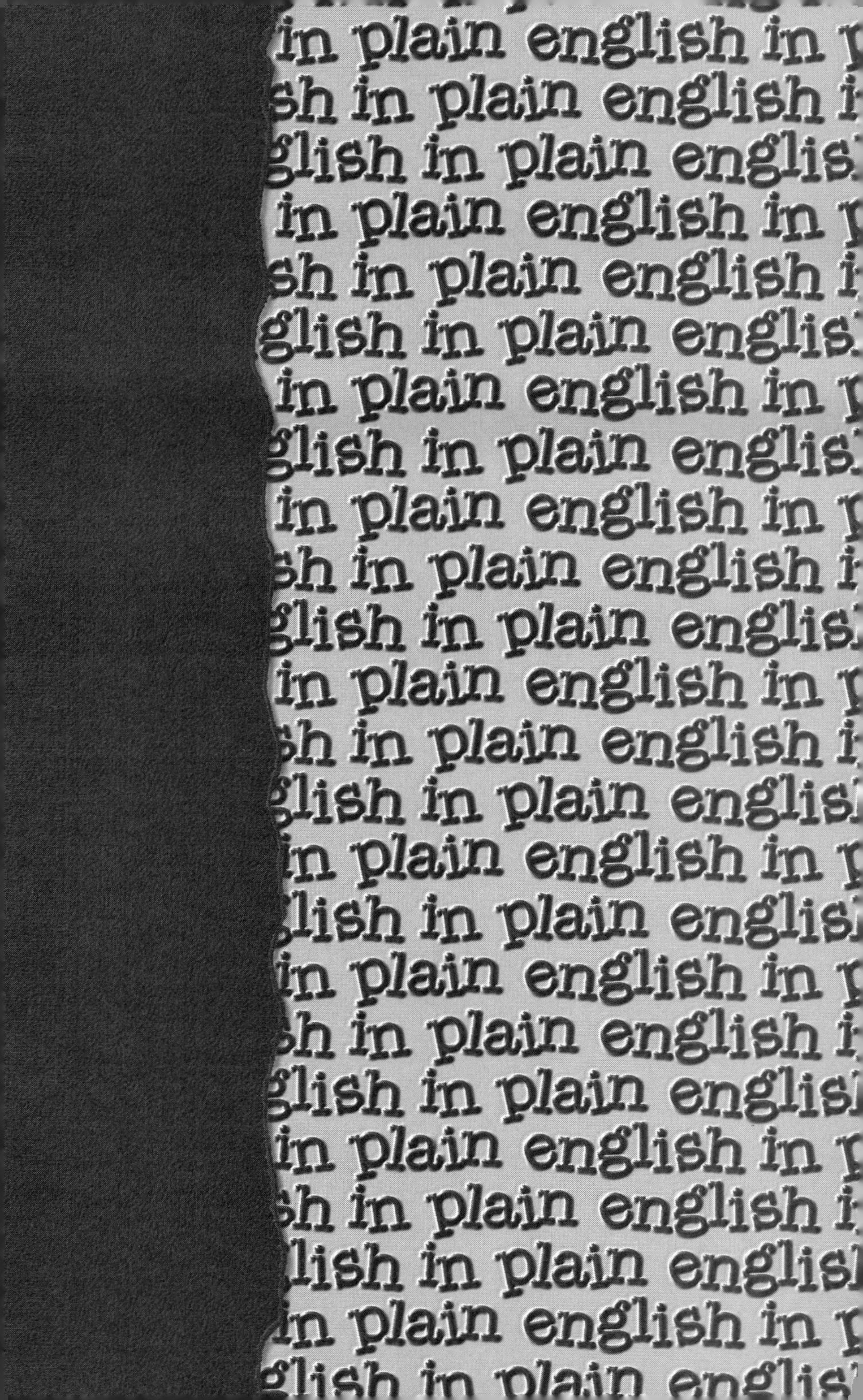
in plain english

The lconv Structure

The setlocale and localeconv functions (pp. 218 and 199) set and get a structure named lconv, which should never be altered directly. The lconv describes formatting conventions for the current locality. An application programmer can consult this information to appropriately format data displays for the end user.

Here is the layout of the lconv structure:

```
#include <locale.h>

struct lconv {
    char *decimal_point;
    char *thousands_sep;
    char *grouping;
    char *int_curr_symbol;
    char *currency_symbol;
    char *mon_decimal_point;
    char *mon_thousands_sep;
    char *positive_sign;
    char *negative_sign;
    char int_frac_digits;
    char frac_digits;
```

```
        char p_cs_precedes;
        char p_sep_by_space;
        char n_cs_precedes;
        char n_sep_by_space;
        char p_sign_pos;
        char n_sign_pos;
    };
```

The following table describes each of the data members. Some of these members have type char; each such member is interpreted as a simple integer value rather than as an ASCII character. In contrast, each char* member is interpreted as a string of text characters, except for grouping, which is interpreted as a series of byte-sized integers.

Data member	String or char?	Description
decimal_point	S	Decimal point character.
thousands_sep	S	Thousands separator character.
grouping	S	Set of numeric values describing grouping of digits; for example, \003 indicates that first three digits are grouped together. See further explanation below.
int_curr_symbol	S	International currency symbol.
currency_symbol	S	Local currency symbol.
mon_decimal_point	S	Decimal point character for monetary figures.
mon_thousands_sep	S	Thousands separator character for monetary figures.
positive_sign	S	Positive-value indicator for monetary figures.
negative_sign	S	Negative-value indicator for monetary figures.
int_frac_digits	C	Number of digits to right of decimal point for monetary figures (international format).
frac_digits	C	Number of digits to right of decimal point for monetary figures.
p_cs_precedes	C	1 = currency symbol precedes a positive value; 0 = currency symbol follows the value.

Data member	String or char?	Description
p_sep_by_space	C	1 = currency symbol is separated from value by a space; 0 = no separation (positive values).
n_cs_precedes	C	1 = currency symbol precedes a negative value; 0 = currency symbol follows the value.
n_sep_by_space	C	1 = currency symbol is separated from value by a space; 0 = no separation (negative values).
p_sign_pos	C	Number indicating positioning of the positive-value sign; see table below.
n_sign_pos	C	Number indicating positioning of the negative-value sign; see table below.

The grouping string, although it has type char*, contains a series of bytes in which each byte is interpreted as a simple integer rather than as an ASCII character. The first byte specifies how the first few digits after the decimal point are grouped. The next byte specifies how the next few digits (going right to left) are grouped. For example, the string "\003\004" indicates that the first three digits are grouped together, followed by a group of four. For example, 123456789 would be grouped as 12 3456 789.

Certain values have special meaning in the grouping string. A value of \0 indicates that the last value is to be repeated indefinitely. A value of CHAR_MAX (usually 127) specifies that no further grouping is performed.

The last two members, p_sign_pos and n_sign_pos, determine how positive and negative signs are placed in monetary figures. Each of these members has a value from 0 to 4, which has the following meaning:

Value	Meaning
0	No sign printed; parentheses surround the number. (This is a possible approach for negative amounts.)
1	The positive/negative sign precedes the rest of the number string, including currency symbol.
2	The positive/negative sign follows the rest of the number string, including currency symbol.
3	The positive/negative sign immediately precedes the currency symbol.
4	The positive/negative sign immediately follows the currency symbol.

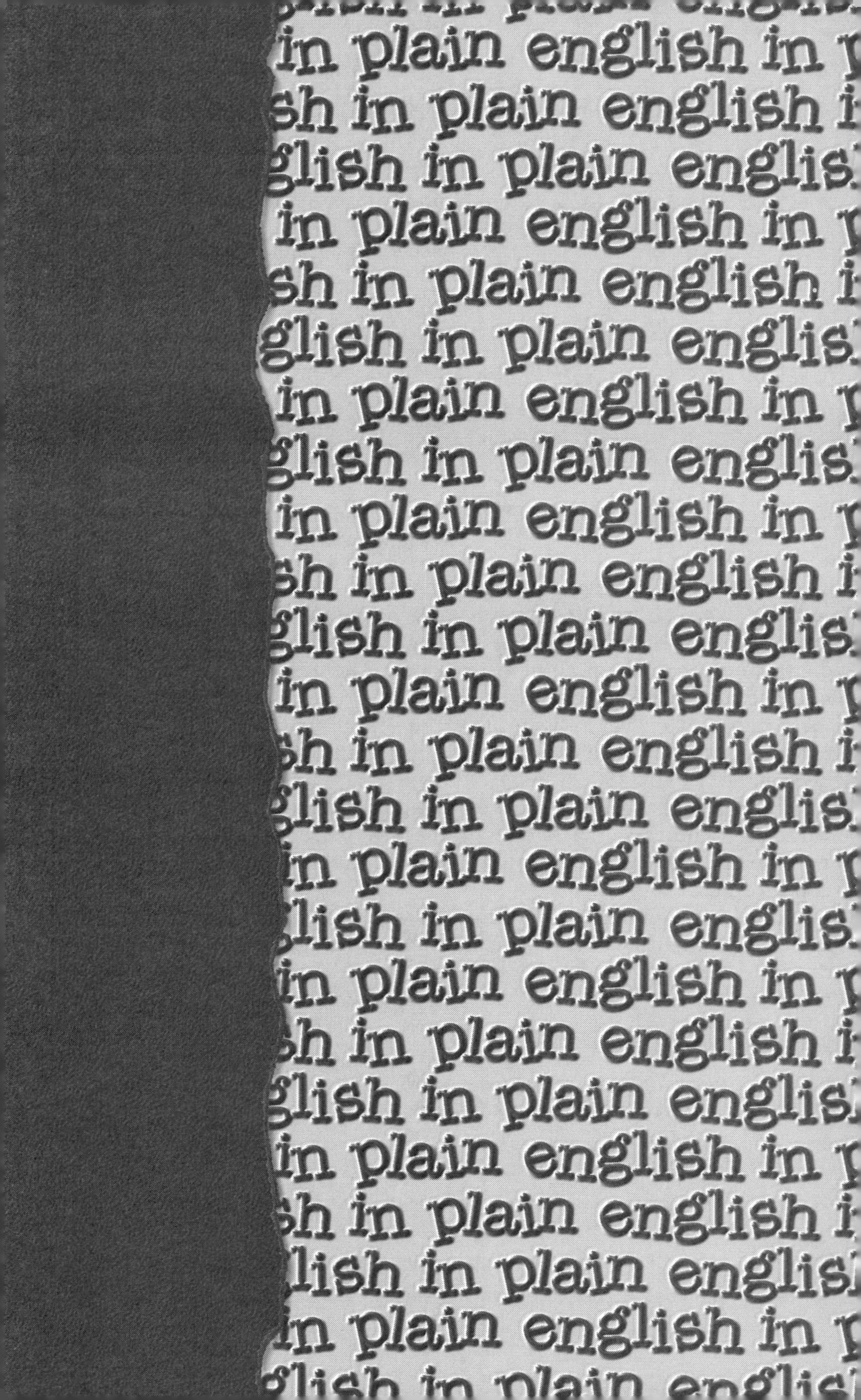

Glossary

abstract class

An abstract class is a class that can't be used to create objects. Such a class can still be useful if you want to create a family of related classes. For example, an abstract class might define a set of general services that other classes then implement with their own function definitions.

Technically speaking, an abstract class is any class with one or more *pure virtual functions*. A pure virtual function has no function definition in the class in which it is declared, but it can be implemented by derived classes. See *pure virtual function* for more information.

abstract data types

One of the potentially confusing terms in object-oriented theory is the phrase *abstract data types*. Theorists love it; other people go crazy.

Generally speaking, an abstract data type is one in which the details are not defined; they may be filled in later or may be hidden. Philosophically, the concept goes to the heart of object orientation: you define the relationships between objects and classes first and work out the details later. Practically speaking, the concept is not always that important, except in one respect: a language such as C++ provides ways to hide implementation details, so that a data type is defined by what it *does* rather than by how it's built.

aggregates

Aggregates, which are lists of constants used to initialize complex data types, come in two forms. The first form is set notation. A set contains one or more items, each of which can be a simple value or another aggregate (such as a string). Here the syntax indicates that the brackets are required and that you can include any number of *items*.

```
{ item [,item]...}
```

The second form of aggregate is the literal string, which is used to initialize arrays of char. The syntax for a literal string is:

```
"text"
```

For example, the following statement initializes an array of char* pointers:

```
char *cats[3] = {"Bill", "CB", "Purrly"};
```

In this case, each of the three pointers is initialized to point to a different string. In the next example, however, not all the pointers are initialized.

```
char *cats[5] = {"Bill", "CB", "Purrly"};
```

The effect here is to create cats as an array of five pointers of type char*, with the first three initialized to point to strings. The last two elements of cats are set to NULL by default.

When you use nested sets to initialize complex structures, each nested set initializes a logical subunit. For example, the following declaration initializes all three rows of matrix1, but it initializes only the first half of each row. Elements not initialized get the default value of 0.

```
int matrix1[3][6] = { {1, 2, 3}, {4, 5, 6},
                      {7, 8, 9} };
```

Aggregates play a special role in the initialization of arrays with empty indexes. In such cases, the aggregate determines how much space to allocate for the array. For example, the following declaration allocates exactly six elements:

```
int lotto_numbers[] = {1, 5, 21, 27, 33, 40};
```

anonymous unions

An anonymous union is a union not given a name. ANSI C++ supports the use of these unions. When you refer to a member of such a union, the member's name makes its union membership clear. For example, assume the following declaration:

```
struct databag {
    char fancy_name[20];
    union{
        char    strdata[20];
        double floatdata;
    };
} bag1;
```

Here you can refer directly to `bag1.strdata` and `bag1.floatdata`, without specifying a union name.

There is one principal limitation to this language feature: the use of an anonymous union must not create any name conflicts. There is no conflict in this case, because `fancy_name` is not the same as either `strdata` or `floatdata`. For more information on unions, see the union topic on page 129.

argument

An argument is a value passed to a function or template. For example, with the factorial function `fact`, `fact(4)` returns the factorial of 4, and `fact(5)` returns the factorial of 5. The numbers 4 and 5, in these examples, are arguments. Within the `fact` function definition, the argument may be declared as `n`:

```
long fact(int n) {
//...
}
```

Some books on programming use the terms *parameter* and *argument* differently, to distinguish between an argument declaration (such as n in this case) and a value passed to a function (4 or 5 in this case). Other books use the terms *formal argument* and *actual argument*, respectively, in the same way. For simplicity's sake, this book uses the term *argument* for both cases. I find that the distinction between declared argument and argument value is sometimes useful, but that there are cases in which the distinction blurs and unnecessarily complicates things.

array

An array is a collection of items of the same type, in which each item — called an *element* — is accessed by index number. By declaring an array, you can repeat a data type any number of times. Array indexing provides an excellent use for loops.

An array declaration of the form `type name[n]` creates an array that runs from `name[0]` to `name[n-1]`. For example, suppose you have the following declaration:

```
int nums[3];
```

This creates these items in memory, each of which is equivalent to an individual `int` variable:

```
nums[0]
nums[1]
nums[2]
```

In C++ as in C, there is a close connection between arrays and pointers. For more information, see Chapter 3.

Note that an array name is a constant. In the previous example, `nums` is a constant equal to the address of `nums[0]`. (An array name is a constant because although array data can normally be changed, the array address cannot be. An array name equates to this address and therefore cannot be changed. A pointer to array data, however, can change as much as you like.)

See also *multidimensional array*.

assignment operators

Assignment places a value into a variable (as in the expression x=1). C and C++ support a whole family of assignment operators. Most of these, such as += and -=, perform some other operation before assigning data. The exception is plain-vanilla assignment (=), which, for lack of a better term, might be called simple assignment.

C and C++ have no assignment statement *per se*. Instead, an assignment is just another kind of expression, and it can appear inside a larger expression. As with all expressions, you can turn an assignment into a statement by appending a semicolon.

```
x = y;
```

One thing that all assignment operators have in common is that they modify the contents of the left operand. This operand must therefore be an *lvalue*: this is an expression, such as a single variable, that has a single, valid address in memory. (See *lvalue*.) An lvalue is usually a variable, but can also be an array element or data member.

See Chapter 2 for more explanation of the quirks of assignment. See Table 2 in Section 3, page 44, for a listing of all the assignment operators.

association

Association of operators determines the order of resolving operators when they have the same level of precedence. (See *precedence*.) For example, addition (+) and subtraction (–) have the same precedence. How, then, do you resolve the following expression?

```
amount = 10 - 5 + n
```

C++ syntax states that addition and subtraction associate left to right. This expression, therefore, is equivalent to:

```
amount = (10 - 5) + n   // amount = 5 + n
```

which produces a different result from the following:

```
amount = 10 - (5 + n)   // amount = 5 - n
```

Association is not difficult to determine yourself. All operators in C++ associate left to right, except for assignment operators, unary operators, and the conditional operator (?:). When in doubt, consult Tables 1 and 2 (p. 44) in Section 3, which give precedence and association for all C++ operators.

It may help to remember that association and precedence in computer languages are consistent with the rules of arithmetic your third-grade teacher, Mrs. Grundy, taught.

base class

A base class contributes members to another class, called the *derived class*. For example, if class B is the base class of C, then all the members of B are automatically members of C. This relationship is an example of inheritance in C++. A base class is sometimes called a *superclass* or *parent class*. For more information, see Chapter 5.

base-class constructor

When you write a constructor, you can invoke a constructor from the base class (if there is one). This is particularly useful if the base class has any private members, because otherwise these members could not be initialized. Here is the general syntax:

```
class::class(args) : base_class(args) {
    statements
}
```

As an example, suppose the class CSportsCar is derived from the class CAuto. The following example demonstrates a call to a base-class constructor. In this example, the arguments h and m are passed along to a CAuto constructor.

```
CSportsCar::CSportsCar(double h, CStr m, double a) :
    CAuto(h, 2, m) {

    accel_0_60 = a;
    stripes = 0;
}
```

This code passes the initialization values h and m to the constructor in the base class, CAuto, along with a constant, 2. For a more complete description of this example, see the last section in Chapter 6.

binary mode
Binary mode is one of two I/O modes in which you can open a file. When you read or write to a file in binary mode, no translation of data is performed. You access data exactly as it is in the file. In contrast, text mode writes a string by translating each newline (a single character in program memory) into a carriage-return/linefeed pair in the file.

Another practice of binary mode that is usually (but not always) observed by programmers is reading and writing numeric values directly, rather than as a series of text characters that represent the value. When using stdio.h functions, you read and write values directly by using the fread and fwrite functions (p. 179). When using the stream classes, you read and write values directly by using the read and write member functions (pp. 283 and 293).

For example, if you write the value 255 as text, the program places the ASCII codes for "2", "5", and "5" into the file: these values are 50, 53, and 53, respectively. If you write the value 255 directly, the program places the value 255 itself into the file (hex 0xFF). If the value 255 is part of a short integer (short), it writes the bytes 0x00 0xFF.

binary operator
A binary operator combines two items (or *operands*) to form a larger expression. Most C++ operators are binary, as are operators in most languages. Common examples include addition, subtraction, and multiplication. For example:

```
x + y
amount * factor
```

Assignment is also a binary operation, because it has both a left operand and a right operand. For example:

```
x = y
```

See also *unary operator*.

bit field

A bit field is a special C/C++ data type that represents a subset of bits within an integer. Such a field can be as small as one bit, but it can optionally be several bits wide. When you write code involving bit fields, the compiler generates instructions to extract, manipulate, and store the bit values. Although the end result is the same as if you used bitwise operations directly, bit fields have the advantage of being easier to read and understand, as well as (in many cases) involving fewer lines of C++ source code. See the last section in Chapter 2 for more information.

Boolean values

A Boolean is an expression that holds one of two values: `true` or `false`. Most data types, in contrast, have a much bigger range than two values. If storage space were at a premium, use of a single bit would be the most efficient way to store a Boolean value. (See *bit field*.) But accessing a bit requires additional instructions; therefore, Boolean values are usually stored as integers.

In early versions of C++, there was no separate Boolean type; 0 was considered false, while any nonzero value was considered true. This can cause strange results if you're not careful. For example, combining 6 and 9 with bitwise AND (`&`) produces 0, which equates to false, even though 6 and 9 are both treated as representing the value *true*. One solution is to favor the use of logical, rather than bitwise, operators. The C/C++ logical operators treat all nonzero values the same way.

ANSI C++ provides another solution, which is to use the new `bool` data type. Any nonzero value assigned to a `bool` variable is automatically converted to 1. See page 72 for more information on this data type.

The term *Boolean* is capitalized because it is an adjective derived from a proper name. In this case, the name is that of George Boole, the inventor of modern symbolic logic. (This is one of the fun facts you may have learned in college and then forgotten.)

callback function

Some function calls require the address of another function that you have written; this latter function is a *callback function*. In effect, you are giving someone else's code the capability to give control back to your own code, at least temporarily. Although this may sound obscure, it is the only way to implement the `qsort` and `bsearch` functions with enough flexibility. When you call one of these functions, you pass the address of your own callback function.

Another significance of callback functions is that they declare function addresses as arguments. This illustrates function-pointer syntax. See `qsort` and `bsearch` topics in Section 6 for more information (pp. 209 and 168).

cast

A cast takes the value of an expression, changes its type, and passes along the result. (If you cast a variable, you have no effect on the original variable's type; you only affect the type of the expression.) In some cases, the effect of the cast is to change the actual bits used to represent a value. For example, casting an integer value to `double` format changes the underlying data.

```
double d = static_cast<double>(i);
```

This operation can also be expressed with the old-style C cast:

```
double d = (double) i;
```

In other cases, a cast has no effect on the data, but only changes the way the expression is interpreted. For example, casting an `int*` pointer as `float*` has no effect on the pointer value itself, but changes the format used to interpret the actual bits. When the pointer is eventually dereferenced, the difference between the data formats is critical.

ANSI C++ supports the new cast operators `const_cast`, `dynamic_cast`, `reinterpret_cast`, and `static_cast`, but it continues support for the old-style C cast as well. For more information on the rules and uses of the new cast operators, see topics in Section 4. See also *promotion*.

class

The concept of class is one of the most central concepts in C++. In general, a class is any user-defined type other than an array or `typedef` type: this includes any data structure defined with the `class`, `struct`, or `union` keywords. When you declare a class, you extend the C++ language by creating a new type of data structure.

After a class is declared, you can use it directly to create any number of instances, or *objects*, each of which has the attributes defined in the class. See Chapter 5 for an introduction to classes and objects.

Classes take the idea of a C structure type, which can contain data fields, and extends it by adding support for functions. These are *member functions:* they define operations on objects of the class. You can also define how operators (such as +, *, /, and so on) work on these objects. (See Chapter 7) Another important feature is private access, which hides selected class members from the rest of the world. (See *encapsulation*.)

class instance

An instance is the same as an object. See also *instance* and *object*.

comments

A comment is text that the compiler ignores. The comment remains part of the source code even though not compiled. In theory, a comment can contain anything. You can, if you want, insert "To be or not to be." Generally, though, programmers add comments that are helpful to humans reading the source code.

C++ supports two varieties of syntax for comments. The syntax most commonly seen in C++ source code is the line comment, which causes the compiler to ignore all text from double backslashes (//) to the end of a line. (This is one of the few cases in C++ code where a line break matters.)

```
x = y;    // This is a comment; x is assigned y.
```

The other syntax — the multiline comment — is inherited from the C language. All text between the symbols /* and */ is ignored by the compiler, including line breaks, if any. For example:

```
/* This is a C-style, multiline
   comment. */
```

When using the multiline comment syntax, remember that begin and end comment symbols do not work like parentheses. You cannot successfully nest these comments. The compiler simply ignores all text from a begin-comment symbol (/*) to the *first* end-comment symbol (*/) found thereafter. The following code, therefore, causes a syntax error.

```
/* This is the outer comment, and
   /* This is an embedded comment. */
   Here is more of the outer comment. */
```

In this example, the compiler reads the end-comment symbol (*/) at the end of the second line as terminating the comment. It therefore attempts to compile the third line as ordinary code. To temporarily block out code, consider using the #if and #endif directives, which can be nested to any level. See Section 5 for more information on these directives.

complex data types

A complex data type is a data type that is built from other types. Complex data types include all arrays, classes, unions, and structures, as well as pointers. The only data types that are not complex are primitive data types such as int, bool, and float.

compound statements

A compound statement consists of one or more statements surrounded by braces ({}). The statements work as a group. Either all or none are executed. The syntax is:

```
{
    statements
}
```

Compound statements have a number of uses. First, they define a statement block. Local variables defined in the block go out of scope after the closing brace (}). Another important use is with control structures. Anywhere you can put a statement, you can put a compound statement. This fact makes possible the following if statement, in which either all the statements are executed or none of them are:

```
if (switch_now) {
    temp = a;
    a = b;
    b = temp;
}
```

In C and C++, a semicolon (;) is a statement terminator, not a statement separator, as in Pascal. This makes C++ syntax easier. The only kind of statement not terminated by a semicolon is the compound statement itself; therefore, a semicolon is not used after the terminating brace (}) except in the case of a class declaration.

conditional compilation

Conditional compilation is a technique for maintaining multiple versions of a program. Rather than rewrite a program each time you compile it for a different target platform, you place the platform-specific lines of code into #if...#endif blocks. This way, you can change what code gets compiled with very little effort. See Section 5 for more information on #if and other directives.

control structure

A control structure is a statement that has the ability to alter the flow of control or make a decision. (But even after Deep Thought's victory over Kasparov, it's still debated whether computers really make decisions. In reality, all a control structure does is execute a simple numeric test and follow instructions.)

Control structures in C++ include if-else, while, do, for, and switch. Functions and goto statements also alter the flow of control. See topics in Section 4 for more information.

constant

C++ supports a number of items that can be called constants. In general, a constant is a value that does not change. There are several kinds of constants:

- Numeric constants such as 100, 4.5, 0xFF, and 018. (The last two use hexadecimal and octal format, respectively.)
- Symbolic constants defined with the #define directive. (These are also called *macros*.)
- Constants defined with the enum keyword.
- String literals such as "This is a string.".
- The name of an array, which is a constant equal to the address of the first element. (Array names are constants, but pointers and indexed items are not.)
- Any variable declared with the const keyword.

The last category differs from the rest in some important ways. A variable declared as const is still a variable, even though it is also a constant. You should assume that a const variable takes up space at runtime, just as any variable does. Moreover, such a variable can have any base type, as well as scope and storage class.

The first two categories are different from const variables because they include constants that may exist at compile time only. Depending on the particular compiler, these constants may be folded together during compilation. For example, an expression such as 2 + 2 is likely to be replaced by 4.

For more information on numeric constants, see Chapter 2; on strings, see Chapter 3; for the #define directive, see page 143; and for the enum and const keywords, see pages 83 and 76, respectively.

constructor

A constructor is an initialization function for a class. Whenever an object is created, a constructor for the object's class is executed. A constructor is the logical place to set initial values for data members and perform other initialization tasks. A constructor always has the same name as its class, and it has no return type, not even void.

You can have multiple constructors for the same class, as long as each has a unique argument list. A constructor's argument list corresponds to the arguments, if any, used to initialize an object of that class. If no values are used to initialize the object, the class's default constructor is executed. (See *default constructor*.) For more information on constructors, see Chapter 6. See also *copy constructor*.

conversion functions

C++ lets you support conversions between types in two ways. A class C can define incoming conversions from a type T through the use of a constructor of the form C(T). The incoming conversion defines how instances of T can be assigned to instances of C (as in c_obj = t_obj).

Conversion operator functions define outgoing conversions. For example, if class C has a conversion function for type T, this function defines how instances of C can be assigned to instances of T (as in t_obj = c_obj). For the syntax of conversion operator functions, see "Writing a Conversion Function" on page 434 of Chapter 7.

Constructors and conversion functions do more than just define how assignments can be carried out; they also create implicit type casts. For example, if the CStr class defines a conversion to char*, then you can pass an instance of CStr wherever a function specifies an argument of char* type.

copy constructor

A copy constructor is called whenever the program initializes a new object from another of the same class. If an object is passed by value, the program automatically makes a copy of the argument and passes it along.

Another example occurs when a function produces an object as its return value, but doesn't use a pointer or reference to do so. The copy constructor is automatically executed to create a permanent copy for the calling function. (This is inefficient, which is why pointers and references are frequently used when a function manipulates an object.)

Each class has exactly one copy constructor. If you don't write your own, the compiler automatically defines an implicit copy constructor. This constructor performs a simple member-by-member copy of each data member. Although this behavior is adequate in many situations, it may be inadequate if the class contains pointers. A copy constructor has the following general syntax for a class C, which indicates that it takes a reference to an object of class C. (See also *reference*.)

```
C(const C&)
```

A copy constructor has similarities to the *assignment operation function* (assign the values of one object to another of the same class) but they are not precisely the same. The copy constructor initializes a completely new object.

For more information on constructors, see Chapter 6.

data abstraction
Data abstraction is the art of defining types in terms of what they do, rather than in terms of their internal structure. When learning C++, it's best not to lose too much sleep over learning this term; it's a bit fuzzy. See *abstract data types*.

data member
Data members are the variables in a class declaration. As a rule, the data members define the data fields for every object of the class. There is one exception: a data member declared with the `static` keyword does not correspond to a data field inside individual objects. Instead, static data members are shared by all objects of the same class — meaning that they really have little to do with individual objects.

data type
See *type*.

declaration
A declaration is a statement that describes a variable, class, or function. Such a description gives type information, which means that it tells the program what kind of item is being referred to. Some declarations actually create a variable or function code; these are called *definitions*. For example:

```
int x, y, z;   // Declare x, y, and z as integers.
```

Other kinds of declarations provide information to interpret forward and external references. These include function prototypes and `extern` declarations. C++ is stricter than many other languages. Before you call a function, it must be declared — either through a function definition or prototype.

To understand complex C/C++ declarations, you need to use reverse logic. Ask yourself: What does it mean when this expression appears in executable code? For example, consider the following declaration:

```
char *sarray[100];
```

To understand this declaration, first apply C++ rules of precedence and association. Because unary operators associate right-to-left, the declaration is equivalent to:

```
char *(sarray[100]);
```

Now, assume the expression `*(sarray[n])` appears in code, in which n runs from 0 to 99. This means that an element from 0 to 99 is indexed and then dereferenced to get a `char` value. Therefore, `sarray` is an array of 100 pointers to `char`. In contrast,

```
char (*ptr_to_array)[100];
```

is a pointer to an array of 100 `char`, not an array of 100 pointers.

Using similar logic, you can see why the following two expressions differ as they do. The first item is a function prototype; the second is a function pointer.

```
int *pfn1(void);       // Function returning ptr to int
int (*pfn2)(void);     // Ptr to function returning int
```

The key to understanding these declarations is to remember that in executable code, `pfn2` must be dereferenced before the function call is made.

decorating

Decorating is the scheme used by a C++ compiler to generate type information along with a name. For example, if you declare an `int` named `Charley`, C++ will not simply output the name `Charley` when it generates an .obj or .o file. Instead, it will output `Charley` and add extra characters to the name, resulting in a longer name identifying `Charley` as an `int`.

There are two main reasons for name decoration. One reason is to support *type-safe linkage*. Because function and variable names placed in .obj (or .o) files are decorated, the linker cannot consider the integer `Charley` and the floating-point variable `Charley` to be the same symbol. This prevents linking of certain kinds of bad code. The other purpose of decoration is to support function overloading. The name decoration scheme is implementation specific. See *overloading, function*.

default argument value

Each argument in a function definition can be given a default value. If the function is called without a value being specified for that argument, the default value is used. For example, assume that you have defined the following function, which takes one required argument and one argument with a default value:

```
void set_vars(char* name, int amt = 0);
```

Now, if `set_vars` is called with only one argument, `amt` is assumed to be 0.

```
set_vars("Joe Schmoe");
```

If, however, `set_vars` is called with two arguments, `amt` gets the value specified.

```
set_vars("Joe Schmoe", 5);
```

C++ imposes some restrictions. First, all arguments with default values come at the end of the list. This is necessary because C++ assigns values to arguments in left-to-right order. For example, if you call a function and specify three arguments, the first three arguments get the values; any remaining arguments take default values. Another restriction relates to function overloading. (See *overloading, function*.) When a function name is overloaded, the function signatures must differ in at least one argument that does *not* have a default value.

default constructor
A default constructor is an initialization function that takes no arguments. Whenever an object is created and no values are used to initialize that object, the default constructor of the object's class is called. For a class C, the signature of the default constructor is:

```
C();
```

If you write no constructors of any kind for a given class, the compiler supplies a hidden default constructor that sets all data members to 0; but if you define *any* constructor, the compiler no longer provides a hidden default constructor. Because of this behavior, it is a good policy to write a default constructor for each of your classes, even if that constructor doesn't do anything.

That the compiler provides a default constructor and then removes it as soon as you write another constructor may seem strange. Contrary to appearances, this is not part of a conspiracy to make your life difficult. C++ provides automatic default constructors to support backward compatibility with `struct` types ported from C. Once you start writing your own classes, you ought to know better than to rely on the compiler.

For information on default constructors and other kinds of constructors, see Chapter 6.

definition
A definition creates a variable or function code. In a large and complex project, a function or variable may be declared many times, but it can only be defined once. (Exception: a virtual function can be defined different ways by different classes.) The definition of a variable is the place in program code where the variable is actually created and, optionally, initialized. For example:

```
int i;
```

A function definition contains the statements to be executed when the function is called. Here is a short example. (Yes, it's yet another example of the factorial function!)

```
long fact(int n) {
    long amount;
    for (amount = 1; n > 1; n—)
        amount *= n;
    return amt;
}
```

Definitions are a kind of declaration, but not all declarations are definitions. For example, extern declarations do not define a variable.

dereference

Dereferencing an address expression gets the contents at the address. For example, if an address expression evaluates to the numeric value 1055, then dereferencing the expression gets the contents at address 1055. Another way of stating this is to say that dereferencing a pointer gets the thing the pointer points to. For example:

```
int n = 5;
int *p = &n;    // Place address of n in p.
cout << *p      // Print what p points to (n).
```

The asterisk (*), applied as a unary operator is the dereference operator (also called the *indirection* operator). When used in a data definition, as in the second statement above, it creates a pointer. When used in an executable statement, it dereferences the pointer.

It's possible to declare pointers to pointers and multidimensional arrays. This complicates things a bit. An address expression must be fully dereferenced to get the data at its address. For example, assume pointer pp holds the value 1055 but has type int**. In that case, it must be dereferenced twice to get an integer:

```
int matrix[2][2] = {{1, 2}, {3, 4}};
int **pp = matrix;    // Point to beginning of matrix.
cout << **pp;         // Print first item in matrix.
```

Note that applying an index dereferences a pointer, just as * does.

derived class

A derived class inherits some or all of its members of another class, called the *base class*. For example, if class C is derived from base class B, then all the members of B are automatically members of C. (But the derived class C can add additional members of its own.) A derived class is sometimes called a *subclass* or *child class*. For more information, see Chapter 5.

destructor

A destructor is the converse of a constructor. Whereas a constructor is executed just after an object is created, a destructor is executed just before the object is removed from memory. You almost never call a destructor directly. An object's destructor is called automatically whenever some action, such as the use of the `delete` operator, causes an object to be destroyed. (Remember that all of an object's code resides in its class.)

Although it isn't required that you write a destructor for every class, such a function can be useful for performing object cleanup and termination-related tasks. For example, you might use a destructor to close files associated with an object of the class. Unlike constructors, destructors are unique: there can be only one destructor for each class. For any given class C, the destructor has the following declaration:

```
~C();
```

For more information, see "Life and death of an object: constructors and destructors" on page 399 of Chapter 5. Despite the harshness of the name (*destructor*) and the syntax (*there can be only one*), destructors are occasionally useful.

directive

A directive is a special command to the compiler that is executed before the rest of the program is compiled and run. Unlike a statement, a directive never corresponds to a runtime action; therefore, anything you accomplish with directives has zero cost in execution speed. One of the more useful directives is `#define`, which creates a symbolic constant:

```
#define PI 3.14159265
```

See Section 5 for a complete list of ANSI-supported directives along with descriptions.

empty statement

In C and C++, it's legal to use an empty statement, which is just a blank statement terminated by a semicolon (`;`). One consequence of this syntax is that you are usually not penalized if your finger should slip and you type extra semicolons. The following code, for example, is perfectly valid.

```
int i = 1;;;
```

Technically, this is not a single statement, but a declaration followed by two empty statements.

Empty statements are useful in at least one context: to help provide the target of a goto statement. Specifically, if you wanted to jump to the very end of a procedure, you would need to follow a label by an empty statement. Otherwise, the label would not precede any statement at all and would be illegal.

```
i = m * 2;
if (i == j)
        goto end_of_func;
//...
end_of_func:
        ;
}
```

encapsulation

Encapsulation means to protect the insides of something. For a data structure to act as a truly self-contained object, it needs to have data integrity. This means that it can communicate with other objects through established channels (much as a nerve cell communicates through tendrils), but the insides of the object are private. C++ supports this approach by enabling you to declare parts of a class as private or protected.

Encapsulation is one of the three pillars of object-oriented programming, the other two being inheritance and polymorphism. Of these three concepts, encapsulation is probably the most important, especially in small-to-medium-sized examples. The advantage of encapsulation is that in each class (and therefore each of the class's objects), you can change or optimize the internals as much as you like without breaking the rest of the program. The term *encapsulation* is close to the term *abstraction*. At bottom, both mean roughly the same thing: hide the details. Chapter 5 explains the benefits of encapsulation in the context of a detailed example.

enumeration

Enumeration is a fancy word for *list*. In C++ programs, declaring an enumeration is a convenient way to create a list of integer constants. You could define a series of constants with the #define keyword, but the use of the enum keyword is easier and more elegant. Here is a simple enumeration:

```
enum number {
        zero, one, two, three;
};
```

In this example, each name has the value you would expect. By default, the first item in an enumeration has the value 0.

Another example creates constants CLUBS, DIAMONDS, HEARTS, and SPADES, and assigns the values 0 through 3. Note that these names appear only in source code — at runtime, the values are printed as 0, 1, 2, or 3.

```
enum suit {
    CLUBS, DIAMONDS, HEARTS, SPADES;
};
//...
cout << HEARTS << endl;    // Print "2".
```

For more information on the use of the enum keyword, see page 83. See also Appendix B for information on ANSI extensions to enum.

escape sequence
An escape sequence is a C/C++ technique for coding a special character in either a quoted string or a single char value. These sequences (such as \n, which indicates a newline) always start with a backslash (\). Because the backslash is interpreted as the beginning of an escape sequence, you have to use a double backslashes (\\) to place a single backslash in a string. For a list of escape-sequence codes, see the char topic on page 74.

exception
An exception is an unusual program occurrence demanding immediate attention. Exceptions that are not handled cause a program to terminate. Typically, an exception is a runtime error, but it is possible to have an exception that is not an error. ANSI C++ provides the keywords try, catch, and throw to handle exceptions. The advantage of C++ exception handling as a way of dealing with errors and other events, is that you can intercept these events and provide responses in whatever part of the program you want. You can therefore centralize all error-handling code or override it as needed. See try on page 122 for more information.

executable statement
An executable statement corresponds to some action at runtime, such as calling a function or performing a calculation. In the C language, the line between declarations and executable statements is well defined — each statement is either one or the other, but never both. In C++, however, the line is blurred. A variable definition that creates an object does not just define data; it also calls a constructor.

The term *executable statement*, therefore, is not quite as precise a concept in C++ as in C. It still makes sense, however, to refer to certain kinds of statements as executable. Most statements — such as control structures, function calls, and statements that move or assign data — can be considered executable. Data definitions may or may not be executable in practice, but for clarity's sake, it helps to classify them as declarations rather than executable statements.

expression

Expressions are the fundamental units of execution in C and C++. Generally speaking, an expression is anything that evaluates to a single value. For example, a simple variable such as x is an expression, but so is a more complex piece of code such as (x * n + 1)/y2k. A unique aspect of C/C++ syntax is that any expression can be turned into a statement by appending a semicolon (;). Furthermore, assignments are expressions, because they return a value — namely, the value that was assigned. All of the following are valid examples of expressions that have been turned into statements through the use of a semicolon:

```
x;
y = x;
y = x = z = 0;
y = (x * n + 1)/y2k;
func1();
y = func1();
```

Note that although x; is a syntactically valid statement, it doesn't actually do anything.

forward reference

In C++, you must declare a symbol (variable, function, or class name) before referring to it. If you want to call a function before defining it, you must place a function prototype at the beginning of your program — or at least before you call it.

C++ even enables you to refer to a class before fully declaring it. This is necessary in the rare situation in which two classes have pointers referring to instances of each other. ("I point at you; you point at me.") This is perfectly legitimate, but it requires forward references to classes. You can do this by placing syntax of the form class *name*; at the beginning of the code (or, for structures, struct *name*;). For example:

```
class A;
class B;

class A {
public:
       B *ptr_to_B;
};

class B {
public:
```

```
    A  *ptr_to A;
};
```

ANSI C++ extends the forward-reference capability to classes nested inside of other classes. (See *nested control structures and classes.*)

function

A function is a group of statements executed as a single unit, which optionally can return a value. The concept of functions is central to all programming languages, although functions are often called *procedures* or *subroutines* in other languages. A unique feature of C and C++ is that all subroutines are considered functions, whether they return a value or not. Functions that don't return a value are declared void; otherwise, there is no difference between functions that return a value and those that don't. Another feature of C/C++ syntax is that you can call a function but ignore its return value. For an introduction to basic function syntax, see Chapter 2.

function member

See *member function.*

function pointer

See *pointer to a function.*

function prototype

See *prototype.*

global variable

A global variable is visible throughout a program, or at least throughout a source file. (You can make a global variable visible throughout a multi-module program by using the extern keyword. See page 86.) In C and C++, you make a variable global by declaring it outside all functions. The variable is visible from the point where it is declared to the end of the source file. Ideally, the number of global variables should be kept to a minimum. However, global variables are often necessary as a way of sharing information between functions. See also *local variable.*

header file

Header files provide common definitions and function prototypes. C++ requires every function to be declared before being called, and some functions in the standard library are implemented as macro functions. All these declarations must be read into a source file before the library functions can be called. Header files, which are read in as if they were source code, save you from having to enter the declaration yourself.

You include a header file by using the #include directive. See the #include topic on page 150 of Section 5 for information on this directive.

In ANSI C++, the new, preferred coding technique replaces library header files with virtual header files. For example, instead of using #include <stdio.h>, the new technique is to use #include <cstdio>. This latter approach enables the possibility of future versions of C++ replacing a physical header file, such as stdio.h, with a series of internally stored declarations, making faster compilation possible.

In addition to supporting standard library functions, customized header files are often useful in individual projects. This is particularly true for projects with multiple source files. The following kinds of declarations should be placed in header files:

- Prototypes of all functions except those intended to be private to one module

- Declarations of all classes used throughout the whole project

- extern declarations for all variables intended to be used across modules

- Definitions of macro functions

- typedef definitions for complex types used throughout the project

Some kinds of code should never be placed in header files, because the intended use of a header file is to be included in multiple sources. For example, placing a function definition into a header (unless it is a macro function) usually causes a linker error.

identifier
An identifier is a name defined in a program. Any word in a program — with the exception of text appearing in quoted strings or comments — is either a keyword or an identifier. Another way of stating this is to say an identifier is any name that *you* make up. In addition, any name defined in a library is also an identifier. (Library names are not keywords.) The names of variables, classes, macros, and functions are all identifiers.

Identifiers in C++, as in C, must be formed according to these rules:

- An identifier cannot be the same as a C++ keyword.

- Each character in the identifier must be either an uppercase or lowercase letter, one of the digits 0 through 9, or the underscore (_).

- The first character cannot be a digit.

In addition, there are some other guidelines that you should observe when devising identifiers. First, although you can begin names with an underscore, doing so is unwise, because the C++ standard library uses some special low-level identifiers (usually unseen by the programmer) and begins these names with an underscore. Second, you should avoid creating two different names that differ only in case: for example, MrBig and mrBIG. Use of two such names is likely to cause errors because even though C++ is case sensitive, the linker may not be. The safest policy is to ensure that all identifiers are unique, and then use a consistent uppercase/lowercase scheme for each. You can certainly mix case within a name, and doing so is a tried-and-true scheme to promote clarity: for example, avgDollarsPerEmp. Just be consistent and never type AVGdollarsPERemp.

implementation

The term *implementation* is used in several ways. First, *implementation* can refer to a function definition. When you derive a class and override the function definition, you are said to be *implementing the function*. Second, *implementation* can refer to all the internals of a class, as opposed to its external part (or *interface*). Chapter 5 uses the term in this sense. Finally, the term *implementation-specific* can refer to behavior specific to a certain C++ compiler.

indirection

The term *indirection* means referring to data through a pointer rather than directly. For example, consider the following statements:

```
int i = 5;
int *pi = &x;
```

The pointer pi contains the address of x. When you use *pi to refer to i rather than using i itself, you are using indirection. Each use of the pointer-dereference operator (*) is another level of indirection. For example, the expression **ppi uses two levels of indirection. See also *dereference*.

inheritance

Inheritance enables you to declare a new class by basing it on an old one — thereby getting all the declarations in the old class for free. Given a declaration for class A, you can declare B as a more specialized kind of A. The relationship is then: "B *is a kind of* A." For example, having declared CAuto, you can declare CSportsCar by specifying just those additional members needed in the new class; all the common members are inherited from CAuto and don't need to be repeated. See Chapter 8 for an introduction to the subject.

Inheritance is one of the three pillars of object orientation, the other two being encapsulation and polymorphism. Not everyone considers inheritance as important as the other two. Microsoft's Component Object Model (COM) deemphasizes inheritance because, as a language feature, it's tied more closely to source code, whereas COM is an object-oriented model emphasizing machine and language independence. Inheritance is often useful — it encourages efficient code reuse — but you can get most of the same benefits through object containment. In C++, the major importance of inheritance is that it provides a syntactical foundation for virtual functions and polymorphism.

inline function

When the compiler sees a call to an inline function, it responds by expanding the function definition into the body of another function. (See the following figure.) Inline functions are similar to macro functions, because neither is executed in the standard way — by transferring control to a different address. However, unlike macros, inline functions follow the same syntax rules that normal functions do.

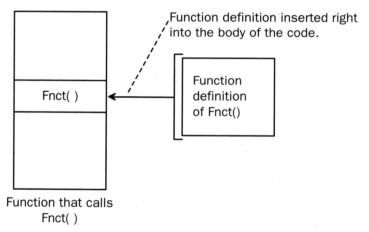

Function definition inserted right into the body of the code.

Fnct( )

Function definition of Fnct()

Function that calls
  Fnct( )

Expansion of an inline function call.

There are two ways to create inline functions in ANSI C++:

- In the case of class-member functions, you can inline a function by placing its definition inside the class declaration. For example:

```
class CHorse {
    CStr name;
    CHorse (CStr nm) {name = nm; }
```

- You can also inline a function by using the `inline` keyword in the definition.

```
inline double cube_it(double x) {
    return x * x * x;
}
```

In addition, some compilers can be enabled to inline functions on their own, as an optimizing technique. For more information on member functions, see "Function Inlining for Fun and Profit," on page 401 of Chapter 5. For more information on the `inline` keyword, see page 92.

instance
The term *instance* is another word for object. Once a class is declared, you can use it to create any number of instances. The relationship between a class and its instances is roughly the same relationship as between the `int` type and individual integer values. The class defines the general type, as well as function code, but the instances hold specific data values.

instantiation
Instantiation is a fancy word that means "to create an object." Another way to define this term is to say it means "to create an instance." (Objects and instances are the same things.) Although, in general, a class can be considered a blueprint for creating objects, there are some classes — notably abstract classes — that cannot be used to create objects, at least not directly. It's common to say that such a class " cannot be instantiated."

I/O stream
See *stream*.

keyword
A keyword is a name defined in the C++ language itself. This does not include library-defined names, which are identifiers. Examples of common keywords are `if`, `while`, `do`, and `for`. For descriptions of keywords, see Section 4.

label
A label, also called a *statement label*, provides a target for a `goto` statement. Because `goto` is used infrequently in most C++ programs, there usually isn't much need to use labels. A statement label has the following syntax:

```
label_name: statement
```

The `case` and `default` keywords also define labels, although these are used only within a `switch` statement. The labeled statements become potential targets for `switch`. (See p. 111.)

One of the fine points of C/C++ syntax is that a labeled statement is itself a statement. The syntax can therefore be applied recursively to give a single statement any number of labels. Some case statements, in fact, take advantage of this syntax.

```
case 1:
case 2:
case 3:
    cout << "Too small\n" // Execute on 1, 2, or 3.
```

literal

A literal is a constant that does not involve a symbolic name. It is *literally* what it is, and nothing more. Literals come in two versions: numbers (such as 0, –3, 12, 5.007, 0x6E20, and 0xFF) and string literals that consist of quoted text. See also *string literal*.

local variable

A local variable is a named storage location, used inside a function and private to that function. Wherever possible, you should make variables local, because doing so avoids conflict with other functions. Each function can have its own variable named `temp`, for example, without affecting what happens inside other functions. This reduces a common source of errors. See also *global variable*.

logic vs. bitwise operators

Unlike Visual Basic, C++ does not have logic operators do double duty; instead, C++ provides two sets of operators for performing AND and OR. One set (logic operators such as `&&` and `||`) combines Boolean values. The other set (bitwise operators such as `&` and `|`) operates on the bit patterns of integers. The logic operators treat all nonzero values the same way, by first converting them to `true` (1). Logic operators are the best choice for creating complex conditions. Bitwise operators are more discriminating — they operate on each individual bit. You can get an unexpected (and wrong) value of 0 in a bitwise expression such as 4 & (2 > 1). In contrast, the logical expression 4 && (2 > 1) correctly evaluates to `true`.

Another difference between the logical and bitwise operators is that logical operators perform *short circuit* logic. For example, if the first half of an AND expression (`&&`) is false, the program does not evaluate the other half. Bitwise operators always evaluate both operands fully.

loop

A loop is a group of one or more statements executed repeatedly. In almost every case, it's important that the loop stop after some finite period of time, so the rest of the program can continue; otherwise, the result is an infinite loop, which is almost always an error. There are several ways to construct a loop in C++: you can repeat the loop while a specified condition is true (while and do) or you can repeat it a fixed number of times (for). You can also set up a loop which is apparently an infinite loop — such as while(true) — but has some internal mechanism for exiting.

Loops are one of the most fundamental concepts in programming. They make many operations possible. For example, you can use a loop, combined with a loop counter, to process an entire array in a few lines of code. The beauty of the technique is that the same amount of code is involved whether the array is a few bytes long or a million; thus, you can use a few lines of code to process a huge array. For more information see do (p. 80), while (p. 136), and for (p. 87).

lvalue

An lvalue (pronounced "ell-value") is an expression that can appear on the left of an assignment. A variable is an lvalue, but a constant (such as 105) is not. An array element is usually an lvalue; so is a data member. The general rule is: *if an expression has a single, valid address in memory, it's an lvalue.*

Constants are never lvalues. The names of arrays are constant address expressions and therefore are not lvalues. This a subtle point, because the *elements* of an array are usually lvalues, as are pointers. For example:

```
char s[] = "a string";    // s is NOT an lvalue
char *p = "b string";     // p is an lvalue...
p++;                      //   therefore, p can be
                          //   incremented.
s[1] = 'A';               // s[1] is an lvalue
```

This treatment of s and p may seem inconsistent, but the difference is this: s is a constant expression that translates into the address of its first element. p is a pointer variable; it is initialized to the address of the string, but it can store other values as well. Therefore, p is an lvalue.

A fully dereferenced address expression is an lvalue. If an expression pd has type double*, then *pd is an lvalue. However, if ppd has type double**, it has to be dereferenced twice before it produces an lvalue (**ppd). A dereferenced address expression can be complex. For example:

```
int n = 5;
int *p;
*(p + 5 + n) = 100;        // This is valid.
```

Notably, p + 5 + n is a complex expression and is therefore not an lvalue, but *(p + 5 + n) is an lvalue. This follows logically; by definition, *(p + 5 + n) does have a single address, namely, the total p + 5 + n.

macro
A macro is a symbolic name defined with the #define directive. During preprocessing, the compiler replaces each occurrence of the name with the substitution text. For example, if PI is defined as 3.14159265, the compiler replaces each occurrence of PI with the numeric string. (See *preprocessing/preprocessor.*) The name *macro* alludes to the fact that a symbolic name is usually expanded during this preprocessing phase; potentially, the substitution text can be fairly large. Some assemblers have a similar capability; this is where the Microsoft Macro Assembler (MASM) gets its name.

The name *macro* is admittedly a little odd, because some macros are actually small. (Thus, you can have a small macro, which is an oxymoron much like "jumbo shrimp"). No one has thought of a better name, and it's too late to change now.

Macros come in at least two flavors: simple macros, such as PI described above, and macro functions that take arguments expanded right into the replacement text. For further explanation, see the #define topic on page 143.

main function
The main keyword defines a function that serves as the program entry point. This means that main is executed first, and when main returns or stops executing, the program normally ends. The main function is only used in a standard console application. Dynamic link library (DLL) code, as well as Windows applications, do not contain a main function. For more information, see main on page 95.

member
A member is a variable or function declared inside a class. See the topics *data member* and *member function.*

member function

A member function is a function declared inside a class, just as a data member is. Member functions provide the intelligence behind all the objects of a particular class. You use an object by calling a member function; the function definition provides the response. When you write a member function, therefore, you are in effect programming behavior into objects. (Exception: static member functions apply to the class, not to individual objects.)

You can also think of a member function as just a function with class scope. A member function can only be called through an object, but once called, it has access to all the object's data members — even those that are private. Here is a sample call to a member function named move declared in class CPnt.

```
CPnt aPoint;
aPoint.move(10, 20);
```

Notably, it is aPoint's data members that get manipulated — and not those of some other point — through this call. For an introduction to member functions, as well as classes, see Chapter 5.

multidimensional array

C and C++ let you apply the array syntax recursively to declare multidimensional arrays. For example, here are two- and three-dimensional arrays:

```
int matrix2D[10][10];
int matrix3D[10][10][10];
```

What kind of expression is the name matrix2D? As with any array name, matrix2D is a constant address expression that, numerically, is equal to the address of the first element. However, matrix2D has to be dereferenced *twice* to get an actual int. The following statements both initialize the first element to 5:

```
matrix2D[0][0] = 5;
**matrix2D = 5;
```

So far, so good. But what kind of expression is matrix2D[0]? The applicable rule is that unless an address expression is fully dereferenced, it does not produce an lvalue—you cannot assign a value to it. The declaration of matrix2D creates an array of arrays, but it does not create an array of pointer variables. However, you can use an expression such as matrix2D[n-1] to get the starting address of the nth row.

`matrix2D[0]` gives the starting address of the first one-dimensional array (or "row"); `matrix2D[1]` gives the starting address of the second row; and so on. Such expressions are constants. They have type `int*` and need to be dereferenced again before they produce an integer. The distance between each row is the size of an `int` times the first dimension — in this case, 10.

To evaluate an expression involving a multidimensional address, each index is multiplied *by the size of the remaining dimensions*, as well as by the base type. This multiplication involves *scaling*, which the compiler does for you automatically. Assuming that the size of an `int` is four bytes:

```
Address of matrix3D[7][2][3] => Address of matrix3D +
                                7 * 10 * 10 * 4 +
                                2 * 10 * 4 +
                                3 * 4
```

As you can see, as you increase the number of dimensions, the array can take up vast amounts of address space, so use multidimensional arrays carefully.

multiple inheritance

In ANSI C++, a class may inherit from multiple base classes. (See *base class* and *inheritance*.) For example, suppose a class D inherits from three classes A, B, and C.

```
class D: public A, public B, public C {
    // Add declarations specific to D...
};
```

The result of this declaration is that class D automatically has all the member declarations from classes A, B, *and* C. Multiple inheritance raises some language issues. For example, if A and B both have a member called x, how are references to x in class D treated? The solution is to use the scope operator. You can use `A::x` and `B::x` to refer to the versions in A or B, respectively. Multiple inheritance also raises issues for the people who implement compilers, which fortunately, you probably never have to worry about.

In any case, multiple inheritance is probably best avoided unless you have a clear need for it. It tends to violate the object-oriented paradigm, or at least greatly complicate it. If D inherits from B, this is supposed to mean that D is a subspecies of B. (D *is a kind of* B.) To say that D is a kind of A but also a kind of B is stretching things — it's like saying a bird is a kind of mammal but also a kind of lizard. It's hard to make that one fly. For a good example of multiple inheritance, see Figure 10-1 (p. 494). In this figure, `fstream` inherits from both `ifstream` and `ofstream`.

namespace

Namespace is a fundamental concept in C++. As a rule, a namespace is a group of names within which conflicts must be avoided. Exceptions include overloaded function names and variables with different scope. (See *overloading, function,* and *scope.*) Names in separate namespaces don't conflict. When you work with a new namespace, you don't have to worry about whether a name was used in another namespace.

Class declarations provide the most common example of namespace. For example, you can use the name `my_address` in two different classes without conflict.

C++ also enables you to define namespaces by using the `namespace` keyword. Such namespaces exist to reduce the possibility of name conflicts and are useful when you are combining names from several different libraries; in such cases, inadvertent name conflicts are possible. See page 97 in Section 3 for more information on this keyword.

Names are also called *identifiers.* See also *identifier.*

nested control structures and classes

In general, nesting is the act of placing one thing inside of another. Think of a bird's eggs safely inside a nest — the eggs are completely inside the nest and protected from anything outside it. (At least until humans come along.)

A nested control structure is one kind of statement placed inside another, totally enclosed as an egg inside a nest. The capability to do this follows from basic syntax. A control structure features one or more *statements* as part of its syntax. However, a control structure itself is a statement. Therefore, an `if` statement can contain a `while` statement, which can contain an `if` statement, ad infinitum. Loops can be nested inside of other loops to any level.

C++ also supports nested classes. A class nested inside of another can be referred to within the enclosing class, but not anywhere else. One of the new, extended features of ANSI C++ is that you can refer to nested classes in forward references. See Appendix B for more information.

newline

A newline is a special character (represented as `\n` in a quoted string or `char` value) that indicates a line break. Printing a newline causes the display to advance to the next line and start in column 1. When you work with the I/O classes and objects such as `cin` and `cout`, you can code a newline as `endl`.

object

An object is a collection of data that (optionally) has functions associated with it. You can think of an object as an intelligent data structure, able to respond to function calls. Each object is an instance of a specific class, which defines its data fields as well as behavior. See Chapter 5 for an introduction to classes and objects.

object orientation

Object orientation is an approach to programming-language design, system building, and application writing designed to integrate code and data rather than to segregate them as in traditional programming. In simple terms, this means building a program around objects that have both state (data) and behavior (code). It's possible to take an object-oriented approach to design even with a traditional language such as C; however, use of an object-oriented language such as C++ makes the task much easier, because of its support for classes. A C++ class defines both data fields and member functions for objects. (See *class*.)

In many ways, the easiest way to understand object orientation is to envision a program as a set of self-contained objects sending messages to each other. The key aspect of this model is that it emphasizes the autonomy, or built-in intelligence, of individual objects. This model deemphasizes the physical layout of a computer system — in which code and data are segregated — in favor of a model that is closer to the way most things work. For example, in a biological system, each individual cell has its own internal state (i.e., data), but it also knows how to respond to stimuli (i.e., it has behavior specified by internal code). Many volumes have been written concerning the requirements of object orientation. The consensus is that there are three major pillars: encapsulation, inheritance, and polymorphism — each of which is defined in this glossary. Encapsulation is probably the most important. It cleanly defines the relations between program units — that is, objects — and keeps the internals of each object private. Polymorphism is also increasingly important as a way of making objects independent.

Object orientation is a natural step in the evolution of programming languages. It builds on the concepts of structured programming but also moves in new directions. One aspect of object orientation that can be frustrating for the novice is that its benefits are rarely apparent in smaller examples. The benefits of object orientation are most apparent in the context of large systems, in which a way is needed for defining how complex parts interact. As programmers do more and more of their work in graphical user interface (GUI) systems, as well as large network environments, the advantage of object orientation is becoming clear.

OOPS

OOPS is an acronym for object-oriented programming systems. Object orientation is the general concept; OOPS is the attempt to apply it to a particular language or architecture. In practice, though, the terms *object orientation* and *OOPS* are nearly synonymous.

operand

An operand is a subexpression that an operator combines into a larger expression. For example, in the expression x + y, the addition operator (+) has two operands, x and y. With a unary-operator expression such as *p, there is just one operand (in this case, p).

operator

An operator is a symbol, defined in the language, that combines subexpressions (called *operands*) into larger expressions. Most, but not all, operators are special symbols such as *, +, &, and /. In a few cases, an operator may be a keyword (sizeof, new, and delete are examples). Still other operators are made up of two-character combinations, such as ++, −, ->, and ==. A simple use of an operator is the use of addition (+) to add two numbers:

    x + y

Operators have many similarities to function calls. (Chapter 7 explains how operators are translated into function calls.) An operator takes one or more inputs and returns a single value. Syntactically, however, there are important differences. First, unlike functions, operators are limited to the set defined in the C++ language. You can overload existing operators with new behavior, but you cannot make up entirely new operators. Second, operators have their own unique syntax and, unlike function calls, do not require parentheses. Where parentheses are omitted, conflicts are resolved through precedence and association rules.

See Tables 1 and 2 in Section 3 (p. 44) for precedence and association of operators, as well as descriptions. See Chapter 7 for information on how to define how operators work with your own classes.

overloading, function

Overloading means "reusing a symbol or name." Function overloading is the capability to write several different functions that share the same name. Another way to think of this is that you can write several different versions of the same function, each version having different arguments.

For example, the following code contains prototypes of three different versions of `Init_var`. In this case, each is used to initialize a different kind of data.

```
void Init_var(int);
void Init_var(double);
void Init_var(char*);
```

Although each of these functions is named `Init_var`, each is actually a separate function, and each must have its own definition. At compile time, the compiler looks at the type of argument passed to `Init_var` and determines which of these functions to call. If no matching declaration can be found, of course, the result is a syntax error.

Function overloading observes certain restrictions. Each overloaded function must have a unique signature, meaning that the arguments must differ in number or type. It is illegal to have definitions of an overloaded function that differ in return type only. Nevertheless, as long as the argument lists are different, each function can have a different return type. (See *signature*.)

Although there are some surface similarities between the two concepts, function overloading should not be confused with virtual functions. With virtual functions, the appropriate function address is determined at run time, not compile time.

overloading, operator
C++ lets you define how operators work on your own classes. For example, you can define what happens when two instances of your own class are combined with the plus sign (+). In effect, then, you get to define what it means to "add" two objects of a particular type. This feature is one of the most flexible and interesting features in C++. Not all object-oriented languages support this feature, although some people consider OOPS incomplete without it. For information on operator overloading in C++, see Chapter 7.

parameter
Parameter means the same thing as a function argument. Some books use *parameter* exclusively to refer to arguments as declared *within* a function, reserving *argument* to mean a value passed *to* a function. However, for simplicity's sake, this book uses *argument* in both situations.

pointer
In C and C++, the idea of pointers is one of the central concepts — and it can also be one of the most baffling ones if you're new to the language. A pointer is simply a variable that contains an address. If you've never worked with addresses before, you may wonder why this is useful.

The truth is that if you've worked in a language such as BASIC, FORTRAN, or Pascal, your programs have probably made extensive use of addresses. In these other languages, however, the use of addresses is hidden from you. (Pascal has pointer variables, but their use is limited.) By exposing address manipulation at the source-code level, C and C++ require that you understand more about how the computer works; but they also present new possibilities for efficient code.

Addresses are used when you pass a variable by reference. When this happens, one function passes the address of a variable to another function, rather than making a copy of the variable. The called function is then able to manipulate the original data. Moreover, it is often far more efficient to pass a 2-byte or 4-byte address (or whatever the address size is) than to make a copy of a large data structure. Pointers have these and many other uses, as explained in Chapter 3.

pointer arithmetic
C and C++ are the only popular higher-level languages that not only have a concept of pointer, but also let you perform a full range of operations on them. Basically, you can perform all the operations that make sense. Here are the addition and subtraction operations supported for address expressions:

```
addr + integer    // Produces addr expression
integer + addr    // Produces addr expression
addr - integer    // Produces addr expression
addr - addr       // Produces integer
```

In each case, the language uses *scaling* to evaluate the terms. In the first three lines of syntax above, *integer* is automatically multiplied by the size of the base type of the address expression *addr*. In the last line of syntax, one amount is subtracted from the other, as normal, and then the result is divided by the size of the base type. This operation could be used to determine the distance, in terms of element positions, between two places in an array.

All this makes perfect sense, if you think about it. Scaling saves you from a couple of laborious computation steps. For example:

```
short scores[20];

        scores[5]
=>      *(scores + 5)  // From definition of []
=>      get contents at: scores + (5 * sizeof(short))
=>      get contents at: scores + (5 * 2)
```

Because the size of each element is two bytes, the address of
`scores[5]` is actually ten bytes away from `scores[0]`, not five bytes
away. Moreover, in the case of multidimensional arrays, the index is
multiplied by the size of the remaining dimensions as well as the base
type. For example, in the case of a three-dimensional array, the first-
dimension index is multiplied by the size of the second and third dimensions, as well as by the base type. See *multidimensional arrays* for
more information.

pointer to a function

One of the advanced uses of C and C++ is declaring a pointer to hold
a function address rather than a data address. (The latter is the more
common use for pointers and is considered the "normal" type of
pointer.) Function pointers have strange-looking declarations, such as
the following declaration of `pf`. In this case, the function pointed to
must return a `double` and take two integer arguments.

```
double (*pf)(int, int);
```

Function-pointer syntax has some specialized uses. One is to specify a callback function. For example, when you call the `qsort` library
function, you give it the address of your own comparison function,
which `qsort` calls each time it compares two elements. (See `qsort` on
p. 209.) Another use is to build tables of function addresses that can
then be accessed for indirect calls. You can use the C language, in fact,
to emulate the behavior of virtual functions by building such tables.

In general, function pointers and addresses confer a special kind of
versatility, which C++ virtual functions take advantage of without using
the function-pointer syntax. A function pointer holds an address that
can be filled in later. Because it's possible to make function calls indirectly, through the pointer, it's possible to write calls to code not yet
written at compile time. The actual code to be executed can be developed at any point in the future.

polymorphism

Polymorphism is the capability to call an object's functions — in effect,
sending it a message — without knowing its type. If you build a network
of objects, then ideally one object ought to be capable of sending a message to another without knowing everything about the recipient. If you are
talking to someone on a phone and you both speak English, the message "Hello" ought to make sense even if you're not sure who the other
person is. This approach makes a message independent of objects
and — more importantly — independent of any particular response.

Polymorphism is one of the three pillars of object orientation, the others being encapsulation and inheritance. Of these three, polymorphism is the subtlest, but in certain kinds of systems, especially graphical user interfaces (GUI), it is essential. Microsoft Windows, for example, is polymorphic because it runs applications by sending them messages. Windows does not know everything about an application to which it sends a message. The application may have been created, in fact, long after Windows was.

It's this very flexibility that gives rise to the name: *polymorphism* is Greek for *many forms*. Responses to a message (or, in C++ terms, a function call) can take many forms — in fact, a limitless number of forms. The traditional approach, in contrast, limits a program to interacting with a specific number of object types that it knows about in advance.

C++ supports polymorphism by using virtual functions, which can be emulated in C by using pointers to functions. For a more thorough introduction to polymorphism and virtual functions, see Chapter 9.

pragma

A pragma is an implementation-specific command that is supported by a particular compiler vendor. By their nature, pragmas tend to result in nonportable code. However, they are sometimes necessary as a way of turning on a special feature of a particular compiler. ANSI C++ supports the #pragma directive for this purpose. See page 152 for more information.

precedence

Precedence determines which operators are applied first within a complex expression. The higher the precedence of an operator, the sooner it is applied. For example, the expression p = x + 2 * n requires three steps to completely evaluate. The precedence order, from high to low, is: *, +, and =. The expression is therefore evaluated this way:

```
p = (x + (2 * n))
```

Certain common sense notions apply in C++ as in most languages. The mathematical operators (+, -, *, and /) follow standard conventions, giving multiplication and division precedence over addition and subtraction. Relational and logic operators have lower precedence, and assignment operators have lower precedence still. Unary operators have fairly high precedence. Where two operators have the same precedence, C++ uses rules of association to resolve the conflict.

Tables 1 and 2 in Section 3 (p 44) list all operators by precedence.

preprocessing/preprocessor

When the C++ compiler translates a program, the first thing it does is preprocess the source code. During this phase the compiler reads through the source code and makes changes to the program specified by directives. For example, the #define directive specifies substitutions, and the #include directive causes the compiler to read in header files. These changes do not affect the original source file. The source code changes are made to an intermediate source file that you don't see, although the compiler may provide an option for printing this intermediate file.

Although having such a phase may seem unnecessary, preprocessing gives certain advantages to C and C++ programmers. Preprocessing enables C and C++ to support a wide set of powerful directives. Among other things, this makes possible conditional compilation, which helps you maintain multiple versions of the same program. Another advantage of preprocessing is that it takes place at compile time only. This, in turn, lets you define substitutions and manipulations that occur before the program ever runs. Consequently, there is no cost in execution speed, although the program might take slightly longer to compile.

Programmers and software manuals often refer to *the preprocessor* as if it were separate entity from the compiler. In the very first C compilers, the preprocessor may have been a separate program, but these days, the process of building a program is so tightly integrated that there's no noticeable delay between preprocessing and compiling. I find it more appropriate to think of preprocessing as simply the first phase of the compiler, although you'll sometimes read about "the preprocessor" as if it were separate from the compiler.

preprocessor directive

See *directive*.

primitive data type

Primitive data types, sometimes referred to just as *primitive types*, make up the set of types defined by the C++ language itself. These include integer types (such as char, int, unsigned int, and long), floating-point types (float and double), and the ANSI-supported bool type, which, although not used as a general-purpose integer, holds the value 0 or 1. Other recently added types are wchar_t, long double, and long long int. For a summary of the types, see Table 1 in Section 4 (p. 68).

All of the C++ primitive types are, at bottom, numeric types — which makes sense because the computer cannot store anything other than numbers. Character values are stored in code as char values. A text string is made up of an array of char.

Primitive types have great importance in C++ as in any other language, because all other types (including classes and arrays) are ultimately made up of combinations of primitive types. Primitive types are the fundamental building blocks for data structures. Structures such as classes and arrays, incidentally, are sometimes called *complex types*.

promotion

Promotion is what happens to a C++ programmer who can write 1,000 lines of perfect code a day or successfully explain what *polymorphism* means to his or her manager.

Promotion is also the process of automatically converting data to a larger type. This happens all the time in expressions that mix types. For example, when you assign an integer to a floating-point variable (as in float f = 1), C++ automatically promotes the integer data by converting it to floating-point format. No explicit cast need be applied here; the cast is implicit. C and C++ promote data, as needed, according to a hierarchy. For example, short is promoted to long as needed and long is promoted to double as needed. See also *cast*.

prototype

A prototype is a function declaration containing complete type information for its return type and all its arguments. In C++ (unlike the C language), every function declaration must contain a prototype to be valid.

Prototypes can be used to declare a function defined later in the code or in another module. These prototypes are not required to use formal argument names, although such names are permitted. The following sample prototype declares a function taking a string argument and returning an integer.

```
int print_items(char*);
```

The word *prototype* has a different meaning to system analysts than it does to user-interface specialists. To user-interface specialists, *prototyping* a system means getting a user interface working along with minimal functional code for demonstration purposes. This has almost no connection at all to the C++ meaning. Before you throw around the term, therefore, it pays to know to whom you're talking — a C++ programmer or a UI designer. Fortunately, these people usually belong to different clubs, thus minimizing the chance of confusion.

pure virtual function

As strange as it may sound, a pure virtual function is a function containing no function-definition code. The pure virtual function acts as a stand-in, or general prototype, for code to be provided by other classes. Any class that has such a function is an abstract class, and you cannot use the class to create objects. The only way to use such a class is to derive other classes from it and then implement all pure virtual functions.

Pure virtual functions use the notation =0. For example, the following statement declares a sample function, `report_stats`.

```
virtual void report_stats(int, char*) = 0;
```

A declaration of a pure virtual function has complete type information, even though the class cannot contain a definition for this function.

recursion
A recursive function is one that calls itself. To avoid an infinite regression, of course, it needs some way of detecting an end condition. The classic example is the factorial function, but for once, I'll spare you.

C++ fully supports recursion, but within such a function, you should be cautious about the use of local static variables. Use of static variables tends to break recursive-function code.

reference
A reference variable is an alias for another variable. For example:

```
int b = 1;
int &a = b;     // a is an alias for b.
a = 5;          // Set b to 5.
```

A reference *argument* is an alias for the variable passed to a function. Changes to the argument permanently affect the variable that was passed. For example:

```
void switch_values(int &a, int &b) {
      int temp;
      temp = a;
      a = b;
      b = temp;
};
```

This function could be written with pointers. However, the advantage of this version is that you call it without using pointer operations (& and *). For example:

```
int x = 1, y = 2;
switch_values(x, y);   // After this call, x=2, y=1.
```

When working with references, remember that a reference argument passes a pointer, but hides the pointer syntax. (This is just like BASIC and FORTRAN's pass by reference.) Similarly, a reference return value means that the function returns a pointer to some object, but pretends it is passing the object itself. References are useful, even essential, in the syntax of member functions such as copy constructors and assignment operator functions — which is the real reason references were added to C++. See Chapters 6 and 7 for more information.

runtime type information (RTTI)

ANSI C++ supports the use of runtime type information (RTTI) in two ways. One way is through the use of the `typeid` operator. See page 126 for more information on this operator. The other way is through the use of the `dynamic_cast` operator, which performs a runtime check on a pointer argument, to see whether it points to an object of a particular class. See Section 4 for information on the cast operators. In both cases, you use RTTI to get information about an object's type at runtime. Some compilers, such as Microsoft Visual C++, require an explicit compiler option to turn on support for RTTI.

scaling

Scaling is the process of multiplying an array index by the size of the array's base type. For example, if you declare one-dimensional `array` of type `short`, the base type is two. Therefore, `array[5]` is not five bytes away from the starting address, but ten bytes away. It would be inconvenient to have to do this conversion yourself, so C and C++ do it for you. The languages are quite specific about when they do this multiplication. It is only performed in expressions such as `array + 5` (see *pointer arithmetic*). Index expressions such as `array[5]` are equivalent to the form `array + 5`, so scaling is performed for indexes, as well. With multidimensional arrays, scaling also considers the size of each dimension. See *multidimensional arrays*.

scope

The scope of a variable or function is its visibility within the program. In C, the most important categories of scope are local and global. (In multiple-module programs, scope can also be external.) A local variable is visible only within the function that calls it. In addition, every compound statement defines another level of scope; variables defined inside a statement block are local to that block. C++ adds one major category of scope — class level — which applies to data members and function members of a class. Such members are visible to each other — function members can access any data member — and are also visible through an object reference if they are public.

An ANSI extension lets you limit scope to an `if` statement by declaring the variable inside the `if` condition. See Appendix B for more information.

sign extension

Sign extension is the process by which a signed integer type is assigned to a larger type. See *two's complement format* for details. This is a machine-level detail that you can mostly ignore, except in cases where you are freely mixing `signed` and `unsigned` data of different sizes. In those cases, you might occasionally need to pay attention to the effects of zero extension and sign extension. For example, consider a signed byte containing −1 and an unsigned byte containing 255. Each has the bit pattern of all 1s (binary 11111111), but each is extended to a different result when assigned to an `int`. To control the effects of sign extension, you might want to cast a value to `signed` or `unsigned` before assigning to a larger value.

signature

A signature uniquely identifies a symbol according to its name, type, and — in the case of functions — its argument list. Note that names of formal arguments are irrelevant in this context. The functions `init (int i)` and `init(int j)` have identical signatures as far as the compiler is concerned. The functions `init(int)` and `init(double)`, however, are distinct. When generating .obj files (or .o files, depending on the platform), the compiler uses a scheme called *decorating* to output a symbolic name with its signature. It is interesting to look at decorated names, but you should never make assumptions about them, because they are implementation specific.

Standard Template Library

The ANSI C++ specification now defines a set of standard templates for compiler vendors to implement. These templates included a set of generalized string and collection classes that can be built around any number of different types. Space limitations prevent covering them in this book because these are complex templates that support many different functions. The string template has capabilities that are a superset of the `CStr` class described in this book, but the string template can be built around different types, such as `char`, `signed char`, `unsigned char`, and `wchar_t`.

statement

Along with expressions, statements are the fundamental units of execution in C/C++. A C++ program consists of function definitions, along with global declarations. Function definitions, in turn, are each made up of one or more statements.

The most common type of statement is an expression terminated by a semicolon. Syntactically, this can be expressed as:

```
expression;
```

Such an expression is usually an assignment expression or function call. For example:

```
a = b + 1;    // Assignment expression
do_the_laundry();
```

The first example above is not a special "assignment statement" (as in most languages), but rather an assignment *expression* terminated by a semicolon. The fact that assignment is an expression makes it possible to place one assignment inside another, until finally the whole thing is terminated by a semicolon — at which point it becomes a statement.

```
a = b = c = e = getdata(x, y);
```

Other examples of statements include if statements, switch statements, and loops (do, for, while). The syntax here is fully recursive. For example, a loop forms a statement, and may therefore be placed in the *statement* part of another loop.

A compound statement forms a statement and may therefore be placed anywhere in C/C++ syntax that calls for a single statement. Compound statement syntax is:

```
{ statements }
```

Here, the *statements* placeholder represents one or more statements. By using this syntax, you can use any number of statements where one is called for.

See also *executable statement*.

STL

See *Standard Template Library*.

storage class

The storage class of a variable or object determines how the compiler allocates a variable in memory: in a data segment, on the stack, or in a register. Variables with automatic storage class are allocated on the stack and are not permanent. As soon as a function returns, the values of its automatic variables are lost. Note that it's quite possible to have static storage class with local scope — this is the case with local variables declared static. The C/C++ storage classes are auto, extern, register, and static. See Section 4 for information on these keywords.

stream

A stream is a place you can get or send a sequence of data. Metaphorically, the word "stream" implies a flow of something. With C++, this flow is a data flow. As long as things go well, you should always be able to get or output the next byte. C++ supports several basic kinds of streams: standard input and output (connected to monitor and keyboard), disk files, and array-based streams. For an introduction to streams, see Chapter 4.

The C++ standard library supports streams in two ways: with stdio functions (these are shared with C) and the I/O stream classes. The stream classes have the advantage of being extensible to any type or class; this demonstrates a basic virtue of object orientation. For information on extending classes, see Chapter 10. For a reference guide to the classes, see Section 7.

string

A string, also called a text string or character string, contains an array of character data. Support for strings in C++ enables you to handle words, sentences, and other text. See Chapter 3. For information on string library functions, see Section 7, page 288. For information on coding special characters, see Table 3-2 on page 360.

string literal

A string literal consists of text surrounded by double quotation marks (″). This is one of the major categories of constants in C++. (See *constants*.) An example of a string literal is:

```
"Hello there, C++!"
```

For information on coding special characters, see Table 3-2 on page 360.

The C++ compiler handles string literals in a specific way. First, it allocates space in the constant data area and places the text there, coded in ASCII form — each number represents a character. Then C++ replaces the string literal in program code with the address of the data (although the actual source code is never altered). Therefore, when a variable is assigned a string, as in this example:

```
char *p;
p = "Hello there, C++!";
```

what happens is that the address of the string data is assigned to the variable, p.

This makes sense if you think about it, because arrays (and a string is just an array) are handled by referring to the address of their first element.

structure

In C, a structure is a compound data type built upon other data types, called *members* or *fields*. Another way to state this is to say that a structure is a data record consisting of a set of variables. C++ extends the concept of structure by making structures just a special case of classes; and because a structure is a class in C++, it may optionally have functions associated with it. See page 111 in Section 4 for information on the `struct` keyword.

structured programming
Structured programming is an important stage in programming evolution. Its principal tenant is that source code should be as well-organized and meaningful as possible. This, in turn, represents a vast improvement over the primitive days of writing in machine code, and even over the days of the early, primitive versions of FORTRAN and COBOL.

There are several ways that structured languages encourage code to be organized. They provide meaningful symbolic names for everything, replace spaghetti code (made up of `goto`s) with rigorous control structures, and encourage the use of local variables and arguments. All of these features are fundamental to object-oriented programming. The difference is that object orientation goes a major step further: it encourages related functions and data to be organized together in classes.

Object orientation does not represent a whole new direction away from structured programming. It is actually just a logical development.

subclass
See *derived class*.

superclass
See *base class*.

text string
See *string*.

template
A template is a declaration containing a generic type. This type, which can be denoted by an identifier such as `T`, is a stand-in for a type to be specified later. Once declared, a template can be used to generate a specific declaration, replacing `T` by an actual type. For example, the following template declaration creates a generic data structure called `pair`, which has two instances of type `T`:

```
template <class T>
class pair {
    T a, b;
}
```

Once this declaration is read by the compiler, the `pair` template can be used to generate a specific type, `pair<int>`, as follows.

```
pair<int> jeans;
```

The data structure `jeans` is now a class containing two integers, a and b. For more information on templates, see the `template` topic on page 113.

two's complement format

Modern mini-computers, as well as nearly all personal computers, use the two's complement format to represent negative values in a signed integer range. In this format, a negative number is produced according to the following transformation:

1. Take the bitwise inversion of the corresponding positive number; for example, to get –1, first change 00000001 to 11111110

2. Add 1; for example, change 11111110 to 11111111

A consequence of this system is that –1 is represented as all 1s for an integer type of any size. Another consequence is that if there is a 1 in the leftmost position, the number is negative. In a signed type, therefore, the upper half of the range is actually used to store negative numbers. In a 2-byte integer, for example, the bit patterns with 0 in the leftmost positive represent values from 0 to 32,767. The bit patterns with 1 if the leftmost position represent values from –32,768 to –1.

You can usually ignore the details of two's complement arithmetic. The compiler generates the appropriate machine-level instructions for operating on each type. Most machine instructions work equally well on both types. (You can verify this by adding –1 to 1 and then ignoring the overflow.) In some situations, however, the compiler must generate different instructions for signed and unsigned types. This is true when an integer value is assigned to a larger integer type.

For example, in the following figure, the same bit pattern is handled differently depending on whether it is considered signed or unsigned. Unsigned data is always zero-extended when it is assigned to a larger integer type, which means that it is padded on the left with all 0s. However, signed data is padded on the left with all 1s or all 0s depending on the value of its leftmost bit. This handling of signed data is called *sign-extension*.

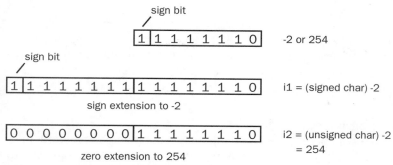

Sign extension and zero extension.

type

A variable's type determines what kind of data it can store. The type also determines the variable's range and how much space it takes up in memory. For example, a variable of type short can represent any whole number from –32,768 to 32,767. A variable of type double has a much greater range. In addition to variables, every expression and value in C++ has a type.

In short, a type is a data format. In addition to the standard types (see *primitive type*), C++ enables you to define your own types. These are called *classes*.

type-safe linkage

C++, unlike the C language, supports type-safe linkage — a feature that prevents the same variable or function name from being declared inconsistently in different modules. With C, it's all too easy to declare the same variable as short in one module and long in another, or to do even worse things. C++ prevents programs with these errors from successfully linking. See *decorating* for information on how type-safe linkage is implemented.

unary operator

A unary operator applies to just one operand — unlike a binary operator, which combines two items. For example, in the following expression, the asterisk (*) acts as the indirection operator; this has the effect of referring to the thing that ptr points to:

```
*ptr
```

Notably, when the asterisk is used to join two items, it specifies multiplication — which is completely different from indirection. C++ uses context to determine which is intended. In the following statement, the first use of the asterisk acts as the multiplication operator (binary); the second use acts as the indirection operator (unary).

```
product = n * *ptr;
```

unsigned data type

C and C++ support both signed and unsigned integer types. Integers are signed by default; you use the `unsigned` keyword to modify an integer to make it unsigned. The unsigned version of any integer is actually simplest to understand. All bit patterns represent either 0 or a positive value. The drawback of using an unsigned type is that it cannot represent negative values. In return for this sacrifice, however, an unsigned type can represent twice as many positive values as its signed counterpart. For example, the range of `unsigned short` is 0 to 65,536 rather than −32,768 to 32,767.

For information on how signed types are handled at the machine-code level, see *two's complement format*.

variable

A variable is a named location for storing data, such as x, y, count, my_data, or amt. Unless declared `const`, a variable can hold different amounts at different times. You can make up almost any name for your variables that you want, subject to some restrictions. (See *identifier*.) In C++, variables can include objects — which are instances of classes — as well as pointers or primitive data. Note that in C and C++, all variables must be formally declared before being used.

virtual base class

When a base class is virtual, objects inherit only one copy of base-class members, no matter how many ways the derived class inherits from the base class. If this all sounds obscure, that's no surprise. Virtual base classes only come into play with complex inheritance hierarchies, involving (at minimum) three generations and multiple inheritance. Unless you're involved with this kind of weirdness, there's no reason to be overly concerned about virtual base classes. See also *base class.*

For an example of the `virtual` keyword applied to base classes, see page 133.

virtual function

A virtual function is a function that can be defined in different ways by different classes, and yet still be correctly executed no matter how an object is accessed. Even if an object is accessed through a base-class pointer or as part of an array of different types of objects, the correct function code is executed.

Another way to think about this is to say that each object contains its own knowledge of how to execute virtual functions. Therefore, it doesn't matter how it's accessed. This supports the concept of objects as autonomous units that can act independently like cells. Moreover, a new type of object can be plugged into an existing framework, bringing with it a pointer to its own implementations of virtual functions. Although it's possible to override a function that is not declared virtual, doing so is risky (and a common programming error). As a rule, any member function that might be overridden in a derived class should be declared virtual in the base class.

Virtual functions are closely related to the object-oriented concept of polymorphism. For an introduction to the subject, see Chapter 9. You declare virtual functions with the use of the `virtual` keyword, described on page 133 in Section 4. *Virtual* originally meant *manly* in Latin. Due to 2000 years of sexism in Western culture, *virtue* has come to mean "to behave well," and *virtual* has come to mean "to have the behavior of." (This is because to the ancient Romans, true manliness emphasized a code of behavior.) Virtual memory is a mechanism that behaves like memory, even though it may be a disk file. A C++ virtual function behaves like a normal function call, even though it is implemented with pointers.

May all your programs behave well; may they be truly virtuous, if not virtual.

wide-character string

A wide character (`wchar_t`) uses two bytes to represent a single text character. All C++ code looks pretty much the same, but the *text data* that your program handles will differ depending on the language of your end users. Wide-character strings were developed to support natural languages that cannot be accommodated by the ASCII set, which is limited to 255 characters. Amendment 1 to the ANSI specification mandates library support for these strings. A wide-character set is always a superset of the ASCII set, so you translate standard C++ strings into wide-character strings by inserting a zero byte in front of each ASCII byte. For a list of new functions in the standard library that support wide-character strings, see page 245.

The importance of supporting natural languages spoken throughout the world is a sign of our times. In the end, C and C++ have had to join the global village.

Index

Symbols

Continued

Notes

Two Books in One!

CONCISE TUTORIALS

Each In Plain English guidebook delivers concise, targeted tutorials—no hand-holding, no coddling, just the skills you need to get up and running fast.

READY-REFERENCE HELP

Each book also features topic-sorted and A-to-Z reference sections that answer your questions quickly and help you get the job done, day after day.

In Plain English. All the tools you need to get up to speed—and get results.

Active Server™ Pages In Plain English
by Patricia Hartman & Timothy Eden
650 pages • $19.99
ISBN 0-7645-4745-3

C++ In Plain English, 3rd Edition
by Brian Overland
700 pages • $19.99
ISBN 0-7645-3545-5

Java™ In Plain English, 3rd Edition
by Brian Overland & Michael Morrison
750 pages • $19.99
ISBN 0-7645-3539-0

JavaScript™ In Plain English
by Sandra Eddy *Available Spring 01!*
700 pages • $19.99
ISBN 0-7645-4792-5

XHTML™ In Plain English
by Sandra Eddy
750 pages • $19.99
ISBN 0-7645-4743-7

XML In Plain English, 2nd Edition
by Sandra Eddy
750 pages • $19.99
ISBN 0-7645-4744-5

For more information, visit our website at:
www.mandtbooks.com

my2cents.idgbooks.com

Register This Book — And Win!

Visit **http://my2cents.idgbooks.com** to register this book and we'll automatically enter you in our fantastic monthly prize giveaway. It's also your opportunity to give us feedback: let us know what you thought of this book and how you would like to see other topics covered.

Discover IDG Books Online!

The IDG Books Online Web site is your online resource for tackling technology — at home and at the office. Frequently updated, the IDG Books Online Web site features exclusive software, insider information, online books, and live events!

10 Productive & Career-Enhancing Things You Can Do at www.idgbooks.com

1. Nab source code for your own programming projects.

2. Download software.

3. Read Web exclusives: special articles and book excerpts by IDG Books Worldwide authors.

4. Take advantage of resources to help you advance your career as a Novell or Microsoft professional.

5. Buy IDG Books Worldwide titles or find a convenient bookstore that carries them.

6. Register your book and win a prize.

7. Chat live online with authors.

8. Sign up for regular e-mail updates about our latest books.

9. Suggest a book you'd like to read or write.

10. Give us your 2¢ about our books and about our Web site.

You say you're not on the Web yet? It's easy to get started with IDG Books' *Discover the Internet,* available at local retailers everywhere.